Letters FROM A SOLDIER

A Memoir of World War II

William M. Kays

Wimke Press

Publication editing, design, art work, page layout production, and
project coordination by members of the author's family.
Published by Wimke Press

*This book is dedicated
to the World War II officers and men of the
First Engineer Combat Battalion, First Infantry Division,
some of whom didn't make it through the war,
and most of whom are no longer with us. I miss them all.*

*I also want to thank my family,
who helped produce this book, as well as provided
moral support while it was being written.*

CONTENTS

PREFACE

In the summer of 1942, I went to war. In October of 1945, I came home. Hundreds of thousands of others did the same. I spent thirty-seven months overseas. I fought in Africa and Sicily, was on Omaha Beach in Normandy soon after "H-hour" on June 6, 1944, and was still fighting in Czechoslovakia when the war ended. Thousands of others did likewise. The only thing that makes my story the least bit unusual is that my mother saved all of my letters home, 123 in total, and it is around these letters that I have built my story. This book was originally written in 1994, and photocopies were distributed to family and friends. It was then revised and expanded into publishable form in 2009.

I was a U.S. Army officer in a combat engineer battalion, in an infantry division, mostly at or near the front lines. Out of three years overseas I was within effective range of German artillery for almost two years; had I been in the infantry, the odds against lasting that long were very low indeed, and my story would likely have been much shorter. In the Engineers the odds were much more favorable, although as it was, over half our battalion officers ultimately became casualties. I was very careful, and kept my "head down." I survived.

This is not a story of heroics; I was no hero. I think I was reasonably competent most of the time, and I managed not to disgrace myself, but I was much more interested in staying alive than in winning a war. We did have some legitimate heroes in my battalion; but more on them later.

The letters are in many places a little bit embarrassing for me to read today, now that I'm in my eighties, for they reveal pretentiousness, and other characteristics of youth and the times that I would like to forget, including elements of racism. I was twenty-two when it all started and thought I was an adult, but the letters sound like they were written by a fourteen year-old. However, they do represent what was going on in my head at the time, and combined with my recollections from a distance of over sixty years, they will perhaps enable a story a little out of the ordinary. The letters provide a framework, and I have filled in the details between them from memory, explaining events in the letters and adding other experiences that were not mentioned.

One of the difficulties of writing letters from a war zone as a soldier was that censorship rules forbade mentioning either place names or military events. That didn't leave much to talk about, but since my mother became quite upset if I didn't write frequently I had to fill my letters with something, so complaining (or "griping," as we called it) became an easy way out. After we had been in action for a few months we all felt very sorry for ourselves, so it was easy to gripe about anything and everything, and especially to complain about all the people who didn't have to fight. The letters are full of self-pity.

Another feature of these letters is I now realize I frequently wrote to impress rather than inform. I felt I was important and ought to be listened to. I wasn't above scaring my parents a little. It is in this effort to impress that a certain pretentiousness creeps in. An interesting thing (to me, at least) is that I can distinctly remember, after over sixty years, carefully thinking up and writing particular sentences that appear in the letters. They were not just random thoughts off the top of my head.

Another thing that should be mentioned is my relationship with my father, although it only tangentially relates to the letters. My father spent his career in the U.S. Navy. I adored my father and as a kid I loved to listen to his stories about his life as a naval officer and his various associated adventures. As I grew up and had a few adventures of my own I couldn't wait to sit him down and tell him all about them. He was a pretty good listener and was always interested. The war was my biggest adventure of all, and, especially in the early part of the war in Africa, I frequently thought of him and how I wanted to describe to him what I was seeing and doing. I was terribly frustrated that censorship prevented me from telling the full story in my letters. One of the things I looked forward to when coming home was to tell him that story. A great disappointment when I finally did come home was that I could never engage him in any real discussions of my adventures. Ultimately I gave up. I never really understood what the problem was.

I usually wrote to my girlfriend, Noma, at the same time I wrote to my parents. I have long since lost track of Noma so I don't know what happened to those letters, although I doubt she saved them. It is just as well — they would be even more embarrassing.

The story starts on the 1st of July, 1942, the day I put on my uniform and boarded a train in San Francisco; it was my first day of active duty. But how did an academic nerd like me, an engineering student, ever get into this predicament in the first place? It certainly was not part of a plan. Some background is required.

My father was a graduate of the Naval Academy at Annapolis and was a naval officer, as were my grandfather and numerous uncles. It was assumed that I would attempt to enter the Naval Academy, but during my high school years my eyes began to fail, and if anything could keep you out of Annapolis in those days it was eyes that did not test 20/20. For a long time, I was afraid to admit to my parents that my eyesight was weak. But the fact was that I badly needed glasses after my sophomore year in high school, and I faced the necessity of taking an eye examination to get my driver's license, so I eventually had to confess. I then needed an alternative plan.

I found I liked high school physics, so I quickly decided that I wanted to be an engineer, and furthermore that I wanted to go to Stanford University. Why Stanford? My mother was horrified at the cost, but my father thought it was a good idea. The sole reason was that my family had lived in Palo Alto during most of 1927 when my father had an assignment in San Francisco and my father became a Stanford football fan. (Stanford won the Pacific Coast Conference Championship that year and went on to play in the Rose Bowl game.) Therefore, to Stanford I went. It wasn't all that difficult to gain admission in those days.

People were beginning to talk about war in 1938 when I entered college, so there was no question but that I would join the Reserve Officers Training Corps (ROTC). If there were any possibility of going to war, it would certainly be preferable to be an officer. This idea was reinforced by an experience I had when I was ten years old. My father took me to see the movie *All Quiet on the Western Front*. I thought it was going to be a cowboy movie! To this day I remember virtually every scene. The impression was overwhelming. I told my friends all about it and for weeks we played "war" in my back yard, practicing how to fall when mowed down by machine guns. But after that experience there was no way I was going to get involved with the infantry and have to go "over the top." (We will hear more about *All Quiet* later.) The point is that Stanford did not have a Naval ROTC, which would have been my natural choice, but it did have an Army Artillery unit. So into the Artillery I went and spent the next two years (to the extent that ROTC took any time at all) driving and mostly cleaning up after horses, since it was a horse artillery unit. But it was far preferable to the infantry.

Then I discovered that Stanford also had an Ordnance ROTC unit that was open to engineering students during their junior and senior years. Ordnance was a non-combatant branch of the army and looked like the safest possible haven, and since the war was now heating up, it was an ideal choice. By the middle of my senior year, December 1941, we were in a war and it was apparent that I would be called up as soon as I graduated in June 1942. Then one of our ROTC officers left Stanford and took a position in the Ordnance Procurement Office in San Francisco. He offered to put in a request that I be assigned there and I took up the offer. Everything was falling into place nicely. But then I saw him a couple of weeks before graduation, and he told me that orders had been changed and all new 2nd Lieutenants were going to be assigned to "the field." In fact, I think he told me they were going to make a "fighting soldier" out of me. This was supposed to be a joke, although I was not amused. But the Ordnance still looked relatively bulletproof; I was just disappointed to get orders to report to Benicia Arsenal at the northern tip of the San Francisco Bay on July 1st, rather than to downtown San Francisco.

Graduation from Stanford was on Sunday, June 14th, and the next day I boarded a train to go spend a week with my girl, Noma, in Norfolk, Virginia. This was a graduation present from my parents.

When I returned to San Francisco from Norfolk on about June 28th, I was greeted by a telegram from the War Department informing me that I had been transferred to the Corps of Engineers and that I should start traveling on July 1st and report for duty at Ft. Leonard Wood, Missouri.

This was a shocking development. It wasn't just that I had no training in the things that Army Engineers do; I was also well aware that Engineer soldiers carry rifles, frequently come under enemy fire, and sometimes even act as infantry. And the idea of Missouri in July was not very appealing either. So much for my plans to spend the war in relative comfort and safety!

MAP 1

Algeria, December 6, 1942-January 25, 1943

MAP 2

Tunisia, December 6, 1942-January 25, 1943

MAP 3

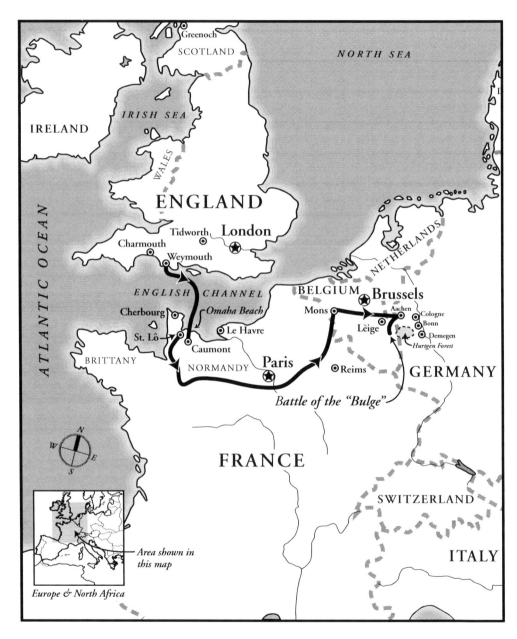

Normandy to the "Bulge", June 6, 1944 - January 31, 1945

MAP 4

Germany, February 1 - May 7, 1945

CHAPTER ONE

FORT LEONARD WOOD

JULY 1 – AUGUST 31, 1942

It was Tuesday, June 30, 1942. My mother and father drove me from where we lived in Berkeley, California, to the old Third and Townsend Street Southern Pacific Station in San Francisco. I remember distinctly going through the gate and walking down the platform and looking back at my parents, my father smiling and looking proud and my mother in tears and looking wretched. I took the Southern Pacific "Daylight" train to Los Angeles as the first step en route to Missouri. From there I took another train through Arizona, New Mexico, Texas, and Oklahoma.

The first letter is written on stationery from the Hulkins Hotel, Oklahoma City.

Thursday, July 2

Dear Mother, Dad, and Sis:

I guess I'd better tell you all my adventures from the beginning. (Not that there is anything extraordinary about them).

The trip down on the "daylight" was very pleasant, except for a bunch of drunk sailors who decided that because they had been in three battles, they had the right to molest everybody on the train. That is quite a train. The conductor talks to you by loud speaker all during the trip. We arrived in L.A. late, but I had plenty of time. There must have been ten thousand people in the station. I've never seen such a confused mess in my life. I got a haircut and shoeshine, and then got myself a lower berth on the 7:30 train. Found one Stanford officer going with me as far as El Paso. There were a dozen U.C.L.A. infantrymen [all R.O.T.C. 2nd Lieutenants] going as far as Oklahoma City, so I had plenty of company.

At El Paso, a navy commander got on and produced a ticket for my berth. He insisted that because of his superior rank, I should move out and go find myself another berth. This I refused to do, and I impressed him greatly with the "insolence" of young army officers. I didn't even get to see the El Paso station, because I knew the minute I left, he'd turn in. Eventually the porter told him to take another berth, and everybody was happy.

I've been enjoying the luxury of first class travel no end. However, yesterday a law went into effect banning the use of lounge cars, so that luxury is gone.

The train lost time consistently, and finally pulled into here three hours late, making me miss my train by a long shot. I've got an upper on the 4:40 train tomorrow, so I have quite a long lay-over. The ticket agent sent me to this hotel, and with a flurry of taxis and bell-hops, I landed in a very nice room with bath for $2.50. After dinner I took in a show. Afterwards I was going to wander around but I couldn't stand the continual saluting so I sneaked back here and took a bath. This is the first town I've been in where the soldiers salute, and every other person on the street is a soldier. An officer walking down the street just about starts a riot.

I'm now lolling on a big double bed, enjoying life at its best. I'll write soon after I arrive and give you all the gory details. Hope I meet someone going there on the train tomorrow. Showing up alone is going to be no fun.

Lots of love to all,
Bill

The UCLA Infantry 2nd Lieutenants that I met on the train were heading for Camp Robinson, Arkansas, and they were talking about what a good place Camp Robinson was supposed to be and what a good time they were going to have. Years later I wondered what became of these guys. I saw some figures on UCLA casualties after the war; 1942 was not a good year for Infantry 2nd Lieutenants to report for duty. The casualty rate for my classmates at Stanford was not nearly so high, and a large part of those were in the Army Air Corps (forerunner of the modern U.S. Air Force). It was the Infantry that made the difference, but then who in his right mind would go into the Infantry? Those were such nice guys, the "all-American" types!

Co. D, 31st E.T. Bn.
Ft. Leonard Wood, Mo.
July 5, 1942

Dear Mother, Dad, and Sis,

This letter is more to give you an address to write to than anything else, as I really don't start work until tomorrow. However, I'll tell you the dope so far.

Arrived in Newburg at 5:00 am yesterday. A soldier met me and subsequently arranged transportation to the post. I spent most of yesterday going through an extraordinary amount of filling out questionnaires. I found they have three categories into which they can put you: - railroad officer, construction officer, and line officer. For each they have a month "refresher" course. I put in for construction, so they promptly turned around and made me into a line officer when I couldn't find a physical reason why I shouldn't be. The result is that tomorrow I draw a rifle, bayonet, gas mask, and all that sort of stuff, and start on a program that begins at 7:10 am, and ends at 8:30 pm.

I have a single room, or hole, in an officer's barracks. The place is inhabited by everything from majors on down, there being no accommodations for families within 30 miles of the post.

The food at the officer's mess seems to be fairly good. Costs me $1.15 a day. I also have to pay $4.00 a month for an orderly who makes my bed and polishes my shoes.

I went to the PX last night and spent $45.00 on uniforms. Charged it all.

Due to my possible temporary stay here, I am receiving my pay by check, and will mail it to the bank. An allotment takes over a month to go through. I get my travel money in a couple of days and will mail that in.

One other fellow from school is here. We expect another soon.

This is a tremendous post. About 40,000 men. It's rolling wooded country, and the post is spread out for miles. None of the neighboring towns amount to anything, and they run a special train to St. Louis every Saturday night.

The weather here is identical with Norfolk. I can see no choice, except that I think the sun itself is probably hotter here.

All I hear around here is about how hard we are going to be worked. This is a far cry from the Ordnance.

Well, I'll draw this to a close now, and next week I'll probably feel like an old timer and be able to tell you more details.

Much love to all,
Bill

The four week "refresher" course was to be virtually my only military training, and certainly my only training as an Engineer. I had spent three years in the High School Cadet Corps in Washington, DC, and that experience ultimately served me well, but my college ROTC experience added little.

After a week in the officer's barracks I introduced myself to the officer in the room across the hall. He had just arrived after graduating from a three-month Officer Candidate School course at Ft. Belvoir, Virginia, and evidently after several months as an enlisted man. This was Bill Barnum, from Minneapolis. He was at this time an officer in one of the training companies, and had no connection with my refresher course. But fate was later to bring us together in a big way. We ultimately served in the same company in Africa and Sicily, and many of the adventures I will describe later involved Bill Barnum. He was badly wounded on Omaha Beach two years later, but for the next fifty years until his death he was my great friend. Bill was about eight years older than I. In the evenings I used to go over to his room and listen to his tales about being an officer in a training company.

July 12, 1942

Dear Mother, Dad, and Sis,

Well, one week is over, and I'm still kicking. I might as well say right now that I hate and detest this place, and the sooner I get out the better. Today is a much needed day of rest, and I shall try to catch up with my letter writing.

I've enjoyed your last two letters very much. Mail is my one form of amusement around here. There just aren't any others. With a working day that begins at 7:00 am and ends at 8:30 pm, you are just too tired to walk a mile to the officers' club, or go to a movie. Besides, there is always a lot of study reading to be done.

I omitted one other form of pleasure. That's the shower. It's the one and only way to keep cool. It rains every other day, but around here it doesn't affect the temperature one bit.

There are three Cal fellows here besides two of us from Stanford. Boy, how we long for that wonderful San Francisco fog.

This last week has been one of sweat and grime and dust. We've worked on demolition, rigging, classroom stuff, and the ever present infantry drill and bayonet drill. The last is the worst of all. One half hour of bayonet drill is about all the average man can stand. Next week we spend the better part of our time on rifle marksmanship. We have long hikes and night problems coming up soon, but not next week. You ought to see me with a full pack. I can hardly walk.

What's the Red Cross doing for me? That's a laugh.   Nobody does anything for officers. With all their money, they're supposed to take care of themselves, but, damn it, you can't spend it. I haven't seen a newspaper or magazine since I've been here, but I wouldn't have time to read them if I had them.

There is no telling where or when anyone is going to get sent. A certain part of the officers will stay here with the training battalions. God forbid!! One thing I do know, if and when they ship me, they can't send me any farther from civilization.

Finally got my travel money, $117.00. Enclosed is $100.00 which I would like you to deposit in the bank for me. I will get my uniform money as soon as I get time. They give you no time whatsoever to take care of that sort of thing. You have to skip a lunch, or something like that. I will credit myself with $100.00 in the check book.

I left a forwarding address at school. Don't know why they didn't send Doug's letter on. Met a guy on the train who said the Quad[1] got misplaced, or rather the freight car they were on got misplaced, and they hadn't yet located it.

I'll have to finish this now, as I've got a lot of letters to write. Please write soon, and enjoy the fog.
Much love to all,
Bill

So, the "griping" or "bitching" or general complaining starts. As I recall, my mother was very disturbed by all the discussion of bayonet drill. At this point I was definitely wondering myself what I had gotten into.

This letter contains the start of what was to become an obsession about getting out of Ft. Leonard Wood. At about this time they were starting to ask our class for volunteers to go various places, evidently in response to War Department requests. I signed up to volunteer for a couple of places, but I wanted to go to the East Coast because my girlfriend Noma was there, and most of the requests were for the West Coast or for the Pacific. Bob Springmeyer, the other Stanford guy in the camp, jumped at a chance to go to Ft. Ord, California, and left in great glee. My impression is that he ended up in the 3rd Infantry Division and got to Africa as fast as I did.

The next letter is postmarked July 21.

Sunday

Dear Mother, Dad, and Sis,
I first want to thank you for the numerous letters. I've received something or other every other day, and it sure has been swell. Also received laundry and newspaper. Got Mother's "airmail" today.

I suppose I'm half an officer now, since I've completed half the course. Our class

---

1   Stanford yearbook

has already begun to break up. A lot of the construction men have been sent out, some of them to Puerto Rico, and more to Texas. Building airports, I believe. Six of the men were sent to a combat unit in a regular division, and ordered to get rid of their cars and heavy baggage. The belief seems to be that most of the younger officers will be sent to combat regiments in regular divisions, and they are of course located from Maine to San Diego.

Spent most of this week on the rifle range. I think we reached the height of our required physical exertion on Friday when we spent the entire morning on that damndest of army pastimes, the bayonet assault course. Thank gosh that's over. Temperature was about 110° without a cloud in the sky. I thought I'd die after the first 1/2 hour, but I managed to half-heartedly struggle through the morning.

The only thermometer I've seen here is one in our classroom that goes up as high as 95°. The red line goes out of sight about 10:00 am, and the tip doesn't appear again till eight in the evening. Where it goes in the meantime no-one knows. It's awfully hot about 2:00 or 3:00, though. However, yesterday the heat broke, and today isn't bad.

I don't think I'll ever enjoy the army. I just don't care for this kind of work. Nothing comes easy for me, I have to learn everything by hard work. I sure envy all my friends who are in laboratories or working at drafting boards.

The men in the class are all ages, me being the youngest of all, I believe. Most of them are married, so on Saturday evening they disappear into the surrounding country, and don't show up again until Monday. Therefore, I get awful lonesome on Sundays. I'll be awfully glad when I get out of this class and start doing something useful, even if I have to be a "scoutmaster" in one of the training companies. At least, that's what the officers here consider themselves.

One officer was telling me about a man in his platoon who can't count above ten. He says the man was firing on the rifle range for a week, and has yet to hit the target. Another told me about a case on the range where he discovered a nigger with his rear sight turned completely off the gun. When he asked him what he thought he was doing, the nigger replied, "Suh, that thing gets in mah road!"

I'm enclosing our first week's program. You might be interested in how it is run.

Next week we take up combat principles and tactics. Also we start building bridges, and manning assault boats.

Dad, you might send me those copies of "Mechanical Engineering." Better keep the other stuff. Otherwise I don't need anything. Can't think of a thing I need for my birthday. Hope I'll be out of this place by then.

I believe I've run out of news, so I'll close and get this into the mail. Think I'll sleep this afternoon.

Much love to all,
Bill

As I indicated in the Preface, I regret the racist remark in this letter (and there will be some more). The reference to the rifle range reminds me that one day I was in the "pits" scoring hits and the guy on my target was getting an incredible number of bulls-eyes. I asked who he was and was told that it was Finley. As was the case with Bill Barnum, fate was to bring Fred and me together for the rest of the war. Fred was an ROTC graduate (1941) of Missouri School of Mines in Rolla. We had many adventures together and served as fellow company commanders during the Battle of the Bulge. Fred stopped a machine gun bullet in Sicily, but recovered and rejoined us later.

Saturday night

Dear Mother, Dad, and Sis,

Again, I have quite a line of letters and what-nots to thank you for. Most especially, I want to thank you for the birthday present. I like it very much, and I am sure it will come in very handy. I remember I had one before, but I wore it out several years ago. Thanks also for the clippings and Sporting Greens.

This place is becoming a little more endurable as I swing into the final week. Had fewer classes, & more outdoor work this last week. Spent two mornings building bridges, and a day or so on combat work. One day we had to crawl on our bellies for about a quarter of a mile. I apparently strained a whole new set of muscles, 'cause my legs were sore for days. We crawled up to a firing line, fired 10 shots at targets 350 yards away, and then staged an infiltration attack. Had to fire with gas masks on, and as you can't use glasses with a gas masks, I couldn't even see the targets. At the end of the attack we all collapsed from exhaustion at the feet of the enemy. Fine fighters we are!!

Has been cool for the whole week, following a heavy storm Sunday and Monday. Rain doesn't affect our program one bit. I've at times been knee-deep in mud. Nice cleaning problem.

Building pontoon bridges is rugged work, but more interesting than some things we've done. We laid a foot-bridge across a 170 ft river in 8 minutes this morning.

Three times a week, now, they portion us out to various training companies, and let us exercise them and give them infantry drill. Rather fun to give a command and then have half a dozen non-coms jump on each guy who makes a mistake.

Dad, you asked about the organization here? I'll start from the top. The E.R.T.C. composes about 1/4 of the post, and is made up of 10,000 men — 7000 whites, and 3000 jigs. These are divided into several training groups that are comparable to regiments. Each group has three battalions, and each battalion, four companies. The officers in the "refresher" course are each attached to a regular training company for administrative purposes only. They are all quartered and messed by their particular "group". The class itself is run by ERTC Hdqrs., and is separate from any "group". The organization is a little split up here, because, for instance, we are carried on the company "morning report", but in the class "sick book". The class itself is organized into a company for instruction purposes only. A new class starts every week now, so there are four overlapping classes, which are entirely separate.

Our class had originally about 60 men. We now have 40, having lost several to El Paso, Puerto Rico, Alaska, and to the 3rd Division at Fort Ord. A good many of the remainder will stay here in training companies, and to get away at all costs, I've put in for the Motor Transport School at Omaha. A new class starts there August 4th. Don't know whether I'll get it or not, but to get a decent job you've got to have experience of some kind, and any officers who have special training will naturally get better jobs when they get out into the field. They also asked for volunteers for the Cooks' and Bakers' School at Fort Riley, Kansas, but I couldn't see that. Anyway, before long I'll know something, because we finish up next Saturday. Doubt if I get any leave to speak of. They have a habit of giving 4 days leave when you are transferred, which wouldn't help me a bit. Don't know what I'll do.

Thanks for the letter, Sis; how about another?

The principle criticism I have about the army is that the drafted men are too old. They all have too many firmly established interests at home. I think congress is mad not to draft them at 18. By the time they're ready to fight, they're plenty old enough. In the Engineers everything depends upon teamwork, and the younger men have a much better team spirit. The older men will do what they are told, and they don't cause so much trouble, but they just don't have the push.

Had a nice long letter from Uncle Marion today. Says he will write Dad soon.

We have an over-night combat problem next week. Hope it doesn't rain. Means a full pack hike and lots of belly scraping.

Bought myself a pair of quartermaster field shoes. Wonderful shoes, but they feel like diver's shoes after you've hiked a ways in them.

Have to quit now, 'cause I'm out of letter paper. Hope this is my last letter from Ft. Wood.

Much love to all,
Bill

This was not to be the last letter from Fort Leonard Wood!

The birthday present referred to was a little leather comb and fingernail file holder. I carried it through the entire war. I remember in particular on Omaha Beach, in France, after I had made my harrowing way to the top of the bluff, and didn't know exactly what to do next, I sat down and cleaned my fingernails, much to the disgust of a nearby soldier who thought I was out of my mind.

Sunday

Dear Mother, Dad, and Sis,

This letter will be mailed a little late because I want to get it registered first. I'm enclosing my pay-check which I wish you would take care of. I will deduct $75 from it as partial payment to you, Dad, and will enter the remainder in my checkbook. As you can see, this miserable room is costing me $40 a month. They work a funny system. The married men get the same quarters, but they get their rental allowance in addition. I haven't collected my uniform allowance yet. They make it just as difficult as possible to get.

I had hoped I would be writing from elsewhere this Sunday, but at least I know I'm leaving soon. I got orders to report to the 8th Group headquarters yesterday, and when I did so the adjutant said "——of course you know you're going to the Motor Transport School". Of "course" I didn't know. Practically everybody else was put in a training company here in the ERTC. They don't know when I'll get my travel orders, but I know the school starts Tuesday, so I suppose they'll get me there late. I don't see why they couldn't have sent me yesterday so I could have been on time.

Certainly glad to get the "refresher" course over. Spent this last week on full pack hikes, machine gun firing, bridges, etc. Had one overnight combat problem.

Has turned hot again. About 105° yesterday. I wonder how Omaha will be. At least I'll be on the beaten track up there so mail and transportation will move faster.

Thanks for all the magazines. I've enjoyed them very much. You'd better hang onto my Quad until I get settled somewhere. I don't know how well I'm going to fit in my trunk as it is.

My QM shoes went thru in the soles after a little over three weeks use. The things were about 1/2" thick, too.

As usual I have nothing to do today except sit around. I think I'll catch up a bit in "Mechanical Engineering". That seems to be the only way I have of keeping in contact with the mechanical engineering profession.

Two soldiers have died of the heat since I've been here. In both cases they have been older drafted men. The average age in some of these companies is 30.
Received a letter from Marion the other day. Says he has command of a company.

I don't see why you don't go on up to Tahoe and stop talking about it. Gosh, you've got all that country right at your doorsteps, and if you don't make use of it now, you probably never will. Maybe nobody will be going anywhere next year. After living 4 years in Palo Alto, I can truthfully say that you'll never get there if you wait for the perfect opportunity to come.

Went up to the club last night and had a couple of beers. I then proceeded to fall asleep in a chair there.

Well, there doesn't seem to be much more news. Once more I hope my next letter will be mailed from elsewhere.

Much love,

Bill

P.S. Here's the other check. I'm taking $50 of it. You take the other $100. In other words I have now paid you $175.00. Please let me know just how much more I owe you.

I detect in this letter, as well in some of the others, a sense that I thought I was going to eventually have some kind of semi-permanent assignment, i.e., I was going to stay in one place for awhile. The idea of a fighting war had not yet sunk in, and indeed there was at that time very little fighting on land going on. However, I do recall that there was increasing discussion in the press about a "second front" in Europe. The Russians were pressing very hard for it, and I have a recollection of feeling that I wanted no part of it. The Dieppe Raid (a Canadian raid on the French coast that proved to be very costly) took place about this time, and that was not encouraging.

I had begun to make a few friends, and one very nice guy was an officer who was a June graduate from Johns Hopkins. One evening he and I walked over to Headquarters to go to a movie. On the way it was clear there was something he needed to talk about. After graduation he had married a girl in Illinois and then they had come almost immediately to Ft. Leonard Wood. She was living in a nearby town and he was spending just his weekends with her. His problem was that after a month of marriage they had not yet successfully "consummated" their marriage, and this had him really upset. She evidently had a friend who had the same problem, but he seemed to need someone else to reassure him. I was certainly of no help! Well, they were going to try again next weekend.

The following letter was evidently written on August 5.

Wednesday night

Dear Mother, Dad, and Sis,

This is going to be the voice of embittered humanity speaking this evening. Maybe if I put my gripes down in writing it will make me feel better.

Principle gripe is that I'm still here. Don't ask me why. They've put me in the plans and training division of the 8th Group headquarters, pending receipt of my orders. There are four people in the office and there is enough work for two. You have no idea what it's like to sit and do nothing for hours on end. If I have to do it for another day I'll scream. If I can get away tomorrow I think I'll go see the colonel who issues orders and find out what the score is. He'll be mad when I bother him, but I don't give a damn any more. I have never in my life been so fed up with anything as I am with this army. It sure doesn't make me feel any better, either, when I get letters from Rog and the other fellows who like their jobs so much.

I don't care in the least for the people I'm supposed to be working with. They don't even seem to know I exist. There's a corporal who comes in a couple of times a day and I heave a sigh of relief when he shows up 'cause I then have someone to talk to.

I've run completely out of clean clothes, but I don't dare send any laundry out, because as soon as I do I'll be shipped out.

They asked for volunteers for duty overseas twice last week, and I volunteered twice, but they passed me up both times. A transfer like that would at least mean leave. There is no other way to get it.

Please write me as much as possible, because you have no idea how I appreciate letters. My present address is on the envelope, and they will forward mail when (and if) I leave.

Been pretty cool here lately. Rained all day Monday.

The government's sure getting gyped paying me $200 a month. The WPA does more work than I do.

Well, I think I'll pull off these filthy clothes and go to bed. There's nothing better to do.

Lots of love,
Bill

Buried in this letter is a significant and fateful statement. I had "volunteered for duty overseas." It was one of my less brilliant moves, and as it turned out it was the source of all my current problems, not to mention future problems, although I did not realize it at the time. What I didn't know was that the decision to invade North Africa had been made no more than a couple of weeks before and among the thousands of plans for that operation were included arrangements for replacement troops to be sent to England.

Saturday, August 8

Dear Mother, Dad, and Sis,

Well, it seems as how I'm here to stay. They changed their minds today and stuck me in a company for keeps. I feel greatly relieved now that all the uncertainty is over, and altho it isn't the kind of work that I'd like best, it'll be plenty of work, and I'll try to do my best. Monday, I get a platoon of 60 raw selectees and start them out on a three month road towards becoming soldiers. I haven't met my sergeant or corporals yet, but I can do that Monday. We don't really start training until week after next. I have the first platoon, and it just happens to be the first to fill up. The men arrive all week. I don't know much about the rest of the officers, but the C.O. seems to be a nice enough guy. I've got to buy a lamp now, because I'll have to learn the stuff the night before the men learn it.

I'm driving into St. Louis tomorrow with another fellow, and we may take in a ball game. Haven't seen a big league game for a long time, and I think a little entertainment of that sort would do me good. Also a nice juicy porterhouse steak is in order.

I'll probably have a lot more to talk about once I get my platoon and get into the swing of things. Right now there isn't much to talk about except that last week was a nightmare, and I hope I won't have any more of that sort of stuff for awhile.

I had a nice long letter from Marge today. I understand Sis got one from her, so I guess you know as much about her as I do.

They are becoming overcrowded with officers here now, so my $40 per only goes for half a room. I moved in with another fellow today.

I guess Sis must be in La Jolla now.

Hey, I thought Doug was going to write me.

Every day or so I read in the St. Louis papers about the Arroff trial.[2] He seems to be quite well known now. I wonder if Bob Dieck has read about it?

I'm not doing anything in particular now. I'm going to spend the evening writing letters, and then get to bed early so I can get up early. Ordinarily, I haven't arisen before 11:00 on Sundays.

Well, as I said before, I'll have more to say next week.

Much love,

Bill

P.S. Please note my new address.

(Co. B, 32nd E.T. Bn.)

This letter is followed by a note in my mother's handwriting. Apparently she sent my letter to my sister who was probably in La Jolla.

This sounds better, doesn't it? We're on our way out to dinner but not movies - Dad has to go to a Scabbard & Blade meeting.

Love, Mother

Evidently my belly-aching was getting to them!

---

2   I have no recollection of what this was about.

Tuesday afternoon

Dear Mother, Dad, and Sis,

For the umpteenth time I've been reassigned, but I think I'm at last at least temporarily permanent. I was transferred yesterday from Co. B to Co A of the 32nd Bn. Right now I'm an extra officer, but I imagine somebody will leave soon, because there is no surplus of officers.

We have a full company now, but regular training doesn't start until next week. Most of the men are from California or Texas. Practically no "ski's" or "vich's". This week they are on work details, and are getting shot, classified, etc.

I like the officers in this company a lot better than the last one, but I wish I had a platoon. Have very little to do right now. I'm sitting in the orderly room writing now.

Had a swell time in St. Louis Sunday. Had a steak dinner, took in a double-header between St. Louis and Detroit, and went to a show. Got back about 2:00 am very tired. It's about 135 miles to St. Louis from here.

My mail seems to be chasing me all over the post, this being my fourth address here.

O.K. I'll send this by airmail. The only trouble is getting to a post office to get stamps.

Received two letters from you all yesterday. Thanks. I guess it's lucky you didn't try to catch me in Omaha. Better not try that; they change their minds too easily.

Now that I've started a second sheet, I've run out of things to say. That's always the way. I can't think of what you said in your last letters.

The weather hasn't been bad lately. Rains every two or three days, and a good deal of cloudy weather in between.

Well, I seem to have definitely run out of material now.

Much love,

Bill

P.S. The written address is a Post Office Department rule, so they tell us.

I now suspect that the transfer from Co. B to Co. A was related to the fact that I was by this time on a list of officers slated to move out soon.

The next letter was probably written on August 13.

Thursday night

Dear Mother, Dad, and Sis,

I'm down at the company orderly room and have temporary access to a very poor typewriter. I want to go to the late show, so this won't be very long.

I'm beginning to sort of enjoy this company duty, so I have no doubt that I will be shipped out any moment now. It's kind of fun to have a bunch of men snapping to attention whenever I appear, and jumping when I open my mouth. I'll have to admit they don't jump very quickly yet, but they'll learn. The non-coms do, though.

I spent today out on the battalion drill field with about 125 men cleaning up the place and making it fit for use. I had them picking up rocks, and they sure didn't like it. I think I'll probably be out there again tomorrow.

I was OD last night, and had to get up early and stand reveille this morning. It's pitch dark at reveille now. I wonder what it will be like this winter.

I'm thinking of making another trip into St. Louis this Sunday if there is a good game on. The fellow I went with last Sunday can't make it, so I may go by bus.

There is some talk of going on a seven day week around here, so I want to make use of my Sundays while I have them.

I don't have any stamps now, so I will probably have to wait till tomorrow to mail this. But you insist on airmail!!

I'm as usual running out of conversation. Nothing much of interest has happened this week. I keep intending to take some pictures, but I don't seem to get around to it.

Much love to all,
Bill

There may be a missing letter here because it is hard to believe that I didn't write during the following week, the week of 17 August. I am sure that I spent that Saturday night in St. Louis. I recall distinctly seeing a Cardinals game. Several of us drove to St. Louis in a car owned by a guy named Weldele. One of these guys spent the entire trip telling us about his sexual exploits and his plan of attack for that night. As I recall his "plan" went somewhat awry. I had begun to make more friends and life was improving. I think Weldele was a neighbor in the officer's barracks. He had a brand new Chevrolet.

We probably got back late Sunday and I didn't have time to write; I usually wrote letters on Sundays. Everything went to pieces the following Saturday morning, so I probably had intended to write on the next Sunday and never got the chance.

On Saturday morning, 22nd August, I was getting my platoon ready for the traditional Saturday morning inspection when word came for me to report immediately to Group Headquarters. I hustled there and found a large group of 2nd Lieutenants, including the aforementioned Barnum and Finley, getting the news that we were being shipped to the New York Port of Embarkation, and they hoped to get the orders cut in time to get on the train that afternoon. We were to report in New York the following Thursday, the 27th, and with four days travel time our generous adjutant said he could get us one day's leave.

We had to scurry around and settle all our bills (mess, laundry, etc.), and do various other similar things before we could leave. I decided I would take the train from St. Louis to Norfolk and spend the extra time with Noma. One of the frustrations that day was that we were not allowed to make phone calls or send telegrams — wartime troop movement information was secret. I did manage to send a telegram that night from St. Louis, but I note that it was not received until Monday morning. I suppose I telephoned Noma at the same time, because I must have arrived in Norfolk on Sunday evening, although I am not clear on that. I may have arrived on Monday. In those days long distance telephoning was sort of a luxury that you seldom used. The telegram to my parents is below.

MRS. H. E. KAYS
200 HILLCREST ROAD, BERKELEY CALIF
SPENDING ONE DAYS LEAVE IN NORFOLK ENROUTE ELSEWHERE
WILL EXPLAIN BY AIRMAIL SPECIAL LATER HOLD UP MAIL UNTIL I
GET NEW ADDRESS LOVE
BILL

I spent Monday, Tuesday, and Wednesday at Noma's parents' house, but evidently never sent that "airmail special." I did send the following telegram on Wednesday.

MRS. H. E. KAYS
200 HILLCREST ROAD, BERKELEY CALIF
HAVE TRIED TO PHONE TWICE LEAVING HERE TONIGHT. WILL TRY
TO PHONE FROM UP NORTH TOMORROW OR THE NEXT NIGHT.
LOVE
BILL

Noma Greene was the daughter of a Naval Officer and lived in officer's quarters at the Naval Operating Base, Norfolk. I knew the area well since my father had been on duty there until the previous November, and I had spent the past two summers there. She was a student at Sweet Briar College in Virginia.

I don't recall precisely what we did during those three days, other than visit some old friends. We probably went dancing at the Cavalier Club at Virginia Beach, because that is the sort of thing that she liked best. All the most famous "big bands" spent time there and people like Frank Sinatra could frequently be found. I do remember her father telling me that where I was going it was going to be "hot in more ways than one," suggesting of course Africa. I recall looking up an old friend, Bob Fogg, who had joined the SeeBees and was in training there.

Wednesday evening Noma took me to the ferry that connected with a train at Cape Charles on the east side of Chesapeake Bay. It was a few hours' boat trip. I remember standing on the deck at night in a cold wind and wondering what could possibly lie ahead, and what had I gotten myself into. I was excited, but not a little fearful. I had time to do a little thinking. For the first time my army experience was beginning to take on the aspects of an "adventure." What I didn't really appreciate at the time was that I was heading for a combat experience with totally inadequate training. I was going to be a combat officer based on essentially four weeks of basic training. Even the rawest recruits who I would presumably lead would have had substantially more training than I, and that is not to mention the more experienced soldiers. My three years in the Western High School Cadet Corps in Washington D.C. had probably contributed more to my being a soldier than any experience I had had since. My background for what lay ahead was pathetic.

And for those curious, I went off to war still a virgin! Perhaps this would be a little surprising in this day and age, but things were different in 1942. Oh, there were plenty of guys who were very experienced, but the fact is I wasn't all that unusual. Fear of pregnancy by the girls and fear of venereal diseases, as well as pregnancy, by the boys made a big difference. And the Army put the fear of God in you about the latter. Besides which, "nice" girls just didn't believe in pre-marital sex.

The New York Port of Embarkation had requested that we report in at Camp Kilmer, near New Brunswick, New Jersey. In fact the whole thing was a little strange. We had formal orders to the N.Y. Port of Embarkation, presumably in Jersey City, but then they had inserted into the envelope a little typewritten note saying that we should report to Camp Kilmer. This was probably some small concession to wartime secrecy — enemy spies were apparently interested in where this little group of 2nd Lieutenants was going! The idiocy was beginning.

I had an upper berth on a train that left about 11:00 pm. Then I discovered the train didn't stop in New Brunswick and that I would have to get off at Newark and take another train back to New Brunswick. The train arrived in Newark at about 6:00 am and as soon as I took the train for New Brunswick I realized that my footlocker, which I had checked through, was not going to arrive with me.

The next four days at Camp Kilmer were chaos compounded by stupidity and incompetence. I found that we were a group of 50 new 2nd Lieutenants assigned to something they called a Task Force with the designation 6088BB. Nobody was in charge. A 1st Lieutenant with a little mustache and a jeep was supposed to be taking care of us, but he knew nothing and seemed incapable of finding out anything. When were we going to leave? Where were we going? What kind of clothes did we need? Idiotic wartime secrecy hid everything, especially from people with a need to know. A major came around and told us we weren't going to a tea party, so we had better get some winter field uniforms. We were all dressed in summer khakis. I put the 1st Lieutenant to work finding my footlocker, but he initially had no luck.

Friday evening several of us went into New Brunswick and found an Army-Navy store open and there we bought wool clothes. I also bought a large metal suitcase that I intended to use to mail a lot of junk home. The previous night I wrote the following letter that I mailed in New Brunswick that Friday night.

Dear Mother, Dad, and Sis,

I've tried to phone you on both Monday and Tuesday nights, but you were out both times. Tonight is my last opportunity to even write a letter, so here goes.

I'm attached to some task force, going somewhere. I don't know the answer to either of the above. I arrived here (secret) today, and tomorrow we are restricted to the post with no communication, so I guess we leave soon. My APO [Army Post Office] will be A.P.O. #3014, c/o Postmaster, New York, N.Y.

I'm going to try to send a lot of excess stuff home tomorrow. Everything is in a hell of a mess here, and nobody has their equipment or proper clothing. They were supposed to equip us before we left Ft. Wood, but they sent us out on too short notice.

Somehow I've got to take care of my financial matters if possible. Will allotment most of my pay to Mother.

Haven't time to say any more now. Will write at my next chance. Don't know when that will be.

Loads of love to all,
Bill

My next letter would be from England. However, in New Brunswick that night I went to the railroad station and called home from a pay phone. I remember my father asking if I was going to England, and I said I didn't know. My mother kept shouting "you're going to be all right!"

At Camp Kilmer I first became well acquainted with Harold Haas. In fact the last letter was written on his imprinted letter paper. Harold was a member of our refresher class, but I hadn't met him till now. He was, like Finley, an ROTC graduate of Missouri School of Mines, and like all of us, an engineering graduate. I don't know whether Finley knew him there or not, because Finley had graduated the previous year. Haas was another of this group, like Barnum and Finley, who I would get to know very well. Harold had one near fatal flaw — he frequently couldn't seem to read a map. Ultimately he was wounded twice, and then finally captured in Germany in 1945, and in every case it was apparently because he didn't know where he was.

From Haas I learned the famous army term, SNAFU (situation normal, all fucked up). Harold must have used the term a hundred times during the next few days, for very good reasons.

The next couple of days were frantic. They finally issued us the new style helmets and gas masks and field packs and officer bed rolls and blankets and all that sort of thing. My footlocker was finally located on Saturday. We were told to paint our names, serial numbers, and 6088BB on everything, but nobody could find either paint or a paintbrush. Our 1st Lt. finally brought a can of white paint but no brush. We used the ends of our pup tent ropes for brushes. And so it went with every single detail. How could we possibly win the war if the Army was run by imbeciles?

Although I thought we were restricted to the post, some of the guys went into New York on Friday night and saw the show "Arsenic and Old Lace." On Saturday evening several of us went to the post movie and saw a war film involving a romance between an English soldier and a girl from the Women's Auxiliary Air Force (WAAF). It was a sentimental film titled "This Above All," starring Joan Fontaine and Tyrone Power. Suddenly we were all excited about the possibility that our destination was England. WAAFs appeared to be something to look forward to, never mind that Joan Fontaine was an American! It was all very romantic; the "adventure" was beginning to unfold. We will come back to that story later.

On Sunday afternoon we were led to a railroad siding where we found 370 enlisted men who were evidently also in 6088BB. This came as something of a shock; nobody had told us that we had any enlisted men to deal with. These were all new Engineer recruits who had received a shortened training course of two months. There were also several large wooden packing cases that they said were to go with us. We were then all loaded into the train, along with the packing cases. The train went to Jersey City where it finally stopped at a ferry dock. We were herded onto a car ferry, along with the packing cases, each of the enlisted men carrying two large blue barracks bags, along with everything else, sweating and cursing. I had a pack on my back, a rather large officer's bedroll on one shoulder, and a heavily packed valise (I think it was called a val-pac) in one hand.

In the late afternoon we pulled out into the Hudson River and turned north. Pretty soon we stopped and drifted south. We did this repeatedly for about two hours. It afforded a good view of Manhattan, but then we also noticed that there was a very large ship at Pier 92, and it appeared that was where we were ultimately going. It was the Queen Elizabeth.

Ultimately we docked at the end of Pier 92 and filed out into the covered dock. Guides led the first of the men to the side of the Elizabeth and they started to go in through a hatch on the side. After most of the officers and some of the enlisted men had gone aboard, the Transportation Corps officer who was directing things turned to two or three of us and said, "Who's in charge here? Who is the commanding officer?" We told him, "Nobody." At this point he turned to the guy next to me, one Lt. Schamp, and said, "As of this moment you are the commanding officer of 6088BB. Open up those boxes and see what's in them." I decided to stay and help Schamp, and we got some of the men to break open the boxes. They were full of clothing and other junk, stuff that evidently was supposed to have been issued to the enlisted men at Camp Kilmer. He ordered us to start issuing it there and then on the dock. In the meantime all loading of the men stopped.

I stayed with Schamp and we finally got all the men aboard about midnight, taking the partially filled boxes aboard too. Schamp and I made our way to our assigned cabin and found it so full of people and baggage that we could hardly get in. There were twelve bunks in what had been originally a small double cabin. Schamp and I couldn't even find our bunks; they were full of somebody else's gear. We decided to go back onto the dock and get a Coca-Cola (we had seen a machine). A guard stopped us at the gangway — nobody goes ashore. I got a sinking feeling that I had stepped off the edge of the earth; we had literally reached a point of no return.

We sailed the next morning, Monday August 31st. My first letter from England gives some description of the trip. There were 17,000 troops on board, and to a large extent 6088BB had disappeared into the crowd. A day or so out a representative of the Commanding Officer of troops came around, found Schamp, and told us to set up a unit headquarters in a space at the top of one of the stairwells and get organized. We used one of our boxes and set up shop. A soldier named Siedlecki claimed that he had been a non-commissioned officer (NCO) in the British army at some time or other and volunteered to act as First Sergeant. He eventually rounded up about two-thirds of the men. I later got to know Siedlecki as a corporal in one of our companies in the 1st Engineers. He never did make sergeant, much less First Sergeant.

The men were double-loaded, twenty-four to a twelve-bunk room. Our unit was assigned a small space on the boat deck and the men were supposed to spend twelve hours there and twelve hours in their bunks. The Queen Elizabeth had very little deck space; most of its space was enclosed. I suppose it was designed for the North Atlantic trade where being on deck was no luxury. Actually the men spent most of their time in the chow line. Only two meals a day were provided and the chow line snaked continuously all over the ship.

Each morning the ship's crew supplied buckets of water and mops to clean the state-rooms, and then there were inspections. With all the gear and barracks bags you couldn't even find the floor. The ship gradually became a mess. Fortunately the trip took only six days for otherwise people might have started dying of suffocation!

The officers ate in grand style in the main dining room, tablecloths and all. There was a huge and comfortable lounge, again for the officers, but it was almost entirely taken over by Air Force officers who apparently didn't have responsibility for any enlisted men. Several large poker games ran continuously twenty-four hours a day with multi-thousand dollar pots. It was my first exposure to these hotshots with their leather flight jackets and floppy caps.

The Queen Elizabeth sailed without escort. At thirty knots she was too fast for German submarines to catch, although this was a very dangerous submarine period.

As we left New York we headed southeast for a couple of days and we began to think we were going to Africa. But then we changed course to almost due north. It got colder and the Big Dipper went high in the sky.

One night Schamp and I were on the boat deck with our enlisted men and he pulled out a little chemical cigarette lighter of which he was very proud. You could light a cigarette without a flame. We both lit up cigarettes. In less that a minute we were accosted by a British Naval Officer who was very nasty about American idiots who lit cigarettes in submarine country.

On another occasion I led some of our men to our little section of the boat deck only to find it occupied by a large number of black troops. I told them to "get the hell out of here." One of them turned to me and said, "You treat us like we's dogs!" I was somewhat taken aback by being talked to like that, but the incident troubled me. I had to admit to myself that he was right, and I felt badly about it.

There was a small contingent of British officers on board. I suppose they were some kind of liaison officers. One seemed to be the senior officer and was deferred to by the others. I remember in particular a Scottish officer in kilts. The senior officer would issue some kind of order in quiet tones and this guy would step up, stamp his feet, bang his heels together with a loud clack, and then give a wildly exaggerated British open handed salute. More orders and the Scottish officer would reply with a loud shout, "Right you ah, suh." Then there would be more stomping and clacking and another salute. This was obviously designed to impress American slobs, and we did stand there looking kind of stupid with our mouths open.

Somebody asked one of the British ship's crew where we were going and he said Greenoch, Scotland. That was the first that we had even a clue. On Saturday afternoon we saw through a fog the blinking signal light of a British destroyer dead ahead, and a little later the incredible green hills of Northern Ireland off to the right. By late afternoon we were past the northern tip of Ireland and were sailing up the Firth of Clyde, a large area of coastal water sheltered from the Atlantic Ocean on the West Coast of Scotland. A British Spitfire flew along side and dipped his wings. At about six o'clock we anchored in the Firth of Clyde a mile or so off Greenoch. Two weeks before we had been in Missouri, seemingly a million miles from the war. Now we were getting somewhere near where the action was — we had been reading about it in the papers for over three years. I was a little awed, but not really fearful. It was all still a grand adventure.

North Carolina, August 1939; Dad, Mother, and Sis.

Norfolk, August 1941; Noma Greene.

Norfolk, June 1942; Noma and me.

Camp Kilmer, August 29, 1942;
In my newly issued equipment.

Chapter Two

England

September 5 - December 6, 1942

We arrived in Greenoch, Scotland, on Saturday, September 5th, and word came over the loud speakers that we would disembark onto lighters (actually a barge) the next morning. This would involve going down the stairs to a hatch just above the waterline. The ship was not at a dock. In fact, there were no docks large enough for the Queen Elizabeth in Scotland. We hoped that our unit, 6088BB, would be the last to disembark, because that was probably the only way we would find everyone. The next morning it was announced that the first unit to go ashore would be 6088BB!

Simply getting down about five decks, carrying all the gear and barracks bags, and with the stairs crowded with hundreds of other men, was an ordeal. When a headcount was made on the lighter, all 370 enlisted men and fifty officers were accounted for! Simple self-preservation had prevailed.

On the dock we were met by British officers and non-coms and led to a nearby train. Suddenly the world changed. Everything was very efficiently handled and, above all, people seemed to know what they were doing. The contrast with Camp Kilmer was striking. I was impressed with the British. Some Red Cross ladies served us tea after we got into our train compartments, and a small bagpipe band (old men with knobby legs) performed up and down the platform.

There followed one of the most exciting days of my life. It is hard to realize today the emotional impact of suddenly being in the United Kingdom in 1942. For three years, we Americans had followed the war on the radio and in the newspapers, as Hitler swept over Europe, and only England held out. We had agonized as the Luftwaffe tried first to destroy the British Royal Air Force (RAF) and then burn up the cities. American sympathies, led by Franklin D. Roosevelt, were overwhelmingly on the British side. Winston Churchill was the hero of the day. Dozens of movies idealizing the British effort added to the effect. The Japanese attack on Pearl Harbor had changed a lot of priorities in American minds, but the feeling about England persisted.

All day that first day on British soil we traveled south in beautiful weather, hanging out of the windows and waving to the small crowds who cheered and waved back. The Yanks had come! The train stopped a few times and more tea and refreshments were served. The only towns I remember were Carlisle and Crewe. After dark we reached our destination, the little town of Lichfield, some miles north of Birmingham, England.

British officers met us and without confusion we boarded trucks. I remember we sang "Over There" in the truck as we drove through a blacked-out Lichfield. We were taken to a British army establishment a couple of miles outside of Lichfield, Whittington Barracks, home of the South Staffordshire Regiment. I was assigned to a rather ample room with Finley and Haas. What had again brought us together, since we had also roomed at Camp Kilmer? Years later it occurred to me that our names were simply close together in the alphabet.

As soon as we had dumped our gear in our rooms, they led us to a mess hall. We were served platters of bread and sliced mutton. The enlisted men had no problem but the British had assumed that we officers had mess kits. We ended up eating the meat with our hands, but we were hungry so it was no problem.

I'll let the letters pick it up from there. The following letter is dated September 7, but that can't be correct unless I merely started the letter that night. A more likely date is Thursday September 9. Evidently writing letters was not yet high on my priority list.

Sept 7, 1942

Dear Mother, Dad, and Sis,

Well, here I am. Not quite at my final destination, but almost there. There's so much I could tell you, and yet there's so much of it that they won't let me tell you, that I don't know where to begin.

First of all, this is an experience that I wouldn't have missed for the world. For the first time in my life, instead of reading and hearing about adventures & big things, I'm right in the midst of it all myself.

The trip over was a little hectic because of the crowded conditions on the ship. I was in a small cabin with 11 other officers. The only good part about it was the mess. The officers ate very well, which I believe is a British custom.

Incidentally, if there are any doubts in your mind, I guess I can tell you that I'm in England. At the present time we're all living in barracks in an old English army post while awaiting our assignments. We've had nothing to do for a few days other than eat & sleep, so we've been seeing the countryside. We've spent some time in the two neighboring villages where I've already been thru a 10th century castle and a 12th century cathedral. Yesterday we took a train into a large city and spent most of the day poking around. There's not much to do. In restaurants, all you can buy is fish and tea. You can apparently always get tea.

There are a lot of things about England that are very different from America. The first thing that impresses you is the amazing cleanliness of the countryside. Every bit of space is used and is very neat. Every house has two stories and a steeply sloping roof. In the south every thing is brick. In the north all the houses are of rock, and even all fences are rock.

The whole country is amazingly green. A cow pasture looks like a well kept up lawn. Also every single house in the country has a flower garden.

The villages look like something out of a storybook. A large cathedral is in the center, and then the houses are jammed in around it. You see very few houses that appear to have been built in this century.

The only bad thing about the place is the vile weather. As one Englishman explained, summer comes on some Thursday afternoon, and you're not quite sure which Thursday at that.

You see very few cars here. If you go any distance, you use the train. Otherwise you walk. We're beginning to catch on to the train system.

The English money has given us no end of headaches. It makes no sense whatsoever. Every time we go into a store to buy something we just about start a riot. At first we'd just hand them a pound note and take the change. Finally our pockets bulged so that we had to figure it out.

I got a haircut the other day, and it ought to last me three or four weeks.

I have yet to see an English house with any form of heating other than a fireplace, and they don't ration coal until October. Brrrr!!

Well, I think I'll close this now and get it mailed. I'll have a new address for you soon, although 3014 will reach me.

Much love to all,
Bill

The morning after we arrived in Lichfield (Monday), the officers were assembled in an auditorium and addressed by a British officer. The burden of his message was that our "chaps" who were going to run this place had not yet arrived, so we were free to do as we liked. We could get to the neighboring towns, Lichfield and Tamworth, by bus, Birmingham was an hour away by train, and London was three hours. And nobody asked us to worry about the enlisted men, so for the time being we forgot them.

Finley and Haas and I, and probably one other, went into Birmingham the next day. It was bombed out and bleak. We talked to a couple of girls on a street corner. One of them said she thought England was likely going to lose the war; I assured her that wasn't possible. After all, Roosevelt had recently announced that the U.S. was going to build 50,000 airplanes, thus assuring victory! We had tea and a few thin slices of bread, and returned to Lichfield.

We went into Lichfield most every night when and we discovered the WAAFs; there was a RAF bomber base near by. We went into a fish and chips joint (it was probably a pub) and through a dense cloud of cigarette smoke we found that the place was crawling with WAAFs. After that movie at Kilmer, we were in seventh heaven. Americans were a novelty, and the WAAFs dropped their RAF buddies instantly. Almost immediately we made several friends, and we saw them frequently afterwards. We even ultimately held a dance at Whittington Barracks. Finley got involved with one named Eileen. She claimed that her husband had been shot down over Germany. Who knows?

The next letter is dated Tuesday, September 14, which is impossible. It must have been written on the 15th. At any rate it follows our first weekend in England.

Tues., Sept 14

Dear Mother, Dad, and Sis,
Haven't as yet received any mail from anyone, so when the mail arrives, I'll expect quite a pile of it.

I've been principally having a wonderful time and doing no work. Spend all day dodging anyone who has work to be done and sleeping, and all night prowling thru the blackout in the nearby towns. We've found ourselves some WAAF's, and they've found that all Americans are millionaires, so everybody has a good time.

Got into London last weekend. It's only about 3 hrs. if you can catch on to the railway system. I'm gradually becoming very acquainted with the London, Midland, and Scottish Railway, better known as the L.M.& S. The trains are very odd. They are divided off into compartments & you enter each compartment from the outside.

In London we had a terrible time finding accommodations. We finally went to the billeting officer at the U.S. Army headquarters and he fixed us up very nicely at the American officer's club for 5 shillings apiece. Got some good old American food, or in other words something other than fish, potatoes, & tea.

The next time we go to London we're going to take somebody with us who knows their way about in the blackout. There's plenty of night life, but you have to know where to look for it. On Sunday, we did manage to get around to most of the more famous points of interest by means of double-decker buses, taxis, and we even ventured into the subway, or tube, as they call it. We went thru Westminster Abbey, saw No. 10 Downing Street, St. Paul's, walked across London Bridge, and had lunch near Piccadilly Circus. There is no lack of American company in London, and you literally wear your arm out saluting. At the officer's club I saw more rank than I've seen since I've been in the army.

We had to stand up most of the way back on the train. Apparently everybody & his uncle goes to London on weekends.

We are now on a 48 hr. alert expecting our assignments, but I've been on so many false alerts during the last few weeks, that I'm not really expecting to move for awhile.

In the future I'll probably be sending you lists of things to send me. When we were at Camp Kilmer they kept telling us that we weren't going to any tea party, and to get rid of our fancy uniforms. As soon as we get here they tell us to put away our old clothes & haul out our dress clothes. We're supposed to be able to get uniforms from the quartermaster, but we can't as yet. This is more of a "tea party" here than it was at home. At present all I would like is some Kleenex. It's unheard of over here.

Altho cold, the weather has really been very nice lately. The British say it is most unusual. However, it just doesn't get warm in this country. And Scotland is worse!!

Every time you walk down the street and meet someone, they move to the left & we move to our right. You always end up by coming to a dead stop & starting over again.

Say, I would appreciate a U.S. newspaper, or rather clippings once in awhile. We get very little U.S. news here except in the movies. They are virtually all American. The British radio plays American music almost continuously also. Popular songs here are "Don't Sit Under the Apple Tree", and the "Three Little Sisters". "One Dozen Roses" is beginning to make an appearance.

The girls tell us that they get Jack Benny once in awhile, but there is very little interest because nobody understands what's so funny about him.

Well, this was a little longer than the last one, & I could go on for pages, but I've got an officers' meeting in a few minutes, so I'll have to close.

Much love to all,

Bill

The group going into London included Finley and Haas, and I believe a guy we called Rabbit (because he looked like a rabbit, not because he acted like one!). We arrived at Euston Station and got directions from an American Military Policeman. The officer's club was on the east side of South Audley Street. When we ventured out into the blackout after dinner we made the mistake of turning right and ended on Oxford Street. We then went west to Marble Arch, and finally went into the Continental Hotel. We had never heard of Piccadilly Circus, so didn't know enough to go the other way. Even today Oxford Street is pretty dull on a Saturday night. However, we did meet two girls on the sidewalk at Marble Arch, and after some conversation they offered to give us a tour of London the next day. We met them at the same place Sunday morning, and they gave us the tour that is described in the letter. The only trouble was that we didn't have a map, and when we emerged from the Underground at various places I had no idea where we were. I do recall coming out of the Underground at St. Paul's and seeing nothing but devastation in all directions.

On the Monday following the London trip the Americans who were supposed to run the establishment at Whittington Barracks showed up. I think they were something called the 4th Replacement Battalion. The officer in charge didn't have a bird of an idea of what he was supposed to be doing — shades of Camp Kilmer again. Then during the next several days various American officers from London would visit and assemble us all in the auditorium for a speech. Each one contradicted the previous one. They said they had jobs for three times our number and would return shortly to take us away. Then we would never see them again, although one needed somebody so badly that he conducted interviews and took Rabbit away with him.

These were apparently all jobs in the Services of Supply (SOS), building airfields and camps and that sort of thing. It sounded good to me. As it turned out, the problem was that the SOS was in charge of the replacement depots, and Lichfield was the first replacement depot established in the European Theater. But in true army fashion the SOS assumed that they owned the replacement depots and thus had first claim on the replacements, for that is what we were. Apparently somebody in the London headquarters woke up to what was happening and issued a stop order. We were destined for combat outfits, although we didn't yet realize it.

One of our visitors was a hard-assed Colonel who stood up on the stage and gave us instructions on how to salute. We were told that we had come to a tea party after all, so we had come full circle from the major at Camp Kilmer who had told us to forget our dress uniforms and get some clothes to wear in the field. This idiot then stood at the door as we filed out and with a ruler measured the placement of the brass emblems on the lapels of our uniforms!

Later I heard that the guy running the 4th Replacement Battalion one day went to the Lichfield station and tried to order a rail ticket to Kansas City (I presume somebody ultimately sent him back to the USA). The story may be apocryphal, but probably is based on an element of fact. Lichfield eventually became the most infamous of the "repo-depo's" established by General John C. H. Lee, chief of the SOS in Europe. ("C.H." was generally understood to stand for "court house").

The next letter is a "V-Mail" letter. V-Mail letters were written on a special one-page form and were then put on microfilm, sent airmail across the Atlantic, and finally printed on a small 3" x 5" paper and sent by regular mail in the U.S. An examination of the postmarks on my V-Mail letters suggest that they were usually slower than ordinary letters. So much for an innovative experiment!

Lt. W. M. Kays
APO 3014
Sept. 17, 1942

Dear Mother, Dad, and Sis,

How do you like this form of mail? Let me know how long it took to get there and if you could read it well.

I wrote you the other day all about my trip to London, so there really isn't much news. My main interest right now is to get some laundry and cleaning done. Also they are beginning to make me work for a living.

They now tell me that I can tell you that I visited the cathedral in Lichfield and the castle in Tamworth. This weekend I may go to Stratford-on-Avon and, for obvious reasons, to Coventry. Also will try to get to Birmingham and squander a few pounds and shillings and things on a bicycle.

Love,
Bill

I was not to get to Stratford or Coventry or to Birmingham for a bicycle. On or around the 22nd of September, six of us, together with a considerable number of the enlisted men, got orders to report to the First Infantry Division, then stationed at Tidworth, near Salisbury, and actually quite near Stonehenge. Besides me, the group of officers included Barnum, Finley, Haas, Ed Dolega, and a guy named Cole. I had not known either Dolega or Cole before. Ed spent most of the war with us, but was badly wounded during the Battle of the Bulge in Germany near the end of 1944. Cole was a musician and something of a misfit in the combat engineers. He was transferred out of the Division in North Africa in December. I hardly remember Barnum at Lichfield at all, although of course I had known him well at Ft. Leonard Wood — he buddied around with an entirely different group of officers.

How had this particular group come together? Barnum, Cole, Dolega, Finley, Haas, Kays - sounds very alphabetic. After Cole was transferred out, the five of us were to serve together in the same battalion through a great deal of the war. All but me were eventually casualties, but we all survived.

We traveled on a special train that passed through the outskirts of London late at night. At one point the train stopped and the few lights in the railroad yard where we were at the time went out. In the distance we could hear the faint wail of the London air raid sirens. At another point the train stopped abruptly and a conductor came running through the cars in great concern. It seems one of our men had pulled an emergency cord that stopped the train. Once pulled out the cord stayed pulled so it was easy to determine in which small compartment the deed had been perpetrated. Of course all six men in the compartment denied responsibility, so without an officer really in charge, we had a problem. I think Haas was the most senior officer (he had the earliest date of rank), so he probably calmed down the railway employees, who were very upset.

The First Infantry Divison consisted of three infantry regiments, four battalions of artillery, and other units of support troops of various kinds. The latter included the First Engineer Battalion. The total strength of the division was about 13,000 men. This was a regular army division and had been highly decorated in World War I. The junior officers were mostly ROTC graduates and some Officer Candidate School (OCS) graduates, but the officers above the rank of lieutenant included many regulars. The same was true of the enlisted men. Most of the NCOs were regulars, but the privates were largely, although not exclusively, draftees. The division had a strong New York flavor because its various units had been stationed in the Northeast before the war. In the year before going overseas the division had moved to the South and there picked up a lot of recruits from the deep South and the mountain country of West Virginia and Kentucky.

At Tidworth we were met and taken to the officers quarters of the 7th Field Artillery Battalion. We spent all the next day there, not knowing what was gong on, and then towards evening two officers from the 1st Engineers, Len Cohn and Charlie Mills, came over in a couple of command cars and took us to their officers' quarters. I learned later what had been the problem. We had originally been designated to go to the 601st Tank Destroyer Battalion, which was attached at that time to the 1st Division. Apparently the 601st had decided that they needed to form a mine-laying group, and engineers were supposed to be the experts in laying and removing mines. I had never even seen a mine! They talked somebody at the American headquarters in London into approving their request. That day the Commanding Officer of the 1st Engineers got wind of what was going on and went to the commanding general saying, "If there are any spare Engineer officers we need them worse than the tank destroyers do." His argument prevailed and we were assigned to the 1st Engineer Battalion.

The 1st Engineers were very short of rank. Most of the officers were 2nd Lieutenants, many being recent ROTC graduates just like our little group. Few had been in the army more than a year, despite the fact that this was a regular army unit. The Commanding Officer was Major Henry Rowland, a Regular Army officer, but the best soldier was undoubtedly the battalion executive officer, 1st Lieutenant William B. Gara. He had come into the Army, I think, in 1940 under a special officer's program after graduating as an ROTC officer from New York University. Bill Gara was by far the dominant personality in the battalion and became its most permanent fixture. Ultimately promoted as a Lt. Colonel, he led the battalion through most of the war.

The 1st Division had crossed the Atlantic on the Queen Mary about one month before we did. By the time we arrived at Tidworth most of the division was in Scotland undergoing landing exercises in preparation for some kind of major operation, as yet unknown except to senior staff. The three "line" companies of our battalion, A, B, and C, were attached to the three infantry regiments and were in Scotland. The contingent left at Tidworth consisted of the battalion staff and the Headquarters and Service (H&S) Company. We were therefore all attached to H&S.

Thursday Sept 24

Dear Mother, Dad, and Sis,

As you can no doubt tell from the new address, I've been doing a little moving about, which will account for the fact that I'm a little late with this letter. The address will tell you that I am now a member of the First Engineers, and it's no secret that the First Engineers are a part of the First Infantry Division. It was apparently by a most wonderful quirk of fate that several of us were put in this outfit. It's a combat engineer battalion, but I can't tell you anything beyond that. On their service uniform, the officers all wear decorations received in the last war. I am told that the battalion was the second unit formed in the U.S. Army, and during the Mexican War, one of our companies was commanded by Robert E. Lee. The executive officer of the division, incidentally, is Gen. Theodore Roosevelt, Jr.

It's sure swell to be in an outfit where everyone is experienced & knows his business. They all groaned when they found how inexperienced we were.

I've made a $100 allotment to Mother which you can handle in any way you see fit. It will start on my November pay, so you won't see it until December. Incidentally, I am now getting $150 plus a 10% increase for overseas duty. I don't get my rental, but of my $21.00 rations, I only have to give up $15.00 per month for food. The result is that I get in cash $171.00. Deducting insurance and the allotment, that leaves me about (pounds) 16, which should be plenty. I took out $10,000 insurance with Mother as the beneficiary. The policy will be sent to her.

I've still received no mail, but mail to this new APO should be here fairly rapidly. Some officers say they get 1 week service on airmail.

Sent the first laundry out today since I left Ft. Wood. I'm in terrible shape.

Principle news here is that it's cold as hell & I'm having a devil's own time rounding up warm clothing. As soon as I can get some ration coupons, I'll see what I can do in town in the way of wool underwear. You have no idea what it's like to have the temperature in the low 40's or colder & not a fire any place except in cooking stoves. This country is really taking it on the chin.

I've been to London again, but this time I didn't see anything.

I don't remember whether I told you much about the trip over or not. There were a lot of thrills that I'll never forget. I remember the skyscrapers & the Statue of Liberty disappearing from sight, and the long low Jersey coast finally passing out of view. I remember the hot days in the Gulf Stream & then the cold rough days. I remember we had a bunch of British officers who sort of ran things. Do you remember that Gen. Percival at Singapore? Put a pair of short pants & a foolish looking Scotch cap on him and you had one of our officers. We had some Poles on board too, and I remember during a boat drill they got in the way & he exclaimed, "Oh, you bad Polish fellows." Gosh!!

I'll never forget when we finally sighted a tiny destroyer bobbing up and down & flashing signals to us, and then a rocky rugged coast appeared. Those are all things that have contributed to a great experience.

The most important news in Britain right now is that Lord somebody-or-other has cornered the world's tea supply in India. I'm getting to be quite a tea drinker, but now that I'm getting down to work, I'm again out of contact with the British, so maybe I'll lose the habit.

Had a very pleasant experience recently. — The band of the North Staffordshire Regiment came to play for us, & following the concert we were talking to a British major & he invited three of us down to his house for tea and cake. They were awfully nice people & it was really the first contact I'd had with the better class of British. They'd been on duty in India & Africa and their house in London had been shattered during the blitz, so they had lots to talk about.

Have played some bridge lately, but none since I arrived here. We have a short wave radio set here in the officers' mess, but I haven't been able to get America. Every other station is German.

Oh, I forgot to mention, we ran into that Scottish fellow in London.

Have you ever heard a Scotch bagpipe band? Your ears howl for hours.

When we first arrived here (England) we were given tea from a portable tea shop run by the Red Cross & which was a gift of the city of Honolulu. You see a great deal of Red Cross activity in this country.

Well, I've about hit the end of my rope for this time so I'll close.

Much love,

Bill

Lt. W.M. Kays

1st Engineer Bn.

A.P.O. #1

N.Y., N.Y.

By this time, Bill Gara, our battalion executive officer, had told us that we were about to take part in an amphibious operation, but he gave little hint of where this was to take place. The papers had been talking for the past month about Dakar on the west coast of Africa, so I was pretty sure that Dakar was to be the target.

Since we were evidently going to be in Tidworth for a while longer, they soon got us involved in training. Gara built our Commanding Officer (CO), Major Rowland, up to be some kind of God, so it was with fear and trepidation that we were introduced to him. We six walked into his office and saluted. He then sat us down and proceeded to give us a brief oral examination on the subject of preparing a small bridge for demolition. My only contribution to the discussion was a suggestion that we ought to bring along a pair of "crimpers" to "crimp" the detonator to the fuse. Barnum suggested that we ought to take along 100 pounds of TNT, and Colonel Rowland thought that was a very good answer but that 200 pounds would be better.

Shortly thereafter he called Barnum and me in and explained to us that in the pending operation there was a concrete pillbox that had to be taken out, and he wanted us to form and train two special squads, equipped with flamethrowers and explosive charges, to work with the infantry to accomplish this mission. Barnum had seen a flamethrower demonstrated at Ft. Belvoir; I had never even heard of a flamethrower. I am sure that Rowland got me mixed up with somebody else in our initial conversation with him. Cole had also come from OCS at Belvoir, so perhaps he got me confused with Cole. The battalion didn't have any flamethrowers, but never mind, the British would supply them when we boarded ship. I was horrified. This was not what I had in mind back in June.

The men for these squads were to come from H&S Company. When Charlie Mills, the CO of H&S, heard about it, he was all enthusiasm and cooperation. He sat down with the First Sergeant and picked out all of the best men in the company, much to the First Sergeant's distress. He had some kind of inferiority complex about H&S Company and wanted to show the line companies that the real gung-ho fighters were in H&S. Charlie paid for this eagerness with his life in Sicily. Basically Henry Rowland had the same problem, probably with respect to the infantry, and this was exacerbated by the fact that he was in the Regular Army. He was eager to get into a fire fight and make a name for himself, and this was to lead to other developments in Africa.

Mills decided that we should call these two squads, each with about twelve men, the "Hell Squads." My squad was headed by Sergeant McCarthy, while I was the officer in charge. Sergeant McCarthy was one of the best soldiers I ever encountered. Rowland and Mills ultimately got their "fire fight," and McCarthy was blown to bits at El Guettar in Tunisia.

Barnum and I spent most of our time at Tidworth training our Hell Squads. We made fake flamethrowers by putting a sandbag in a backpack and tying a piece of rope to a stick. We did use live explosives and blew up a simulated pillbox on the side of a hill. Rowland had picked out the spot as being nearly identical to the real pillbox that he expected us to encounter.

At this time I began to have a bit of a problem with Bill Barnum. He out-ranked me (by a few days), and was about eight years older, and it was natural that he should be the leader of our little contingent. He had been drafted into the Army about a year before and then had gone through the six-month Engineer officers training course at Ft. Belvoir, Virginia. He was miles ahead of me in terms of training and experience. But rather than help me he treated me as if I was a total dumbbell, and in front of the enlisted men this became embarrassing. Later we were to be in the same company and this problem continued. Bill and I were to become great friends in our later lives, but this was not a good start to our relationship.

One time we were on a rifle range, trying to teach the new sixty-day recruits to shoot. At 300 yards and in a miserable rain most of them couldn't even hit the target. Sergeant Wright, who was in charge of things, became totally disgusted and announced that he was going to show them how easy it was to hit the target. He called over the telephone to the men in the target pits and made a great point that "Sergeant Wright" was going to shoot. I was puzzled. He then fired off a clip of eight shots very rapidly. I distinctly saw some of them splash in the water puddles that were everywhere between us and the targets. Then the target markers went up and indicated that Sergeant Wright had scored eight bulls eyes!

On one occasion the whole outfit, i.e., H&S Company and the entire staff, went on a full pack route march. What made this memorable was that it was led by Harold Haas. When we six reported in to Major Rowland upon our arrival at Tidworth, Harold stepped up and gave a very snappy, heel-clicking salute. Commanding officers always fall for that and Harold was immediately spotted as a coming star. For that reason he was on this occasion made chief of the advance party, the "point," and he had the map. We were hiking on paved roads, but the British had removed all direction signs for the duration of the war. Harold took a wrong turn at one point and added several miles to our journey. We finally hiked about twenty-two miles. The troops were thrilled to have this opportunity to improve their hiking skills!

There was a movie theater on the post and my principal recollection is of the dense cloud of cigarette smoke through which the projector beam had to penetrate.

On another occasion there was a Navy, Army, Air Force Institute (NAAFI) show in the same place (this was the British equivalent of a USO show). A small band was on stage and in the corner there was a bald-headed man on the drums with a silly grin on his face, lightly tapping a drum with one of those wire brushes. At one point he got up and pranced across the stage, tapping on the metal footlight cover as he went. One of my friends said later, "I didn't know whether to laugh or cry!" Gene Krupa he wasn't!

Sunday Oct 3

Dear Mother, Dad, and Sis,

I've delayed a little in writing this letter due to the lack of anything to say. That is, the lack of things that I can say. I can't tell you where I am or what I am doing, and that's my main source of writing material. For the first time I've really appreciated the necessity of keeping my mouth shut. One word of what we're doing at the present time would give away the whole show.

I haven't received my mail yet. I don't know what in the world has happened to it.

We officers who were sent to this battalion are all extra officers; that is, there is no regular place for us in the battalion. We're sort of tagging along to learn what it's all about, and then to fill in when necessary.

There are some amazing things about this battalion. Altho it is supposedly the combat engineer battalion of the army, there is not a single West Point officer in it. Another thing is the lack of rank. Practically every job is held by an under-ranked officer. In the whole battalion, we have one major, two captains, and all the rest are lieutenants.

We took a trip to Cheltenham yesterday to get some warm clothing. It's probably the prettiest town I've seen in England. It's quite a wool center.

Watched a soccer game yesterday.

We've been getting reasonably up-to-date sports results from the States. The papers briefly cover the World Series, and every Sunday night an American gives us football results of the preceding Saturday. Haven't heard yesterday's results yet. I hear Cal beat St. Marys.

Hope you got my cable. I got that brainstorm after I'd written my last letter. That was supposed to be the fastest type, as I paid about 11/6 for it.

I think I'll get a money order and send about $130 home next week. This British money is very bulky, and I'm now carrying around about 65 (pounds) in 1 (pound) notes. Higher denominations are like travelers checks — they have to be signed, etc., so you seldom see them.

Spent a day firing the rifle the other day. It was the rainiest, windiest, coldest day I've ever spent. On these British rifle ranges, if you get a little wild & shoot over the hill your bullet is likely to land in some town.

We have a good radio with short wave & everything, but we can't get a peep out of the U.S. Do you remember how easily we got Britain & Germany from Norfolk? I'm getting quite discouraged with the BBC. All they have is two programs — The Home Program, & The Forces Program. Most of it is very uninteresting to us. The best music still comes from Berlin. The funniest program is the daily propaganda from Italy. German propaganda is a little more subtle.

Well, that is about the end of the line for me today. I've tried to be fairly regular with my letters, but if in the future there should be any gaps, don't let it worry you.
Much love to all,
Bill
P.S. Saw a western thriller recently taken near Death Valley. When I get home I'm going down there and spend a month drying and baking out.

Despite all the talk about "keeping my mouth shut," I was doing my best to let them know that something big was about to happen, and I was also going to some pains to let them know where I was (see for example the reference to Cheltenham). At this time I was still obsessed with football at home. By the time I received a lot of newspaper clippings that my father sent me I had lost all interest, and in fact as time went on I gradually lost interest in things at home in general.

The next letter is postmarked November 2, despite the October 14 written on it by me. Evidently the mail was held up for security reasons. Furthermore a pencil note by my father on the letter says "Money order put in bank Nov. 28 HEK," so my parents were now many weeks behind the events. Actually other evidence suggests this letter was written on October 7. A later reference suggests this letter was mailed aboard ship, but it was undoubtedly written earlier. My continual confusion on dates simply suggests that there were no calendars hanging around, and I never carried a pocket diary.

Oct 14

Dear Mother, Dad, & Sis,
This will be a very short letter, the principle object being to get the enclosed $200 to you. Hope you get it.
Received my first mail the other day — three V-mail letters from the three of you. You have no idea how swell it was to hear from home. Outside of those, I have received nothing. I suppose the others will catch up to me some day. I discovered that APO #640 is the Base Censor in England, so I at least ought to get that some day.
As to Christmas, practically everybody is writing home and telling everybody to just skip it this time. Besides, I have absolutely no room for anything. Our footlockers have been taken away, so I'm living out of my suitcase and field pack, and they are very full.
Anything that I could say about what I'm now doing would be censored, so I'll close before I get into trouble.
Much love to all,
Bill

Despite the censorship I am giving big hints that some kind of action is imminent.
I had sent a cablegram home on about the 25th or 26th giving my new address. That accounts for the three "V-mails" from home. These were to be my only letters from home until January.
The time had come to join the major part of the Division in Scotland. Presumably we would join them and then embark for whatever this big operation was going to be. I believe it was Saturday, October 10, that we boarded a train at a place near Tidworth and

traveled north all that night. The previous night I came down with a miserable cold that made the trip a nightmare. In the early morning we arrived at Gouroch, Scotland and were immediately transferred by boat to a small steamer called the Royal Ulsterman. Bill Barnum and I had a cabin together.

That day my cold began to develop into bronchitis, with much wheezing and breathing difficulty. I remember distinctly that evening (Sunday) being in the officers' mess and having a "gin and lime." A radio was on and I was eager to hear the American sports program. What I was waiting for finally came — Notre Dame 27, Stanford 0. Now I was really sick!

The next day the Battalion Surgeon, Doc Marcus, made me stay in bed and plied me with sulfanilamide. I was running a temperature. On Tuesday he decided to put me ashore into a hospital, and that night I was lowered over the side in a canvas sack and into a launch. I recall that I was placed in a stretcher near a coal-burning stove. The heat was lovely.

I had presumed that I was being sent to a British hospital. My feeling at the time was that this was going to be another adventure, and I would treat it as such and enjoy. Marcus assured me they weren't going off without me.

There was a long wait at a dock, and then some people came aboard the launch with a stretcher. To my surprise I heard American English being spoken, and then two American sailors appeared and transferred me to their stretcher. I remember the warm feeling of a blue wool uniform pressing against my head. They had trouble getting the stretcher to fit properly into the ambulance they had brought, and cursed, "these damned Limey ambulances."

The hospital was a small American naval establishment directly across the Firth of Clyde from Greenoch near a place called Rosneath. It was constructed entirely of Quonset, or Nissen, huts, corrugated metal structures that looked like half of a piece of culvert pipe. The officer's ward contained nine beds with real sheets on them. An oil heater kept the place wonderfully warm. A doctor examined me soon after my arrival and told me I had acute bronchitis. Later I discovered he wrote on my record "bronchial pneumonia."

There followed four weeks of relative comfort. Outside of breathing difficulty, which gradually abated, I was not in any distress. While I was there the Division went on a landing maneuver in northern Scotland, and then returned. I learned later that Doc Marcus phoned about me when they got back and was told that I was still running a temperature. So they ultimately left without me.

Most of the officers in the ward were army officers from various units of the 1st Division. They either had ailments similar to mine or had been hurt in things like jeep accidents. There was one Navy Lt. who had been on a Murmansk convoy that had been badly roughed up by German air attacks. His ship had been sunk, he spent forty-five minutes in the icy water, and he had a broken ankle. My recollection is that we talked about twenty hours a day.

One of these people was an officer from the 7th Field Artillery Battalion. He kept talking about "Obie," his Battery Commander, T. J. Obrian. Obrian was eventually to become something of a legend as an artilleryman, but he couldn't get along with Colonels. He was one of several Harvard ROTC graduates in the 7th Field. None of them were particularly impressed by military pomp and nonsense, and had little use for idiocy.

The commander of the 7th Field apparently wanted to get rid of him and he was ulti-mately transferred to the 16th Infantry Regiment to command their Cannon Company. Each infantry regiment had a six-gun battery of its own artillery that was called Cannon Company. The infantry loved Obrian; he was always on the front lines with them, and he knew how to get the best out of artillery. I ultimately got to know him quite well because we were cabin mates on the ship that took us to Omaha Beach in Normandy in 1944. T. J. Obrian was to die along with so many others in the Battle of the Hurtgen Forest in Germany in November 1944.

Another was a guy named Brooks from Anti-Tank Company of the 16th Infantry Regiment. He was an army junior and had lived in Washington D.C. where he had dated a girl that I also had dated in high school. She had been killed in an auto accident a couple of years before and we talked about her. I was to see Brooks later in the war.

The next letter is postmarked November 5, so it probably reached home before the previous one.

Nov. 2, 1942

Dear Mother, Dad. and Sis,

I understand that "V-Mail" will from now on go a lot faster than ordinary mail, so I've been waiting around trying to find a "V-Mail" form, but have given up. Hope you get this some time before Christmas.

You'd better hold up all mail to me until I get another address. To be absolutely frank, I'm no longer in the 1st, or at least I don't think I am. I really don't know where I stand because I'm now rounding out my third week in a naval hospital. Acute Bronchitis, they call it. I'm OK now, and they let me get dressed & take a little walk each day. I'm good for a few hundred yards now, and am rapidly improving. I think a little California sunshine, orange juice, butter, milk, eggs, decent meat would make a lot of difference. The sun shone a few hours the other day, but it was pretty cold out.

This is an amazing hospital, architecturally, I mean. I'll describe it to you some day. We have an officer's ward with about 9 beds, and there are more army officers than naval officers here. We have one jg from the "Armed Guard" who started out at Little Creek. Have the craziest corpsmen I've ever seen. We were inspected by an Admiral the other day. He had stripes up to his elbow, thick white hair, and glasses. You know him? We'll probably see "Eleanor" one of these days. She's been visiting service hospitals, etc., and now I hear she's going to venture up into this neck of the woods. The officer's ward is the only one with regular hospital beds, so they always show us off.

One of the guys here has a radio, so life isn't so bad. On Monday nights about 7:00 we hear "Command Performance" from the U.S.A. That's all we hear from the U.S.

I expect to be out of here soon. Doctor says I can go as soon as I stop coughing. Don't know where in hell to go, though. The Navy is trying to find out where to send me.

(The letter continues with the following confusing date; perhaps the first date was in error.)

Tuesday, Nov 2

Just took my longest walk. Walked to the nearby village & bought a newspaper. Had to see "My Day".[1]

You ought to see my beard. The dogs run away from me, & the cats hiss at me when I try to pet them.

We have a great time here talking about what we could do with a hamburger, or a milk shake, or a coke.

As near as I can ascertain from bits of football scores I pick up, UCLA is the red hot team on the coast this year. Our Sunday night sports reporter doesn't know there are any football teams west of Chicago. Every time I hear a Stanford score I shudder.

This is a great life. Sleep all you want; get up when you feel like it; get all the service you want. The food is pretty awful, but that's a universal thing in this country. Every time you turn around, they throw beans at you. I like beans, but they have a habit of dumping them from the can onto the plate & by-passing the stove. Had the first bacon I've seen in months yesterday, and it was absolutely raw. Did we raise hell!!

They have these dried eggs which they scramble, but in my opinion they might just as well use the cargo space for something else. Nobody will eat the stuff, despite all the cries of glee of the Dept. of Agriculture.

The sun was shining today, and I thought it was quite warm until I noticed all the mud puddles frozen over. It hasn't rained for a week, but it's always wet, and there's always mud.

One blessing about this hospital is the fact that they keep it warm. This is the only time I've felt comfortable since I've been in this country.

We're eight hours ahead of you here. Seems funny to wake up at 700 and know that you are all just going to bed the night before. It's 1600 now and the sun is starting to go down while you are just going to work.

We listen to "Germany Calling" every night. I'm afraid the announcer doesn't have the respect for Americans that he should have. Very interesting, though.

Being in the hospital has given me the opportunity to do a lot of studying of my field manuals. I'm learning a lot but I'd like a chance to use it. In my four months service, I've done two weeks useful work.

Well, this is about the longest letter I've written, so I've run dry.

Much love,

Bill

P.S. Hope you got the $200 in the last letter. I've received no October pay, of course. Also no mail, except those three "V-Mails." When I give you a new address, you'd better start giving me all the news since Aug. 15, as I have reason to believe I won't see any of that other mail for many months.

I am very surprised to find that I waited three weeks in the hospital before I wrote a letter, especially after writing so often during the preceding weeks. Perhaps my illness had something to do with it, but it is more probable that it was associated with the fact that I didn't have a definite address for them to write to. I have no recollection of being so incapacitated that I couldn't write.

On about October 23 the Battle of El Alamein in Egypt started and the radio was

---

1   Eleanor Roosevelt's daily column.

filled with commentary. At first it sounded like the usual feeble attempt to do something, but by early November it became apparent that a major defeat had been dealt to
Rommel, who commanded the German Afrika Korps, and that he was in retreat. Then
on November 8 came the news of a large American/British series of landings in Algeria
and Morocco. The opposition was Vichy-French, mostly colonial troops. They put up
a fight for three days and then quit. The French at that time were very resentful of the
British whom they accused of deserting them at Dunkirk, and who had killed Frenchmen when they sank part of the French fleet at Oran in 1940 to keep the ships out of
German hands.

It was now apparent where my 1st Engineer friends had gone. The officer from the
7th Field Artillery Battalion then told us that the 1st Division had gone ashore at Oran.
He had known the plan all along.

On about November 13th I was discharged from the hospital and sent to an American army establishment in nearby Rosneath. This unit turned out to be the rear echelon
of the 1st Engineer Amphibious Brigade (not part of the 1st Infantry Division and not
to be confused with my First Engineer Battalion) — the other parts of the brigade were
already in Africa, having participated in the landings there. I soon learned that they were
in fact in Oran, and that the remainder of the brigade was scheduled to join them soon.

When I reported to them I was told that they were going to send me to the replacement depot at Lichfield. I panicked at the thought. I suggested they take me to Africa
with them, and after a little discussion they decided to attach me to their quartermaster
battalion, the 361st, which was the only unit of any consequence remaining at Rosneath.

The next letter is a V-Mail letter. It is typewritten.

Co. C, 361st QM Bn
Nov. 17, 1942

Dear Mother, Dad, and Sis,

Unless you have received my letter of a couple of weeks ago, this letter won't make
much sense to you, so you'd better just put it aside until you receive the other letter.

I am now out of the hospital, and am rapidly regaining my health. Life in the hospital became so pleasant that I honestly hated to leave. All together I spent just shy of
four weeks there. I discovered that after I spent the first week there I developed bronco-
pneumonia, and that accounted for my being there so long. It must now be obvious to
you why my becoming sick was more a great disappointment to me than anything else,
and my distress was caused by that rather than by any physical discomfort. However,
things are not now so bad as they might have been. Upon discharge from the hospital
I turned myself into the nearest Army establishment and they deduced that I was a free
agent, and were all for sending me to a replacement pool, which would have amounted
to my having gone in one big circle since I've been over here. I then approached the
Personnel Adjutant as if I was asking a business executive for a job, and after much talk
and telephoning, they decided to temporarily attach me to this 1st Engineer Amphibian
Brigade. Right now they are trying to get permission to assign me to it. Then if I ever
get near my old outfit I can request reassignment, although they were probably very glad
to get rid of me. Right now I am attached to the brigade quartermaster battalion, and as
I have always been in the army, I am "excess baggage." However, this being an engineer

brigade, I suppose they will eventually put me in one of the engineer regiments. I am living very well now, and they aren't working me hard. I know nothing about how the QM operates, so they let me more or less take care of the combat training which all branches have to dabble in nowadays.

The food here is the best that I have had since I've been overseas. Dad, it's too bad you can't get yourself overseas; your outfit eats the best of anyone. Don't know what I weigh now, but I ought to be back to normal before long.

The only trouble with this place is the hours they keep. We have to be up to stand at 6:00 reveille, and I'm not kidding when I say that the sun puts in it's first appearance at 9:00. I think they are trying to defeat nature. Outside of providing a certain amount of light, however, the sun here serves no useful purpose. It certainly radiates no heat. And there's the ever present drizzle (they call it rain). As long as I've been in the British Isles I've never seen a day when you could sit on the ground without getting a very cold and wet seat. You couldn't possibly picnic in this country. None of it goes very well with my nose, but I have been very encouraged to see the war developing in the warmer parts of the globe. However, don't worry about me, I always have been a pretty good planner.

Everybody is already talking about Christmas and how they'd like to be home. "Home" becomes a very attractive word when you're 6000 miles away.

Since I first went to the hospital I have become extraordinarily studious and I have read every field manual that I could lay my hands on. For the first time I feel that I'm beginning to know a little something about the army.

Much love to all,
Bill

The following letter has "Don't Open Before Xmas" written all over it, and evidently it was intended to be read on Christmas morning.

November 19, 1942
Great Britain

Dear Sis,

Merry Christmas!! (Or if the mail service ain't what it might be, — Happy New Year!!) Let's assume this is Christmas morning, though, so I can figure out what you're doing. It ought to be about nine o'clock (AM) now, and you are all sitting around the tree in the living room. (Or maybe you're out at the Manners', in which case the scene is the same, except the crowd is a little larger, and I can hear Jackie screaming about your getting a letter from that "Stanford pill".) Mother is sitting on the most uncomfortable chair she can find, and Dad is probably on his knees, reaching under the tree and exclaiming "joy and rapture" every time he opens a package. Now please don't go and upset your ordinary routine, because I'm thinking about you all now, and that's the scene that I see. It's five PM here, and getting dark. We're going to stand "retreat" in a few minutes. I don't know where I am yet, but I've got a pretty good idea. I like this type of country; I always have. So much for Christmas Day and take a big bite of that Turkey for me.

Sis, I haven't written you for quite awhile, so I thought that possibly better than anything else, you'd like a nice long letter. Please excuse me if it rambles. Not being able to devote much space to facts, I'll have to resort to a collection of random thoughts.

Got a 24 hour pass yesterday, so I took off for the nearby large and famous city, it being the first time I've been away from this immediate vicinity in over five weeks. It's the first time I've been in a city of any kind since my visit to London in the middle of September. I put up at the swankiest hotel in town, and then proceeded to have a very quiet afternoon and evening. Did some shopping, and finally got into a "cinema" and saw "To the Shores of Tripoli", after standing in a "queue" for quite awhile. The British are the greatest people for "queuing" that I ever saw. They "queue" to get on buses & street cars, to get up to a counter, to go to the movies, and everything. None of the American "every man for himself" stuff! The whole populace here is far better disciplined than Americans, and that goes for the army, too. I believe that it is a thing that has accounted for democracy working better here than any place else. Nobody ever gets excited or flies off the handle. For instance, when you are walking down a street you can always spot Canadian or Australian soldiers, altho their uniforms are similar to the British. They are always talking loud & shoving each other around, while the Britisher looks straight ahead and minds his own business. This business of minding his own business is another British trait. When an Englishman buys a house, his first act is to erect a tall fence or hedge between him & his neighbors, and it will probably be months before he knows his neighbor's name, although every morning he will very politely speak to his neighbor and comment on the weather. However, I seem to be wandering away from my trip to the city.

I went to the Post Office & got what they had which is enclosed. (Please take one copy of each & put in an envelope in my album.) All they had was the current issue. I should have gone to the P.O. while I was in London. I figured England would be the best place for Empire stamps, but once more, when you say England, you really mean London. I couldn't find any good Stamp Cos. here, so these stamps I got for you are just scattered sets of Empire recent issues. I should have liked to have taken some province or colony & really filled it out for you, & I could have done it, had I had time in London[2]. The Polish stamps are the ones used by the Polish government in exile in London. This stamp company that I found was just part of a bookstore. Speaking of bookstores, every little village in this country has bookstores. I've never seen a place where people read so much. They read an awful lot of non-fiction. There must be hundreds of books with such titles as "Our Glorious Navy," "Our Wonderful Air Force," or "Our Army." (They don't think much of the army in this country. They openly speak of the navy as the senior service, and of course the air force is literally worshipped. They are completely shocked at the American idea of not building battleships, and the radio never tires of talking about such things as the "Murmansk Convoy". I'm not kidding when I say that for four days in a row we heard four different sailors describe a certain "Murmansk Convoy." Incidentally, we had an officer in the hospital from the American armed guard on a "Murmansk Convoy" & he had some hair raising stories including one of a 45 minute swim or ducking in the Arctic Ocean. My, I'm wandering!!) Because they read so much, I think the British public

---

2   Both my sister and I had been avid stamp collectors, so I was trying to buy stamps for both of us.

is much better read on the whole than the American, although college education isn't extended to the masses at all as it is in the U.S. After all, I guess a library is the best university, and every Britisher has a library, a leather soft chair, and a pipe.

Now for a few more or less administrative matters. The mail situation is unchanged. No use writing to this address, cause by the time you get this letter, I may have most any address. I haven't drawn any pay since September, but I guess Uncle Sam can take care of it for me. I still don't know whether you got that $200 I sent home. I have enough to take care of me & I'm trying to skin down anyway.

The clipping is from the "Stars & Stripes", our service newspaper.

"Eleanor" has left telling us that we should acquaint the English with America by talking about it to them. I think the British could have wrung her neck. If there's anything they don't want to hear us talking about all the time, it's America. You know — "California is OK, but back East —."

Loads of love to all & a Merry Christmas,

Bill

The next is a Christmas card postmarked November 21st, but undoubtedly written before that. The following note is included:

Dear Mother, Dad, and Sis,

(Sent Sis an extensive letter, so this is just to you).

You know how much I wish I could be with you, but there are plenty of Christmases to come and then I can settle back with a pipe in an easy chair and tell you all about the Christmases I spent in the four corners of the globe. We won't have the comforts of home this Christmas, nor will we have our families, but there will be lots of Christmas cheer and song here, because you'd be surprised how sentimental and soft the toughest American soldier is.

Say Merry Christmas to everyone for me.

Love, Bill

A week with the 361st soon convinced me that I was destined to spend the war with idiots. The 1st Engineers had spoiled me. (The "1st Engineers" are not to be confused with the "1st Engineer Amphibious Brigade". It is confusing.) I actually missed the spit and polish. The CO, Major Smith, was a pompous little jackass; the officers were mostly slobs who were only interested in their own comfort, well-being and entertainment. I was particularly offended by the way they treated the enlisted men. In my few weeks with the 1st Engineers it had been drilled into me, mostly by Bill Gara, that "you take care of your men first." I set my heart on going to Africa with the 361st and then getting back to the 1st Engineers. I didn't realize at the time that they had no intention of helping me get back.

I remember getting a bit sentimental each day when we stood for retreat and the flag was lowered and the bugle sounded "colors." (The bugler was awful.) It was at sunset, which was at about four o'clock pm, and we looked out over the Firth of Clyde, and somehow I felt very proud despite the idiocy and incompetence with which I was living.

At other times I led the men in various combat exercises and even in bayonet drill —

me of all people! They regarded me as an expert. Well, it was satisfying to be thought worth something.

Among the army field manuals that I found in the company office was one on mine-laying. I figured this outfit would have no use for it so I swiped it. It will appear again in our story.

Another V-Mail follows.

Co. "C" 361 QMBn
APO #302, N.Y.
Nov. 22, 1942

Dear Mother, Dad, and Sis,

I sent you Christmas cards, etc., but after noticing how miserable the mail service has been lately, and the number of wet, faded letters that are arriving here, I decided that I'd better take a more sure method of wishing you all a very Merry Christmas. Please say Merry Christmas to the Manners and everyone else for me.

If I didn't say so before, don't write to me at this address. By the time you get this I hope to be in an engineer outfit, my ultimate plan being to get back to the "1st". I've induced higher headquarters to look the other way while I pull one of the greatest hitching stunts of all time. Everything is working smoothly at present.

The course of our intervention in the European war now seems apparent. I only hope they do it on a large enough scale to avert disaster and don't try to expend too much energy on the bastard Japs. Their day will come.

Well, Merry Christmas, and I hope you get the other letters before the poppies bloom.

Much love,
Bill

The other officers had been getting into Glasgow fairly regularly. I finally went with them, and spent the night at the Beresford Hotel. The letter to my sister describes that trip rather completely.

A day or so before Thanksgiving we loaded up on a train and went to Liverpool. There we boarded a British transport, the Derbyshire, and pulled out into the harbor where we anchored and spent the next several days. I recall a Thanksgiving dinner while we were there. Liverpool looked gray and bleak. We sailed on November 30 and joined an absolutely huge convoy, going around the northern coast of Ireland and then heading south. We didn't seem to have much of an escort, but some of them may have been over the horizon. On occasion we saw the splashes of depth charges far in the distance, but as far as I know we were never attacked, and I don't remember having any fear of a submarine attack. All through the war I always enjoyed the periods when we were aboard ships. The beds were more comfortable and the food was very much better. Somehow the fear of submarine attack hardly entered my head.

The ship was carrying an assortment of "rear area" people, including a bunch of officers who were going to Oran to set up the Mediterranean Base Section of the SOS. I got well acquainted with some of these types at the dinner table; as usual the officers ate in great style in the main dining room. These officers were mostly captains and majors who had served in World War I, and were thus in their forties and fifties. I remember a captain who told me he "couldn't wait to experience the smell of burned gunpowder." His chances of smelling "burned gunpowder" would have been greater in New York. They all seemed to be little small-minded men who had lived boring lives through the Depression and were now going to have the times of their lives. Their first priority would be to find the best place in town to set up an officer's club, and being in the SOS would give them first access to all the more desirable supplies coming through, as well as to the best wine and (probably) women.

A major sat at the head of our table and let it be known that he wanted his rank respected. Near the end of the trip he announced that we would all contribute some rather large amount for a tip to the waiter. The last night the CO of troops announced that we would tip a very much smaller amount, much to the major's chagrin.

The enlisted men lived in a much different style. Their quarters were essentially mess halls. To sleep they took hammocks from lockers and slung them from the ceiling over the tables. Each table operated as a unit, and at mess time sent two men to the galley to draw food. A typical meal consisted of a platter of loaves of bread and a platter of fish with the eyes and tails intact. We were told that the ship was loaded with American food at Liverpool. The men became increasingly upset. The American CO of troops carried on a continual argument with the ship's officers, but to no avail. The American food was never located.

The weather got warmer, which I enjoyed. While at anchor in Liverpool I began to develop my chest trouble again. This time I decided to sweat it out, at least until we were at sea. We each came aboard with a bottle of Teachers Highland Scotch in our packs, and that helped. I arrived in Africa in pretty good shape.

On the evening of the 4th of December we entered the Straits of Gibraltar and anchored in Gibraltar harbor. In a following letter I describe the incredible beauty of the sparkling lights of an African city in the distance on our right, probably Tangier, an extraordinary sight after months of blackout. Of course the convoy was blacked out.

We spent the following day in the harbor where we gazed at Spain and wondered in which house there were Germans counting our ships and sending radio messages.

After dark we weighed anchor and made an overnight run to Oran on the Algerian coast. In the morning we pulled up to a dock at Mers El Kebir, the port of Oran. Rowboats with French-speaking men came alongside as we slowly moved in. It was December 6th. Africa and warm weather at last!

CHAPTER THREE

ALGERIA

DECEMBER 6, 1942 - JANUARY 29, 1943

My group was the last to disembark when we arrived at the port of Oran, so I watched my SOS friends go ashore. They assured me that they would be met by buses. The last I saw of them they were trudging along a dusty road, no buses in sight, each carrying a typewriter. What a way to fight a war!

When the 361st Battalion arrived ashore later we hiked for miles, and well into the night. The men were carrying far too much junk and we had a hard time keeping them moving. We were finally met by trucks, loaded up, and then were taken around Oran to the town of Arzew west of Oran. Arzew had a little harbor and was apparently where part of my 1st Engineer Battalion friends had landed the previous month. That night we spread out our bedrolls on the floor of an old concrete fort.

"North Africa"
Dec. 12, 1942

Dear Mother, Dad, and Sis,

The Air Corps says they will get this home by Christmas, so you may get it before my last letters from Scotland. If it does get there, Merry Christmas and a happy New Year. Wish I could be there.

Been in North Africa some little time. Am still with this Amph. Brigade. My old battalion is about 35 miles from here, but I don't know yet what they are going to do with me. Better hold off mail until I let you know. Forwarding just doesn't seem to work. Except for those three "V-Mails" written in Sept. I have received no mail.

We are camped on the shores of the Mediterranean and are definitely "roughing it." The men live in pup tents, but we [the officers] now have pyramidal tents & cots. The country is very much like inland So. Calif. or southern Ariz. Vegetation: palm trees, scrubby bushes, century plants, prickly pears, and a great deal of plain old Arizona mesquite with very long thorns. The weather is also like So. Cal. & Ariz. When it isn't raining, the days are warm, but the nights quite cold. However, lately I've been living in rubber boots. The men have been swimming a couple of times, but it's a little too cold for me. The country is characterized by filth, flies, & Arabs, all three of which are very closely associated. Mark Twain describes them in "Innocents Abroad" much better than I ever could. They literally infiltrate our camps along with the flies about an hour after sun-up. The children stand by our garbage cans during mess and intercept our dumpings with cans. There is a large French population, especially in the towns. They don't seem to object strenuously to our being here. My small knowledge of French comes in very handy. The houses here are mostly desert type with flat roofs and are made of tiles put together with mud mortar.

We are now living on a "B" ration which means no fresh food. However, there seems to be an endless supply of nice big oranges which we buy from the Arabs. Also wine is 13c a quart. (10 francs). Hope we can get back on the "A" ration which we had in Scotland and England before too long.

I saw Gibraltar, and also a sight that is music to a soldier's eyes nowadays, a lighted city. I believe it was Tangier in Spanish Morocco. Also of course saw Spain.

When I get a chance I'll get some local stamps. Hope they let me send them because they would fix my position a little more definitely.

If you aren't getting my allotment you'd better raise hell with the War Dept. You also should have received my insurance policy.

The first North African Stars & Stripes just came out & I see the Big Game[1] came out to the satisfaction of all.

Well, I hope you get this by Christmas.

Merry Christmas.

Love, Bill

The next letter has written on it in my father's handwriting: "Rec'd 29 Dec".

No. 1
"North Africa"
Dec. 15, 1942

Dear Mother, Dad, and Sis,

From now on I'm numbering my letters so that you can tell what you are and are not getting. This will be no. 1, and is the second from Africa. The other was the Xmas airmail that should have reached you by Christmas if it got there at all. There is no V-Mail service here yet, so I will send this straight. From Scotland you should have received a couple of Christmas cards (or letters) and a couple of "V-Mails". I also think I wrote a letter from the hospital there. In October I mailed a letter aboard ship in which I enclosed $200 in money orders. I wish there was some way to check on that as I still have the stubs if it didn't get through. I'm going to have to send another wad of money at the end of the month as I haven't been paid since September. There's one thing good about this God forsaken life; I'm saving plenty of money. Hope I can use it some day.

If you have missed some of my letters I'm afraid there will be serious gaps in your attempts to follow me. I believe I am now completely recovered from my illness. I feel swell and this outdoor camp life seems to agree with me.

Sis, I hope you received the stamps I sent you from Britain. I am enclosing some stamps I got here. My negotiations with the post office girl reminded me of your tales from Quebec. There seems to be no complete sets available so these are just an assort-

---

1   The Stanford-UC Berkeley football game, which Stanford won.

ment. Perhaps in a later town I can get more. Wish I could have stopped off at some of the places I saw from the ship and bought some stamps. Hope this damp weather does not stick them together too badly.

I'm not keeping terribly busy right now. I wish to hell they would make up their minds what they're going to do with me. I was going to say that I've wasted an awful lot of time with this outfit, but I guess I've learned considerable about troop movements, handling men, bivouacking, etc.

Went to my first movie in months last night. The army takes over the local cinema two nights a week. It's a little bit of a place, but does the trick. The heading said it was donated (the film) by the "motion picture industry" to the AEF. I'm afraid the "motion picture industry" didn't over-exert itself for that miserable picture.

Wish the damn ocean wasn't so damn cold. It looks like I won't get a bath until spring. I wash and shave with our rather precious but cold water every morning. I've built a fire-place of tile from a ruined house, & made a kettle from half a gasoline can, so I can now have hot water if I make the effort, however.

On Dec. 7 I was thinking back to Dec. 7 a year ago, and remembering what I was doing at that time, and remembering how remote the thought was that I'd be off in a place like this within a year.

Had one of those "this is a small world" coincidences on the boat (coming here). On the train last summer when I was on my way to Ft. Leonard Wood I met a classmate of mine who was on his way to Florida to join the Air Corps. On the boat coming down here I found the same guy quartered two cabins from me. The last I'd seen him was in El Paso. He said I was the first familiar face he'd seen since that time.

I think you all get a much better coverage of the news on our front than we do here. Every day or so I see the official bulletin that comes out, but I only get a vague idea of what is going on. This isn't the first time Rommel's been on the run, and they tell us too little to tell whether he is beaten or not.

Well, I have to go to an officer's class so I will close. Hope to be able to give you a permanent address before too long so I can hear some of the news at home. There aren't many soldiers in the AEF who have gone for over two months without any mail.

Much love to all,
Bill

This letter was a bit damaged, and the stamps had indeed stuck to it.

I am a little surprised that I had not by this time taken some steps on my own to get back to the 1st Engineers, since I evidently knew they were only thirty-five miles away. I probably didn't realize that there was a field telephone network, although it was very poor and the security regulations would have made it hard to get through without knowing the code names of various units. However, I could have written, and I believe that I did write to Finley a few days later. I don't think he got the letter until long after I had rejoined the 1st. However, at this particular time I was completely trusting in the Brigade Personnel Adjutant who was responsible for such things. He seemed a nice guy, and of course I was a green 2nd Lieutenant expecting to be told what to do. As it turned out my trust was totally misplaced — they had not the slightest intention of giving me back if they could get away with it.

No. 2

North Africa
Tues., Dec. 22, 1942

Dear Mother, Dad, and Sis,

This letter will probably deal principally with my present status. I should have known that this outfit was too easy to get into, as I am now going to have trouble getting out. As far as ever getting back to the 1st Div. is concerned, I guess that's out. They are getting me assigned to this 1st Engineer Amphibian Brigade, which is OK, except that I am in the Quartermaster Battalion of the brigade, and it is short of officers, and the Engineer regiments of the brigade apparently aren't. The longer I stay with this battalion the harder it will be to get out, and although they assure me that I won't get transferred into the QMC that can very easily happen, and would be the greatest catastrophe of my military career. I not only don't want to be in the QMC, but I'll be in a terrible disadvantage in training for a long time to come. This battalion is a trucking and gasoline supply outfit and could be fairly interesting, I believe, if some policy could be formulated on top as to what our mission is. As it is, we just catch the lousy odd job details and never know what we're doing, or what we're going to do next. Knowing nothing about trucking, I catch the lousiest of the lousy details. I suppose the best thing to do is to start studying up on motor transport and make the best of it. There's one thing about this outfit, it'll never get near enough to the front lines to even hear the guns. However, the main point of this letter is to start you writing to this address pronto so I can get some mail. You'd better give me all the news of all fall, because I'll probably never see all the other mail you've sent. Also, there are a few items I'd like you to send me. First of all, I ought to have an extra pair of glasses. The Jenkel-Davidson Optical Co. of Palo Alto has all the dope on my glasses, and I imagine their office in Berkeley can get that for you very easily. Next, I want a pocket slide rule (6 inch or less). Just something cheap that I can make rough calculations on. Thirdly, I'd like a small lantern-type flashlight, preferably the type that has a spot-light on the side and another bulb on the bottom. That may be difficult to find nowadays, especially since it's got to be small or else it's too bulky to cart around in baggage.

I've made another allotment out, bringing the total up to $140 a month. The $40 will be taken out of my January pay presumably. Have very little use for money here and besides the exchange is very advantageous to us. I'm getting my back pay this month & it will amount to about $260 cash or about 20,000 francs. I think I'll send home about 18,000 francs. The fact that a haircut cost 10 francs will show you how rich I am. Trouble is that the American army is causing a regular inflation around here.

Much love to all, Bill

My concern about never receiving the mail should not have troubled me. All through the Tunisian campaign I got great quantities of mail, most of it months old. By that time I was losing interest in events at home. My father sent me clippings from the San Francisco Chronicle Sporting Green each week, and there was all the football news. I couldn't care less. The Kleenex arrived; I had no use for it. The glasses did arrive in late April; I promptly stepped on them. A crummy little cardboard slide rule arrived; I doubt that I ever used it. Warm underwear came, but by this time I had adequate GI underwear, and of course I wasn't in England. Hand knit wool socks arrived, and these I did use, both in Tunisia and later in England, France, and Germany. I think my mother enlisted all her friends to make socks, and they arrived throughout the rest of the war.

My comment about the 361st never getting near the front is interesting. They didn't go to Tunisia, but my company, "C," was converted later to a DUKW company. DUKW's were amphibious trucks that were used extensively in landing operations because they could sail in as boats, and then drive right up onto beaches and then go inland. The 361st apparently participated in the landing in Sicily, where they saw a lot of action, and I suspect they went in at Salerno, and probably at Anzio.

No. 3
North Africa
"Christmas Day", 1942

Dear Mother, Dad, and Sis,

It is 4:00 PM here now, and as I write I guess you are all having breakfast and getting ready to open packages. I'm thinking of home today more than ever before. I've sent you greetings via several routes so that you should have received at least one. Christmas here has been a work day just like any other day, except that there were a few "Merry Christmases" passed around this morning. I am the officer of the day, but it makes little difference in whether you are officer of the day or not now. Spent a rather sleepless Christmas eve due to the Darlan excitement[2], of which you probably know a lot more than I. Got myself drenched from head to foot inspecting the guard last night, and was very glad to see that at least Christmas Day turned out to be a beautiful day. My blankets are all stretched over my tent drying for the first time in many a day. This country is beginning to remind me more of Northern Calif. than Southern Calif. At least the weather is. Even matches under cover become too damp to light. In order to go from my tent to the battalion headquarters, there is no alternative but to wade through a quagmire of soupy mud. I've heard it said that it isn't the shooting that makes wars hard on men, but it's the cold, and the wet, sleepless nights. Thank gosh for my rubber boots, altho I feel guilty about wearing them when I see our men with feet that are never dry, never warm. Why they aren't equipped with the light leather field boots of the German army I'll never know. Sometimes you wonder whether the people in warm offices who specify equipment have ever been with an army in the field. I guess it's all an experience that I wouldn't miss for the world, and will never forget. I have to go to guard mount now — I'll finish this later.

5:00

I'll try to finish this before retreat. Every few minutes I have to chase Arab children from my tent. They beg cigarettes and sell oranges and attract flies, and are a general nuisance. They know it's near chow time, and they are all gathering around with tin cans to collect slop.

They had hoped to have turkey for us today, but no dice, so we had a Christmas dinner of Heintz's spagetti. I'm company mess officer now, but about the only thing I have to do is inspect for sanitation, and provide a decent garbage disposal, which is

2   Refers to the assassination of French Admiral Darlan on Dec. 24, 1942

incidentally quite a problem due to the fly menace. Because of the great scarcity of wood fuel, burning garbage is impractical, and the only alternative is to strain out the water into a drainage pit, and then bury the remainder. Bed rock is near the surface and digging is difficult. This fly problem is going to be terrible when warm whether comes.

I get very disgusted with this Quartermaster outfit. I guess even being with a crack organization a short time spoiled me. We have a major who is a dead ringer for Admiral Simons. (And I don't mean he looks like him.) Enough said! I get my share of the hell that is passed out, but like everyone else, I figure they can send me home if they don't want me here. Every other man in this battalion is a New York or Pennsylvania "vich" or "ski" or "off" or "stein". Nothing like the just plain Americans we had at Ft. Wood. I'm the only man from California, and as I guess I've said before, I'm fighting the wrong war.

I suppose it will be February before you get this letter, and Christmas will have long since been forgotten, but I just wanted you to know that I was thinking of you on this day that has always meant so much to our family.

Just a few passing thoughts: Don't under rate the British army. We can learn an awful lot from them. They are organized to a point that we can't approach. They are set in their ways, pig-headed, and difficult to work with, however. They are much more efficient than we are and I would estimate that it costs about half as much to put a British army in the field as an American army. Due to the standard of living that they have been used to, they can thrive in conditions that the American soldier won't stand for. That is also true of all other armies, and puts us at quite a disadvantage. It's not that the American soldier can't take it, it's that he won't take it.

Well, I'll have to close now as I have to take a detail of men to the movie in the neighboring town. ("Tarzan in New York"). 10% of our strength can go twice a week.

Much love to all,

Bill

P.S. If you didn't get my letter of a few days ago, you can start writing to this address.

I'm amused now by my dissertation about the British army. I hadn't been near the British army for months, and there were no British around us at Oran, so this must have been the result of conversations with other people. My statement that being "cold and wet" was the worst feature of war was an opinion that I was soon to revise. Cold and wet and mud are bad enough, but guns and bullets and shells and bombs are quite another matter.

At this point I had begun to be rather fond of the enlisted men in the company. I had made a considerable point of not assuming special privileges until I felt that I had earned them. For example, I refused to cut into the chow line as the other officers did. As the result of this and numerous other trivial things, I began to get their respect, and they were responding by trying to please me. I was learning by trial and error something about leadership, and it was rewarding. I was not so unhappy about my situation as I had been a couple of weeks before. When I got back to the 1st Engineers I would find it much more difficult to gain the confidence of the men, because they were more used to good leadership. Also a large number of them were from the Regular Army, not "citizen soldiers."

I also sent a cable home for Christmas. It was probably some kind of package deal; it doesn't sound like my words. It was delivered on January 13.

The next letter was written to my sister, although it was evidently intended for all.

No. 4
North Africa
Dec. 28, 1942

Dear Sis:

I'll start a letter to you now, although I may not be able to finish it till later.

Having written to you all just a few days ago, (Christmas Day), there isn't much news of myself that I can give you. I'm assuming that you got that letter.

I hope you received the stamps that I sent from here, and also from England. If you didn't, please let me know and I will get some more. As long as I'm seeing the world I might as well make the best of it. Incidentally, if you haven't yet received that other letter, you can start writing to this address — I'm stuck here. As soon as I get a chance I'm going to start a tracer going after that lost mail of mine. Gosh, I must have hundreds of letters.

Sis, I think you'd be interested in this country, although a little of it would go a long ways. I've been trying to think what this little dump of a town reminded me of, and it occurred to me that what I was thinking of was Tijuana. There isn't much difference that I can see between a Mexican and an Arab outside of their clothing, and the Arabs seem to be gradually stocking up on GI army stuff. My tent-mate has already lost two pairs of shoes and a pair of pants right out of the tent. One interesting thing is the way the more well-to-do Arab women dress. They cover their entire body with a white sheet, & all you can see of their eyes is one eye. They are sort of mysterious looking.

Dec. 29, 1942

I got interrupted to start a new job. I'm now working nights with a band of horrible crumby Arabs. My day is now turned upside down, but I think I can work it out. Trouble is that I have company duties besides this job. There's one thing about working with Arabs; they are scared to death of water, and refuse to work in the rain. It rains for at least half of every night, the Arabs pile into the back of every covered truck, and I curl up in the cab and go to sleep. Our Major, however, has a nasty little trick of calling out troops who have worked all day, to work in place of the Arabs in the rain.

Today, my field jacket is missing from my tent. It'll be a dead Arab that I find wearing it.

Seeing as how I'm in a truck company I decided to learn to drive a truck, and have now got an army license. It really feels good to get behind the wheel again. I sneaked a "jeep" out the other day and took a look at the country.

Enclosed are a couple of clippings from the weekly "Stars & Stripes."

Our promised Christmas turkey arrived yesterday, so at noon today we had a

Christmas dinner. We also got some fresh potatoes. Had a dinner of turkey, boiled potatoes, dressing, canned corn, canned blackberries, and coffee. I really gorged myself.

Poking around my mess tent, I can find a regular glossary of California towns on the cans of food. The brands are ones I've never heard of.

Dad asked me in his Sept. V-Mail how my uniform was holding out. The blouse & pinks that I left home in will last the duration as I seldom have to wear them. Around here I wear an O.D. shirt, a one-piece coverall fatigue suit (green), rubber boots, and an overseas cap. A field jacket or short-coat goes over that for warmth, and my slicker keeps me dry.

Well, that's enough for the present; write soon.

Love, Bill

In a way it's too bad that I did not write to my sister more often, because for some reason I wrote more to her about the local color and the small domestic details.

No. 5
"North Africa"
Dec 30,, 1942

Dear Mother, Dad, and Sis,

I've been doing considerable writing lately, but this being my 6 months anniversary in the army, I thought I'd celebrate. Little did I think six months ago today that this is where I'd be within six months. I've been in the army for six months and I'm already entitled to wear an overseas stripe on my sleeve. It was four months ago tonight that I last set foot on American soil. Things have sure moved fast since I last saw you all at Third and Townsend.

"And the rains came"!! That is the only thing that will describe life here now. The natives say that it will last two more months. I wonder if we will! If you would like to see how we are living, you might picture this: In the middle of January when California is going full tilt, build a little platform about 6 ft square & 6 inches off the ground in the nearest vacant lot. Over it pitch a pup tent, and throw a few blankets & whatever else you want to keep dry into it. Incidentally, pick a lot with no grass, because grass retains the mud too well. Then go out and live in that tent through the worst of the storms. No fair making a fire when the rain stops, 'cause firewood is too valuable. You can have a candle in the tent if you wish. Better spread your raincoat over the entrance to keep out the wind & rain. Your worst problem will be this — after you've crawled in and out a few times, it's as wet inside as out. Also it's cold as hell. 'Course I have a bigger tent and a cot, but the problems are similar.

I'm working nights now. I'm supposed to work all night, but I quit at 400 so I can get all my sleep in by noon. Nobody knows the difference, and it makes it much easier. I dread tonight, but I've a suspicion that my Arabs have no intention of making an appearance tonight, in which case I'll send everyone to bed and do likewise myself. Hope the major doesn't come snooping around & decide to call out the troops.

As I write I have a pair of socks drying out over a candle. I don't wear my boots during the day now, because my feet get too cold in them. I just let my feet stay wet all day & then put on dry socks & boots at night. Do you suppose you could send me two pairs of heavy wool socks. The rains will probably be over by the time they get here, but they will be good for hiking. Army socks are totally inadequate for any place except the tropics. Don't send me more than two pairs, 'cause I have too much baggage now.

I'm going to try to make breakfast in the morning as we've got the first fresh eggs I've seen since I left the states. The A rations are beginning to roll in now, and our mess tent is full of frozen meat. If they don't issue us enough, the boys on the trucks see to it that we get plenty by other methods.

In case you haven't yet received letters No. 3 and 4, you can start writing to this address, and you can also get me some glasses. Jenkel-Davidson in Palo Alto has the dope on them. Chocolate bars and Milky-Ways can always be used, even if they start selling them to us. Otherwise, I need nothing.

I'll close now & brave the elements.

Lots of love,

Bill

The "work" I was doing at night consisted of supervising a work team of Arabs loading ammunition onto railroad cars. The night before this letter one of the cars at another location a mile up the road, and at a slightly higher elevation, got loose and careened down the track and hit my ammunition-loaded cars with a great smash. A couple of Arabs were injured, and the whole gang was very upset and generally shaken up. I told them they could go home, but they still were not happy. Then I told them they would get paid for a full night's work. This was greeted with smiles and contentment.

(5)
North Africa
Jan 4

Dear Mother, Dad, and Sis,

I'm O.D. tonight, so I thought I'd drop you a line to help pass the time. Being as how I've been working nights, being O.D. is really a vacation, because all I have to do is inspect the guard once after midnight, and then I'll set up a cot here in battalion headquarters and sleep until it's time to get up and raise the flag.

We've had a couple of beautiful days. It's probably the best weather we'll have here, because the nights are still cold enough to keep the flies down to a minimum. In the daytime it's warm enough to be comfortable in shirt sleeves.

We've been getting fresh food for the last week. A fried egg tastes awful good when you haven't had one for four months. The crowning glory was the arrival of a boatload of oranges, oranges being the only thing in the world that we have plenty of. How can you win a war with brains like that running things?

Saw some good news on the battalion bulletin board tonight. A mobile shower unit has set up near by, so you see that life is definitely becoming more luxurious.

One of my cooks is a very accomplished accordionist, so we have lots of music around here.

I see the Rose Bowl game didn't turn out so good.

Pop, you might ask Col. Thomas what an Engineer Amphibious Brigade is good for. Nobody around here is quite sure.

Well, that's about enough for tonight. Write soon.

Love, Bill

The Col. Thomas mentioned was the CO of the Army ROTC unit at UC Berkeley; my father was at that time commanding the Naval ROTC at Berkeley. His son and I were good friends, as were he and my father.

That was to be my last letter from the 361st QM Battalion. The next day my good friend the Personnel Adjutant of the brigade sent for me and announced that I was going back to the 1st Division. I would go into Oran the next day, January 6, with the mail truck (or something) and meet a representative of the 1st Engineer Battalion in the lobby of a hotel that was also some kind of headquarters. I left with no regrets and in great excitement.

> *No. 6 (I think)*
> *North Africa*
> *Jan. 8, 1943*

Dear Mother, Dad, and Sis,

I'll start this letter before supper, but it's going to be a long one, so I'll probably have to finish it later. I've at last got lots of wonderful news for you. First of all, look at the address on the envelope, and you will get the general idea. I'm an engineer; I'm in the 1st Infantry Division; I'm in the 1st Engineers. How do you like that? It all happened very suddenly, and is a long story. Mother, I know you would rather have me in a "behind the lines" service outfit, but I'm sure Dad appreciates how happy I am to get back to the best fighting outfit in the U.S. Army. I know he'd give his eye teeth to be in the Solomons right now, and that's the way I feel about it too. If I've got to fight a war I want to be with the best of them even if the life is going to be a lot tougher.

The second news item is that I have at long last got some wonderful mail: 11 letters, several newspapers, a "Time", and of all things, a package of Kleenex. They've had lots of mail for me, but they sent it up to Scotland. This mail is mostly Oct. and early Nov. mail. (A letter from Aunt Bern is dated Dec. 12). It is by no means complete, as there are big gaps in your stories. I gathered that Sis had joined a sorority, for instance, but it was a letter from Betty Manners that finally let me know which one. More comments on your letters later.

I discovered that the battalion had learned from an enlisted man who was on the same transport as I, that I was in Africa. They have been combing all of North Africa for me & finally located me & told that other outfit in no uncertain terms that I was their property.[3]

To get here I had to spend several hours in a large city, and had a most interesting time, altho they had a regular cloud burst while I was there. I ducked in a door entrance for shelter, and there had quite a conversation with a Frenchman who was

---

3   Apparently the orders issued by the Brigade attaching me had finally drifted through channels and down to the 1st Division

interested in learning some English. I shopped around and found a good stamp store. I thought stamps would make good souvenirs of my travels, and besides, they are dirt cheap here. I'm sending them home in installments to make sure that at least some get there.

I find that French cities are much more American than British. There are lots of women's hat & shoe shops, and women run around in high heels and furs. Seems funny to see them mixed in with Arabs who look like something out of the bible with their white sheets, and riding astride donkeys half the size of a man.

I got a genuine American woman, Red Cross woman, to find me a place to get lunch. They have places for enlisted men, but the officers as usual have to shift for themselves. I guess that'll be the last I'll see of a city for quite awhile, but I made the best of it. It's the first city I've seen since Glasgow. For your information, other large cities I was in while in England were London, Birmingham, and Liverpool, altho I didn't get a chance to really see the latter.

I am now in "A" Co. of the battalion and am the administration officer handling the mess, supply, motors, company fund, etc. I like the job because it will give me an opportunity to get acquainted with the company and what they do before I have to take much responsibility in operations.

I thought I was roughing it before, but I'm really roughing it now, & it's going to get rougher. I'm living in a pup tent, but it's not so bad because we've built up the sides about 2 ft. so I can put a cot into it. I don't know how our company rates cots for the officers, because the Col. & the staff are on the ground.

We are in very pretty country now. Our camp is in one of the few woods in North Africa. We made a march this afternoon up a mountain. I'm pretty soft, & my feet are now in bad shape.

Much love to all,
Bill

Note the new macho attitude in this letter. Up until this point I had very mixed feelings about being a "fighting" soldier; my experiences in the 361st had turned me around.

At the designated place in Oran I met Bill Gara, Captain Gara now. We got into an ambulance that was being used by our battalion for a bus, and as we drove Gara explained what they had in mind for me. Colonel Rowland (he was now a Lt. Colonel) had received permission from the General to form a new company, to be known as "D" Company, in which he was going to concentrate all the heavy weapons of the battalion, which were considerable. Under the regular organization each platoon in "A," "B," and "C" Companies had a lightly armored halftrack vehicle mounting a 50-caliber machine gun and two 30-caliber machine guns. In addition each platoon had a jeep that towed a 37 mm anti-tank gun. So there were available nine halftracks, nine jeeps, and nine anti-tank guns. He then threw in the two "Hell Squads" from H&S Company, obtained for them two 81 mm infantry mortars, and apparently felt he had a miniature armored division with which he was going to ride to great glory. (I was soon to find that this move was very controversial; the regular platoon commanders especially resented losing their jeeps. Other consequences of the formation of "D" Company will be better appreciated later when I describe what the combat engineers actually did when in action.) I assumed that Gara was telling me that I was going to be assigned to "D" Company. But no, this was leading up to the fact that Finley and Haas had been assigned to "D" Company, along with Charlie Kelly who was in "C" Company and would take command of "D" Company. I was going to be assigned to "A" Company to replace Haas as the Administrative Officer.

The 1st Engineer Battalion was camped at a place called Oggaz a few miles inland from Oran. The heavy rains that day had caused a flood, and most of "A" Company were out placing sandbags to protect the company area from inundation. When I met Charlie Murphy, the company commander, he was wearing hip boots and was wading around in the flood.

The next sub-unit below a company is a platoon. "A" Company had a Headquarters Platoon, and then three "line" Platoons, each with about thirty-six men.

The other officers in the company were Fred Rutledge commanding the 1st Platoon, Bill Barnum with the 2nd, and Simeon Alexander ("Knocker") Box with the 3rd. I was to be the company "Administrative" officer. Let me introduce them all because they were to play a big part in my life.

1st Lt. Charles E. Murphy, "Murph," was an electrical engineering graduate of the Univ. of Tennessee in 1941, and had joined the battalion sometime early in 1942. He had evidently worked for a while as an engineer for Lockheed in Southern California following his graduation. He was married and had a baby daughter. There was probably nobody with whom I was closer than Murph during the entire war. I soon discovered that the other officers resented him, since he had been moved over from "B" Company to take over "A," and a very popular officer, John Oxford, had been transferred from "A" to "B." Murphy sort of took me under his wing, with the result that I was excluded initially from the little fraternity of platoon commanders. It seemed to me they were always whispering together in the corner and leaving me out.

The Colonel had appointed Murphy as company commander because he felt he had "dash," as a result of some action during the battle for Oran. Murphy was a bit outrageous at times and was perhaps born a century too late. He would have been very happy in the Confederate Army, probably riding with Jeb Stuart, the famous Confederate cavalry commander in the Civil War (Murph was in fact a horseman.) A further complication was that Murph didn't get along with Gara, and that was not the best way to get ahead in the 1st Engineers. But Col. Rowland thought he had what the French so highly prize, élan. And there was no question that Murphy was what we would call a "take charge" guy. Gara had commanded "A" Company in the States the previous year and knew more about the company than Murphy did, and that didn't help. We all had our complaints about Murphy as time went on, but I loved the guy. One of the most distinguishing characteristics of Murph was his wild imagination and his outrageous memory. He often got the two mixed up, so Murph's memories of shared events were likely to be very different than that of others. He often clashed with the enlisted men on all kinds of disciplinary issues, leaving the rest of us to pick up the pieces. Eventually I was to become the peacemaker between Murph and the platoon commanders, but this would be much later.

Fred Rutledge was a very tall, blond South Carolinian from Clemson, with a lovely drawl and a twinkle in his eye. Like all of the officers except Barnum, Rutledge was, like me, an ROTC graduate. That is, he received his officer's commission when he graduated from college and thus never served as an enlisted man. He was not married, and I assume he was from the college graduating class of 1942 like me. Rut would be described today as "laid back." He was a good person to go out on the town with. It took me awhile to really get close to Rut, but we ultimately became great friends. At the end of the war we were fellow company commanders.

You have already met Bill Barnum. Very serious, very dedicated, definitely not "laid back." He was about six or eight years older than the rest of us. He had been an enlisted man before going to OCS and probably had a somewhat different attitude than the rest of us schoolboys. He was an engineering graduate of the University of Minnesota.

"Knocker" Box was another Southerner, a graduate of Louisiana State (probably class of 1942 like me), and a native of Mississippi. He had been quite an athlete, a guard on the football team and apparently a great catcher on the baseball team. Box was already a legitimate hero, and very popular with the enlisted men. When the infantry had been pinned down outside of a small town near Oran, Box had taken his halftrack and stormed into the town with machine guns blazing and effectively captured the place all by himself. For this he was awarded the Distinguished Service Cross (DSC). He was short but very husky and undoubtedly could whip any man in his platoon. I found him to be a nice pleasant guy but I doubt he had much use for me. He had a great sense of humor and was fun to be around. He usually dominated the conversation. He seemed to be more knowledgeable about what was going on than anybody else, and I think Box genuinely enjoyed being in the army and being in combat situations.

I should also mention Charlie Kelly at this time. He was an MIT graduate (class of 1941) and another of the current "heroes." He had also used his halftrack to help the infantry out of a tight spot in the battle for Oran, for which he had been awarded the Silver Star. These two halftrack episodes undoubtedly gave Rowland his inspiration for "D" Company, which was the reason for Kelly becoming the company commander of "D" Company. We will see more of Kelly later.

The enlisted men were for the most part from New York and its environs (especially Brooklyn), but there was a considerable contingent from the deep South, and from Kentucky and West Virginia. There was nobody from the Midwest, the Mountain States, or the Pacific Coast. A good fraction were old Regular Army types, including many of the NCOs. The average soldier was five to ten years older than me; that is, they were in their late twenties and early thirties. These men were not as easy to win over as the draftees in the 361st. It took me many months to feel comfortable.

I was terribly excited about rejoining the 1st Engineers. My experience with the 361st had made me wonder whether the war was indeed winnable. Suddenly I was back with real professionals and I had the feeling that people actually knew what they were doing.

At this point it is appropriate to digress a bit and describe the organization of the 1st Infantry Division, because some understanding of the relationship between the various units, and especially their names and designations, will be helpful in making sense of much that is to follow.

The Division, with about 13,000 men, had a "triangular" organization, which simply means that every unit was composed of three parts. The main units were three infantry regiments, the 16th, the 18th and the 26th, each with about 3,000 men. These each had three battalions of about 700 men, supported by some other components; each battalion had three rifle companies of about 180 men, supported by a heavy weapons company; each rifle company had three rifle platoons of about forty men, supported by a weapons platoon (a 60 mm mortar and light machine guns), each platoon had three squads of about a dozen men. Associated with each infantry regiment was a battalion of light artillery (105 mm howitzers), the 7th Field Artillery Battalion with the 16th Infantry Regiment, the 32nd Field Artillery with the 18th Infantry, and the 33rd Field Artillery with the 26th Infantry. In addition there was a battalion of medium artillery (155 mm howitzers), the 5th Field Artillery Battalion.

Then there were support troops at the Division level, and these included the 1st Engineer Battalion. The 1st Engineers also had a triangular organization. Company "A" was associated with the 16th Infantry Regiment, "B," with the 18th, and "C" with the 26th. Sometimes this association was carried a level lower with the 1st Platoon of each company associated with the 1st Battalion of the infantry regiment, the 2nd Platoon with the 2nd Battalion, and so on. Our "D" Company was totally separate and had no association with the infantry regiments.

Sometimes the division subdivided itself into three independent groups known as regimental combat teams. Thus there would be the 16th Regimental Combat Team, comprising the 16th Infantry Regiment, the 7th Field Artillery Battalion, and "A" Company of the 1st Engineers. In some cases, especially in landing operations, battalion combat teams would be formed in essentially the same way.

To further confuse matters, other outside units would frequently be attached to the division, and then sometimes they too would be broken down and attached to the combat teams, always using the same scheme. Thus the 601st Tank Destroyer Battalion was attached to the 1st Infantry Division in Africa, and the 745th Tank Battalion (medium tanks) was attached in Europe. In Africa we had no tanks in direct support, which was probably one of our problems, although our tanks were no match for either the German anti-tank guns or the German tanks. Our tanks were all in the 1st Armored Division, which operated independently. In a similar manner, in Africa we had no direct air support; all of the air forces were "strategic" and carried on their own war completely independent of the ground forces. On the Continent later we did have tactical air forces in direct support of the infantry, and these were completely independent of the strategic air forces that carried out the bombing of cities, etc.

In contrast, the German infantry in Africa was always associated in some way with tanks, and the Germans always had tactical air support. A result of this was that we would find ourselves in Tunisia being bombed and strafed while at the same time B17s and P38s were flying far overhead on their way to rear area targets. All of this would change on the Continent after the Normandy landings, but it had a lot to do with our experiences in Tunisia, as we shall see.

Jan. 13, 1943

Dear Mother, Dad, and Sis,

This letter is mostly to let you know that I am getting mail, and to restate that I am back with the old outfit, in case you didn't get my last letter.

I have been back almost a week now, and I have received something in the mail every day. For instance, yesterday I got three letters from you dated Sept. 7, Sept. 11, and then Nov. 13. Also I guess you recognize this stationery — thanks. Best of all, I got your Christmas package for which I thank you all ever so much for. A lot of the fellows have those picture wallets, and the cards are always hard to get. What do you think of the chess set Liz sent? My company commander soundly beat me in chess last night, so I will have to scare up some less formidable opposition. As I told Liz, everything you sent fits in nicely with the necessity of keeping my personal baggage light. Incidentally, what's that Cal sticker on my car windshield? Fine stuff!!

I've also received several Sporting Greens which are gradually catching me up on the football situation.

Better not send any more Kleenex. I find it's really just a crutch that I can easily get along without, when necessary.

Enclosed is the second money order installment. I sent $100 in the last letter. As I said in that letter, and many before it, I still don't know whether or not you got the $200 sent in October. Also, no mention has ever been made to whether or not you received the suitcase I asked them to send for me at Camp Kilmer, N.J.

Later

I am sitting in my pup tent having just finished looking over the "Berkeley Daily Gazette" in which I see Sis is a Gamma Phi. Well, well, well!! Congratulations, — do you live at the "house", or at home? If I got half as many letters from home as I get newspapers, I'd be a very happy man. I think letters will start coming in a few days, or at least as soon as they get the package situation straightened out. Poor APO #1 is completely snowed under with Christmas packages still.

A new ruling has just been passed down concerning what we can say about where we've been. Before they change their minds again, I'll tell you what is legal. We'll put it this way. I am familiar with the city of Oran and the town of Arzew. Everybody else can write that they have been in action and under fire. Much to my regret, I can't. I can say that in England I was in such places as Tidworth (north of Southhampton), Lichfield, Tamworth, Stafford, Liverpool, London, Rugby, etc. In Scotland, I am familiar with Glasgow, Greenoch, Gurock, Helensburgh, Kilcreggan, and places which you'd never find on a map. What I was doing when I was at these places is another matter, however. Dad, if you know anything of the U.S. Navy setup in Scotland, you shouldn't have any trouble in placing me for part of the time, at any rate. One last word about Scotland: it's the coldest, wettest place I've ever been in. I'll leave it to the Scotch.

I'm enclosing the first of two installments of stamps. Altho I'm collecting stamps as souvenirs, more or less, don't let them confuse you too much as to where I've been. Let's just say that having had the opportunity to buy some of them first hand, and having muffed it, I bought them at a stamp store in Oran. I got two of each kind, and will send the duplicates in the next letter. You can see by the prices what bargains they are. A franc is worth 1-1/3 c, which is an exchange rate having very little relation to the buying power of the money.

Well, I'll close now & thank you once more for everything you've sent.

Lots of love,

Bill

#8   1st Engineer Bn.

APO#1, New York

January 16, 1948[4]

Dear Mother, Dad, and Sis,

Here are the rest of the stamps, and the rest of the money. Yesterday I signed my pay voucher for January & that will send another $140. I may not be earning as much money as lots of people back home, but it's a cinch I'm saving more.

If you haven't received my recent letters, note the above address. I'm still keeping up my record of getting something in the mail every day. Guess I'm gradually catching up. I even got two post cards from Sis from Idlewyld, dated Aug. 24, and addressed to Ft. Leonard Wood. Also got some underwear, which I am now wearing. Took my first bath, since I arrived in Africa, yesterday, and put on some clean clothes.

The "Sporting Greens" have taken me up to the week before the Big Game, and then they stopped coming. Fine thing!

Here are a couple of post cards from Sidi-Bel-Abbès. I'm going to try to get some pictures out of the battalion photographer, and will send them. It would be a pity to go through the war without some pictures of it.

We had a battalion review for General Allen[5] today. Not much like garrison reviews. Everybody wears steel helmets and field dress. As a matter of fact, we wear our helmets when we're doing duty of any kind.

The colonel has got himself a police pup. I'll be interested to see how it acts under fire. We seem to have collected innumerable dogs here. Hope they don't eat us out of house & home when the going gets tough.

Just got my sixth pair of shoes since I've been in the army. Six pairs in 6-1/2 months, and that includes a month in the hospital, and a month aboard ship.

Africa has definitely taken a turn for the cold. It's been nice and clear, though, and reasonably warm in the sun. I finally got another field jacket, but I find my short-coat is necessary in the mornings & evenings.

Definitely don't eat as well here as in the QM. "Vienna sausage" and field ration "C" provides most of the meat.

One of the fellows got a letter dated Jan. 1. Sometimes if airmail letters are timed right they hit one the few planes that bring mail. Sometimes they hit a slow convoy and take months.

Well, that's about all I can think of tonight.

Much love,

Bill

---

4   That's how the year was written!

5   Division Commander

P.S. I just finished beating my company commander in chess.

From the day I arrived at Oggaz they were all talking about going to Tunisia, and it was apparent that we would soon be moving. Tunisia was a name I only knew through stamp collecting. Murphy told me that he expected that ninety percent of us would become casualties in Tunisia. But this was typical Murphy talk. I soon discovered that I had opinions that were at least as good as his.

American units that landed in Algeria were committed piecemeal to various parts of Tunisia in an attempt to cut off Rommel who was retreating from Egypt. The distances were great and I suppose logistical problems made it impossible to do otherwise, but it was always too little too late, and the resulting fragmentation of units led to ineffective battle formations. Paratroops who had landed at Algiers went to central Tunisia a week or two after the landings. Parts of the 26th Infantry Regiment were in central Tunisia in late November, and the remainder of the regiment a little later. In the meantime British troops, which became the British 1st Army, moved into northern Tunisia, but failed in an attempt to capture the city and port of Tunis. Our 18th Infantry Regiment went to reinforce the British in December. French colonial troops joined and moved into central Tunisia. (These were Vichy French troops who came over to the Allied side.) All of the 1st Division units were attached to other commands as they arrived in Tunisia, and were scattered from one end of the country to the other, mostly in battalion size groups. As the American General in charge of American operations in Europe, this was not Dwight Eisenhower's finest hour and heads were to roll before it was over.

When I arrived at Oggaz there remained only Division Headquarters, the 16th Infantry, the 1st Engineers, and some other support troops. So most of General Allen's command was in Tunisia, but he was still hundreds of miles away in Oggaz.

I explained before that our company consisted of three platoons of about forty men, each under the command of a lieutenant, plus a headquarters section. Whenever we went into action, one of our platoons was detached from the company and came directly under the control of the associated infantry regiment. We called these platoons the "combat platoons." When I arrived at Oggaz the combat platoons from "B" and "C" companies had long since gone to Tunisia. It was a long time before I ever got to know these particular platoon commanders. In fact in one case it was years after the war.

On the 17th of January we started the long truck convoy to Tunisia. I don't recall whether our battalion moved independently of the other Division units or not.

The first evening we camped out on an open field only a couple of miles from our camp at Oggaz. As soon as we left Oggaz, the Arabs descended on the place and started digging up the trash that we had buried. The Colonel sent somebody back to inspect the area and found the Arabs digging up 50 caliber machine gun ammunition. One of our halftrack crews had evidently found themselves with an excess of ammunition and had simply buried it. It turned out to be an "A" Company halftrack, and although the halftrack was at that time attached to the newly formed "D" Company, the Colonel still considered the discipline of the men to be Murphy's responsibility. Murphy was furious at both the Colonel and the halftrack crews, and the sergeant in charge of the halftrack had to be instantly broken to private. The whole incident caused a lot of hard feelings and didn't serve to endear "D" Company to the rest of the battalion.

Despite the fact that I was "administrative" officer of the company, I don't recall anything about the logistics of the trip. How did we get gasoline? How did we get food and water? I suspect the motor sergeant and the mess sergeant simply ignored me and dealt directly with the battalion supply office.

For hundreds of miles the road was lined with Arabs selling oranges and other stuff. I remember camping near Orleansville, and then on the outskirts of Algiers. The latter reminded me of the countryside near Los Angeles. I guess it was the orange orchards. East of Algiers we got into mountains and I recall camping in cold, bleak country, with few Arabs around. On one occasion we stopped after dark in high mountain country and simply circled the trucks, covered-wagon style, reminiscent of the wagon trains of American history. We passed through Constantine, and on the 23rd of January stopped for a few days at a place called Guelma, still in Algeria. There was heavy frost at night, but there were hot springs nearby, and we were able to let the men take a bath in a warm creek. But it was generally cold and wet and there was mud everywhere. In fact if there is one impression of the war that sticks with one it is the mud, whether in North Africa or in France or in Germany. Only in the summer in Sicily did we not have to deal with mud.

I believe we did a little training while camped near Constantine, because I remember that we prepared a bridge for demolition.

Our food was a British "compo" ration. This was a box with enough for a British squad for one day. It contained, among other things, a tin of instant tea (no coffee), and a tin of English cigarettes, which our men wouldn't smoke. At Guelma I took a large supply of these tins of cigarettes and bartered with some Arabs for fresh eggs. I got enough for the entire company for breakfast, perhaps the first useful thing I did in the 1st Engineers.

We had a well-equipped kitchen truck in each company. But with the British compo ration the cooks had to open hundreds of small cans for each meal. The compo ration was really meant for individual soldiers to prepare for themselves, similar to our less elaborate "C" ration. Initially in Tunisia we were apparently being completely supplied by the British.

At Guelma, one night Murphy got into a big argument with our First Sergeant, Quesenberry. Quesenberry was a very fine soldier, but he came from a small town in West Virginia and was a religious fundamentalist. He was very disturbed to find that Murph didn't believe in God. When I was censoring the men's mail the next day (we officers were required to censor our men's mail) I read Quesenberry's letter home, and it was apparent that he was extremely upset. He was going into battle with a commander who didn't believe in God! He ultimately became so disturbed that he had to be reduced in rank to corporal and was transferred to H&S Company. He spent the rest of the war driving a truck.

While we were at Guelma our trucks were briefly requisitioned to carry infantry forward to meet a combat emergency of some kind. In this case a regiment was hastily formed from one battalion of the 16th Infantry, one battalion of the 26th, and a British battalion, all under the command of Col. Matthews, the Executive Officer of the 16th Infantry. Once more, troops were being committed piecemeal with a hopeless command structure.

At this time the German 21st Panzer Division was conducting a series of probing attacks in the central sector of Tunisia, designed primarily to get us out of the way in preparation for the withdrawal of Rommel's Afrika Korps which was at that time entering southern Tunisia. Great panic was being caused because neither the American forces, nor the French colonial troops who were in that area, had any weapons that could effectively stop German tanks.

Our anti-tank guns were 37 mm "pea-shooters" that required a very lucky hit to do any damage. The "bazooka," a fairly effective rocket gun, had yet to arrive. Our armor was all in the 1st Armored Division operating further south, but it was having its own troubles with an atrocious medium tank (the General Grant), and light tanks armed with 37 mm guns. It was now three and a half years since the Germans introduced the blitzkrieg in Poland, and over two and a half years since they overwhelmed France, and yet Americans were being put into battle against them with weapons that would have been barely adequate in 1939. Our tank destroyer battalion, the 601st, was armed with thin-skinned halftrack vehicles mounting WW1 French 75s. (The Grant also had 75s.) This was a rather low muzzle-velocity gun that required one to be at very close range, a good trick for a vehicle with virtually no armor. In addition the Germans had just introduced the Mark VI tank, the "Tiger," a sixty-ton monster that was totally immune to 75s, and mounted the dreaded 88 mm gun. The 21st Panzers had a number of these. It is no wonder that there was a good deal of panic on our side. The British were somewhat better off, having an effective six-pounder (57 mm) anti-tank gun. Near the end of the Tunisian campaign we were issued the British gun, but by that time a far better tank destroyer vehicle had arrived, mounting a high-velocity three-inch naval gun, which was to prove effective, and the new "Sherman" tank had replaced the hopeless "Grant." But even the Sherman initially had the low velcity 75 mm gun; it was later equipped with the better three-inch gun. We eventually discovered that massed artillery was effective against tanks, but nowhere did we have "mass" in January and February. Americans do move quickly in an emergency, and the new weapons did arrive sooner than might have been expected, but one has to question why we get ourselves into these situations in the first place? These inadequate weapons cost a lot of money and time, not to mention a lot of lives.

Sometime while we were at Guelma, Rutledge and the 1st Platoon left as a "combat platoon" with the 16th Infantry.

The rest of us finally crossed the border into Tunisia and camped near the town of Makhtar. I recall passing an ordnance repair depot that afternoon, and saw a number of badly damaged tank destroyer vehicles. There had been some kind of major action a day or so before over the next mountain range, and that was the reason we had been moved there. We were getting close. It was the 28th of January.

We were put on an alert that night for the possibility of leaving for the "front" at any time. There was trouble ahead and we were evidently going to be used as infantry, not as engineers, or at least that was what we were told. At about one o'clock in the morning our runner (we maintained a runner at our battalion headquarters to relay messages) at headquarters, Pvt. Grassi, came back to the company bivouac area calling for "Lt. Murphy." I woke up and crawled out of my bedroll and got my stuff together.

Murphy soon came back from a company commander's meeting and said we were moving out immediately and going to a place called Ousseltia over the next range of mountains, where the Germans were threatening to break through. (Murphy pronounced it so that I thought he said Sausalito, a town on San Francisco Bay.)

Since we had no jeeps, nor did we have a command car, Murphy used a weapons carrier (a small truck) for a command car. I sat in the back with the First Sergeant and the company clerks and all our gear. For hours we struggled over a mountain range in pitch dark on awful roads. In the back of the vehicle we talked about what kind of food we each liked best — steak, roast beef, etc. Nobody would admit to being nervous. But what lay ahead? Were we going to intercept an armored division at dawn? I couldn't visualize what was going to be involved, and I certainly couldn't visualize what I personally was going to be doing. There was no point in asking Murph; he didn't know either, but he wasn't going to admit it.

Oggaz, Algeria, January 6, 1943; A flood on the day I returned to the Battalion.

Oggaz, Algeria, January 1943; "A" Company officer's tents.

Oggaz, Algeria, November 1942; Len Cohn, Adjutant, Bill Gara, Exec. Officer, Henry Rowland, Battalion Commander.

Oggaz, Algeria, November 1942; Fred Rutledge, "Knocker" Box, Fred Finley

CHAPTER FOUR

TUNISIA - PHASE I

JANUARY 29 - APRIL 15, 1943

As dawn broke on January 29th, we found ourselves out of the mountains and on an undulating plain, which was actually the Ousseltia Valley. It was grassy with scattered small trees, low brush, and here and there clumps of prickly pear cactus. It reminded me of some of the country near Prescott, Arizona, where I spent time with my grandparents as a young boy. Just at dawn we pulled off the road and scattered the vehicles as best we could under or near the few trees on a low hillside. No armored division, or anybody else, faced us! Nobody seemed to know anything. I don't recall fear or anything like that. I was just confused and didn't know what to think.

Just as we finished spreading camouflage nets over the vehicles I heard the sound of planes and looked up and saw what looked to me like two American P40s. A few seconds later there was a clatter of sustained machine gun fire, and I caught a glimpse of tracers through the trees. In an instant my thoughts went back thirteen years to *All Quiet on the Western Front*, and to Corporal Katczinsky telling his squad to hit the dirt - "Mother Earth, dig your faces into it." I was on the ground in a flash. As it turned out, a good part of the gunfire was from our own 50 caliber machine guns on our halftracks, and from a nearby artillery battery. But actually this was the German "dawn patrol," two Messerschmidt 109s that patrolled the Ousseltia Valley during daylight hours strafing any and all vehicles that happened to be on the roads.

During the entire three weeks we were in the Ousseltia Valley these planes arrived regularly, unchallenged by allied aircraft. They apparently came from Kairouan, which was in the desert over the next range of mountains and perhaps forty miles away. We could usually chase them off with 50 caliber machine guns, but a lone vehicle or convoy on the road didn't have a chance. The valley roads were strewn with burned-out vehicle carcasses. So the valley was very quiet during daylight hours and erupted with life when the sun went down. Fortunately it was January and not June, and the nights were long. But this was the story all over Tunisia until at least late March. Whenever you ventured out in daylight your eyes combed the skies until you weren't quite sure whether you were seeing planes or not. It was like being a hunted animal, a squirrel waiting for a hawk to pounce upon it.

A little while later that same morning I heard a whining sound overhead, and once more my childhood memory sent me to "Mother Earth." Several shells burst in a field

100 yards to the rear of us. What was going on? I couldn't figure it out. Where was the "front," or didn't it exist? A mountain on the enemy side looked down on us. Were they looking at us from there? A partial answer came a little while later when a battery of our own artillery a couple of hundred yards to our rear, and well hidden amongst some small trees, opened up with a deafening series of bangs. It was a battery of the 7th Field Artillery Battalion. The Germans were evidently after them, not us.

I spent the next few hours trying to dig a foxhole in the rocky ground. It was a sad affair. The enlisted men were doing much better. But I had a hard time finding a decent shovel. The little entrenching shovels that one ordinarily carried were close to useless in the hard and rocky ground. Since we were Engineer troops we did have regular big shovels in our trucks, but the enlisted men were using all of them.

Feeling a call of nature, I walked down the other side of our little hill to get well away from the vehicles and dug myself a little toilet hole in the soft bottom of a sandy wash. There were no trees. I no sooner had squatted over it than the two planes appeared again. Suddenly I felt like a giant and I was sure they were looking at me.

The chronology of the next several days eludes me. Unfortunately there are no letters from this period to inform my memory, and when I did write, I said little. Perhaps it was that first day when the 16th Infantry Regiment requested that Knocker Box, in charge of our 3rd platoon, be sent to their headquarters nearby as a liaison officer, and this meant that if we had anything to do I would have to take over his command. I recall going out at night with a detail to get water at the "water point" some miles away. The place was alive with French Arab soldiers and horses (or mules), all being watered. They were part of the French 19th Corps, and in fact we were at that time serving in the 19th Corps, commanded by General Juin. I have no idea where the French soldiers were dug in; I only saw them at night.

I should add a few details about where we got our water at what was known as a water point. The supply of fresh water for the Division was a responsibility of the 1st Engineers. Each of our three line companies had a team of several soldiers with a sergeant in charge, a couple of vehicles with pumps, hose, a collapsible canvas water tank, and water treatment equipment. We virtually never saw these people because they were generally several miles away wherever they found an abundant supply of water. Effectively they were under the control of one of our staff officers, designated the Assistant Division Engineer (our Battalion Commander Officer was designated Division Engineer) who spent most of his time at Division Headquarters. In fact we seldom saw him either. So we in the company really had nothing to do with the water supply, but we always seemed to be able to send trucks to the nearest water point and fill up five-gallon water cans, and all the other units in the Division did the same. I can never recall a time when there was any question about fresh decontaminated water being available. Thinking back on it, it seems amazing that the water point teams were always able to find adequate water and to operate so efficiently. An adequate supply of fresh water is as important to an army in the field as ammunition, and probably more important than food. These guys were certainly underappreciated.

Some time during the first two or three days we were told that the infantry wanted an extensive anti-tank minefield laid across the valley at the extreme left end where we effectively didn't have any troops in position. One battalion of the 16th Infantry Regiment was located in a side valley near the proposed minefield, but otherwise the area was deserted, essentially "no-man's land." "A" Company was chosen to do the job, and Murphy told Barnum and me to join Colonel Rowland and him on a reconnaissance.

I went to my pack and retrieved the Field Manual on Mine-Laying that I had lifted from the 361st. I stuffed it into my back pocket.

With a couple of vehicles we ventured out onto a road and down the valley with furtive eyes directed towards the sky. I envied those who didn't bother to look up; I certainly kept my eyes sweeping the sky. We passed evidence of a tank-tank destroyer battle of a few days before, little piles of 75 mm cartridge cases and tracks in the mud. I recall one place where the tank destroyers had apparently gone into a thick cactus growth to get partial cover. I have never known precisely what had happened in that valley before we arrived. Our tank destroyers had obviously challenged German tanks, and I suspect we came off second best. The thought of our thin-skinned halftrack tank destroyers, mounting French 75s, challenging a group of German tanks still gives me the creeps. I do know that German troops had occupied positions near where we were presently camped because there was a lot of German trash around.

To continue the minefield story, farther on we came across tank tracks, and to my horror we saw fresh tracks at least two feet or more wide. It was like running across fresh dinosaur tracks, and sent a chill up my spine. I knew which vehicle had made those tracks. German Mark VI tanks! They had just been introduced onto the Russian front; we hadn't expected to see them so soon in Africa. I was well aware that we had no weapons that would stop them, and our little anti-tank mines were not going to stop them either.

We reached the appointed place where we were to start laying the mines a mile or so further on and got out and walked over part of the area. It was approaching dusk. Rowland turned to Murphy and said, "I want you to lay a standard minefield across the valley." Murphy turned to Barnum and me and said, "Barnum and Kays, lay a standard minefield." I didn't know what a "standard" minefield was; I was sure that Murph didn't have a clue. They decided to leave Barnum and me there to make plans while they returned to get the remainder of the company and to get the several truckloads of mines that would be required. In a few minutes Bill Barnum and I found ourselves all alone in the middle of nowhere.

I pulled out my Field Manual and we read it. I guess Barnum had seen this particular type of minefield at OCS. We figured out the scheme and made our plans. Barnum would take his platoon and work to the right from the road. I would take Box's 3rd platoon and work to the left.

Then it got dark, and we sat down against a small tree and waited, and waited, and waited. It was moonlight and slightly windy and it felt to us like every moving tree limb was a German patrol. We heard dogs barking in the distance, and then heard barking from a different direction. Our imaginations ran wild.

The company and the mines finally arrived around eleven o'clock that night. "D" Company provided security with several halftracks. As described earlier, the halftracks were open-topped armored cars, with quarter-inch armor plating on the sides and half-inch armor over the windshield. The armor would essentially stop machine-gun bullets and small shell fragments, but not much more. They had truck wheels and tires in front, but had tank tracks in the rear so that they could negotiate fairly rough terrain. They were armed with a 50-caliber machine-gun mounted just to the right of and above the driver, and two water-cooled 30-caliber machine-guns, one on each side. Their primary function, for us, was to provide security for engineer work parties, but we also used them extensively for anti-aircraft work.

In the dark we had to explain to the NCOs how to lay out the field, and that was a bit of a hassle. The mines were British, and we had to figure out how to assemble and arm them. I got into a terrible argument with Sgt. Ziegler, an old Regular Army type and the platoon sergeant of the 3rd Platoon, because I insisted in holding things up while I prepared a map of the field using a compass as a surveying instrument. The Field Manual had been very insistent that the mine-field be accurately mapped. (A couple of weeks later we pulled up the mine-field; we didn't need my map; you could easily see every mine.) We used up our supply of about 2,000 mines by three o'clock in the morning and returned to camp.

The argument with Ziegler continued the next day when Murphy got into the fray. Ziegler insisted the mine-field wouldn't stop a tank. Apparently a "standard minefield" was a little three-row layout with closely spaced mines, something the NCOs had learned to lay some time in the past. My minefield was a four-row scheme recently developed at the Engineer School at Ft. Belvoir. It was easy to lay out and was effective. I stood my ground. I knew from my readings that the British were using much deeper minefields than ours, and certainly much deeper than the "standard." Basically Ziegler was miffed because I was directing operations rather than he. And he obviously had no respect for me, a fresh ROTC 2nd Lieutenant who couldn't compare with Knocker Box.

The next night "B" Company continued to lay the minefield. They came to me and borrowed my manual. We laid numerous minefields in Tunisia, most of them the same type. As to effectiveness, a couple of nights later one of the "D" Company halftracks drove through the minefield and blew up the front end. Fortunately nobody was killed. As far as I know the Germans never tried to run a Mark VI tank through one of our minefields. They didn't have too many and used them carefully.

A day or so later I was sent to the Command Post (CP) of the 16th Infantry Regiment to relieve Box. The CP consisted of a pyramidal tent pitched under a small tree in an otherwise open field, a couple of miles from where our battalion was bivouacked. There I saw my first German machine gun, which had been captured in a clash of patrols the night before. I admired the beautiful mechanism.

The CO was Col. d'Alary Fechet (pronounced fe-shay), a strange old bird and a veteran of the trenches of WWI. As we sat in the grass and ate lunch he asked me where I was from. "California — I knew there was something I liked about you, Kays." He was a bachelor and had a home in Carmel.

While I was there General Roosevelt, the son of former President Teddy Roosevelt and the Division Executive Officer, came up in a jeep. He told us that General Montgomery with the British 8th Army was now entering southern Tunisia with three armored divisions and four motorized infantry divisions. He also said that we were now expecting to be attacked at a place called Pichon, some miles south of where we were. He talked just as I imagined his father had talked. He got on the telephone and had difficulty explaining to somebody who he was, since everybody was very careful about security, worried that the telephone lines might be compromised. He kept saying, "This is R," but apparently got no response. Finally he said, "This is Rough Rider." Finally they saw the light!

A few days later the bulk of our battalion was withdrawn into a mountain pass at the western side of the valley, but "A" Company was left behind to relieve "F" Company of the 16th Infantry. We were to provide an infantry outpost for the 5th Field Artillery Battalion, not far from where we had been camped before. While the relief was taking place I conversed with an Infantry 2nd Lieutenant named John Kersey (at least, I think his name was John). I admired his beautiful officer's short-coat. As the war progressed, I saw Kersey often and had numerous discussions with him, the last time being in England in 1944. He seemed to be a survivor. Unhappily, "F" Company was one of the assault companies on Omaha Beach, and Kersey commanded one of the boat sections. All of the section commanders of "F" Company died on the beach.

Our engineer "D" Company sent a detachment, including halftracks, with us to provide some heavy weapons. Fred Finley was in charge of this detachment. It also included Master Sergeant Valerie Kosorek, undoubtedly the best soldier in the battalion. Korsorek was Regular Army and was eventually given a battlefield commission as an officer. He later served with me in "A" Company, so we will run into him again.

We were not in direct contact with the enemy; in fact there wasn't any definable "front line" in the Ousseltia Valley. We kept the men under cover during the day and sent out extensive patrols all night, but we never did have any enemy contact.

Finley and I played chess on the little set that my aunt had sent me for Christmas. He beat me so consistently that I don't think I ever played again.

One night a German bomber, probably a Ju88, came over and flew back and forth over our positions, lower and lower with each pass. It was a brightly moonlit night and he was probably looking for the artillery positions. He finally came so low we could see him; in fact I felt I could hit him with a rock. His belly machine gunner then sprayed our positions with fire. He was trying to draw fire so he could attack them, but fortunately our gunners on the halftracks didn't bite. He finally dropped his stick of bombs on a road intersection a few hundred yards away. In the quiet night they went off with a deafening series of cracks and the flashes lit up the countryside.

While we were in these positions I took a jeep one day and went out to see if I could buy some fresh eggs from the Arabs. I had seen what looked like a prosperous farm off in the distance on the day we had gone down the valley to lay the minefield. I found the farm, they did have lots of chickens, and I had a conversation in my schoolboy French with a well-dressed gentleman wearing a sort of gold colored shawl. My idea was, as I had done at Guelma, to trade British cigarettes for eggs. As I mentioned before, we were on a British ration that included cans of cigarettes, but we did have our own ration of cigarettes and the men wouldn't smoke the British ones, so we had lots of them available. The gentleman seemed to like the idea, so we struck a bargain, and he issued orders to some other Arabs to gather eggs. I wanted enough for two eggs per man ("quatre cent"). While they were gathering eggs, other people were cooking a kind of flat round bread in beehive shaped ovens. When he delivered the eggs to me he presented me with a dozen of these loaves, hot and fresh.

Gordon Pope, our Battalion S3 (Operations Officer), visited us that afternoon and stayed for the evening meal. I was very proud that each of the officers could be served a loaf of this Arab bread. Pope liked it and asked where we got it. I told him and he instantly spat it out. Well, I liked it anyway.

A bag of mail was sent out to us and included a large box of brownies from my mother. When we finally left to rejoin the battalion, Finley and I ate the entire box while riding in the truck. I think I ate them partially in self-defense, for otherwise he would have eaten them all! Nothing in my life has ever tasted so good.

I am not sure exactly where we were when this next letter was written, but it may have been at this time. I was so intimidated by the censorship that it isn't very informative. This letter is in pencil, as are all of my Tunisian letters. I actually carried my Parker fountain pen all through the war, but I guess I didn't have any ink at this time.

Feb. 10, 1942

Dear Mother, Dad, and Sis,

Please forgive me for the almost one month's gap in my mail. I'm sure you'll understand. I haven't had much time, and when I have had, I've been too cold, or wet, or something like that.

It's the middle of the afternoon now and I'm inside my bedding roll to keep warm. It's been well over a month since I slept under anything better than a pup-tent, and for the better part of the time I've just slept under the stars and a few pine limbs. There have been times when I've awakened in the morning to find my blankets white with frost. I guess it's all part of the game. Life has been interesting, and I've seen and done things that I've only read about before. I've found that there are a lot of real men in the army, and it takes a lot to keep up with them.

Got a lot of mail the other day. Mostly December mail, altho the latest was Jan. 10. Best of all was your Christmas letter. There seems to be a big gap in November. Your "Free" letters seem to get here as fast as any. Had a nice letter from Mrs. Morrison.

Some General made the statement that this division would get a big surprise at the end of the African campaign. Your guess is as good as mine, but you know what we're thinking!!! It's all the men talk about.

Gosh, there's so much I could tell you, but can't. I'll sure do a lot of talking one of these days. I'd better close now before I say something I shouldn't.

Loads of love to all,

Bill

P.S. My face is tan, but I think it's only dirt.

Here was the beginning of an almost continual thing about going home. All through Tunisia we were sure it was going to happen. As it turned out, the "big surprise" that I referred to in my letter home was that we were going to get to invade Sicily! Or it may have been that we were already slated to return to England. After Sicily it began to sink in that we weren't going home until the war was over, but in Africa we actively cultivated this illusion.

Everybody pulled out of the Ousseltia Valley at about this time (I think it was the 15th of February); evidently the German 21st Panzer Division was stirring around to the south of us. One had the feeling that we were a bunch of little animals trying to control some kind of monster. "A" Company was ordered to re-join the battalion at a little side valley where the road entered the main valley, and we stayed there several days. We had been given very sudden orders to withdraw, and we assumed that we would be on the road again as soon as we got back to where the remainder of the battalion was camped. We arrived late at night and most everybody in the rest of the battalion was asleep. Murphy reported in to the Colonel who was also apparently asleep. He came back somewhat perplexed, saying, "The Colonel says to have our men bed down and cook their rabbits." He was drunk.

There were the remains of a beautiful Roman high arch bridge near our bivouac, so this road was not a new one. About a half-mile down the road into the main valley there were further Roman ruins. Finley and I went down there and climbed around. I was fascinated. Obviously nobody had ever done any archeology here.

We had a battery of British 40 mm anti-aircraft guns nearby, and we enjoyed watching them fire away at the two German Messerschmidt 109s (Me109s) that had been our constant companions, when they came nosing around. One day a squadron of American B17s passed over very high up, along with a half dozen P38s as escort. Suddenly we heard machine-gun fire and saw little puffs of smoke. Our two Me109s were attacking that whole crowd! They soon broke off, but I was impressed.

On about the 19th of February, Knocker Box and his platoon went out to put mines in the road just where it emerged from the mountains and went into the Ousseltia Valley. It was a hard-surfaced road and they used our air compressor and pavement breakers to dig holes in the pavement for the mines. Suddenly there was an enormous explosion, and when the smoke cleared, Box and about six others were dead, and several more (including Sgt. Ziegler who had argued with me earlier about how to lay the mines) were injured. I think the man with the pavement breaker had accidentally touched a mine, which then detonated several others. This accident cast a pall over the whole company that night; our first casualties. I was now to be a platoon commander, albeit with an under-strength 3rd Platoon.

A further note on Alex Knocker Box: Many years later I was sitting in front of the TV watching a College World Series baseball game. This particular game was being played at Louisiana State University, and at one point the camera focused on the stadium name on the outfield fence - ALEX BOX STADIUM!

This is probably a good point to say that I was at this time, as I was going into action against a dangerous enemy, probably the most inexperienced and under-trained officer in the entire army. My ROTC training in the Ordnance was of little use in the Engineers, and my entire training of any real significance was four weeks at Ft. Leonard Wood the previous summer. I hardly realized how little I knew. It was no wonder that the enlisted men, and especially the NCOs who were mostly Regular Army, took a very dim view of me. And I was going to replace Box. It was going to be a long time before I got any respect. In fact it wasn't until an incident in Sicily the next July that they began to trust me. But I don't recall that it bothered me terribly at the time.

At about this time the German 21st Panzer Division was breaking through Kasserine Pass a hundred miles south of us, and threatening to envelop the whole American position. This breakthrough had followed some other disasters at American positions east of Kasserine. The pass was defended by a battalion of the 26th Infantry Regiment, plus the 19th Engineer Regiment. The 19th Engineers were a Corps level unit, that is, a regiment attached to the 2nd Corps, which is the next unit up the ladder from a division. Neither had the weapons to stop the tanks.

Soon after rejoining the rest of the battalion, we were immediately sent on a long all-night motor convoy to a point in the mountains just south of Kasserine. I believe it was the 20th of February. During the night I remember going through a town in which our motor column intersected a British column at right angles. We had a terrible traffic jam. The British were moving south to meet the Germans head on, and we were trying to move around to the other side of the breakthrough. My driver, Corporal Kling, kept offering me Camel cigarettes that he evidently had received in a package from home. I convinced myself that they were very superior to the cigarettes we were being issued.

The next day our battalion left its trucks and deployed into the mountains over-looking Kasserine Pass from the south. I was left behind with my platoon to guard the vehicles. We didn't know what was going on, but we could, off and on, hear intense machine-gun fire. At one point we were moving the kitchen truck when a flight of German planes went over fairly high. Cannici, one of the cooks, insisted that the engine be turned off "so they won't hear us"!

The next day the battalion moved farther south to occupy a deserted valley as a precautionary matter, but there was no enemy activity in that area, and we had a chance to catch our breaths and clean up a little. We went through Box's stuff and divided up what we weren't going to send home. I got his air mattress, and somebody else (probably Barnum) got his sleeping bag. We found a couple of condoms in his coat pocket. We decided that they didn't need to be sent home!

General Allen (our Division Commander) came by and said he wanted to talk to the officers and NCOs. We gathered around and he gave us a football locker-room pep talk. He talked about how our "D" Company with all its halftracks and heavy machine guns was going to do great things in the days ahead. He was drunk.

I believe the next letter was written at this place.

Feb. 24, 1942

Dear Mother, Dad, and Sis,

At last I have a few minutes to write, plus the inspiration of several letters yesterday, dated Oct. 2, 7, and 12. All in all, yesterday was a fine day as I got a chance to shave & wash my face for the first time in over a week. My hair got in such terrible shape that I had the company barber cut all but a little fuzz off. Now my helmet fits too loose — you can't win. Also we got some sunshine yesterday, so I got my blankets fairly dry for the first time in a week.

I'm now sitting under a pine tree on my bedding roll. I've got my feet sticking out in the sun trying to warm them. Boy, this is a winter I'll never forget! The men still get letters asking how they like the African heat.

One thing that interests me is what the reaction at home is to the battle over here. They tell us that this is the second front, and that due to the supply problem of both sides, 10,000 men here is worth 100,000 in Russia. I don't know!

I don't quite understand why you should be having a food shortage at home. We don't get it here. Take coffee, for instance. I've had one cup in the last month, and it didn't have any sugar in it. Here is our daily menu: breakfast — "corned willy"[1] and tea, lunch — stew and tea, supper — stew and tea. In addition we have hard tack, and every day or so a little jam to put on it. Once in a while we get a little canned fruit. Stew is the only thing you can get full on. It's the same thing day after day, week after week. However, that stew tastes awful good when you're hungry and cold. Nobody's complaining.

Received "Sporting Greens" up thru the 21st of December. Oh, did I tell you that I got your Christmas letter and also a box of wonderful brownies? I had no idea anything could taste so good. The other officers & I ate them all in one sitting, completely gorging ourselves.

I seem to remember numbering my letters at one time, but I lost track of the numbers so I gave it up.

I had a terrific dream the other night. It seems I did nothing but roll up my bedding roll & un-roll it. Boy, whatta life!

I haven't been paid in a couple of months, but I don't even want the money. I'm glad that I allotted most of it. You should start getting $140 out of January's pay. I have never yet received confirmation on the $200 I sent in Oct. or the $300 in early January.

I'm once more running out of things that can be told, so I'll close.

Much love to all,

Bill

P.S. Dad, you might tell Col. Thomas to tip off his class of Engineers that they'd better learn their infantry stuff just as thoroughly as their engineering. I can't elaborate further, but I'm sure he knows what I mean. These infantry generals can't stand to see the engineer weapons idle.

The reference to 10,000 men, etc., was from Terry Allen's pep-talk, which helps me place this letter. Evidently we were still on British rations at the time. My reference to a dream is probably a lie. I don't recall ever dreaming during the war. Dreams usually involve past events; in war you tend to live only in the present, and think about the future (will I be alive?). It is also evident that the battles and all the associated excitement didn't keep me from being concerned about my money!

Soon afterwards we were told that the 16th Infantry Regiment, and apparently part of the 1st Armored Division, were going to re-take Kasserine Pass, and we were going to follow them in. This was the first time I saw American tanks, the high General Grants with a 75 mm gun mounted on the side, not in a turret. (They were mercifully not long for this world.) But the Germans withdrew as we rushed in, so there was no fight. They had pretty much accomplished their mission of pushing us out of the way as they got ready to take on the British who were entering southern Tunisia in force.

That day Bill Barnum had an interesting experience. He had driven down to the edge of the town of Kasserine, basically to find out how far he could go and see if the road was mined. In the distance he saw what looked like some kind of staff car driving off. He stopped and talked to some locals. They told him, "That was General Rommel driving off."

We bivouacked that night right at the neck of the Kasserine Pass. It reminded me of

1   Corned beef

Palm Springs without the people, and on a much smaller scale. The geology and vegetation were much the same. For the first time we were really in desert country.

We stayed there several days and I had two or three experiences worthy of note.

The first thing we did was scour the original battlefield to pick up mines. In the process of doing so I found the infantry bringing in the body of a 2nd Lieutenant. He was very young and blond and had a machine gun hole through his head. I looked at his dog tag: Francis J. DeLacy, St. Albans, NY. For some reason, perhaps because he looked so alive, I remembered his name, and many years later looking at the 1st Division Monument just below the White House in Washington, I found his name etched in bronze. He was listed under the 26th Infantry.

During this little exercise I came across an American helmet full of holes, all going from the inside out. Looking around we found scraps of clothing, and then a finger and a few other small remains of what had been a man. We couldn't find his "dog tags," but on the sweat band of the helmet was printed "J. Fitzwater." Much later, I found that there is also a "J. Fitzwater" listed under the 26th Infantry at the monument in Washington.

A day or so later the whole company went out of the pass and down through the town of Kasserine and started work repairing some small bridges and culverts that had been blown. There I had my first experience with anti-personnel mines and learned how to disarm the infamous "Bouncing Betty." They had been planted in the soft sand all around the site of a blown culvert. We managed to find and remove several without stepping on any ourselves. We had previously learned how to handle Teller anti-tank mines at Ousseltia, and mines were becoming something about which I felt I could become a specialist. I badly wanted to find something I could do well, and I wasn't nearly as afraid of mines as I was of people with guns.

While at this task, two planes flew over very high up so that I couldn't identify them. Everybody else shrugged them off, but I had a nervous feeling about them. A little later I distinctly saw two planes dive down towards the ground a long way off, and then disappear over the horizon, so I kept my eyes open. Sure enough, in a few minutes they suddenly appeared, skimming along fifty feet off the ground and coming straight at us. I yelled and had time to pull out my pistol and take a futile shot at one of them. Each let out a short burst of fire and then zoomed up and disappeared in the distance. One of the planes hit one of my trucks, which went up in flames (along with some of my gear, including my overcoat), and the other hit and destroyed a British reconnaissance vehicle that was parked on the other side of the culvert. There were a few people hit, but nobody killed. The plane that hit my truck evidently fired one 20 mm round, as well as a short burst from its machine guns. The 20 mm shell hit the gas tank. Good shooting!

In the meantime our kitchen truck was on the way to bring us some lunch. One of our motorcycle runners happened to intercept them and told them what happened. Cannici, one of our cooks, refused to go further! Well, he could cook, so what the hell!

The next was a more amusing incident. The day we finally left our bivouac in Kasserine Pass I built a little fire and burned up my mail. We were usually very good about cleaning up when we left an area. One of the letters was from Noma and she evidently used her college roommate's engraved stationery. Some time later her roommate got a letter from a soldier in the 47th Infantry Regiment, a unit of the 9th Division that had moved into our area when we left. He told her a story of being in a shell-hole in the middle of a battle and finding her name and address on a partially burned envelope at the bottom of the hole. He had vowed if he got out alive he would write to her. At the time there was no enemy within forty miles of Kasserine!

The next letter was probably written at about the same time.

March 2

Dear Mother, Dad, and Sis,

12 letters yesterday! Boy, this is the life. They ranged from Sept 1 to Feb. 1. I see you got my January letters very quickly. I also got a Christmas package of toilet articles. Don't use toilet articles much these days but maybe they'll inspire me to greater heights. I manage to wash and shave about once a week now. We hope soon to go to a place where we can have the men bathe. Lice have begun to rear their ugly heads.

Beautiful weather lately. The first few days have shown signs of things to come. It will have to get awful hot before I'll object.

Everybody who writes asks about Roosevelt's visit. Hell, we didn't know he'd been over here until a week later. I don't know what he gained by going to Casa Blanca. That's an awful long ways from the "hot spots".

A truck just came in from battalion headquarters with a big bag of mail. I've got my fingers crossed.

Can you request to have cookies sent? If so, I'm requesting now. This corned willy & stew is getting a little boring. When I get home, I'll shoot you all if you serve corned willy.

Well, they won't let me say anything more, so I'll close.
Love to all,
Bill

This letter had a censor's stamp and initial near my signature, so I guess I really was being censored. Ordinarily officers censored their own mail with a signature on the envelope.

The "everybody" referred to in the letter was Noma. I was irritated that she didn't get the concept that I wasn't in some place like Casablanca. It wasn't going to be the last time she "was unclear on the concept." As I recall she also asked whether I had seen the movie "Casablanca." It also appears that I didn't attach any importance to presidential summit conferences!

At that time packages could only be sent if the soldier requested something. That accounts for the request for cookies.

Soon after this we moved a considerable distance to the rear to a place called Morsott where the whole Division was finally assembled. General Fredendall, the American commander in Tunisia, had been sacked and the days of operating in small ad hoc units was over. A guy named Patton was taking over 2nd Corps (that was what we were now in), and a lot of things were going to change. Morsott was in low mountain country with lots of pine trees, and was altogether a pleasant place. There we pulled ourselves together, cleaned up, and even engaged in some training exercises. The revolutionary new "bazooka" was issued, and we tried it out. The bazooka was the first rocket weapon, an anti-tank rocket fired from the shoulder. Since its range was very limited it was not the complete answer to tanks in the desert, but it gave us the feeling that we had a fighting chance. But not against Mark VI tanks!

The next letter may have been written from Morsott, but the first paragraph suggests that it was more probably written while we were in the Gafsa operation that followed Morsott.

March 12, 1943

Dear Mother, Dad, and Sis,

I had thought that I would have time to write to you several days ago, but I was apparently mistaken. However, after having washed & shaved, I find a little time today.

I've received lots of mail from you lately, — mostly only a month old. I can't remember when I last wrote, though, so I may tend to repeat.

I at last got a chance to bathe last week. It was the first time since late in January. It's going to be difficult to get back in the habit of bathing and shaving when this is all over. I'm lucky if I shave & wash once a week.

I saw a recent "Time" the other day, and discovered something that I suspect was true for a long time. On the "War" section the fight over here is given last mention, and only a small paragraph at that. The Jap war covered pages. It's rather obvious that the American people are far more interested in licking Japan than they are in licking Germany. All the ads in magazines give the same indication. The Jap may be more treacherous, but I believe anyone that knows anything about it will agree that the real professionals in the war are on this side of the water, and when we finish with Germany, despite the fact that we'll have a long tough Jap war ahead, we'll be on the downhill side. It's rather discouraging to these boys over here who go thru what they do to find that the people at home aren't even particularly interested in this affair.

The chow situation has considerably improved lately, and our kitchen finally got together enough flour and other necessities to bake a cake today. I've never in my life tasted anything so good.

Had a nice long letter from Uncle Marion the other day. He gave me Marion Jr's address and I shall write them both soon.

I got a notification from the War Dept. that my last allotment went thru, so I now ought to be completely straightened out. I got my January pay on the 75 fr. to the dollar basis and bought money orders on the basis of 50 fr to the dollar, so I made a bit. Also got $100 more of uniform allowance. Soon as the money orders get back, I'll send them ($160). That'll make $660 in money orders I've sent home plus $480 you ought to have by this time in the way of allotments. Don't know what I'm going to do with all the money. By summer I'll have $1500. The night after we paid the men you could hear the dice clicking all over the camp, and the next day some men were putting in for seven and eight hundred dollars in money orders.

We're on the downhill side of this winter now, but it still is a bit winterish. The sun is warm, but you don't see too much of it.

Well, it's beginning to get dark, so I'll close. This is longer than my usual effort, at that.

Much love,

Bill

P. S. A "V-Mail" station is going to open over here soon. You might enquire about it. "V-Mails" having been coming straight up till now.

I have to get the Colonel's permission for those socks. Haven't gotten around to it yet.

This is probably a good time to describe just what it was that combat engineers did, because up until this time we had not really been involved much in our traditional mission. We had been used primarily as extra bodies to throw into gaps where there was insufficient infantry. This was always an option we faced, but it wasn't really the mission for which we were primarily trained or equipped. Mercifully we had not really been tested as infantry.

First and foremost the job of the division-level engineers, the "combat" engineers, was to make possible the movement of motor vehicles to and from the front lines, and the vehicles ranged from jeeps carrying ammunition and food to tanks in an attack. Our responsibilities extended from the front lines back, sometimes a mile or more. If we had to work at or near the front lines it could get very dicey; farther back we usually had less to worry about.

For this work each of the three squads (about twelve men each) in a platoon had picks and shovels, carpenter's tools, and demolition equipment including a supply of TNT. At the company level we had a bulldozer, an air compressor with jackhammers and other such power tools. There was a larger bulldozer at battalion level.

We used bulldozers and/or explosives to demolish obstacles placed by the enemy, and we used bulldozers extensively to cut bypasses around blown out bridges. We built bridges where necessary. Sometimes we cut crude roads where there was no previous road. For crossing broad rivers we built floating bridges for vehicles, and sometimes floating footbridges. The material for bridges, floating or otherwise, was supplied by special bridge companies stationed in the rear area, but we did the actual construction. However, in Africa we didn't have or need this kind of support.

One of the principal devices the enemy used to impede our progress was explosive mines, so mine detection and removal became our responsibility, for both large anti-tank (and vehicle) mines and smaller anti-personnel mines. For this job we had electronic mine detectors, but largely we had to rely on our wits. In Africa mines were probably our biggest single problem because there were few rivers or other natural obstacles. Four-wheel drive vehicles and tanks could not often move forward without our help. In Sicily with thousands of small bridges over ravines, and no rain, we were kept busy cutting bypasses. On the Continent in France and Germany we had hundreds of rivers, large and small, mud in which vehicles (including tanks) could get stuck, and many man-made obstacles.

Another of our missions was to create obstacles to impede the enemy, and thus mine-laying was our responsibility, frequently out ahead of the "front lines." We were also responsible for blowing up bridges and creating other obstacles during a withdrawal.

Now back to our story.

Soon after our arrival at Morsott I was called to the Colonel's tent, along with Finley, Haas, and Kelly. He said that I was being temporarily detached from "A" Company and assigned to "D" Company for a special mission. Apparently he still thought I was some kind of fighting fool; shades of the "Hell Squads" when they were formed in England! He explained that the Division was going to attack and retake the town of Gafsa in southern Tunisia, that there was a forty-mile gap of desert between Gafsa and the nearest American troops in Fériana, and our mission was to carry out a reconnaissance of that area preparatory to the remainder of the battalion coming down to get things ready for the infantry to advance.

The next day we started out, Finley, Haas, and I each in a halftrack, and Kelly with a couple of jeeps. This was Wild West stuff. Seventy years earlier we would have been on horses riding out ahead of General Custer's main force! The halftracks were ideal for this kind of mission and I felt very confident. This was more exciting than scary. Finley was to take the main road straight down to as near as he could get to Gafsa, Haas was to go over the desert to the left, and I was to do the same on the right. Fériana was perhaps 100 miles south of Morsott; by afternoon we were south of Fériana and off into the unknown.

The area we were now in was true desert; at least it was the kind of desert I had come to know in Southern California and Arizona — rugged mountains with little or no vegetation, flat land between the mountains, cut here and there by dry washes, and a certain amount of desert shrubbery and grasses. Gafsa lay between two mountain ranges in the distance.

I ran into no difficulties. Finley got close enough to Gafsa to uncover and excite an enemy outpost. I believe he did have to remove mines at more than one place in the road. He also reported that the shoulders of the road (it was paved) were heavily mined. That night we came back to a previously abandoned American airfield north of Fériana and camped. I loved it. It was just our little task force with guys I liked, and we didn't have all the hassle of majors and colonels and all the junk they can think up. We slept in the open, and although it rained during the night, I didn't even mind it. Besides the weather was becoming warmer.

The next day the rest of "A" Company joined us and we started the work of removing the mines in the shoulders of the road. Some were "booby-trapped," that is, they had detonators on the side or bottom that would activate them if you tried to remove them. I was proud that we learned to handle this problem with no casualties. I insisted that the men tie a length of rope to the handle of the mines, and then retire a distance, or behind something, and pull the mine out of its hole. One day I had some of Barnum's men working with me and I noticed an idiot named Jaeger simply pulling up mines by hand. I ordered them to resort to the rope method and was met with expressions of great disgust. I got the distinct feeling that Barnum had given his platoon the impression that I was some kind of lightweight. Never mind; a couple of hours later one of the mines exploded as it was pulled up by the rope. Nobody thanked me for saving his life!

On the road that day a jeep coming from the Gafsa direction stopped and the driver said, "I have Lt. Kelly's body in the back!" Kelly, in a jeep, had turned around on the road and backed over a mine. A chill went up my spine. We hadn't even seen the enemy yet, and already two of our officers were dead. I thought about what Murphy had said at

Oggaz about how only ten percent of us would survive Tunisia. What lay ahead for the rest of us?

This is the time to digress a bit and talk about "heroes." After the Battle of Oran (in which I didn't participate because I was in the hospital in Scotland), our battalion had two genuine officer heroes, Knocker Box and Charlie Kelly. Both had distinguished themselves in operations involving the halftracks. Box got the DSC and Kelly the Silver Star. Both had given evidence even before Oran that they were more eager to expose themselves to enemy fire than most of the rest of us. But were they unnecessarily reckless? Well, now they were both dead, our first two officer casualties of any kind. Interestingly, the battalion had had another "hero," a guy named Bob Emery (I never met him) who was such an eager fighter that the Assistant Division Commander, General Roosevelt, took him to be his aide before the Battle of Oran. He was killed at Oran when he personally tried to take out an enemy machine gunner! In Sicily Charlie Mills, the CO of Headquarters Company, tried to be a hero by walking out in front of the Infantry on a reconnaissance. That was the end of Mills! After those four incidents our officer dead became few and far between. Nobody else (least of all me) wanted to be a "hero." As I got to know the 16th Infantry Regiment better, I began to notice the same phenomena there. The gung-ho 2nd Lieutenants died like flies, but those who became company commanders seemed to go on and on and became the real backbone of the regiment – the guys who knew how to fight the Germans effectively and yet did not take foolish risks.

Getting back to our story, the remainder of the battalion moved to Fériana and we spent several days working on the roads, getting as close to Gafsa as practicable. I built my first bridge at that time. It was a small culvert that had been blown out and we used nearby railroad tracks for beams. Here I got into an argument with my platoon sergeant, William Wood. He was another Regular Army soldier and had little use for young 2nd Lieutenants. I knew tanks were going to use the bridge eventually and I wanted it to be sufficiently strong. He didn't want to use as many beams as did I, insisting that the bridge was strong enough. I thought I knew more than he did about the strength of steel beams. The argument only ended with a compromise. Woody had been up and down the enlisted ranks several times in his career, and was now once again on the way up. I never did win him over completely. Eventually we made him First Sergeant in England, and just before D-Day he and several others overstayed their leave in London. They had to be demoted, or "broken" back down to privates, in the traditional Army style. Murphy was so angry that he made Woody his runner for the landing at Omaha Beach, which meant going in at H plus 1/2 hour, rather than hours later as would have been the case had he been First Sergeant. He died on Omaha Beach.

One day I drove out across the desert for some reason or other and saw an Arab frantically waving his arms at me. We had been getting some intelligence from Arabs so I figured I'd better stop and talk to him. When we got close he reached into the rags he was wearing and brought forth his hand with an egg in it. "Icks?" he said!

We spent perhaps a week preparing the Fériana-Gafsa road. The company moved to a tiny deserted town about half way along. There somebody found a desk drawer full of stamps, and I appropriated them. I also found a small German box that was apparently a kit for preparing anti-personnel mines. It was full of detonators and other accessories. I was quite excited with my good luck. This was the sort of thing that I liked.

The attack on Gafsa was to be just before dawn on March 17th. We served as outposts on either side of the road while our trucks were used to bring up the infantry, and then they marched through our positions. Infantry patrols far out ahead stirred up the enemy. Long-range machine gun fire from the enemy sent colored tracers arching through the sky. It was really quite beautiful.

It turned out that Gafsa was held by a small Italian contingent which quickly abandoned the town and withdrew ten to twenty miles to the southeast where a low ridge across part of the desert, between still more mountains, provided a much more favorable defensive position. So all our elaborate preparation produced a fizzle. In retrospect, I find it surprising that General Patton didn't realize that there would not be a fight.

We quickly occupied the town and "A" Company moved into a date grove. Actually, date trees were the main feature of Gafsa. That afternoon the heavens opened and we had a real deluge. A dry wash that passed through the town became a raging torrent and held up everything. The rains lasted for a day or so more. I recall waking up in my pup-tent the next morning in the date grove and realizing that, although warm, I was in the middle of a lake. Box's air mattress kept me slightly above it. Corporal Horman came around and offered me "breakfast in bed" — a cup of tea and two Raleigh cigarettes. I accepted.

We stayed in Gafsa several days. We placed the "A" company CP in a deserted photographer's shop. The men were fascinated by some pornographic film negatives we found!

At this time we were joined by a Lt. Ingersoll, who had been sent from the States as an observer; by whom, I have no idea. He stayed with us for several days and participated in our operations. We called him "Lt. Clock," in reference to Ingersoll Watches! It was only after he had left that we learned he was Ralph Ingersoll, owner of PM newspaper, and later a prominent newspaper publisher. He did seem very urbane and knowledgeable about the world. He later featured our company officers in a book he wrote called *The Battle is the Payoff.*

We had at this time a change in our officer complement. Tom Crowley, an officer in "B" Company, was transferred to "A" and it was decided to make him Executive Officer of the company, i.e. second in command (or "2 ic" as the British would term it). Thus we did away with the idea of the most junior officer being the "administrative officer", and I retained my platoon. Tom was another MIT ROTC graduate, a Bostonian, or at least a New Englander, ultimately destined to become battalion executive officer, and certainly one of our most outstanding officers. Tom was a perfect counter-balance to Murph and his nutty ideas. He was one of those people everybody respects, and the company began operating very smoothly under his leadership. We were back to five officers, but with one usually out with the combat platoon we still had a good bridge foursome. We became a very close group. They called me "Junior." I was never sure whether that was supposed to be complimentary or not! I think Barnum thought up the name.

By this time we were beginning to learn something about this General Patton who had taken over 2nd Corps. He ordered that officers were to shave and wear neckties. I'm surprised we even had any. He drove around in a special command car equipped with a railing in the back seat so he could stand up and wave a stick and chew people out.

The infantry had quickly established contact with a main enemy line of resistance ten or twenty miles to the southeast. The desert spread out in this direction with a large mountain range going directly east on the left, another to the right several miles, and then a smaller range that split the valley a few miles beyond the town, or oasis, of El Guettar. It was at the start of this double valley that the Italian "Centauro" Division had dug in. An extensive Italian minefield extended across the more open part of the valley to the right. An attack was planned which involved the use of a battalion of Rangers (a special purpose force of highly trained "elite" infantry) to climb along the mountains to the left and come down on the Italians from behind, while the 18th Infantry attacked straight ahead. For this operation the "Hell Squads" of our "D" Company, with their 81 mm mortars, were attached to the Rangers. Ralph Ingersoll left us and accompanied the "D" Company group with Gordon Pope, the new commanding officer of "D" (after Charlie Kelly).

The all-night march and the dawn attack were highly successful and the Italians were routed. The Germans reacted quickly to come to the aid of the Italians, and started with a German Stuka dive-bombing attack that caught our "Hell Squads," among others, in an exposed position, killing Sgt. McCarthy and several others.

In the meantime our battalion moved to El Guettar, and bivouacked in another date grove.

I believe it was the next day, March 23rd, that the Germans reacted in a much bigger way. They were obviously sensitive to this threat to their right flank while they were attempting to stop the British 8th Army farther south. At dawn, the 10th Panzer Division launched a full-scale assault on the positions of the 18th Infantry Regiment that were in some low but rugged hills at the head of the valley to the right. This attack was beaten off with the help of massive artillery concentrations and a new type of "tank destroyer" vehicle. Rutledge was with the 16th with his combat platoon, and during the morning Murph and Tom Crowley went out with Colonel Rowland, and I was not sure exactly where they were. Barney and I and our two platoons were left in the date grove, along with two truckloads of mines, and were told to await orders. Battalion Headquarters was there also, but both the Colonel and Captain Gara were up front somewhere, and the other companies were out assisting the infantry.

From the edge of the grove I had a clear view across the desert for several miles to the ridge where our defensive positions were located. This was very flat and arid desert. Most of the Division artillery was between the ridge and me. Around mid-day, the Germans launched another attack, which was preceded by wave after wave of dive bombers attacking our artillery positions. I had a grandstand seat and watched the planes approach, the 40 mm anti-aircraft guns go after them to no effect, and the planes diving through it all dropping their bombs, accompanied by lots of noise, smoke and dust. I didn't feel particularly comfortable about going out and laying mines in all of that; which is a considerable understatement! Somewhere in the middle of all of this I wrote the following letter, but I think it must have been before the air attacks because I'm sure I was much too nervous to write afterwards, and worse was to come.

March 23

Dear Mother, Dad, and Sis,

I know it's been a long time since I've written, and I can't even remember when I last wrote. The last few weeks have been terrifically hectic, and even when I have had short times when I could write, I just couldn't mentally relax enough to write a decent letter. If you don't understand what I mean, I'll explain more fully some day. A little of this life goes a long ways.

Enclosed is my laundry bill from Ft. Leonard Wood. Will you please take care of it for me?

I'm enclosing $160 in money orders, and also $5.00 that Aunt Amy sent me. I have a mess of stamps to send, but I don't know yet whether the censor will let them pass. I got them in a rather unique way. One of my men found a whole collection in a deserted house.

I've sure received a pile of mail in the last couple of days. It's the first I've got in over three weeks. It was mail dating from Aug. 29 to Feb. 26. I even got a letter addressed to APO CO-14.

I'm writing in a rather nice spot right now. I'm lying under some palm trees at the edge of an oasis and looking out over a desert with rugged mountains in the background. If this isn't Palm Springs, I never saw it.

Well, that's about all the news. I'm well, and outside of needing a shave, I'm in fine shape.

Loads of love,

Bill

P.S. I forgot to tell you something. While out on a job for the 16th Infantry I ran into a Lt. Col. Wells (Exec. of the 16th) who said he'd had a letter from Col. Thomas telling him to look me up. I had quite a talk with him, and he apparently knows the Thomas' quite well.

The tone of this letter suggests that I didn't really have any idea what was going on just a few miles up the road.

Sometime around mid-afternoon we got a call from battalion headquarters saying the 10th Panzer Division was going to attack at sixteen hundred hours – four o'clock that afternoon. A little later another call said that the German H-hour had been postponed forty minutes, and the 10th Panzers would attack at 1640. This intelligence must have been from some kind of radio intercept. Soon after that our motorcycle messenger, Augustine, showed up with a message from Murphy: "Bring up the 2nd and 3rd Platoons and the two truckloads of mines." It sounded like Custer's last message: "Benteen, bring up the packs." Fine and dandy; we and the whole 10th Panzer Division would arrive at the same place at the same time!

Barnum decided that he would get on the motorcycle with Augustine and ride up to find out where we were to bring the trucks; I would follow with the men and the mines as soon as we could get ready. He took off and I followed soon after. I looked at my watch; it was approaching 1640.

I rode with the driver in the cab of the lead truck. (Remember, we had no Jeeps.) We followed a fairly straight paved road over absolutely flat desert for several miles and soon got to an area with artillery batteries scattered over the desert to the right and various vehicles moving about. Then I spotted Barnum and Augustine on the right side of the road ahead, Barney waving his arm slowly up and down as a signal for us to slow down. As we pulled up near him he suddenly started to wave his arm frantically. I glanced to the left and saw a whole line of Me109s skimming over the desert and coming towards us about thirty feet off the ground. It was exactly 1640.

I grabbed the door handle, leaped out of the truck, and headed for the ground on the shoulder of the road. As I went down I glimpsed the wings of a plane go overhead and a pair of bombs sailing below it. The noise of machine gun fire was so intense that I have no recollection of the sound of the bombs. It was all over in a second, and then I heard people screaming "medic, medic" all around me. A great flood of blood was oozing from the back of a guy a few feet away. Another guy was running around in circles holding his left arm. Gasoline was pouring out of the ruptured gas tank just behind me, the tires were flat, and my cab door was riddled with holes. The truck following mine was on fire.

One's first reaction in such circumstances is not one of fear, but rather "what do I do next?" The men pulled a lot of stuff out of the following truck and stopped the fire, and my first thought was to gather the men together, transfer to the second truck, which seemed otherwise intact, and then move on. At that moment I heard whistles blowing and the anti-aircraft noise started again. I looked up and the sky seemed full of Ju88s coming down at us. I simply ran as far as I could to get away from the vehicles and the mines, glancing upwards all the time, hit the dirt, and then looked up and watched almost in fascination as what looked like a school of sardines dropped out from under each plane. The bombs were silver and seemed to twinkle. At the last second I buried my head in my hands and an instant later the earth exploded around me. A moment later I looked up and all was smoke and dust and the smell of TNT.

After this second attack I decided that the best thing to do was look for cover, and I found nearby a shallow slit trench, perhaps a foot deep. It was none too soon, because once again the whistles sounded and the 40 mm guns and machine guns began their deafening racket. Another huge flight of Ju88s was diving down on us (actually, it was the artillery they were after). I watched once more in fascination as the twinkling sardines appeared, and then ducked at the last instant. The earth bounced and it seemed like I was somewhere in the depths of hell.

By this time the men were well scattered and I spent some time trying to gather them together. Meanwhile the artillery was firing continuously, enemy shells were coming in, and obviously something big was going on. I think that Barney and Augustine went on to find Murph, although I don't remember the exact details. At any rate, we next got an order to forget the minefield and move to the right flank, or right side, of the 18th Infantry and take up positions as infantry. This we did on foot, leaving the trucks behind. The "right flank" was where the low ridge ended and nothing but flat desert lay beyond. As we approached the last of the ridge we met Murph and Tom coming down from the ridge. "The German tanks are withdrawing," Tom said, "it's all over." We dug in on the rear slope of the ridge.

The 10th Panzer Division had failed to break through. For the first time an American unit had stood its ground. We were exhilarated! Rowland and Gara got Silver Stars for "re-organizing 'A' Company"; Murphy was incensed, and rightfully so!

A few days later the second phase of the Battle of El Guettar started in earnest. It was now to be a Corps affair, not just a division. Our attack was to go down the main road to the coastal city of Gabes, the extension the same road I had followed during the 10th Panzer attack. The 1st Division was to attack along the foothills on the left side of the valley, and the newly arrived 9th Division was to take the right side. On the flat open desert in between, perhaps a mile or two wide, the 1st Armored Division was to attempt to break through, and Patton's dream was to hit the Afrika Korps from the rear as they fought the British 8th Army coming up from the south.

About this time I drove back on some errand to our battalion supply depot, which was at that time in Gafsa. As I returned I saw a large colored billboard with the insignia of the 2nd Corps (We were now in the 2nd Corps, a unit with more than one division) and the words, "II Corps, Gone to Gabes." Somehow I deeply resented this kind of rah-rah stuff engaged in by people who were so far back they couldn't even hear the guns.

The 16th Infantry Regiment and the 26th Infantry now took the lead for our division, and our "A" Company was attached to the 16th, outside of our own battalion control. In the meantime, Bill Barnum was sent to the rear to attend some kind of British "battle school" and Murphy sprained his ankle badly enough to be evacuated to a hospital. We were down to three officers, Tom in command, plus Rutledge and me. We moved the company into the foothills, essentially the low ridge occupied by the 18th in the previous battle. It all started with a night attack, and for the first time I heard the term "pinned down," because soon after daylight, the infantry found they couldn't move during the day. The terrain was a series of rocky ridges with little vegetation, opening out onto the flat plain to the right, where the armor was supposed to operate. (The infantry soon found that to attack in daylight in Africa was just too costly. Later, in Europe, the infantry virtually always attacked with accompanying tanks.)

Rutledge was sent as liaison officer to the headquarters of the 16th Infantry. This turned out to be a somewhat hazardous mission because Col. Fechet, the CO of the 16th Infantry, insisted on a regimental CP virtually on the front lines. The result was that the CP itself was continuously "pinned down," telephone wires were knocked out by artillery, and Fechet was out of communication and out of control. Daylight operations were close to impossible; if you just stuck your head over a rock to take a look you drew instant artillery fire.

Then Fechet, and also the regimental S2 (intelligence officer), were both hit by machine gun fire and evacuated. Col. Wells took over. Fechet was probably the last regimental commander in the Division to be hit by machine gun fire; it was no longer WWI and the trenches of northern France!

As the 16th very slowly advanced, mostly by night attacks, we moved our company by stages up behind them. There was not much engineering work to do; mostly pick and shovel road work and some mine removal work. Each day the 1st Armored Division attempted to move down the main valley to our right, and each day they failed. Patton apparently became hysterical and blamed the infantry, venting his wrath to the war correspondents. The 9th Division was having no better luck on the right side of the valley. Many of the troops being encountered were Italian, but increasingly we were hitting Germans.

The battle went on for days and was so confused, and the terrain was so confusing, that it is difficult to paint a coherent picture of what happened. The following are random impressions: an endless stream of ambulances coming to the rear; the occasional truckloads of prisoners; an Italian boy with an incredibly long nose, "Pinocchio"; the dust of the 1st Armored Division's tanks in the valley to the right; German planes at night dropping amber-colored "chandelier flares" that lit up the whole valley, and the tracers of hundreds of 50 caliber machine guns trying to knock out the flares; bombs that woke me up in the middle of the night, lighting up the sky like daylight; a Stuka dive-bombing attack on artillery positions right behind us, in which the planes came absolutely straight down; endless artillery firing; the almost continuous singing sound of enemy shells coming in and the crack of exploding shells; and the rather quiet sound of the shells of our 155 mm "long Tom" guns passing far overhead late at night.

One day Tom and Rut went out in a jeep to find the 16th CP, which was not simple because of the confusing terrain. They ran into a German officer and a machine gunner. In an exchange of fire the jeep driver, Obrian, using his M1 rifle, killed the machine gunner and wounded the officer. They brought the officer in for questioning. Tom got a Luger pistol, and all three got Silver Stars.

After a few days, Tom decided that Rut had had enough and that I should go up as liaison officer. He and I started out at night to find the 16th CP, but nobody knew quite where it was. We got to the 3rd Battalion rear CP in a little ravine, and Major Horner, the battalion executive officer, said, "You're sitting in a pool of blood." Several shells had come into the ravine during the afternoon and found their targets. We walked past a tent that was the 3rd Battalion aid station. As soon as it turned dark, the wounded were brought in and there were rows of stretchers were on the ground. The battalion surgeon came out of the tent shaking his head, and another officer patted him on the shoulder, gave him a cigarette, and said, "Take it easy, Doc." The wounded were mostly victims of artillery shells, but I remember that among the wounded were burn victims from 1st Armored Division tanks.

We decided the only way we were going to find the regimental CP was to wait until morning and follow the telephone wires, which the men had laid along the ground. Tom and I went out again in the morning. It was quiet and the weather was beautiful. I remember following the wire across a grassy field covered with lovely wild flowers. In the middle of the field we passed a dead soldier, pitched straight onto his face, his rifle still slung over his soldier.

We finally found the 16th Infantry CP, about twenty yards back from a little embankment in which men from one of the rifle companies were dug in. In other words, the regimental CP was virtually on the front line. The CP was in a ravine, or dry wash, about four feet deep, several feet across, and maybe twenty feet long. In it were Col. Wells, Capt. Plitt, the S3 (operations officer), and a few others. They were out of contact with Division Headquarters; the telephone lines broken somewhere. Nothing seemed to be going on. Every now and then a single shell would come singing in and land nearby. At one point, Lt. Armilino, the commander of the reconnaissance platoon, came by in some agitation. He had been manning a regimental observation point (OP) that apparently was on a hill a few hundred yards away. They had been seen and shelled, and there were casualties. "I couldn't stop the bleeding," I heard Armilino say, referring to somebody they all evidently knew. A shell came screaming in and landed a few feet from our ditch. It was a dud and didn't explode; a handful of sand scattered onto our heads.

"That was an act of God," said Col. Wells.

I recall that at this time we finally had some air cover, and a squadron of British Spitfires cruised back and forth over the Corps area. I was confused at first because they had American insignias, but apparently the Americans didn't have any planes appropriate for this kind of work, and these ones had been loaned to the Air Corps by the British. At one time that day we saw a squadron of Me109s coming from one direction and our Spitfires moving towards them from the opposite direction. A large billowy cloud separated them. Suddenly one of the groups emerged from the cloud with the other group directly ahead. It was fascinating to observe the two- or three-second reaction time before anything happened. There were machine gun bursts from both sides, and everybody scattered. The Germans were apparently under orders not to get into a fight.

I soon got the impression that Col. Wells had no idea what he was doing. Capt. Plitt seemed to be running things, to the extent that anybody was doing anything. Wells seemed to be happy to sit there and let Division Headquarters find him.

In the late afternoon a patrol was sent out to see if the next ridge was occupied. It returned with a negative report and Plitt wrote a field order for the battalions to advance to the next ridge after dark.

That night, or perhaps the next day, the Germans withdrew. Patton's tanks went streaming through the valley and beyond. But what they met was the British 8th Army, not the rear of the Afrika Korps. It had escaped to the north.

The Battle of El Guettar was over, destined to be one of the forgotten engagements of the war. We had completely destroyed the Italian Centauro Division and badly mauled the German 10th Panzer Division, but they had accomplished their mission to protect their flank. The 16th Infantry took 600 casualties; I don't know how the other two regiments of the 1st Division fared.

The Division was pulled back to Morsott to recuperate in preparation for the battle for Tunis and Bizerta, in northern Tunisia. Murphy and Barnum returned and "A" Company was left behind for a week to clean up the battlefield, which meant taking up mines, both ours and theirs. An Italian mine field gave us some trouble, and one of Rutledge's men was blown to pieces.

The next letter must have been written while we were still at El Guettar.

April 4 (I think)

Dear Mother, Dad, and Sis,

Just a few moments to dash off a note to let you know that I'm OK. Haven't written since March 23, but time seems to fly now. Spring is really here now, and we've had some pretty hot days.

Finally received the glasses for which many thanks. The metal frames are swell. The others are about to break.

Had a letter from Marion Jr. recently. He had looked up my APO number and figured he was about 500 miles east of me. He apparently got some old dope, because I think he's not far from me now. If we ever get a rest I'll try to find him.

I have a form filled out to get the socks, but I have to get the Colonel to sign it and I can't get to him right now. I'll do it as soon as possible.

Well, I want to write a couple more, so I'll cut this short.
Much love,
Bill

Tom and I took the command car (we now had one) and drove to Gabes on the coast to "see the British 8th Army". This was about a sixty-mile trip and I recall that we amused ourselves on the way shooting Tom's newly acquired Luger at cans along the road. We went to a beach, stripped, and took a symbolic swim in the Mediterranean. There was no surf.

The 16th Infantry was also left behind, and since we were now a hundred miles behind the action area, they had movies at night under the stars. I remember sitting with Murph in the company command car watching a movie. The weather was warm; it was delightful.

Soon afterwards our company rejoined the others in Morsott. The first phase of the Tunisian campaign was at an end.

Oggaz, Algeria, November 1942; Front row: Charlie Murphy, Tom Crowley
Back row: Francis Rudolph (H & S Company), Charlie Kelly, Harold Haas.

Ousseltia Valley, Tunisia, February 1943; Barnum, Kays, Box, Murphy.

Ousseltia Valley, Tunisia, February 1943; Laying our first minefield.

El Guettar, Tunisia, March 23, 1943; "A" Company digs in after attack of the 10th Panzer Division.

CHAPTER FIVE

TUNISIA - PHASE II

APRIL 15 - MAY 15, 1943

The next letter was written while we were at Morsott, where we rested for about a week.

April 16

Dear Mother, Dad, and Sis,

I'm going to try to write a little longer letter now, as I think I have a little time.

I'm really getting your mail in a hurry now. The latest letter I got was dated March 22. I see that the papers have finally announced that the Division is in Tunisia, and apparently went so far as to mention the Gafsa operation. I guess you realized that I've been in Tunisia for a long time, and understand why some of my letters have been few and far between. Everything is very bright now, but we had some hectic times back in February. I'm going to take a chance on the censorship and tell you a few things that I see no reason why I can't say.

When we first got here we had strict orders about hiding the identity of the Division. Now we have to have the Division insignia on our helmets and sewed on our shirts. The reason is obvious, -- we want the Germans to know when they are up against the First Division. The First Division has never given an inch in the face of everything that Rommel has thrown at us. We have never been completely stopped in an attack. I think it is truly the finest fighting unit that the U.S. can field today. We're no longer afraid of the Panzers; we've seen the best they have to offer.

I consider myself to be pretty much of an expert on enemy mines now. Tomorrow I'm conducting a mine school for one of the infantry regiments. Incidentally, I built my first military bridge in the Gafsa deal. It's still carrying traffic.

Tell Col. Thomas that I got to know Col. Wells pretty well as I spent an entire day cowering in the bottom of a hole with him and his staff while being shelled. I was glad to see the sun go down that day.

Dad, you might tell your students that no matter what theater they go into this problem of plane identification is going to be all important. Famous last words --- "They're ours". We have a little song to tune of the Marine hymn which is self-explanatory:

From the dumps at old Tebessa,
To the shores of Gabes bay,
You will find the Stukas bombing,
In the night as in the day;
Desperation and frustration,
As we watch those bastards play,
For the Air Corps' on vacation,
Just another holiday.

The weather has been very pleasant lately. I've even had a bath and seen a movie. Today, the boys are butchering a cow, -- our first fresh meat in many a month.

Oh, -- one last word about the war. The newspaper accounts are very distorted. The most accurate information will be found in "Time".

Had a half-day off recently, and another officer and I drove to the sea and had a very refreshing swim. Also got a good look at the 8th army. It's a whale of an outfit. Seems to be mostly turbaned Indians, slant-eyed Malays, and just plain African niggers, with a few Englishmen thrown in. Also a lot of tough looking Aussies.

Well, that's enough for this sitting, more later.
Much love,
Bill

This letter was clearly written from Morsott. The date, and that of some of the subsequent letters, may be in error since one account of the next battle that I have read says that we kicked off on the night of April 16/17. On the other hand, those dates could also be in error; I have other evidence that we moved from Morsott on the 19th or 20th.

Sometime between the date of that letter and that of the next, we moved to northern Tunisia and the Division took up positions near the little town of Beja. We were to be part of a major coordinated attack, the American 2nd Corps and the British 8th Army (I don't recall what became of the 1st Army), with the objective of driving the Germans out of Africa, and of course capturing Tunis and the port of Bizerta. The Americans took over the entire left hand side of the line. In the meantime General Patton had moved on to plan for the Sicilian invasion, and General Bradley took over. Everybody seemed much happier with Bradley; the nonsense was over and I think the whole army was thereafter more effective. The American forces included the 1st, 9th, and 34th Infantry Divisions, and the 1st Armored Division. We finally had a formidable force.

Soon after our arrival in the Béja area we broke up into regimental combat teams, and "A" Company was attached to the 16th Infantry. Our platoons were then attached to the infantry battalions, at least for the initial attack, and my 3rd Platoon was attached to the 3rd Battalion of the 16th Infantry. In the meantime Col. Wells disappeared and was replaced by Col. George Taylor, who moved over from the 26th Infantry. Taylor was somebody very different, and I (and everybody else) developed the greatest respect for him. He was to lead the 16th for the next year and a half.

The country north of Beja towards the town of Mateur, where our attack was headed, was different from any we had seen, neither desert nor wooded mountains. Grassy hills would be the best description. It would probably have been very dry in the summer, but in April it was green with six-inch grass and few trees. The hills were rather steep in places, and the highest was Hill 609 (it was 609 meters in elevation, or about 2,000 feet). One writer described the land as "biblical," a place where you expected to see shepherds tending their sheep. It was not particularly rocky, and had few of the "wadis" (gullies or streambeds that remain dry except during rainy season) that characterize central and southern Tunisia. For an infantry soldier there was little cover, except behind a hill.

The 3rd Battalion commander, Col. Stone, wanted me with him, while my platoon with its vehicles was to come along with the infantry rear headquarters and their various vehicles. On the night before the attack we set out on a long approach march, starting soon after dark; the actual attack would kick off at about two o'clock a.m. (There must have been some kind of thin covering force up close to the enemy.) I started out at the rear of the column and was late to get moving; I spent several hours trying to catch up with the Colonel who was the head of the column. The battalion was one long string of men, stumbling and grunting and groaning under the weight of weapons, ammunition, and backpacks in the dark. Fortunately I reached the Colonel and his staff before we reached our destination. We stopped at the rear side of a rather conical shaped hill a few hundred feet high; our forward positions, whatever they were, were on the other side.

Col. Stone suggested that he and the company commanders go to the top of the hill and take a look. It was about midnight and there was a bright moon. I asked if I could accompany them, and we set out to climb the hill. At the top there was very short grass and a small level area. We all lay down because the moon was so bright that we could possibly be seen. Before us was a series of depressions and small hills, rolling country, all very clear. They could clearly read their map in the moonlight, and were able to pick out the various battalion objectives on the ground that lay before us. "K" and "L" were to lead, and "I" Company was to follow. "K" Company was commanded by Dick Cole, and "I" Company had a newly appointed CO named Kim Richmond. Dick was pretty badly wounded a few days later; Kim Richmond was to later become a legend as one of the best company commanders in the regiment.

Col. Stone told his company commanders that he was going to direct the attack from an OP using telephones. He wasn't going to get himself "pinned down" by small arms fire and lose control as had so often happened at El Guettar.

They then left, and I got Stone's permission to stay there and watch the start of the attack. I lay there alone; it was very still with not a sign of life. I distinctly remember thinking about how I would describe this experience to my father.

Around one thirty in the morning, I heard the rumble of artillery to my rear, and then the gentle rustling sound of "friendly" artillery shells (our own) going over my head. The hills ahead burst with white phosphorous smoke shells used to register the artillery (that is, set the range and direction) and then there were hundreds of flashes of high explosive shells. It was like the 4th of July. Then the artillery stopped, as suddenly as it had started. I watched for a long time, but saw only occasional machine gun tracers -- white German ones. After about an hour I went back down the hill and rejoined the battalion rear headquarters group.

The attack went on in its confused way for about two weeks. The infantry charged German positions at night, and were generally pinned down during the day. It was much the same as at El Guettar, except more progress was made. I had the same impressions of endless artillery firing; the continuous whining and sharp cracks of enemy shells coming in; the seemingly endless string of ambulances working their way to the rear. We mostly did road work (literally making roads for at least jeep travel), but I hardly remember where we camped. I do know that the next letter must have been written during the first few days because I recall the incident of tearing down Arab houses to get stone for roads.

April 28

Dear Mother, Dad, and Sis,

They've clamped down on censorship regulations now, so I can once more only say I'm in North Africa. Also I can't send those stamps. How silly!

Boy, how time does fly. It was three months ago tomorrow that I got my first glimpse of the enemy. The campaign is going slowly, but always forward.

Africa is full of more odd insects than you can shake a stick at. You get so you don't mind them after while. The fleas are the only things that really bother me. I've had to stop wearing leggings because my legs are so badly flea bitten. We tear down Arab villages in order to get rock for road material, and Arab villages are alive with fleas. These Arab houses in this part of the country are quite something. They are built up with rock sides and grass roofs, all plastered together with cattle manure.

This is really pretty country. It's all grassy mountains with all sorts of wild flowers.

I haven't sent a package request slip home because you can ship packages up to eight ounces without a request. I also need a scout knife, incidentally.

Well, this is about all I have time for right now, so I'll close.

Much love,

Bill

Sometime during the first few days, Col. Taylor, the regimental commander, called me to his CP and told me that the remainder of our company had gone into the line as infantry and that I was to follow with my men. He showed me the map and explained the situation, and explained why we had to go. This was impressive (and new)! I should add that Taylor's CP was well behind the front lines and he fought the regiment mostly by telephone and maps, although the maps of Tunisia were not very good. Gone were the days when the regimental commander (at least Fechet) was up with the assault companies, too close to effectively control the regiment.

I remember marching my platoon across grassy fields, spread out in a long line. I worried about when the German artillery would come in on us. We reached a ridge where I found the company right where Taylor showed me on the map. The Germans had counter-attacked the night before and we were there to secure a gap. I dug a slit trench on the rear side of the ridge. It was tough digging, especially with the lousy entrenching tools we had (of course the Germans had superb entrenching tools; we were later to copy theirs). I finally got the foxhole big enough so I could roll up in a blanket and sleep in it. The enemy left us alone, and the next day we resumed our engineering work.

Soon after this we cut a road out of pure rock over a rather low ridge that was otherwise a total obstacle to any kind of vehicle, using picks, shovels, explosives, and our bulldozer. This feat turned out to be a rather important contribution to the infantry's advance, since the Germans evidently felt the ridge was a good barrier and didn't prepare for an advance in this direction. We moved the entire company up to a valley just behind this ridge, and were there for several days. My next letter was written from that spot.

May 2, 1943

Dear Mother, Dad, and Sis,

I suddenly got inspired to write a letter today. I don't know why. My platoon is working within 100 yards of our bivouac, so I guess that's the reason I have a chance.

I take back all I said about the accuracy of "Time" on the Tunisian war. The April 12 issue (the overseas edition) was distributed to the Division, and I understand the General[1] was so mad that he wrote scorching letters to "Time" & several other magazines. I'm referring to certain remarks about the battle of El Guettar. Apparently the news correspondents didn't get close enough to the action to know what was going on. It's the same old story -- the courageous air corps and armor get all the credit & medals, but the boys who go thru indescribable hell, the boys who get the worst food and only Mother Earth for a bed, and have twice the guts of all the others combined are the poor old infantry. And yet they never complain, they just go right on taking it on the chin. Those are the real Americans, and some day America will wake up to the fact. It's very easy to be brave when you have hot cakes & coffee for breakfast and know that when your days work is done you'll have an eatable dinner and a cot to sleep on. It's easy to be brave when you've got four inches of steel in front of you.

I've received your mail up as late as April 7. However, I've never received the flashlight or slide rule.

Sister's prospect of a job in Yosemite sounds very interesting. However, just now the great "out-of-doors" has temporarily lost its appeal for me. I have now been camping for five months straight.

I wonder if the censor would mind if I described the sensation of a dive-bombing attack. The censor has probably never been dive-bombed, so I don't suppose he'll like it. Anyway, here goes. The first thing you see is a flight of planes, some of which appear larger than the others. They move rather slowly, and then the larger ones slowly start a dive. By this time you can identify them. If they are silver with two black motors, they are Ju88's. If they have visible landing gears, they are Stukas. The Stukas dive steeper and come lower. The dive is amazingly slow, and you die a thousand deaths as they come down. You've got to watch them, or you'll go crazy. As they get near, the motors sound like nothing I've ever heard outside the movies. And then you see a half dozen shining silver objects drop from the belly of each plane. They fascinate you so that you can hardly take your eyes off of them. And then as they near the ground, Mother Earth becomes the most important thing in the world. In the meantime the roar of machine guns and AA is deafening. It drowns out the sound of the bombs, but the concussion lifts you six inches off the ground. When it's all over you stand up terrified & shake your fist at the sky, and then you look with admiration at the gunners who stayed with their guns while you groveled in a hole. That's a dive bombing.

Well, there's chow call, so I'll get this in the mail.

---

1   General Allen, our Division Commander

Loads of love,
Bill

I'm sure my mother enjoyed hearing about a dive-bombing attack!!

I distinctly recall writing that letter. I was lying down in my pup tent and Tom Crowley came along and gave me hell for being in my tent while my platoon was on a job, albeit close by. However, I can't pick out the point in the letter where he interrupted me. I remember being a bit sulky afterwards.

We had started to live less primitively, despite the fact that we were in the midst of a major attack and German artillery shells were frequently coming into the company area. At El Guettar we had found an Italian officer's folding table, and we officers were having our meals served at the table while we sat on water cans. We even started playing bridge. At about this time a portable shower unit was set up about a mile to the rear and I got a shower.

It was when we were bivouacked in the valley just behind the ridge over which we built the road that we finally got some replacements, straight from the States. "A" Company got a new 2nd Lieutenant, George Johnson from Minneapolis. He had a lot in common with Bill Barnum, who was also from Minneapolis. George and I served together for the rest of the war, although he was wounded in the Hurtgen Forest in Germany, and was hospitalized for quite awhile. George was an easygoing Swede with lots of guts, but also good sense. He was a joy to have around.

The next day I took George out to "see the front." We crossed the ridge and as we were walking up the next ridge I looked up and saw a flight of fifteen planes coming our way, three parallel rows of five each. Since they had radial engines I told George they were American. At that instant the three rows converged into a single row of fifteen and down they came in a dive-bombing attack. But I was wrong, they were German Focke-Wulfe 190s, the first we had seen. I popped away at them in a futile gesture with my carbine, surprising George in the process. They came right down onto our company area, but of course we weren't there. I think they mistook our kitchen truck under its camouflage net for an artillery piece. There was a lot of artillery nearby. I don't recall that we suffered any casualties, but our four-ton supply truck was hit by a few bomb fragments, some of which showed up weeks later when the truck was being unloaded.

A little later Col. Rowland came along in a jeep with the objective of going up and taking a look at the battle. He returned a little while later, obviously shaken. He had stuck his head up to take a look and German artillery had almost instantly zeroed in, killing either his driver or his runner. About the same time, General Lesley McNair, Chief of the Army Ground Forces, arrived on an inspection trip. He too wanted to go up and see what was going on. He soon came back on a stretcher. The German artillery was incredible; if you stuck your head up you could expect a response. It was not surprising that the infantry were continually pinned down during daylight hours, and attacks were always at night.

Soon after this, the 1st Battalion of the 16th Infantry was overrun in a night counterattack, many were captured, and the battalion virtually ceased to exist. A big gap in the lines resulted, and "A" Company was once again sent in to fill the gap. For some reason that I don't remember, my platoon was held back, so I didn't share in this pleasure!

Then the 34th division, on our immediate left, finally captured Hill 609, and the pressure on the whole front diminished. The Germans had to withdraw and we soon found ourselves out of the hills and on a grassy plain. The 1st Armored Division on our right was able to break through, and the Tunisian Campaign was coming to a close.

The next letter must have been written at about the same time.

May 8

Dear Mother, Dad, and Sis,

Just a short note, the main object being to enclose this rather exaggerated, but nevertheless detailed account of the events of March 23, which I believe I mentioned once before as being a memorable day. I can't tell you now just how I was involved in that affair, but I aged a bit, I can assure you.

Haven't had much mail recently, but I expect some soon. I believe I got a letter from Mother the other day about a month old. The flashlight, slide rule, and sewing kit arrived today -- many thanks.

Well, that's about all for now. I hope to have some time for more soon, especially after I get some mail.

Love to all,
Bill

The final surrender was on May 13th, but by that time I was long gone. Soon after we emerged from the hill country, I woke up in the middle of the night with terrible stomach cramps. In the morning I had a temperature of 104 degrees, and they sent me back to an evacuation hospital. But before going on with my personal story, let me digress for a moment and discuss some of the implications of this six-month campaign in Tunisia, which was now finally and completely over.

I have read various histories of the war, some very complete, but the Tunisian Campaign is given little space. To the extent that the American effort is mentioned at all, almost all history books speak of the disgraceful American "failure," with emphasis on the Battle of Kasserine Pass. This failure is variously attributed to "poor discipline," "lack of training," "inexperienced troops," "poor leadership," etc. Most of this is nonsense. The American difficulties in Tunisia, difficulties that began to be corrected in March, were primarily due to inadequate weapons. Whoever specified and designed our original tanks probably should have been hung; they were no match for the German machines. Our 37 mm anti-tank guns were hopeless against German tanks, especially in the desert where ranges were long. The Germans by this time were using 88 mm anti-aircraft guns for anti-tank work, and they were so effective that it got to the point where our soldiers were referring to "them 88s" when describing any kind of artillery fire. Our World War I French 75s mounted on thin-skinned halftrack vehicles could inflict a little damage if they got close enough, but usually only at fearful costs. In naval analogy, it was like sending destroyers against battleships. The German machine gun fired 900 rounds per minute, ours 450. The German Tellermine, their standard anti-tank mine, contained eleven pounds of TNT; ours contained five and a half pounds. Our rifle, the famous M1, was superior, but this was not a rifleman's war. Only our artillery was on a par with the Germans, and it was thus not surprising that artillery became our primary weapon and ultimately won the battle for us. And I should mention one other area in which we were actually superior: The General Motors two and a half ton truck had no peer, nor did the ubiquitous little jeep. (It is interesting to note that of all the materials that we pushed upon Russia during the war, only the two and a half-ton truck really made a difference.)

Why is anybody surprised that we couldn't hold Kasserine Pass with one battalion of infantry and one regiment of engineers (the 19th Engineer Regiment), or that parts of the 34th Division were over-run at Faid Pass a few days earlier? The 21st Panzer Division could move around virtually at will with little to fear.

I should add that it was not just in weapons that we had to catch up. Even our water and gasoline cans had to be copied from the Germans - "jerry-cans" they used to be called. Our new entrenching tool, introduced the next year, was a direct copy of a very superior German model that we saw in Tunisia. And eventually we got boots instead of canvas leggings.

Despite the problems and a lot of delays, the Tunisian Campaign ended in a very great and significant victory for the British and the smaller American contingent. The Germans and Italians had been completely driven out of Africa, and the Mediterranean had been effectively opened up from Gibraltar to Suez. Several hundred thousand Germans had been captured, and for the Germans it was a disaster comparable in magnitude to Stalingrad of a few months earlier.

Now let's get back to my story. It was a few days before the final German surrender, and I was on the way to an evacuation hospital.

I recall a large tent full of cots and battle casualties, but I remember little else because I was so miserable. There wasn't much sympathy for my particular ailment; I recall a medic cutting off my underpants with a pair of scissors and dumping them in the bedpan. They managed to get me stopped up in a day or so, and I next found myself on a plane flying to Oran. I remember looking out through a small porthole from my stretcher and seeing that we were flying over the ocean about a mile away from the coast.

They took me to a hospital in the city of Sidi-Bel-Abbès, some distance inland from Oran. It was a large permanent building, and I shared a small room with an Air Force officer. The following letter was written there.

May 15, 1943

Dear Mother, Dad, and Sis,

I'm going to try to write an uncensorable letter this time. My last several letters have been a little "risque," and as the old army saying goes, I'm "sweating" them out.

Well, the first round is over, and I can't say that I'm entirely unhappy about it. Tunisia got to be too much of a good thing (or bad thing). I don't know what happens next, and if I did I couldn't say, so I suppose there's not much use discussing it.

Incidentally, I'm in a hospital now. Got a touch of the old army scourge – dysentery. It's been a nice rest, and I got my first airplane ride out of it. It seems unbelievable to be sleeping on a bed between sheets, with good-looking nurses waiting on you. In fact I have trouble sleeping — I keep wanting to take a blanket and roll up on the floor. I'm OK now, and the doc is initiating proceedings to get me out. (That takes time in the army).

Don't know whether this will go to you straight, or by V-Mail. It's about time that

they photo them.
Much love to all,
Bill

I don't know why I was so casual and flippant about being in the hospital. I do note that all talk about going home has vanished.

I got out of the hospital soon after; I was probably there for less than a week. They sent me to the Replacement Depot in Oran, a place called Canastel near the coast just east of Oran. I had heard about Canastel before from George Johnson, who had come there before joining the 1st Division. It was infamous for disciplinary nonsense. I was in a tent with several infantry 2nd Lieutenants, fresh from the States. Since I had been in "action" I was the center of attention and they listened to my every word. I was also distinguished by my wool olive drab (OD) uniform, as opposed their summer khakis.

Each day these guys had to undergo training in which I simply refused to participate. I could afford to be a little arrogant; there was already developing a gulf between those who had been under fire, and the rear area people.

An example of the training going on there was a "saluting obstacle course." A road intersection was set up and officers were posted at various points within it. Then the men were made to walk through and salute at unexpected encounters with officers. Only an SOS colonel could think this one up.

I became well acquainted with two or three of the 2nd Lieutenants there. Two of them ended up in the 16th Infantry and I saw them later. One, a real nice guy named Griffin, was in the 2nd Battalion of the 16th and was killed soon in Sicily; another was the "mine platoon" officer in the 16th Infantry's Anti-Tank Company for quite some time. I don't know whatever happened to him; I never saw him again after Sicily.

One night we were attending an outdoor movie, and there were several thousand soldiers sitting on a gentle hillside. Anti-aircraft tracers began going up all over Oran. Some idiot came on the loud speaker and yelled "Take cover, on the double." A mad stampede started. Then another voice said, "Stay where you are, don't move." The movie resumed. A moment later over the loud speaker came, "It is an air-raid, take cover." More stampede! I think it was all a false alarm, although the anti-aircraft fire was real enough.

I probably was at Canastel about a week, and then was returned to the 1st Engineers, who were camped at a place called Sidi Shami, not far from where we had been five months earlier. They had just arrived back from Tunisia and were starting training for the Sicilian invasion. This was the first I had heard of a Sicilian operation. My next letter was written from Sidi Shami.

May 26

Dear Mother, Dad, and Sis,
    Have received lots of mail lately, the latest being dated May 9. The V-Mails are doing pretty well. Also I'm wearing now a pair of very welcome wool socks.
    You said you hoped I was now having a rest. You don't know the 1st Division.

These people just don't have that word in their vocabulary. In my 3-1/2 months on the front lines I got a total of 5 days when you had nothing to worry about — I'd hardly call them days of rest. Of course, there were lots of times when we weren't doing much of anything, but there was always that front line tension which precludes rest. I used to read about how the Japs and Germans pushed their troops & how terrible that was, and now I'm beginning to wonder if we're much better.

I received all the clippings you sent, & in every case the outfit mentioned was ours, although the way these newspaper writers distort & paint up stories is astonishing. Why even in the Army-Navy Journal recently I read the most amazing accounts of our experiences. My whole faith in the American press has been horribly shaken.

When we finally got back to a city we had to give the men unlimited passes to keep them all from going over the hill. You can imagine the results when you turn loose thousands of men who haven't seen a city for 3 to 5 months. (Especially in a country of cheap wine.)

I now have a campaign ribbon, but the 1st Division has refused to wear it, because every office clerk 500 miles from the front gets the same ribbon.

In the Officers' Red Cross club the other day I ran into an Ensign who was a classmate & good friend of mine at Stanford.

They've relaxed mail censorship now & we're allowed to relate experiences in Tunisia. It would take me a week to tell you all about it. I guess the most scared I ever was after I had been on the front a total of 30 minutes.

Two nosey little Messerschmitts came ambling over and the men all jumped up and yelled "Look, P-40's." Ten seconds later there was a terrific rattle of machine guns, and I was hugging the ground vowing that I would dig a hole six feet deep if they'd only leave me alone. There were times later when I had much more reason to be scared, but the first time lead is coming your way is the worst. I finally found out that the worst thing of all is artillery. Bombs are hard on your nerves, but the bastards can't hit the broad side of a barn with them, and they attack you once & then they leave you alone for awhile. Artillery can hound you hour after hour in day or night, and it's deadly accurate.

Well, that's enough for the time being. I'll write again soon.

Love,

Bill

The Stanford friend I ran into in Oran was Bob Hinze. I was to see him again four months later in Palermo, and many times since the war.

The 1st Division more or less took over Oran. Our men were in wool ODs and the SOS people were in summer khakis, so it was easy to distinguish who was a "fighting soldier" and who wasn't. The city was also full of men from the 36th Division who had not yet been in action, and who were also distinguished by their summer uniforms. Fights broke out everywhere, mostly over the rights to be in a bar and things like that. I went to a movie theater and saw Jimmy Cagney in "Yankee Doodle Dandy," which was a real flag-waver and got us all excited. The soldiers went around town singing, "I'm a 1st Division Soldier" to the tune of "I'm a Yankee Doodle Dandy," but what really stirred us up was Frances Langford singing "Over There" in the finale.

I recall one night when George Johnson came back late from Oran after having had too much wine for perhaps the first time in his life. Apparently some of the enlisted men had found him and brought him home. At any rate, he tripped over our tent ropes and fell on top of me in my pup tent.

The next letter was written shortly thereafter, but I believe we had moved to an amphibious training center very close to my old town of Arzew when I was in the 361 QM. As part of the training for the Sicilian invasion we spent some time aboard a small naval transport, the Samuel B. Chase, but I think that was probably after this letter. (The next year I sailed on the Chase for the Normandy landing.)

We loved the Chase. I remember spending hours in the officer's mess where we gorged ourselves on fresh bread and butter. By this time we had shifted uniform to OD fatigue clothes, and this is what we wore throughout Sicily. We were a crummy looking bunch in the officer's mess.

From the Chase we practiced going ashore from small landing craft, although the Chase itself stayed anchored in the harbor.

June 2

Dear Mother, Dad, and Sis,

Time seems to buzz along and I don't know when I last wrote, but I think it was fairly recently. Tunisia and all its horrors seems awful far away now. Life is boring and uninteresting principally because there is not one earthly thing that is pleasant to look forward to. I can get an evening off and go to town now and then, but there's nothing to do when you get there.

There doesn't seem to be much to talk about. We're working pretty hard, and that's about all the news there is. It's pretty hot, and lately we've had a hot wind that is covering everything with dust. There isn't a tree within 40 miles of this place and the dust blows for miles.

We have movies every other night now, and for the first time I can go to army movies without seeing one I'd already seen — I'm just that far behind in my movies.

I went to the Red Cross club recently and had some real ice cream. They serve it every afternoon at 3 o'clock and you have to sweat a terrific line. It's a real luxury. Some of the guys have talked their way aboard naval vessels and got cokes and chocolate bars. Gosh, I haven't seen a coke since last summer.

Well, I'll try to write again soon.

Loads of love

Bill

This letter begins to reveal some of the depression I felt at the prospect of having to immediately participate in an amphibious operation and probably an endless campaign after that. We had thought that at the very least we would get a rest and somebody else would lead the way in the next operation. Gradually I became fatalistic about it, as did everybody else. There was going to be no end to it; the only way you were going to go home was in a box.

About the 15th of June we loaded onto the Chase and went by sea to Algiers. We established camp near the coast about fifteen miles west of the city at a place called

Staouli. I am not sure whether the next letter was written before or after the move, although I think it was written from Algiers. It's a V-Mail letter, but it went direct and not by photocopy.

June 15, 1943

Dear Mother, Dad, and Sis,

Having just gorged myself with a little "vin," I'm a little tight, so this letter may seem a little cockeyed. (That sentence doesn't even sound right.) However, I'm thankful for the chance to cut loose once and awhile and feeling very good indeed.

Haven't had any mail for some time, but I guess I'll get a pile of it soon. The last I heard from you, you were still sweating out a letter from me dated after the end of the campaign. By this time you should have several.

You ask "what's next." I can't say I don't know what's next, because we all know damn well what's next. All the "heroes" who sit back behind the lines on their fannies are in a great sweat to get us going, but we unfortunate creatures who have to stick our necks out are perfectly happy to sit right where we are. When I read that only one man in six in the army is in a combatant outfit, I wonder what happened to my luck. The great mystery in the battalion is why I didn't follow in the footsteps of my old man. When I eat their food and sleep on their beds, it's a mystery to me also.

I'm in a Red Cross Officer's club now. I don't know what we'd do without these clubs of theirs. They even serve ice cream in the afternoons.

I'll try to write you more of a letter soon.

Love, Bill

We were fairly comfortably camped in a little pine forest. The surrounding country was hilly and covered with vineyards. We carried on a lot of training exercises. Sometimes in the morning Murphy would take the company for a run on the beach, the men grumbling and griping. We got into Algiers frequently in the evenings. The main problem at this place was the flies. The men all got diarrhea, probably from a combination of the wine and the flies. The company carpenter built a large multi-hole sit-down latrine, but it was usually one hundred percent occupied.

Murphy managed to have a much more active social life than the rest of us. Through friends in the 16th Infantry he met a gang of nurses at a nearby field hospital, and they used to be out on beach parties till all hours of the night. We never could figure out how Murph had so much energy to run in the mornings. As I recall, one of his buddies was Johnny Armilino who eventually married one of the nurses. He later became a company commander in the 3rd Battalion and then lost a leg on Omaha Beach.

On one occasion we had the company on the beach practicing a drill to cut a path through a minefield. Fred Finley had written the drill into a "standard operating procedure," an SOP as we called it. Along came General Roosevelt. He asked what we were doing and we showed him the sheet of paper on which the drill was written. "This is good; this is God-damned good!" he exclaimed. The men crowded around him and somebody mumbled something about going home. "Who said something about going home?" he said. "Do you know when we go home? When there are no more Germans to kill." Everybody laughed. He could get away with this kind of talk. Few commanding officers could.

The next two letters were written from this camp.

June 24

Dear Mother, Dad, and Sis,

Just got your "V-Mails" of June 5 and 6, so I see that you are no longer sweating out my "post-campaign" mail. I wish I could say "post-war" mail, but that is apparently a long ways off. You all seem to go into an awful stew when you don't hear from me for a long time. Gosh, there are millions of reasons why you should not hear from me for a long time. We had an amazing case in the battalion. A man was wounded one night and taken to the rear to a hospital. The next morning the hospital was bombed and strafed and he was wounded twice more. The shock of it all caused him to lose his memory. He had lost his dog-tags, and was turned in as K.I.A. It was a month before he remembered who he was, and in the meantime his family had been notified. Of course, that's a rather odd case, but those sort of things were happening.

What happened to Sis' plan to go to Canada this summer? Is she definitely going back to school this summer? Sounds like a darned nuisance.

Went to the city the other night with a guy and got two quarts of champagne which we finished off in about an hour in addition to a quart of muscatel at dinner. It was really a very delightful evening. These people over here drink wine like water.

Now that I've started another page I find nothing to say. My activities are taboo and they occupy practically all my time. I'm trying to write and carry on a conversation at the same time and I'm having sort of a tough time. Maybe I can do better sometime soon.

Loads of love,
Bill

I'm sure my mother was very reassured by the story of the guy who lost his memory! It sounds far-fetched to me now.

The next letter is dated May 30, but this is obviously an error, and it must have been written on June 30. It was my last letter before the Sicily landings.

May 30

Dear Mother, Dad, and Sis,

I thought I would celebrate my first year in the army with a letter. (Also my first year as a 2nd Lt.) It was a year ago today that I boarded the train at 3rd and Townsend.

I have received several "V-Mails" lately dating up to about June 8. I see you got that stuff I sent home early in May. You speak of being confused as to my whereabouts on March 23. Yes, I wrote you a letter on March 23. The oasis I spoke of was the town of El Guettar, and was four or five miles behind the lines. We were there all morning and could see and hear that something was going on, but were not quite sure what. At noon they decided they wanted the minefield reinforced, and just as we moved out to do it we got a message saying that the entire 10th Panzer would attack at 1600. They had attacked that morning, but I didn't realize it till later. We never did get a chance to reinforce the minefield despite the fact that the enemy advanced their H-hour 40 minutes at the last minute. We were moved into the right flank as infantry after going thru the worst dive-bombing to get there that I ever hope to see. At 1640 on the dot the attack came and it was the kind of thing you read about. Waves of Stukas and Messerschmitts came after our artillery and OP's, an artillery barrage came in with an odd mixture of ground-burst, air-burst, and smoke shells, and then the tanks and infantry. They either didn't know we had so much artillery, or thought the Luftwaffe would do a better job, but at any rate the barrage we laid on them was a surprise, and they gave it up after it turned into a slaughter. The 10th Panzer never bothered anybody after that. They allotted the 21st Pz. for our benefit later, but the second phase of El Guettar is another story.

The coal strikes are certainly a happy story. Don't those people know there's a war on?

I used to get letters from you telling of picnics, etc., and the description would always end with, "and the boys painted." What goes on here?

Took a cold shower at the Red Cross the other night. I never did like cold showers, but I was getting so I couldn't live with myself. I never have told you much about the other officers in the battalion. Col. Rowland has gone upstairs and the C.O. is Maj. Bill Gara. He'll probably be a Lt. Col. soon and he's only 27. Graduated from N.Y.U. a few years back. "B" company is commanded by Lt. Forbes who is from Honolulu and knew "Chokey" Denison and Joe Austin. "C" co. is commanded by Capt. John Oxford who is from somewhere in the south. Our company commander is Capt. Charlie Murphy who is from Tennessee. The first platoon commander is 2nd Lt. George Johnson from Minnesota. The 2nd is 1st Lt. Bill Barnum from Minnesota also, and I have the third. The company exec. is 1st Lt. Fred Rutledge from So. Carolina. We also have two new officers who we use as assistant platoon leaders of the 1st and 2nd Platoons. I had an assistant, but he was transferred out.

Well, chow is on, and I've got to take the pass truck into the city tonight, so I'd better eat.

Much love to all,
Bill

As can be noted in the letter, we had some re-shuffling of officers. The company commanders of both our "B" and "C" had been wounded, and in fact "C" Company had lost most of its original officers. Tom Crowley left us to become battalion executive officer in place of Gara, who was now CO. Rut was now our company exec, and George Johnson had taken his 1st Platoon. The two new officers were Bob Conant and Phil Suna. Conant and I ultimately became great friends. He was a biochemistry PhD from Johns Hopkins; I don't know how he ended up in the Combat Engineers. Conant was wounded in Sicily, but rejoined us and was in the company until November 1944, when he was captured in Germany. He spent most of the rest of the war walking as a POW across Germany in mid-winter.

Suna was from Long Island (or "Long Guyland", as he called it) and was still with the company when we went to England a few months later. I don't recall what ever became of him. A big change at this time was that "D" Company was disbanded. The halftracks and jeeps returned to the line platoons in "A", "B," and "C," and the 37 mm anti-tank guns were junked as useless. The "Hell Squads" returned to H&S Company to be clerks, mechanics, and truck drivers. Fred Finley went to "C" Company, and Harold Haas to "B." Gordon Pope, who had been CO of "D," left the battalion with Rowland.

Near the end of June we went aboard transports and made a practice landing a little distance west of Algiers, near Staouli. After the real landing in Sicily, I was surprised to find that this dress rehearsal was actually quite realistic.

On the 5th of July we loaded up again in Algiers harbor for the Sicily invasion on the same transports. My platoon was once more attached to the 3rd Battalion of the 16th Infantry, so the company was separated and various parts were on different ships. I think that perhaps George and his platoon were on my ship, the U.S.S. Stanton.

That day I was promoted to 1st Lieutenant.

Near Hill 609, Northern Tunisia, April 1943; My platoon moves up into a defensive position.

Somewhere near Algiers, June 1943; Glisson and Cendroski of my platoon (4th and 3rd from right) sample wine at a bar.

CHAPTER SIX

SICILY

JULY 10 - NOVEMBER 5, 1943

I was careless about writing from Sicily, so I will have to rely primarily on my memory of events. In fact I only wrote two letters during the battle.

We sailed from Algiers on Tuesday, July 6th. The landing was scheduled for Saturday morning, July 10th.

The idea of landing in Sicily had apparently been very controversial. The American high command, and in particular General Marshall, the Chief of Staff, was in favor of concentrating all available forces in England and carrying out a cross-channel operation as soon as possible. Sicily, and then Italy, could compromise that possibility, and their argument was that Germany could never be defeated by an invasion of Italy. On the other hand, Sicily occupied a very strategic spot threatening commerce through the Mediterranean, and seemed to be there for the taking.

The Sicily invasion was a very large operation, in fact the largest amphibious operation of the war to that time. Two complete armies were involved from the very beginning: the 7th U.S. Army under General Patton, and the 8th British Army under Montgomery. We were in the 7th (yes, we were back under Patton again!), and we landed three divisions abreast, and the British had about the same size force, so at least six divisions landed simultaneously. The 7th Army was on the left and we were the center division of those three, landing just to the right of the town of Gela on the south coast. The 3rd Division landed to our left, and the 45th to our right. A battalion of Rangers was used to land in Gela itself. The British landed to the right of the 45th. All of the landings were on the south coast. The 1st Division landed two regiments abreast: the 16th on the right, and the 26th on the left, with the 18th in reserve. Parts of the 82nd Airborne Division were to be dropped ahead of the 1st Division landings. This was the first airborne operation of the war.

During the afternoon of July 9th, the whole armada sailed through the narrow straits separating Sicily and Tunisia while the Air Force evidently kept the Luftwaffe at bay. Towards evening we could see Malta. Just after dark we suddenly turned north towards the landing beaches. The sea was unusually rough.

At that stage of the war this was a scary operation. We were landing in Europe itself for the first time, and did not have a clear picture of what lay ahead. Hitler and Mussolini threatened terrible things. We knew that the beaches were to a certain extent fortified, and that we would face both Italian and German troops.

The initial landings were scheduled for about two o'clock a.m. After the Tunisian experience we wanted nothing to do with daylight attacks. The 1st and 2nd Battalions of the 16th Infantry Regiment were the two assault battalions, and the 3rd Battalion was in reserve. Since I was attached to the 3rd, I lucked out again, and I wasn't scheduled to land until about six o'clock, after dawn.

On the ship I ran into a navy ensign who I had known casually at Stanford, Mickey Levee. I was sleeping down in the hold with a bunch of Infantry 2nd Lieutenants. and Mickey suggested I use his cabin on the night of the landing since he had to man a battle station right after dark. I did sleep in his bed for a while, but then I decided that I wanted to be on deck when the action started, so I got up at about twelve thirty in the morning.

I particularly remember a specific infantry 2nd Lieutenant while I was sleeping in the hold. He was a new replacement and his proudest possession was a Thompson sub-machine-gun. He kept playing with it. Later I heard that he shot himself in the foot with it. Accident?

The ship dropped anchor around midnight, perhaps ten miles off shore, and the first wave of infantry were lowered to the water before one o'clock. I watched them sail off, and then came the long silent wait. My legs shook as I stood at the railing. Eventually we saw anti-aircraft fire, which presumably meant that paratroopers from the 82nd Airborne were landing. Just before two o'clock, one or two searchlights came on from the direction of Gela to the left front. They lit up the whole ocean for miles around. They swept back and forth and I could see landing craft silhouetted in the distance. Then I noticed what appeared to be three small white stars slowly moving in a huge arc from my left rear and toward Gela and the searchlights. As they descended, I then saw four red lights moving more rapidly in a flat trajectory from my left front and towards the searchlights. The first three were large shells from a cruiser; the other four were from a destroyer. All seven seemed to arrive together in the vicinity of the searchlights, and the lights went out. Straight ahead on our beach I saw a flash of light just at two o'clock, and then all was dark, and all was quiet.

Nobody told us what was going on, but in a couple of hours we climbed into the small landing boats (LCVPs - Landing Craft, Vehicle, Personnel) and were lowered to the water. Dawn broke as we neared the beach, but all looked quiet ahead. The beach was about 100 yards deep, backed by sand dunes, and beyond that was low, gently rolling country covered with vineyards. As it turned out, our beach was only lightly held by a few Italian machine guns in sandbagged positions. They had been quickly overrun by our assault troops in the dark, with few casualties on either side. The Italians didn't have their hearts in it. There actually were concrete pillboxes at some places along the south coast of Sicily, but not on this beach. There apparently was resistance in the town of Gela, but that was overcome sometime after daylight.

Here and there I saw little groups of paratroopers from the 82nd Airborne (groups of two or three men). They had evidently been dropped, obviously not intentionally, over about a 100 square mile area, some of them ten or more miles inland. Nowhere were they able to fight as coherent units, but as it turned out they were able to accomplish a certain amount of disruption during the next two days.

Our two leading infantry battalions were now about a mile inland, and we followed them. Col. Taylor set up a regimental CP on the near side of a little ridge about a half-mile inland, and I spent the morning there. The infantry was now running into some resistance, and since we didn't yet have much artillery ashore, a navy cruiser was being used for artillery support. A couple of their seaplanes were flying overhead to aid in directing this support fire. At about seven thirty, a German Me109 flew by us, paralleling the coast at about 100 feet altitude. I remember him rolling the plane from one side to the other, apparently to get a good look at what was going on. I could see the pilot very distinctly, all in black. I heard Col. Taylor on the phone say, "Where's that air cover we're supposed to have?"

A little while later I saw one of the Navy seaplanes go over our heads, fairly low and heading for the sea. Suddenly an Me109 was directly on its tail, but flying at about four times its speed. There was a burst of machine gun fire and then the 109 abruptly turned and flew straight up for a couple of thousand feet, barely missing a collision. Smoke came out of the seaplane and it disappeared beyond the sand dunes.

Later in the day I found Murphy and we established a company bivouac in a vineyard a little farther inland. Johnson and Barnum were still out with their respective infantry battalions, but I was released from the 3rd Battalion and rejoined the company. Actually my platoon constituted most of the company at that point. Rutledge was still all the ways back in Oran with some of our heavy equipment, and didn't join us for at least a week, so the company headquarters group was small.

During the rest of that first day the major effort was to bring supplies ashore and prepare for a major push inland the next morning. Before dawn on the 11th, the 16th Infantry started forward against virtually no opposition (and I presume that the 26th was doing the same from Gela), unaware that the Hermann Goering Panzer Division was coming the other way in two or three columns.

The 11th was a wild day. The forward infantry units were easily overrun by the Panzers. Bill Barnum and Bob Conant, with the 2nd Battalion of the 16th, got into a culvert under a highway while the tanks passed over them. Col. Crawford, CO of the 2nd Battalion, was a casualty. George Johnson, along with Col. Denholm, CO of the 1st Battalion and Capt. Berry, one of the company commanders, manned a 57 mm anti-tank gun that had been abandoned by its crew in an olive orchard, and fired on the tanks point-blank. The gun crew had taken the gun-sight with them and George and Denholm and Berry sited the gun by looking down the barrel. When that became hopeless, they hopped into a jeep, and with the Colonel driving, they went over a ridge into a ravine, only to have German artillery follow them. A shell burst behind them, and Capt. Berry was killed and Denholm was wounded, but George took over as driver and brought them out.

(My friend Brooks, from the hospital in Scotland, was at that time the CO of the Anti-Tank Company. I understand that he lost his command as a result of the behavior of his gun crews. Years later I met him at a 1st Division Officers Reunion. He was a general!)

Back nearer the beach I didn't know what was going on, although I heard a lot of noise. A large German air attack took place, the principal targets being the ships anchored off Gela. The naval anti-aircraft fire added to the excitement. I saw a huge cloud of smoke in the distance; an ammunition ship was hit and disappeared. But still we had no air cover.

At one point I returned to the beach to see about something. Coming back inland I passed a battery of the 5th Field Artillery Battalion with their 155 mm howitzers, perhaps two or three hundred yards from the beach in the midst of the sand dunes. They were firing very rapidly, and continuously. Suddenly I saw that they were firing airbursts, which were exploding just over the hill a few hundred yards away; German infantry was that near. The tanks got very close to the beach and were not turned back until naval destroyers were brought in close to shore and were able to use direct fire on them, although this is something I didn't actually see.

Back in our vineyard I recall at one point a lone plane coming over very low. Everybody opened fire on it, including our halftracks using their 50 caliber machine guns, and for a moment, I thought it was one of ours. He must have been lost, because he acted surprised and tried to go into a climb, which slowed him down. Red tracers poured into his belly, a small stream of smoke came out, and then flames and black smoke. He nosed over and disappeared behind a hill. A huge cloud of black smoke went up.

We had some battery-powered radios that could pick up regular broadcasts from Italy. Some of these were evidently for our benefit. I remember that evening hearing Ezra Pound babbling on about the terrible carnage on the beaches, and how the "Jew Roosevelt" had got us into this predicament.

Everybody was jumpy that night, and soon after dark the fleet offshore opened up with Anti-Aircraft fire sending millions of tracers up until the sky was red with them. We heard planes, somebody shouted "paratroops," and our 50 caliber machine guns opened up, along with hundreds of others. I looked up and in the starlit sky and I recognized distinctly the outline of an American C47 transport flying a few hundred feet above me. A flare came out of a window on the plane. I screamed for everybody to cease firing. It turned out the high command had decided to reinforce the beachhead by sending in another part of the 82nd Airborne by parachute. The trouble is they didn't notify anybody; this was not the Airborne's greatest hour. I heard later that the Navy shot down twenty-three transports full of paratroopers.

That night the mosquitoes in our nice vineyard were a terrible nuisance. We would hear more from them later!

The Panzers had been driven off and withdrew from the whole beachhead area. The next day George and I drove to where he and Denholm and Berry had fired the anti-tank gun. Two guns were still there in the olive orchard, along with several German bodies. George took a watch from one of the bodies.

This was essentially the end of the battle for the beachhead. The Italian troops largely disappeared, and the Germans withdrew towards the center of the island. During the next several days everybody moved rapidly inland, and "A" company was only minimally involved in the fighting. The main thing we did was cut detours around blown-up bridges and culverts. It was summer and there was no water in any of the streambeds, so this was a fairly easy task. We finally stopped at a place that I believe was near the town of Barrafranca, and the whole battalion was able to re-assemble in an olive orchard and catch our collective breaths.

I do remember one incident at that spot. We were right on the main road and General Patton came driving along in his famous command car with his whole entourage.

Through the trees he apparently spotted one of our halftrack crewmen wearing a mechanic's cap, a sort of baseball cap that Patton despised. Patton wanted everybody in steel helmets at all times. His whole column came to a halt, he leaped out and came storming through the orchard waving a walking stick that he carried. We spotted him coming, and the officers all ran and hid behind bushes and trees. He accosted the unfortunate soldier, bellowed something, and then demanded to know where the soldier's officers were. The poor guy was dumfounded. Patton stalked off. Either on that occasion, or sometime soon after, I understand that he went up to the 1st Division CP and found General Allen and General Roosevelt both wearing gear that he had expressly forbidden. This apparently had something to do with the fact that he relieved them both of their commands about a week or so later. Patton simply couldn't stand the independence and arrogance that he seemed to see in the 1st Division. To him it was just lack of discipline.

I was with Bill Gara at the same place when we both noticed a halftrack pulling out of the battalion area with Murph standing up in it and pointing forward. He had a long white scarf around his neck, flowing in the wind behind him, and he had a white lanyard attached to his pistol; the whole scene had a John Wayne look about it. Gara said, "Murphy was born 500 years too late; he should be riding a white stallion with a lance in his arms!"

The Germans and Italians continued to retreat across the island and it was important to pursue them rapidly. Intelligence reports that I read later indicate that the enemy units facing us were "the I and II Grenadier Regiments of the German 15th Panzer Division, the 382nd German Separate Infantry Regiment, the 71st Nebelwerfer (heavy mortar) Battalion, tank elements of the Herman Goering Division, and the beaten up Italian Aosta Division."

The 70th Light Tank Battalion was at that time attached to the 1st Division, and despite the mountainous country we were approaching, it was felt that the tanks could take advantage of this situation since they could move more rapidly than the infantry. Col. Wellborn, the CO of the 70th, insisted that he needed some Engineers to take out the inevitable mines that would be encountered. Accordingly, George Johnson and I were selected to each take a halftrack and a mine detector crew and report to Col. Wellborn on the morning of the 20th of July. He then gave us maps and instructions, the gist of which was that we would lead the tank battalion and take out any mines that we saw. If we ran into any enemy opposition we were to get out of the way and let his tanks come through us. It all sounded very simple!

The 70th Light Tank Battalion consisted of a considerable number of small tanks armed with the same 37 mm guns that had proved so ineffective in Tunisia. However, attached to the 70th was a company of medium tanks (Shermans) that would presumably supply some real fire-power. I soon got acquainted with the CO of the medium tank company, and found him to be not a happy man. He said that whenever they got near the enemy, his superior, Col Wellborn, would put his medium tanks out front, and he had already lost half his tanks. I understood the mine removal mission we had, but I suspected that Wellborn was really using George and I primarily to draw fire, and thereby locate enemy guns. This was not going to be a happy association! Our halftracks were open-topped, lightly armored vehicles, capable of withstanding small arms fire and shell fragments, but little more. We were armed with one 50 caliber machine gun and two 30 caliber machine guns. We carried a crew of four, plus two mine detector operators, plus me. My vehicle was commanded by Sgt. Lowe, who also manned the 50 caliber machine gun. It was actually the same halftrack and crew that Knocker Box had used so effectively in the battle for Oran the year before.

On the first day our objective was the city of Enna, perched on a mountain top right in the center of Sicily. We crept along; I was in the lead with George right behind me. In the meantime the infantry was approaching Enna from a different direction, and when we got there the infantry was already there. The enemy had chosen not to defend Enna, so the whole day's operation was sort of a lark.

The next day was a little different. We left George and his halftrack behind and set out on a long road into much higher mountain country, with the objective being the town of Alimena. This time, the lead was taken by the 1st Reconnaissance Company, a cavalry unit attached to 1st Division Headquarters. They had a string of jeeps and I followed them up the winding mountain road. As we approached a summit I found the cavalry jeeps pulled over to the side. The light tank behind me was in radio communication with Wellborn, and I could hear him giving orders. (They used a loud speaker rather than earphones.) He ordered me to bypass the jeeps and proceed forward. I finally reached what was evidently the lead reconnaissance jeep near a right bend in the road. There was a steep bank on the right side so that one couldn't directly see what was ahead. I stopped, wondering what to do. An officer in the lead jeep said that the town of Alimena was just ahead, and that it was occupied by the enemy. Furthermore, he told me, "We're a reconnaissance unit, our mission is to find the enemy, not to fight him, and we have found him." I said our mission was to remove mines, not to fight! But that impressed nobody!

About this time we heard a huge explosion just ahead, and saw a cloud of black smoke. Somebody was obviously up there. Then I heard Wellborn over the radio saying, "Tell the engineer halftracks to move out and go into that town." I looked back at the sergeant in the tank behind me and he shrugged his shoulders. He was standing with his head and shoulders sticking out of the turret. We closed down the steel windshield of the halftrack, leaving a slit to see through, and we moved slowly forward, everybody manning their guns. The town was only about a quarter mile away. I visualized soldiers throwing hand grenades at us from the second stories of the houses. But as we approached the town I saw the road lined with people cheering and waving flags!

We went into Alimena and to what was apparently the town square, and people crowded all around us. A guy climbed up on my vehicle and said, "I'm from Chicago, boys. The Germans just pulled out and blew out the road on the other side of the town." We decided to go on and investigate the road, and he cautioned, "Be careful, boys." True enough, they had done a good job, and it was not going to be possible to get out of town by the main road. This was mountainous country and you couldn't just go overland.

Returning to the center of the town we found the place full of tanks, jeeps, command cars, artillery forward observation teams, and even Charlie Murphy. I hadn't realized what a long line of vehicles was behind me. Somebody found another way to get out of the town by a narrow dirt road. I went there and parked near the lead tank, and waited for further orders. It wasn't clear to me who was running the show.

(Forty years later I read an account of the Sicily campaign, apparently written by our Commanding General, Terry Allen: "ALIMENA, 24 miles further north, was captured by the 26th Infantry, on July 21st, after continued hard fighting." Hard fighting? By whom?)

Alimena was in a sort of saddle in the hills and the road leading out to the north went down a gentle slope for about a half-mile where it reached a low ridge. The road then turned to the left and went around the ridge to the right in a hairpin turn and came out into another small valley. We could see over the ridge and see the road coming out of that valley and leading to the left again. It appeared that some kind of defense had been set up on that ridge.

Some enemy artillery shells came in, landing on the roofs of houses and scattering broken roof tile everywhere. Murph and I ducked into the backyard of a house and discovered something about Sicilian plumbing. There evidently were no toilets in the houses, nor were there outhouses. They just used the backyard. For us it was a choice of the backyards or the shells. We chose the latter.

Somebody sent a jeep down the road to draw enemy fire, which it promptly did. I saw two guys leap out of it as it ran up a bank and turned over. But that gave away the defensive system. The Italians had set up several fairly large caliber howitzers behind a rough stonewall on the ridge so that they could use direct fire on anybody coming out of the town and down the road. It was not exactly the way in which howitzers were intended for use. They are relatively low muzzle-velocity guns that usually fire shells over and down on a target.

Preparations were made to attack and Wellborn's voice came over the radio, "Engineer halftrack, move out." Fortunately Murphy was there, and he yelled to the first tank, "If you think this halftrack is going to attack those guns, you're crazy." The sergeant shrugged and buttoned up his tank. I noted that the medium Sherman tanks were in the lead. If Murph had not been there I don't know what I would have done because I had been given a direct order to attack, but Wellborn never mentioned the incident later.

The tanks went down the road at top speed. Some of our artillery was fired onto the ridge, since by this time at least one battery of the 33rd Field Artillery Battalion was in position behind Alimena. Beyond the ridge we could make out some vehicles and motorcycles scampering away. Then there started a continuous rattling of machine gun fire as the tanks went down to and around the ridge with all guns firing. The dry grass on the ridge caught fire, so there was now smoke everywhere. The tanks went into the little valley beyond and stopped.

After a little while Wellborn got on the radio and ordered me to join them. As we went down the hill and around the ridge, a great deal of enemy artillery was falling all over the ridge. As we came around the far side we were greeted by an incredible rolling barrage of artillery shells moving across the next little valley towards us. It looked as if the field in the valley had suddenly sprouted an orchard, and the shell bursts kept getting closer and closer until they were less than 100 yards away. Somehow I felt relatively safe in our halftrack vehicle with its quarter inch of armor, but one of our 30 caliber machine gunners panicked and started screaming about turning around. We finally did turn around (which was not easy because the paved road was rather narrow) and withdrew to the hairpin turn at the left end of the ridge where there was a bit of cover. This was rocket artillery, the "Nebelwerfer," the first we had seen, and unmistakable evidence that we were now encountering Germans, not Italians.

The Nebelwerfer was a five-barreled rocket launcher that carried rocket shells about 120 mm in diameter. A battery of Nebelwerfers could lay down an incredible barrage. I remember realizing that it was something new and different when we were coming around the ridge and they were landing all over the ridge just above us. As each shell exploded, what looked like a tin can flew high into the air and then tumbled down the ridge. This was apparently the empty tail end of the rocket. The Nebelwerfer was apparently originally designed to lay down smoke screens (hence the name), but had been converted to use high explosive shells on the Russian Front where rocket artillery was by that time being extensively used.

We got rid of our panicky gunner and decided to go on with just one 30 caliber machine gun (plus the 50) from then on. It was at that time late afternoon and everything came to a halt while further plans were made. Col. Wellborn set up his CP near where I was at the hairpin turn, so I just stayed there. Some of the tanks were below us in the little valley just ahead, but nobody was beyond the next ridge. When night fell I took a blanket and went to sleep on the ground beside my halftrack.

About dawn Col. Wellborn shook me awake and told me the plan. He said that during the night the infantry (presumably the 26th Infantry) had moved up into the town of Bompietro, the next town ahead, and he wanted me to lead the tanks to Bompietro. It sounded relatively harmless.

We started out with several light tanks behind us, followed by the medium tanks. After the next ridge everything seemed awfully quiet with not a person in sight. The local Italian farmers had simply melted away. We went along for about a mile, winding over small ridges and across little valleys. We came out into a larger rather shallow valley and at the center of it there were a couple of farmhouses and a road intersection with another road going to the right. There were few, if any, trees. The country, including the hills, was mostly dry grass. Perhaps it was wheat.

A sign pointed to Bompietro to the right. I was confused because that wasn't what my map indicated. I looked back and shrugged my arms at the sergeant in the light tank behind me. He gave a frantic motion to go straight ahead. I was puzzled, but we went ahead. The road approached a low hill and then turned right and gradually rose along the hillside. Shortly thereafter I saw what appeared to be two or three figures in khaki running towards the right along the hillside ahead, above the road. Aha, the 26th Infantry, I thought.

Moments later I heard the crack of anti-tank fire. Sgt. Lowe, standing above me and manning the 50 caliber machine gun, instantly opened up a steady stream of fire onto the hillside ahead and to the right front, where the enemy shots seemed to be coming from. Our plan had been to get out of the way when any shooting started, but there was no place to go where there was any kind of cover, and there was a fair-sized ditch on both sides of the road. The only thing I could see to do was continue forward until the road came up against the hill and bent to the right. I could see a cut in the hillside, a place where we could pull over, half hidden, and let the tanks pass us. I told Merschrod, the driver, what to do, he stepped on the gas, and we charged to the hill, almost straight at the enemy guns which were farther up the hill but slightly to the right.

There is no time for fear in these situations - the adrenalin flows, and you do what you have to do.

We pulled up to my chosen spot, which was just beyond a very small stone bridge over a little ravine that came directly down the hill from the left. I stood up and looked back, and to my astonishment all of the light tanks had disappeared. They had apparently jumped the ditch running along the road and had scurried off to the left and around another hill; their one virtue was that they were fast. Four medium (Sherman) tanks were slowly coming up the road and were at about where I had been when the shooting started. At this moment I distinctly heard shouting voices ahead - Germans shouting fire commands. The guns cracked and white tracers sailed by me. I watched one hit the lead tank and bounce high into the sky. The next disappeared into the tank, a hatch flew open, a couple of figures leaped out, and black smoke poured out. The second tank got it the same way. Their guns had swung around in our direction, but they never got a chance to fire a shot. The next two tanks backed up and disappeared over a ridge - obviously nobody had been able to spot the gun (or guns).

Perhaps a half minute later I heard what sounded like a thousand artillery shells going overhead. The whole area around and beyond our tanks exploded in what must have been hundreds of shell bursts. I saw a couple of the tank crewmen running wildly through all of this. One guy dove into a small depression around a bush, and then the bush went up in smoke. This was the artillery of the Nebelwerfers again. They continued for a few minutes, and then all was silent, and I had a chance to think. A few hundred yards behind me were two burning tanks and not a living soul in sight. We were at least a half-mile ahead of the only friendly people around, and I knew there was somebody very unfriendly about 100 yards up the road ahead. What the hell were we going to do?

My first thought was that soon the enemy would come over the hill ahead to flush us out. I was sure that at least part of the halftrack could be seen from up the road, so we climbed out, going into the little ravine and under the bridge. We dismounted a 30 caliber machine gun and some boxes of ammunition, but it wasn't clear from which direction our tormentors would come, and in any case hand grenades could easily have cleaned us out. Because of the way the hill sloped up and away from us, we couldn't see very far in the enemy's direction, and the tall, dry grass made it even more difficult.

While we were pondering all this we heard the sound of artillery shells coming from the friendly direction. A couple of white phosphorous smoke shells landed on either side of our ravine a little distance down the hill from us - our artillery was registering, but on us and not on the German anti-tank guns ahead! Now I was really scared. We all climbed down under the little bridge and lay down. Soon it came. American artillery fire plastered the entire area, ahead of us as well as behind. Apparently an entire battalion of 105 mm howitzers (twelve guns) was zeroed in on us. All we could do was lie there and pray. Now I knew what the Germans went through when we used concentrated artillery to dig them out of fortified positions. Shell fragments occasionally came spinning in under our little bridge, but the big bad one never came.

The artillery barrage went on for what seemed an eternity, but was probably about fifteen minutes. Then it became quiet again. We waited a long time. I wondered whether the Germans had withdrawn, because it had been pretty clear that they were fighting a rear-guard action and were not trying to make a determined stand. In this kind of mountainous country a few well-armed people could hold up a large force with few losses if they could trade space for time.

But then it started again. From up ahead we heard a terrific and continuous amount of very close German machine gun fire (unmistakable because of their rapid-fire guns). What was worse, ricochets were whining over our heads, so it was coming in our direction. Once more we were sure we were under attack. We grabbed our guns, not knowing what to expect. Suddenly I noticed out of the corner of my eye a couple of people jumping into our little ravine, but about fifty yards up the hill from us. We couldn't see them, but I was almost sure I had had a fleeting glimpse of an American helmet. I shouted, "Hey Joe, hey G.I. Joe." Three GIs slowly peered over a bank, and then stood up and stumbled down to us. They were so breathless they couldn't talk, and one was spattered with blood. We finally learned that they were the remnants of an 81 mm mortar team from the 26th Infantry. They had advanced the night before, somewhere to our left, and had been pinned down when daylight came. German mortar fire had caught them in an impossible place, and the survivors had decided to make a run for it, which meant running across about 1,000 yards of open grassy slope and down into our little ravine. A machine gun had followed them the whole way. The blood was from one of their buddies who got hit by mortar fire before they started their dash.

So now our little group was eight. It was past noon.

There were grass fires everywhere, ignited by the artillery shells. Later on I heard the irregular popping sound of small arms ammunition burning up. I again suspected that the Germans had pulled out their anti-tank guns and were probably digging them in a mile or so farther on, ready for another ambush. But that machine gun fire was worrisome. Forty years later I visited the scene and decided that the machine gun must have been hidden by some bushes at the top of small hill about 300 yards away. It probably had been sited there by the Germans to cover the withdrawal of their anti-tank guns. But it obviously looked down on us and could have given us a bad time had we loaded into the halftrack and attempted to turn around on the narrow road. So for the time being it seemed best to stay put.

From under our bridge we could see a long ways across a valley. The American positions were presumably to our right as we looked down the gently sloping hill, so we were looking at enemy country. At one time I could see what appeared to be a squad of probably Italian soldiers coming along a hill in the distance from the left. They disappeared into what looked like trenches. At another time we distinctly saw a lone American soldier down the hill from us, picking his way slowly from the left. Where had he come from? I presume he was somebody lost in the confusion of the advance of the 26th Infantry the night before.

As I sat there in the silence I thought how ironic it was that I was, at that moment, probably the point man in the whole huge American effort to destroy Adolf Hitler. All I had wanted to do was sit in the Ordnance Procurement Office in San Francisco! I thought it was the 23rd of July, my mother's birthday, although it was probably the 22nd; I wondered what they were doing, 6,000 miles away. How had I gotten myself into this mess?

At about four o'clock in the afternoon we decided to make a run for it. I didn't want to wait until after dark. It was going to be tricky getting the halftrack turned around on the narrow road, but that worked out and we sped back down the road. Then I realized that the two burned-out tanks were in the way with their guns swung around across the road. We passed under them with inches to spare and ultimately found one of the medium tanks over the next ridge. A tank officer said, "You guys are sure lucky, I thought you were Germans and almost took a shot at you."   We went back to Wellborn's CP and I reported to him, telling him all I knew. He was very surprised to see me; he had forgotten all about us, and he wasn't much interested in what I had to say. Then I headed back towards Alimena.

On the road I met Gara and Tom Crowley. They were more delighted to see me. They said they were on the way up to "pick up the bodies"!

I found the company bivouacked on the other side of Alimena. As we drove up, most of the company was crowded around the kitchen truck having spaghetti for dinner. They greeted us with considerable satisfaction, and just as we were shaking hands with everyone, we heard the scream of artillery shells, and several burst in the company area. A shell fragment hit the large aluminum spaghetti tray and red spaghetti sauce splattered on dozens of men. Several were wounded, but because of the splattered sauce, it took a while to find out who was really hit. Then, over in the woods fifty yards away, I saw Private Fringi lying dead, his mess kit still on his lap, and a hole through his head. He had been sitting against a tree. I remember the name because a year and a half later, when I was company commander, his sister Rose Fringi wrote me a letter. She didn't understand why he was listed as "Private Fringi," because she thought he was "Sergeant Fringi." I had to write to her that Fringi had been AWOL in Oran and had been broken to Private in June. She replied, thanking me, and invited me to come for some of her home-made spaghetti if I was ever in Brooklyn.

I believe that Fred Rutledge had rejoined the company that day. He had been left behind in Algiers (or maybe it was Oran) to take care of the heavy equipment that was scheduled to land in Sicily a week or so after us.

I learned that the company had also had some interesting adventures that day. Somebody had reported seeing soldiers in a ravine in the woods a few hundred yards from Alimena. Murphy and Johnson went to investigate, and ended up taking the surrender of several hundred Italian soldiers. My buddies were all sporting neat little Italian Beretta pistols, but they didn't save one for me!

This letter, my first from Sicily, is dated July 22. If the date is correct, it must have been written the same day, although there is no mention of the bloody events of the day. I suspect I suddenly felt badly that I had not written, and had a sense at that moment that I was not immortal.

July 22

Dear Mother, Dad, and Sis,

Now, stop fussing, I'm OK, just like I said I'd be. This letter won't be much, but it's been so long since I've had any chance at all to write, that I thought I'd just get a note off anyhow.

I'm getting to be a much travelled young man, but I can think of more pleasant ways to travel. Don't know what I can tell you now, so I'll wait till later with the details of my recent experiences. Needless to say, I am once more dirty and grimy & need a shave and haircut.

Finally got a big pile of mail yesterday dating up as far as July 1. It was of course very welcome.

Don't know now whether I sent any of those Tunisian stamps I found home or not. Anyway, I'll send part of them now. I found them in an abandoned house in a little place slightly reminiscent of "Desert Center" between Feriana and Gafsa.

This is all I have time for now. More later.

Much love,

Bill

P.S. Incidentally, it's "1st Lt." Kays now.

At about six o'clock that evening, the 70th Light Tanks attacked once more, but this time Wellborn didn't demand an Engineer escort. I'd like to think it was because he felt badly about using us to draw enemy fire, but it is more likely that he decided these Germans didn't have any mines. The attack evidently carried through and the infantry was soon in the town of Petralia, and the next day turned east toward the town of Gangi and beyond.

We moved the company to the valley on the near side of Gangi, but by a different route.

A day or so later I drove back to where I had my "longest day," when my halftrack had been pinned down in the ravine. A couple of miles before that spot I found a whole line of burned out light tanks, charred bodies still inside. This time the light tanks apparently didn't get away; I don't know what happened to the remainder of the medium tanks. I wondered about my sergeant in the tank that followed me. Some men did seem to get out of the medium tanks when they were hit; nobody got out of the light tanks. I think that was the end of the 70th Light Tank Battalion.

So ended the "battle of Alimena." The war consisted of a few big battles and many little battles. Alimena was one of the littlest of the little, soon forgotten by even the participants. It had cost us perhaps a dozen tanks, the lives of two or three dozen tank crewmen, a few infantrymen, and Private Fringi. The Germans probably lost nobody. In the end we prevailed, but they had bought themselves twenty-four hours of time. The battle was little and was forgotten by most, but not by me. It was still "my battle" because I had played a central, if not very important, role.

Forty years later I went back to Alimena. I met the local parish priest and had a good visit with him. Through an interpreter, a local schoolteacher whose English was almost as non-existent as my Sicilian Italian, he told me that he had been a boy of fifteen in 1943, and had been part of a group of boys holding up a white flag as we entered the town.

But let us go on with the war story. The city of Gangi was on the west side of a steep hill. I recall the thunderous echo of our artillery as the sound bounced off the city on the mountainside.

The whole country was by then much more mountainous than it had been previously, and the one paved road wound through a narrow valley with steep hillsides. George and I went out in a jeep to investigate the possibility of pushing a road through the mountains to the right of the main paved road that led east from Gangi. The 3rd Battalion of the 16th Infantry was dug in a mile or so east of the town and was having difficulty getting supplies forward because the main road was under enemy observation. We stopped at the CP of the 3rd Battalion, and I recall that we talked with Capt. Altomarianas, whom I had known in Africa. ("Alto" was killed a day or so later). It was a quiet morning and we drove right up into infantry positions on the rear side of a steep hill. A sleepy Lieutenant got up out of a foxhole. Nearby were a dozen or so bodies piled like cordwood. They were all black after a day in the hot sun. I'm not even sure whether they were American or German.

We drove back down and through a little valley in order to intersect the main road. As we went across a flat field just before the road, an anti-tank shell screamed by us and exploded against a hillside about a hundred yards to our left. We leaped out of the jeep and ran to the cover of a little orchard. A few minutes later we went back to the jeep and started again. Again, another shell whistled by, and again we ran. At this point we decided to be a little more clever. The jeep driver would run to the jeep, start it up and race up to the road. George and I would go through the orchard and run up and leap into the jeep on the paved road. All went as planned, and I jumped into the jeep on the road. I looked for George. He was still in the orchard picking fruit, for it was a fig orchard. He trotted up to the jeep with a silly grin on his face while I screamed, "For God's sake, George, we have to get the hell out of here." We did.

Although I didn't realize it at the time, the German opposition had suddenly stiffened and the days of rapid movement had come to an end. The road east from Petralia and Gangi led through Nicosia and Troina and on to Mt. Etna in increasingly difficult country. The heaviest fighting in Sicily lay ahead. But I was to miss all of that.

My last letter from Sicily was written either that day or the next.

Sicily July 26

Dear Mother, Dad, and Sis,

They've clarified a bit what I can say so I can use Sicily as my heading. I arrived on July 10 by way of a small boat on a beach, the principle incident being that I stepped off into water up to my waist. My platoon was in reserve so I luckily didn't go ashore until about 0600. However, nobody had much trouble & it was definitely no Dieppe[1] as the Axis would have you believe.

So far this has been nothing like Tunisia. The Ities put up no fight at all, altho the Germans are as mean as ever. Unfortunately we have had to face more Jerries than anyone else. The second day they damn near kicked us off the beach with tanks. The Air Corps has done an excellent job here and the Luftwaffe has been unable to do us much harm. Have seen nothing of the Italian air force.

The welcome by the Italian people is extraordinary. We are much more welcome than in North Africa. When you enter a town everybody claps & offers wine. Some have lived in America & a typical expression is "Da son-of-a-bitch, da Mussolini."

This country is terribly poor and filthy. A peculiar thing is that all the towns are either on top of a mountain, or on the side, like Jerome — never in a valley. All houses are stone and grey in color — probably very old. The country is mountainous with some trees and covered with wild oats. Haven't seen any evergreens yet. We're kept pretty busy with bridge & road work as the Jerries have blown every bridge from here

---

1   Refers to the failed Allied attack on the German-occupied port of Dieppe on the northern coast of France on 19 August 1942.

to kingdom-come and cratered all the mountain roads.

I don't care in the least for amphibious operations but the one redeeming feature is that you get to ride on naval vessels which means good food, especially for the officers who get to eat in the wardroom. Ice in your water and real butter is a treat. One of the ships I was on during a move I believe was fitted out while you were at Norfolk. They said they were fitted out at Norfolk and the name is very familiar. The naval forces in our direct support were commanded by names very familiar to you all. I found an ensign on our ship who was a classmate of mine at Stanford and while aboard I had two showers in his private bathroom & slept once in his classroom.[2]

This is enough for now.

Much love,

Bill

That afternoon I got chills and a 104 degree fever. A number of the men had had the same experience during the preceding couple of days. The next day I was sent to an evacuation hospital, a few miles back near the town of Petralia. By the time I got there I felt fine — a peculiarity of this ailment was that you got chills and a fever every other day. In between, you were fine, so you felt that you were sort of a fraud. On my tag they wrote "FUO" (fever unknown origin). Eventually I found out that I had malaria.

I was in a large tent with rows of cots. On either side of me were battle casualties. During the night the guy on my left began thrashing around and rolled out of his cot, tangling up all the tubes and bottles that were connected to him. The guy on my right lay perfectly still. I yelled for the nurse and she and a doctor came. The doctor said, "I don't worry about these guys who fight it; I'm more worried about those who don't move like that guy over there."

The next day I felt great and was ready to leave. Sometime during that day, or the next, the nurses were all agitated because they said that General Patton had come into one of the ward tents and had slapped a soldier in the face because he didn't see anything wrong with him. Nurses were saying things like, "He better not come into my ward." I think this must have been the famous face-slapping incident that was reported to the columnist Drew Pearson, caused a public uproar, and finally caused Eisenhower to relieve Patton of his command. The story has always been that the soldier was suffering from "shell-shock." I doubt that many soldiers suffered from shell-shock in Sicily; I have always been convinced that it was a malaria case like mine. Patton saw his command succumbing to an unknown illness and went to a hospital to see what was going on.

The following day I was sure they were going to discharge me, but again I got the chills and a worse fever than the one before. When the fever broke, I was drenched in sweat. I had never experienced anything like it.

That night I woke up and heard voices at the other end of the tent. Somebody was telling tales of incredible feats of arms. It sounded like a Congressional Medal of Honor winner, at least. Then the voice sounded familiar - Murphy! He had also come down with the fever. Soon after we were all loaded up into ambulances, and as luck would have it, Murph and I were in the same ambulance. All night the ambulance struggled along

---

2   Surely "classroom" must really be "stateroom"

over bumpy roads. We were going to Palermo, which was now in American hands.

We spent the next day in Palermo sitting on our stretchers in a room in a little building. A doctor came to see us, and after listening to our descriptions of symptoms said that it was undoubtedly malaria, but until lab tests confirmed it, our tags would still say FUO. We received no medication.

Later in the day we boarded a hospital ship - as I recall, we walked aboard. On the ship we were put in three-high bunks, and then finally they took a blood sample. The next day I again got the chills and my temperature soared. I had weird dreams and was pretty much out of my head. A nurse took my temperature and looked startled when she read it. She brought a doctor. It was 106.2 degrees. Then my temperature came down and I was drenched in sweat. A nurse tried to give me a routine bath, but she couldn't dry me off. Later my lab report came back, confirming malaria, and they immediately gave me quinine. That was my last fever attack, at least for that year. It seems significant that Murphy and one other officer and I were the only officers in the company who contracted malaria, and we were also the only ones in the vineyard near the beach on the night of July 11th.

The hospital ship sailed on August 1st for Bizerta in Tunisia. I was taken to a Field Hospital out in the desert somewhere south of Tunis. I don't know where Murphy went. I was put into an officer's ward, a tent, with a dozen others. We had nice hospital beds with white sheets, the weather was superb, and they kept the tent walls rolled up so that it was airy and cheerful.

The next letter is a V-Mail that was sent direct.

Aug. 5, 1943

Dear Mother, Dad, and Sis,

Well, I'm back in Africa again doing my periodic sojourn in a hospital. This time it's malaria. My company commander and another company officer are here with me so I'm by no means alone. I haven't run a temperature in several days, but I don't know how soon they are going to let me out. After 18 days on that damned island this is a nice rest and infinitely better than dodging German shells.

There isn't much news as I was taken sick the same day I wrote the last letter from Sicily. Naturally I haven't received much mail from you lately. You keep talking about wanting a package request. They tell us you don't need them anymore, so how about sending me some cookies.

If you receive this before my letters from Sicily, you're probably in a fog. Well, I'm OK, anyhow.

Love, Bill

Most of the other officers in the ward were infantry battle casualties, all lieutenants. They were very happy to be there and talked continually about going home. I remember one from the 3rd Division, one from the 47th Infantry in the 9th Division, one from the 18th Infantry, and one from the 26th. I do know that the latter two rejoined the Division, and the name of the guy from the 26th, John Simon, is now etched in bronze on the 1st Division memorial monument in Washington, D.C. He was an ROTC graduate of Lafayette College and had just been married a week before he sailed overseas. I think that the guy from the 47th Infantry was killed at St. Lô in Normandy. He was always singing, "Give my regards to Broadway" and was sure he was going home. He proudly displayed a shell fragment that had been dug out of a mean wound in his gut.

Significantly, all of these infantry officers were wounded by either artillery or mortar shells - machine gun wounds were much more rare. You could seldom see the people who were shooting artillery or mortars at you, and this was one of the maddening frustrations of the infantry. I learned a lot about what it was like to be an infantry lieutenant from these guys because we talked all the time. I recall John Simon telling me about what it was like to approach the enemy lines in a night attack. He would have to look at one of his squad sergeants and say "Your squad will lead the platoon tonight" and the poor guy would just look back at him with wide-open eyes, suggesting that he had just received a death sentence.

I remember we had another guy in the ward from Aiken, South Carolina. He seemed to spend half his time ranting about Roosevelt, and especially Mrs. Roosevelt. As far as he was concerned, Roosevelt was worse than Hitler. Roosevelt's sin was that he was "stirring up" the blacks (that wasn't the term he used). The South was very touchy about anybody disturbing its social order. This guy was from the 5th Field Artillery Battalion in my Division. He told us a story of the big German tank attack the day after the Sicily landing. The 5th Field was firing almost point blank at the Germans, and about this time General Roosevelt came by in his jeep. He paused and yelled, "Dog Battery will kill them all!" "Dog" Battery was "D" Battery; ordinarily artillery battalions had only "A", "B", and "C" Batteries, but for some historical reason the 5th Field had a "D" Battery and no "C" Battery. Once more, Teddy Roosevelt got away with this kind of cheerleading.

Every day a Red Cross lady came through our tent with a bag of paperback books, as well as shaving gear and that kind of thing. I did a lot of reading. I recall reading Arrowsmith.

The next three letters are V-Mails that had been photographed. The first is dated June 9, which has to be simply one my frequent errors.

June 9, 1943

Dear Mother, Dad, and Sis,

I got the nurse to clean and fill my pen, as I've been a little worried about how well pencil works with this V-Mail. I'm still in the hospital, but more or less for observation. I think we'll all be out in a couple of days. Then we go through a replacement depot, and I guess eventually start my third crossing of the Mediterranean. It's a funny thing, the night before the invasion the wind came up and the sea was the roughest I've ever seen it. I was on a transport which wasn't so bad, but a lot of the troops were on these little things that look like sub-chasers. Those boats tossed so that at times you could see the keels half way back. Then as we dropped anchor and began to lower the boats the wind died completely. There were an awful lot of sea sick soldiers who landed on that beach. When I came back on the hospital ship we went over the glassiest sea I've ever seen. It was like a lake cruise.

Well, once more space stops me, so

Love to all, Bill

Aug. 16, 1943

Dear Mother, Dad, and Sis,

Since I'm still in the hospital, I'll have to admit that I've been letting you down on the writing situation. The fact is that I'm getting wonderfully lazy. They're keeping me here just for observation now, and I'd just as soon be "observed" for the rest of the war.

I wish I could get some of my mail and find out what you are doing. I guess Sis is back in school again and you are back to your old winter routine. I suppose I'll go back to my old "winter" routine soon too. The summer shows some signs of breaking, and I expect we'll have the demon rain before too long. Sicily would have been a hell of a mess if we had run into any rain.

The food is getting better at the hospital and every third day we get some fresh meat. Also every couple of days we get some kind of pie or cobbler. Between meals we get fruit juice. Not bad?

Love, Bill

Aug. 22

Dear Mother, Dad, and Sis,

I've still been able to keep up enough symptoms to keep me in the hospital, but the doc says I'm about running out. We even had Bob Hope and Francis Langford here the other day. What a racket! I have a few gripes, but the fact that you live longer in a hospital far over-shadows them. The temperature in our tent is only 110o today, but that's endurable. Scarcity of food is universal overseas gripe. I still don't see how we're going to feed an entire army in Europe when we can't even ship over enough to feed this puny little advanced guard! Of course, the fact still remains that if you want to be sure the front line soldier gets a pound of sugar, you've got to send over a hundred pounds so that the rear echelons can get their cut. One officer here says the worst blow to morale in his company was the boat trip to Sicily when his men ate lousy "C" rations and watched the sailors eat cake, pie, and ice cream. The bigwigs are going to learn that the Amer. soldier isn't a machine that goes on forever. Hope it won't be too late.

Love to all,
Bill

This letter touches on a point about overseas supplies that is worth expanding upon. In Tunisia we had an ample cigarette ration, but they were all some brand we had never heard of called Chelsea. Apparently, enough letters home complained about this peculiar phenomenon that some congressmen were alerted. When asked to explain, the War Department said that only three percent of their cigarette purchases were Chelseas. Investigation revealed that each echelon in the supply and other rear-area services picked out the preferred brands (Camels, Lucky Strike, etc.) for themselves, and by the time the remainder got to the front line troops, only Chelseas were left. This problem was actually solved, and fairly quickly, by the expedient of packing the cases of cigarettes with an assortment of cartons of various brands. It was the kind of thing, repeated thousands of times over in various contexts, that not even Eisenhower could solve by issuing direct orders.

Tunisia
Sept. 2, 1943

Dear Mother, Dad, and Sis,

I'm in a replacement depot now awaiting shipment back to the battalion. I got out of the hospital five days ago. I stretched my luck for all it was worth, and finally the doc said I had hospitalitis and threw me out. Life is tolerable here, although the chow is a little short, but I'd rather sit here than make invasions so I'm not trying to expedite things. The only trouble is that I sort of miss my mail.

I ran into a merchant marine officer the other day and after I heard the pay he got I was so mad I couldn't see straight. He gets the same base pay and allowances as I. His base pay doubled because the country is at war. He gets $5.00 per day because he is in the Mediterranean, and the first time a bomb drops within 10 miles (no kidding) of his ship while he's in port, he gets a bonus of $100.00. How in hell do they figure that they have such a dangerous life. We look forward to ship movements because it's a rest with nothing to sweat out.

I'm enclosing a money order that I took out in June and keep forgetting to send. I have three months pay coming so I'll probably send a lot more money soon. Right now I don't know exactly what I'm drawing.

It seems funny for a whole summer to go by without my having any idea what you have been doing. A year ago today I was on the Atlantic, having sailed August 31. I guess now that a year has passed that it is safe to say that I went across on the Queen Elizabeth which is a considerable amount of steamship. She cruises at a mere 30 knots. You'd be appalled at the number of men they cram aboard her.

Well, this is about the end of the line for this conversation. Maybe I can do better when I get my mail.

Love,
Bill

I was now in the 7th Replacement Depot near the town of Ferryville in Tunisia, on my way back to the 1st Division. A tent-mate in the replacement depot was Captain Jimmy Dowd of the 7th Field Artillery Battalion. Dowd was a close friend of T.J. Obrian's, whom I had first heard about from a fellow officer when I was hospitalized in Scotland. Dowd was another of the Harvard ROTC artillerymen, a Boston Irishman who, like Obrian, had little respect for Colonels. He told me all sorts of stories about Obrian as well as tales about Boston politics. I enjoyed Jimmy immensely. He was killed on Omaha Beach, and the story was that Obrian saw Dowd's body on the beach and just about went out of his mind. He ran up and down the beach pushing people to get moving. A tank nearby got hit, and the crew opened the hatch and jumped out. Obrian grabbed the crew members and said, "That tank cost Uncle Sam $30,000, and right now it's worth $30,000,000. Get back in there." Obrian will appear again later in this story.

At the time I wrote the previous letter, the news was full of the impending invasion of mainland Italy. My lack of interest in getting back to the battalion in a hurry was probably related to the thought that the 1st Division might be involved. A few days later the Salerno landing took place. It was soon apparent the 1st Division was not there, but I still wasn't sure whether or not we would be involved as follow-up troops.

The invasion of Italy, following the conquest of Sicily, was again very controversial and for the same reasons. Mainland Italy was probably of less strategic value than Sicily, but the trouble was that Mussolini had been deposed and the Italians wanted to capitulate. Again, it looked like like easy pickings. The idea that the Germans would make a determined stand in Italy was apparently not anticipated. But it is a narrow and mountainous country, relatively easy to defend against an enemy driving up the peninsula.

Getting back to my story, on September 8th we were put aboard a little troop carrier called a landing craft infantry (LCI) and crossed the Mediterranean that afternoon and night. An LCI was about the most unseaworthy ship developed during the war. It was designed to carry about 200 men and land directly on a beach. During the afternoon a storm blew up. I had read stories of the ancient Greeks and the terrible storms they had encountered, but I had always thought this was an exaggeration; the real storms were in the Atlantic and the Pacific. Well, the Med put on a show that afternoon. Looking out a little porthole, I could see the line of LCIs sailing parallel to us; as they pitched up and down I could alternately see their propellers spinning in the air and then the bow and the bottom of the ship half way to the stern. At the same time our little tub was rolling at least sixty degrees from side to side. I had gone to sea with my father on a destroyer when I was very young, and I have never been seasick since; I didn't get seasick that day. But I went down to check on the troops' compartment, and it was a sight to behold. They were all sprawled on bunks and a wave of vomit was flowing back and forth along the deck. I didn't dare step off the bottom rung of the ladder. I had dinner with the three ship's officers in their tiny wardroom, but I didn't eat much.

The ship landed in Palermo harbor on the Northwestern side of Sicily. Jimmy Dowd suggested that we slip away from the group we were with and spend a night in Palermo. He was a Captain, so who was I to object?! He found a hotel and we took a room. But in a little while a woman came to the door and took him away. He appeared the next morning and we caught a ride in a vehicle going to where the 1st Division was camped. For all I knew, the Division wasn't even on the island, but Dowd seemed to know everything.

The next letter was written several days later.

Sept. 14, 1943

Dear Mother, Dad, and Sis,

Got back to the outfit last Wednesday, and was delighted to find everybody had settled down to a more permanent life than we had in Oran last winter. It seems funny to sit down and listen to war reports without creating the news yourself.

Came back to Sicily in a little LCI which literally turned up its nose every time a breath of wind stirred. An artillery captain and myself "went over the hill" in Palermo and had a very enjoyable drunk. We met an officer from the division at a bar and he agreed to take us back with him the next day.

We had a battalion officer's dance recently with nurses from a nearby evacuation hospital. It was the best battalion function we've ever had. We used the very fancy office of the mayor of a nearby town. We had more ice cream, cake, and punch than we could eat. Ice cream freezers are plentiful in this country. All you have to do is supply the ingredients.

Enclosed is a self-explanatory citation of the battalion.

Of course I received a tremendous amount of mail when I got here. I'm glad to see that brownies are on the way. Was glad to hear from Charlie Walker. I wish I'd known he was in Africa earlier as I was in the same city as he in late May. His outfit is in action now. I have a suspicion that his father commands that division which would account for his being in div. hq. co.

Will try to get some Italian stamps soon. Will write at the earliest opportunity. We're pretty busy with routine training & I find myself studying nights.

Love to all,
Bill

If I sound considerably more contented with life in that letter, it's because I was just that. We were not scheduled to go into Italy. In fact the word had gotten around that we were going back to England. That could only mean we were going to be involved in the cross-channel operation that the papers were all talking about, but it was now apparent that it couldn't happen before the spring of 1944, eight or nine months off. When you live from day to day, eight or nine months seem like forever.

We were bivouacked on the south coast of Sicily near a miserable little town called Palma di Montechiaro. The town was "off-limits," so there wasn't much to do. The dance referred to took place in Licata, a few miles to the east of us. Licata was to be the scene of the famous book by John Hersey, "A Bell for Adano," and in fact the local American officer featured in the story, the Town Major, probably attended our party.

Forty years later I visited Palma di Montechiaro and instead of what I had recalled as a small village I found a veritable metropolis with high-rise buildings, traffic lights, and traffic jams.

Charlie Walker had been my sophomore roommate at Stanford. He (and his father) were in the 36th Division, which at that moment was having a tough time at Salerno, Italy. His father was the division commander, as I had thought.

I found that some changes in the Division had taken place during my absence. They had been involved in heavy fighting soon after I left, as the Germans made a major stand at the town of Troina. After a couple of weeks, heavy casualties and malaria losses had so weakened the Division that it was pulled out of the line. Generals Allen and Roosevelt had been relieved of command by Patton, and the new CO was a very hard-nosed disciplinarian, General Huebner (Patton thought we lacked discipline – but we just didn't like Patton). Terry Allen went back to the States to command the 104th Infantry Division and a year and a half later brought a very effective division into battle. Teddy Roosevelt became Assistant Division Commander of the 4th Infantry Division and died in Normandy.

Huebner found the Division way under-strength and apparently prevailed upon Patton to give him replacements immediately so that he could get back into the fight. Generals are always eager that way. Patton used a trick that we would see again, over a year later - he simply ordered all the rear area service units in his army to produce so many warm bodies. So, of course, we got all the goofballs and misfits in the army, including some officers. I don't think we ever completely recovered from that infusion of replacements.

The Division was out of the fighting for a week after Huebner took over. He apparently ordered training to start immediately and had the infantry out doing rifle practice. The rifle was probably the most useless weapon of all in Sicily, but Huebner had some notion left over from World War I that being good rifle marksmen was a key to success.

Rutledge had run the company while Murphy was away, but Murph had evidently returned just before I had. When I returned, I found there had been some changes in the officer assignments. Fred Rutledge had been moved to "B" Company as Executive Officer, Bill Barnum had become our Exec, and Bob Conant had taken over the 2nd Platoon. (I think Phil Suna had been running my platoon while I was away.)

Sept 26

Dear Mother, Dad, and Sis,

Sorry I haven't written much lately, but they keep us pretty busy during the day, and at night it is difficult to write. I haven't received much mail from anybody for quite some time. The mail service is very poor, but I guess there are a lot of people more important than us at present.

Life has been very comfortable of late. I guess I told you last time about all the ice cream & what not we get now and then. Al Jolson was here recently, and tonight Jack Benny will entertain. Every night there are four different movies throughout the division and if you have transportation you can take your choice. They're all old, but they can be pretty old before we've seen them.

The Italian post offices are not open at present, so we'll have to sweat out the stamps for awhile.

Well, that's about all the news there is. So long, & I'll try to write soon.

Love to all,
Bill

Oct 6
Sicily

Dear Mother, Dad, & Sis,

Tomorrow I have to take the men on a three day pass to Palermo, so I thought I'd better write now, or I won't be able to for the next few days. It will be nice for the men as they haven't been to a city since they were in Algiers before the invasion. Palermo is quite a modern city, which can't be said for the rest of Sicily.

Had a rain storm the other day, which gave indications of things to come. This place is going to be quite a mud hole. It's cool now & summer is definitely over.

Mail is still very slow and your letters come in such odd order that it is difficult to carry on any kind of conversation. You mentioned the pictures in the August 2 Life. We finally got it. No, the picture in Gela isn't me. At the time that picture was taken I was several miles up the beach on the right flank of the division. I didn't get into Gela until three days later when the Germans withdrew. The picture might just as well be me for I was dressed like that and dead Italians & Germans are no novelty. If you will notice the picture of the tank attack, the tanks are heading towards where I was. I remember about that time I was beginning to sweat out where I was going to move if they got any closer. Two officers in my company were out there under a culvert and the tanks passed over them. I understand there is a later Life with pictures of my co. commander and some men from my platoon removing mines. That was about the time I got malaria.

Life goes on as usual, which isn't bad. I sure wish those cookies you sent would hurry up. My mouth's watering. Cookies are about the only thing I need. I don't have room enough to carry anything else.

That seems to be about all for now. I'll try to get some postcards in Palermo.

Love to all,

Bill

Sicily
Oct. 14, 1943

Dear Mother, Dad, & Sis,

Been raining a great deal lately and it is beginning to get cold. Life is much the same, but going a little slower due to rain.

Have received a couple of letters in the last couple of weeks. Nothing very recent, however.

My trip to Palermo was quite successful. I had plenty of spaghetti, and even got a little steak. Also got a shave, haircut, and shoeshine. I was really pretty spiffy. I did some shopping at the PX and in town. Bought myself a $32.00 trench-coat which will serve as a raincoat and an overcoat. It has a hood which fits right over my helmet and a heavy wool liner which may be taken out. Really an all-around coat for the field. I got some little things for Sis & Noma for Xmas. I've mailed them & only hope they get there. I found a good stamp place and bought some new German stamps and a book of 250 different Italian stamps. I'm enclosing the German ones. Sis, you can divide these stamps between our collections, but I wouldn't break sets. I'll send the Italian ones later and you can do the same with them. We won't have spaces for most of these stamps because they are new.

The Aug. 30 Life just arrived with pictures of the 1st Division. I wish you would cut out & save the three pictures at the top of page 26. They show several of my men and my company commander removing mines near Nicosia. The picture was taken the day after I went to the hospital, or else I probably would have been in it.

How do you like our new writing paper? Our map section turned it out. That's the battalion insignia which you wear on your shoulder straps. I don't have any. Wish I could get a pair.

That's about all the news for the present.

Love to all,

Bill

In Palermo, I ran across Ensign Bob Hinze, my Stanford classmate, again. Bob said he knew a place where we could have a dinner with a real waiter and a white tablecloth. We went to a little hotel near the edge of the city, and although there were few people there (maybe three!), we did have a white tablecloth. We ordered the "steak" mentioned in the letter. It was without question the toughest little piece of leather that I have ever encountered. It was simply not possible to cut it. Well, it didn't cost much.

Sicily
Oct. 19, 1943

Dear Mother, Dad, & Sis,

I've been doing much celebrating lately. I received a box of brownies and a box of Hershey chocolate. All the officers in the battalion have been mobbing me. The brownies had a little mold on some of them, but when you haven't had brownies for eight months a little mold doesn't bother you. Thanks a lot for both.

I don't believe I told you I received the knife. I bought one at the PX in ————- so I'll keep yours until I lose this one. I believe I've had and lost two others since I first asked you for one.

I got a V-Mail yesterday dated Oct. 4 which gets me a little up to date. I gather from the text of it that I am missing some mail that should have come before it.

If I can find an envelope I think I'll send the rest of the stamps presently. I'm keeping my fingers crossed till they get there.

No more news, so I'll close.
Love to all,
Bill

Incredibly, the word "Palermo" has been neatly removed from that letter. The letter is in ink, so some kind of very effective ink remover was used.

That was my last letter from Sicily. On October 23rd we loaded onto trucks and were taken to Port Augusta on the east coast of the island. There we boarded a Cunard liner, the Stirling Castle, for Algiers. The Stirling Castle had come from Cairo and was returning a group of American engineers to the U.S. from the Middle East. We became very excited. But, at a dock in Algiers, we changed ships to another British transport, the Franconia. This ship was going to England! We then joined a convoy for the trip to Liverpool, which took about eight days.

During the short trip from Palermo to Algiers I developed the same wheezing and associated chest troubles that had plagued me onboard ship before. Now I had the clue — I was apparently allergic to something used in the mattresses on British troop ships. I remembered that I had even had some of this trouble on the Queen Elizabeth, so this was the fourth time it had hit me. On the Franconia I got rid of the mattress and used some blankets for a mattress, and the trouble gradually disappeared.

The trip was uneventful, except that we had Division Headquarters onboard, which always produced a certain amount of what was known in the army as "chicken shit." General Huebner dreamed up some kind of contest for the junior officers involving giving speeches on leadership, or some such subject. I think Barnum actually won the contest, or some part of it. Nobody even asked me to participate, which was just as well. We arrived in Liverpool on about the 4th or 5th of November.

The preliminaries were over; the big show was about to start.

Oran, November 1942; One of our armored halftrack vehicles identical to the one I used at Alimena, Sicily.

Palma di Montechiara, Sicily, September 1943; We drink a toast to Len Cohn who has been chosen to go home. Left to right: Kays, Gara, Rudolph, Barnum, Cohn, Gregg, Crowley, and Stowell.

Palma di Montechiara, Sicily, August 1943; Bill Barnum and Fred Rutledge

CHAPTER SEVEN

ENGLAND

NOVEMBER 5, 1943 – JUNE 3, 1944

We disembarked from the ship at Liverpool in the evening of November 5th and immediately boarded a train. I had a miserable dripping cold, so I don't remember much about the trip except that we detrained around one or two o'clock in the morning in the city of Axminster, in Dorset. Trucks met us and took my company, "A," to the little town of Charmouth, on the coast a few miles east of Lyme Regis.

I remember Murphy talking to the officer who was in charge of the arrangements. Murph kept talking about "tomorrow" and I wasn't clear whether "tomorrow" meant "today" or the next day.

"A" Company had Charmouth all to itself, and it was the perfect size in which to billet a company. The men were scattered about the town, one platoon in a small hotel, another in a church hall, a third in Nissen (Quonset) huts. Company headquarters was above some garages behind the Coach and Horses Inn. The kitchen and a mess hall were in Nissen huts, and the motor pool was in a large commercial garage. The officers were billeted in a two-story cottage called "The Haven." I roomed with Ed Sherburne, a new officer who had joined us in Sicily. We settled down for the night at about 3:00 a.m. Amazingly, I awoke a few hours later with my cold virtually gone. It was probably hay fever.

The Division was spread out along the coast from Lyme Regis in the west to Bournemouth in the east. Our battalion headquarters was in Blandford, near Division headquarters and a long distance from us, a fact that didn't distress us in the least. The 16th Infantry Regiment was in our sector, with the 1st Battalion just over the hill in Lyme Regis, and the 2nd Battalion in Bridport, a couple miles to the east.

England
Monday, Nov. 8

Dear Mother, Dad, & Sis,

This letter will probably be of especial interest to you if for nothing more than the address that you see in the upper right hand corner. Yes, I'm once more in England. I'll reserve my feelings about the whole thing. It was just a year ago that I was tearing my hair to get to Africa and get away from this damp cold place. So here I am right back where I started from.

I got a nice pile of mail today including one from Sis from Carmel dated Oct. 27, so apparently mail service is going to be pretty good. I'm really sweating out all these cookies you speak of. I hope they don't get all tangled up in North Africa or Sicily. I'll have to write Bob Dieckerhoff and see if I can contact him, altho I think he is quite a ways from here.

We are billeted in a little village, and for the time being life is going to be rather interesting and unusual. We officers are in a very attractive house complete with lawns and roses and elderly neighbors. We spend the day talking to old ladies and petting their cocker spaniels. The village parson came over to welcome us today and I'm sweating out having to have tea with him soon. We've made arrangements with the proprietor of one of the three local inns to reserve the officers a back room and to set aside one bottle of scotch a week for us. As soon as I finish this letter I think I'll drop down for a glass of beer before going to bed. Our principle problem is of course heat. Right now four of us are huddled in the smallest room in the house trying to nurse along a miserable little fire which refuses to survive on this awful British coal. We've given up trying to have hot water because the water heater is coal fired.

I hope to get a little leave before too long and spend a little time in London. I didn't have much time there last time.

I still haven't sent those Italian stamps. I tried it once & they came back because they were improperly addressed.

Well, this is enough for now. I'll write soon.

Lots of love,
Bill

Before we left Sicily, Fred Rutledge was transferred to "B" Company to become Executive Officer, and Bill Barnum replaced him as our Exec. I think that Ed Sherburne took over Barney's 2nd Platoon at that time. Soon after we settled down in Charmouth, invitations began to arrive for "Captain Murphy and his 2 ic[1]" to come for tea, dinner, etc. As a result, Murph and Barney got all the social attention for awhile.

Down the little alley on which "The Haven" was situated, and across the street, there was a duplex house. In one of houses lived Joan Everett with her little daughter, Anna. In the other was Phyllis (I don't recall her last name). Joan's husband was in the army in the Middle East somewhere, and Phyllis' husband had just recently been killed at Salerno. She was initially very resentful of Americans because she felt that American ineptitude had led to her husband's death. Murph very soon laid a claim to Joan, and Barnum did the same with Phyllis. The result was that both Murph and Barney spent most of their evenings at the duplex. None of the rest of us officers had any kind of social life at all, until I finally became more active in the spring (more on that later). I really don't know why I was so backward at that time, but I just couldn't generate any interest in women. As a later letter reveals, we certainly had opportunities! The enlisted men, on the other hand, had a ball. Charmouth was full of unattached women, as were the nearby villages. There were virtually no men in the age range fifteen to sixty, but many young women, especially those with small children, had moved to

---

1   2nd in command

Charmouth to get out of the big cities and the bombs. The company assembled before the 1st Sergeant each morning at about seven o'clock, long before daylight. The 1st Sergeant, William Wood, took a report from each of the platoon sergeants, and I remember that it was so dark he used a flashlight to record the reports. It was a long time before I realized that the morning reports were largely phony, and that a substantial proportion of the company was not there.

We were ordered to engage in intensive and continuous training, and each week we had to submit to battalion headquarters our training schedule. The training was left up to the companies and at that time the basic training unit was the platoon. As a result the platoon commanders had a vested interest in the training schedule. Soon, it was the three platoon commanders, Johnson, Sherburne, and me, who were doing all the planning as well as the implementation of the training schedule. One very irksome thing was the necessity to prepare a "rainy day schedule," i.e., something useful we could do indoors. One runs out of ideas quickly, but in England a rainy day schedule was one that had a high probability of being implemented. I remember sitting in company headquarters nights working on the schedule. Since we spent all day carrying out the training schedule we were exhausted by evening. Also, we had to have an officer of the day (OD) at company headquarters each night, and the platoon commanders caught that duty. Our only alternative was to persuade Murphy and Barnum to do the planning, but since they didn't have to carry out the plan, we felt we were better off doing it ourselves. In the meantime Murph and Barney spent the evenings with their friends. This probably explains why the three of us (Johnson, Sherburne, and me) had almost no social life during those first few months, and also why I didn't apply for leave to London during this period.

The next correspondence is a V-Mail letter.

Nov. 14, 1943

Dear Mother, Dad, & Sis,

I wrote you a letter several days ago but couldn't send it as they have suddenly clamped down on censorship regulations. I'll send it as soon as I can. The long gap has been due to a little moving, but I can't tell you where I am.

I've received a great deal of mail, some dated as late as Oct. 27. I've got packages from Liz, Amy, Cousin Elsa, and Aunt Lucile, and now I wish you would send me their addresses (except Liz's) because I burned up all the wrappings before I thought. I'm still sweating out your 45 pounds of cookies.

When they've decided that they are no longer fooling (?) the enemy I'll let you know where I am, and my letters ought to be a bit more interesting. Until then they will have to be just like this.

Love to all,
Bill

Liz and Amy were my mother's sisters, my aunts. Cousin Elsa was my mother's cousin, and Aunt Lucile was my father's sister.

Nov. 23, 1943

Dear Mother, Dad, & Sis,

I'm still "somewhere" and therefore not particularly interested in writing letters as you've probably found out. I've been getting an occasional letter from you all, but apparently not all of them. And still no cookies, which I can't figure out, because I got a mess of Christmas packages from all the rest of my relatives. Everybody's getting packages & we've set up a snack bar in the living room. I think I'm getting gypped because I have more than anyone else at this moment. Aunt Lucile sent me a wonderful box of cookies which I should have hid, because they lasted just one day. Also Liz's "Mounds" were much too popular. However if I have 30 lbs on the way I imagine I'll make out.

Thanksgiving is day after tomorrow. We're all sweating out turkey. I remember just a year ago we were eating Thanksgiving dinner in a ship in Liverpool harbor. An awful lot of water has passed under the bridge since that time.

I hope to see Bob D. soon. I haven't written him yet, but intend to.

Did I tell you that I received the subscription to "Time," for which many thanks. It is only about two weeks old when it gets here.

I can't figure this mail situation out. I got a Nov. 1st Sporting Green the other day which is later than any letter I've received except a Nov. 5 "V-Mail".

Well, that's about all for now.

Love to all,

Bill

P.S. Send me some homemade wool socks & also some more cookies of any description. I have a terrific appetite for some reason.

Bob D. (Bob Dieckerhoff) was my second cousin, son of Cousin Elsa. He was a photography officer with the Air Force. As it turned out I never did make contact with him.

That letter, like many others, has the stamp mark of the Berkeley post office, and an initial over the P.S. Apparently my mother had to produce a "request" in order to send a package.

The next letter is a Christmas card with our battalion crest on it.

Dec. 2

Dear Mother, Dad, & Sis,

Just received sweater, socks, and "play kit." They are all swell - thanks loads. (Hope you don't mind my opening them before Christmas.)

Don't worry about me for Xmas day. It won't be like last year when I had "corned willy" and had to look at the calendar to tell what day it was. We are all going to dinner (barring accidents such as OD) with some British "army widows," and we ought to definitely know it's Xmas. We got a ration of 1 qt. of Scotch which we'll take along as our contribution to the day. You feel so guilty when you go to dinner with these people, but they're so nice you can't refuse. I've been out to dinner twice, and it's sure a thrill to sit on a sofa before a fire with your feet on a soft rug.

Many thanks again.

Merry Xmas,

Bill

Curiously, the next letter is written on Ft. Leonard Wood stationary. The paper must have been in my footlocker. We had brought footlockers to England in 1942, but they were stored when we went to Africa. When we returned to England we got them back. They contained our dress uniforms, among other things, so we could socialize in some kind of style.

Sometime in December the officers of the Division were assembled and addressed by the corps commander. We were now in the 7th Corps and we got the message that the initial assault on the continent was going to be made by the 5th Corps. In other words, we were going to come into France after somebody else had secured the beachhead. This was the kind of news I liked to hear. My anxiety about the coming invasion diminished.

Dec. 19, 1943
Sunday afternoon

Dear Mother, Dad, & Sis,

First, I must apologize for not having written for so long. I don't know exactly why I've taken so long other than the fact that I'm in such a rut of work that when I do have the time I'm so tired my only interest is going to bed. The colonel is insisting that I take some leave so I think I will go to London for a week sometime in January. I promise to catch up on my letter writing at that time, and also my sleep. Everybody who has taken leave so far has come back in greatly improved spirits, so maybe it's a good idea. However, when I think about what lies ahead, it'll take a great deal to improve my spirits. Well, I'm laying my money on Gen. Arnold, because if he fails none of us are going to need any money.

I gather from your letters that the face-slapping incident made quite a splurge in the home papers. You say you'll reserve judgment until you know more of the facts. I hope someday to be able to tell you those facts because you & the papers don't know the half of it. What a ridiculous old idiot!

Boy, what a pile of cookies I have now. Up on the shelf is a big box of cookies from Mrs. Morrison which my company commander is now digging into with much relish. In reserve I have a large box from you which I haven't investigated fully. Also two large cans of cookies from Amy, and a box from Sister's friend, Alison Lindh.

Getting up for 7:00 breakfast is getting to be quite an ordeal here. It doesn't even begin to get light until 8:15 or 8:30. Usually the ground is frozen and all the puddles are frozen over. The only time it warms up is in order to rain. They say that once in a while they have a white Christmas here, but not often.

About the only mail I've been receiving lately has been V-Mails, Dec. 2 being the latest.

I do wish I could be home some weekend when Eddy & everyone is there. It really sounds like old times.

I've been about three hours writing this letter. About every two minutes I'm interrupted by any number of people. My room is the only one with a decent fireplace, so it is a very popular meeting place.

I hope you got the Christmas card before Christmas. I'll be thinking about you all. I hope I receive a letter sometime soon telling me something of your plans for the day. I told you that I was going out to dinner.

Well, that's about all for now -- cherrio (as the British say).
Love to all,
Bill

General Arnold was the commander of the 8th Air Force and was going to finish off the war by bombing Hitler back into the Stone Age!

Thurs. night
Dec. 23

Dear Mother, Dad, & Sis,
(and everyone else who reads these letters -- there seems to be plenty of them)
    Well, mail finally began to come in today, so I'm in a very good writing mood. Letters were dated Oct. 30 to Nov. 3, and V-Mails -- up to Dec. 3. The V-Mails are much quicker, but I still like to get ordinary straight mail. How about you? On Dec. 3 you still had no word from me in England, so the b------- apparently held up our mail when we first got here. So if you want to hear from me more regularly you'd better write to your congressmen. After the big stink they raised last month, I'm all for congressmen.
    Christmas is just around the corner and I must say Christmas is a little more Christmassy than in Oran. As I remember I was OD Christmas eve and Darlan got assassinated & it was pouring rain and we had "corned willy" for dinner and in general it was anything but Christmas. Here we have such things as little brats singing carols and we have a tree and we've borrowed ornaments and we've got candy for all the kids in town. We're going to a party Christmas night, two more on Sunday, and one Monday night, so there will be plenty going on. All the women in town think we officers are very unsocial, so they are trying to draw us out, I believe. What I gather is that the various widows are trying to outdo each other entertaining us. I get along very well with the older British but the younger ones get in my hair at times -- especially these widows. They can't understand why we don't take them out every night, and they aren't the least bit reserved about telling you so.
    Glad you received the stamps. But it reminds me that I still haven't sent this tremendous bunch of Italian stamps that I got in Palermo. Maybe I can get them fixed up this weekend. (Oh yeah)
    Got your Thanksgiving "round-robin" letter and enjoyed it very much. "Round-robin" letters are always lots of fun to read. I've also been getting thousands of "Sporting Greens" which keep me well up to date on the sports world. They also have another important use. When we build a coal fire in my room we've found that it's necessary to hold something over the front of the fireplace to induce a draft in order to make this miserable British coal start burning. We've discovered that the S.F. Chronicle Sporting Green is infinitely superior to the London Times or the Daily Mail because the latter catch fire too easily.
    I still haven't written Bob D. for which I feel very badly, but I'll surely do so before I go on leave, because I want to get his telephone number & maybe we can have a spree together in the big city. Everybody back from London on leave has had a great time, altho they've spent one hell of a lot of money. They say it costs twelve shillings

to see a movie.

I'm now living in a wonderland of cookies and what not and I feel like an awful heel for not having thanked anyone as yet. Your packages have been arriving very regularly, and Liz seems to be competing with you to see who can send the most. Right now we are working on two large cans of cookies from Amy. I'm afraid I'm going to forget who sent me what.

I've spent all evening writing this. As usual the mob is in here and between sentences we've been having violent discussions & arguments about things that were done wrong at Gela, reaching no conclusions -- you seldom do when you discuss battles. It's like an automobile accident -- everyone has a different version of what happened, and therefore different ideas. Battles are intensely interesting things after it's all over and enough time has elapsed for the shock to wear off. I've been reading some campaign studies on the British battles in Libya, and when you can really visualize how each man felt & what it looked like, it's much more interesting than it was when I had to rely upon my imagination only to picture the scene. Well, so much for tonight.

Love to all,
Bill

Obviously our social life was improving. I don't recall four Christmas parties, but I do recall two. The first was given by a woman who was French, or at any rate had some kind of French connection. Her name was Yvonne. I think Murph had played tennis with her sometime in the previous two months. She was definitely intent on putting on the premier party in town. It may have been on Christmas Eve. The trouble was, I had one of my lousy colds, so I didn't have much fun. It was a large party and included some British military people from out of town. The thing I remember most was that we played "charades." I found it frustrating as it was not a game that translated easily between cultures.

The other party I recall was definitely on Christmas night. It was put on by a Mrs. Battisil (I'm not sure of the spelling; we referred to her as Mrs. Basingstoke). She was a middle-aged lady and had two grown daughters, for whom the party was apparently arranged. Everybody got very drunk. At one point Mrs. Battisil came running into the room and said, "I've just been sitting on Lt. Johnson's lap!" On another occasion, Yvonne (yes, she was there) came over and gave me a gratuitous kiss. There was also a young lady there named Pat Baker. She lived across the street, and had brought her fifteen months old baby boy, Alvin, to the party. Ultimately somebody had to escort Pat home, with the baby pram, and George Johnson did the honors. I hadn't paid much attention to Pat, but I definitely noticed her.

Mrs. Battisil, and Pat Baker, lived on Upper Sea Lane, which was more or less parallel to our street, Lower Sea Lane. In fact Charmouth had only two streets besides the High Street. High Street ran parallel to the sea and was the main highway. Upper and Lower Sea Lanes ran perpendicular and connected High Street to the beach and the cliffs, for Charmouth was on the side of a valley. The River Char ran along the lower side of the town. Lower Sea Lane ran near the little river and Upper Sea Lane was farther up the hill. The other side of the valley, the east side, was all meadows separated by hedgerows.

Coming home that night George and I tried to take a short cut through some fields and backyards rather than go over to High Street and then down the hill to Lower Sea Lane. George got all tangled up in barbed wire as we attempted to negotiate a fence. I practically had to carry him home.

Monday night, Jan. 3

Dear Mother, Dad, & Sis,

Three "V-Mails" today dated Dec. 14,16,16, so I'm inspired to write a letter altho it is way past my bedtime. I can't remember what I said in my last letter, but I hope I've written since Christmas and told you all about it. It was a pleasant, if un-sober, day, and night.

New Years was very uneventful. I went to bed fairly early after a couple of beers. Slept most of New Years day, and also all yesterday morning. Yesterday afternoon five of us went up to Col. Pass' place again to play squash, drink tea, and sit in front of the fire, -- all very reminiscent of many a Sunday afternoon I have spent in the past. These people have a very nice and palatial estate in the country a couple of miles from here, and we have a standing Sunday afternoon invitation. There are always some British officers of one type or another, and we always have a swell time. They also have horses and grooms and that sort of thing and one of the fellows went riding with the eldest daughter instead of playing squash.

I'm sure I've received everything you've sent, because packages have ceased arriving and I have knives and socks and jam and play kits and all sorts of things which I won't attempt to enumerate. Thanks loads for everything.

I remember last year at New Years I wrote a recapitulation of the year adding that it had been the most eventful year of my life. Little did I know what lay ahead at that time. Little did I know that within 29 days I'd be on the front lines in Tunisia and would be there until the 7th of May. Golly, Tunisia seems like the Dark Ages now. We never realized what a thin edge we were on, but we knew it was the beginning of a long road. The campaign dragged so that it looked at times like a hopelessly long road. Then there were the gloomy days in Oran and Algiers, when, still tired from Tunisia, we were furiously preparing for an invasion of somewhere. We had a pretty good idea where, but not until all the women at the bars assured us were we sure. No wonder all the Italians greeted us with, "What's been holding you up, we've been waiting for you?" We weren't too happy about the whole thing at that time, and I guess my letters reflected it. I remember the horrible sweat I worked up reaching a climax on the morning of July 10. I remember looking at the cruisers with us and wondering how many friends were aboard. This was a holiday for them, they said, and would be lots of fun. It didn't look like much fun to us. The first sight of Sicily was a terrific sheet of AA fire going up on the horizon about 10:30 pm. The Air Corps was giving them a last minute going over. Later the AA went up again & we knew that our paratroops were in there. Next overhead clusters of amber flares appeared and we knew the Luftwaffe was on the prowl. We'd seen too many of them at El Guettar. Every man feels like the whole German air force is looking at him alone. Being in reserve, I stood at the rail and watched the first waves land. The whole coast lit up with searchlights. Then here & there were machine gun tracers -- they didn't last long. A battery of artillery opened up at one point and some searchlights stayed on while others went out. The cruisers took them under fire and I watched a cruiser lay three shells right in on a searchlight from what must have been 12 miles range. The shells looked like slow moving stars. For the next several hours there was nothing interesting except continual flashes of enemy artillery landing all along the beach and a couple of large explosions in the town. About dawn I started down a landing net and commenced the long trip in. As it got light I realized we were much farther out to sea than I had thought and what a defenseless target our little boat was for strafing, but no planes appeared. As a matter of fact, the first German planes I saw were a couple of ME's at about 0930 which were merely looking around and doing a little annoying strafing to boot. They made quick work of a couple of Navy observation planes from the cruisers, and then disappeared. As I landed on the beach they conveniently moved the artillery inland a few hundred yards, so we didn't even have that to sweat out. On the whole D-day ran off very smoothly with everything going ahead of schedule, after the initial waves had overcome the beach defenses so easily. Towards town they had considerably more trouble with heavier casualties, but by afternoon everything was under control. It had almost seemed too easy. The next day wasn't easy, but you've read all about that. During the Sicilian campaign some of the going was easy and some was a tough as anything I ever hope to see. The enemy was fighting a rearguard action after the first week, and there was never any doubt of the outcome, but a withdrawing enemy can make you pay a terrible bloody price for every mile, and there's no place better for defense than a rugged mountain country where you can't even get jeeps very far off the roads because the valleys & canyons are so steep. Incidentally, along about the second week I had one of the most harrowing experiences I ever hope to live through, but it's too long a story to tell here. In fact by all the laws of warfare, I had no right under the sun to live thru it.

Well, you've complained that I never give you any battle details, -- was that any better? I hope I won't have many more details to give you, but I'm afraid we've only begun. Maybe not.

I don't think another sheet will go without excess postage, so cherrio -- as the British say,

Love to all,
Bill

I had hoped I had written since Christmas, but I obviously had not.

Col. Pass was a retired British military officer and one of the landowners of the neighborhood surrounding Charmouth, with an elegant manor house.

Friday night
Jan. 7, 1944

Dear Mother, Dad, & Sis,

I got your Christmas letter yesterday, and it came through so quick that I just had to sit down and answer it. Incidentally, I received at the same time a Dec. 23 'V-Mail', so the airmail letters are now apparently actually going airmail.

I can't tell you how much I enjoyed your swell letter. Those 'round-robin' letters are always lots of fun. It seems funny to hear so soon what you were doing, because it seems just a few days ago that it was Christmas and I was periodically looking at my watch, subtracting 8, and visualizing you all. I wasn't quite sure what you were doing, but I figured you'd get together with the Manners in some way or other. I sure would have liked to have been there. The picture of a big family sitting around a table with someone carving a turkey is just about my idea of the most wonderful thing in the world.

My leave is fairly definitely set to commence on the 13th for one week. I haven't yet had an answer from Bob, but it sure will be swell if I can see him. They say you do just about everything in London (if you have the price), and the Red Cross officer's clubs are supposed to be very good. I don't know exactly what I'm going to do there, except I'm definitely going to get my picture taken. Maybe I'll do some stamping. Some guys spend all their time either on or sobering up from wild parties, and others take in the sights and the theater, etc. I think I'll see "Arsenic & Old Lace" if it's still playing.

Hope you have read "The Battle is the Payoff" by Ralph Ingersoll. The names are fictitious, but you ought to be able to recognize me in it. As a matter of fact he didn't mention me by name. Golly, we didn't know what a real fight was when he was with us. It was too bad he couldn't have stayed with us just a week longer. He's in London now, and I'd like to see him if I can.

Well, I haven't enough to say to start another sheet so this will have to suffice. Oh, incidentally, thanks for the subscription to Readers Digest. Also, my Times seem to be coming thru very nicely.

Love to all,
Bill

As previously mentioned, Ralph Ingersoll stayed with us for several days and participated in our operations as an observer in Tunisia the previous March.

On Thursday, January 13th, I took the train from Axminster to Waterloo station, about a two hour trip. The next letter is on American Red Cross stationery.

London
Friday, January 14

Dear Mother, Dad, & Sis,

Well, here I am on my first leave. I got here yesterday, and will leave next Wednesday afternoon. Boy, what a life! Not a worry in the world for six days. I'm staying at a Red Cross officer's club and it's really swell. I have a soft bed with sheets, good food, and plenty of people to tell me where to go and what to do. Yesterday I took in a movie and last night went to a dance at the women's officer's club (nurses & wacs) Slept most of this morning, got a haircut and since then I've been shopping and getting my picture taken and whatnot. I have a ticket to "Arsenic & Old Lace" for tonight and I'm soon going to start out and find the theater. If this venture proves interesting, I'm going to see some other plays as this city is full of them. I don't know what else I'm going to do. I guess I'll just let each day take care of itself. I'm really getting to "know" London (with the aid of a good map). As near as I can tell everything centers around Piccadilly Circus and distances aren't as far as in New York for instance. Everything of interest is within walking distance of this club which is on New Bond Street, but I'm going to try and figure out the subway and bus system and move around a little more. Taxis are abundant & cheap in the day-time, but are difficult to get ahold of at night. Most prices are sky-high due principally to the American soldiers' bulging pocket-book. The city is overrun with Americans, most of them being aircorps. Some have just finished their 25 missions and are just waiting around to go home.

The weather is beautiful and clear and much warmer than where we live. I'm not even wearing my overcoat.

I think I'd better run now because I want to scout out a place to eat after the show. You can't find anything after blackout. I think I'll probably eat at the Savoy Hotel.

Much love to all
Bill

I evidently accomplished a great deal during my first twenty-four hours in London, and even got to "know" London!

I still have the playbill for "Arsenic and Old Lace." It was at the Strand Theater. I recall going to the women's club because there was a pea-soup fog and a friend (it may have been Tom Crowley, whom I ran into in London) and I tried to cut across Berkeley Square, getting all tangled up in trenches and anti-aircraft stuff.

I don't know why I said that the Red Cross club was on New Bond Street. It was actually on a little street, Heddon Street, just west of Regent Street.

The statement that I was going to have dinner at the Savoy Hotel amuses me now. I did in fact go there, but when I stepped inside I saw people in evening dress, and I lost my courage and backed out.

Tom Crowley and I went to the European Theater of Operations, United States Army (ETOUSA) Headquarters on Grosvenor Square and looked up old Col. Fechet, who had now recovered and was on duty there. He invited us out to dinner and a show. He took us to Choy's Chinese Restaurant in Soho because he said it was the only place where we could get enough to eat (at that time they had a five-shilling limit on dinners in London). At Choy's, Fechet ordered various Chinese dishes until the waiter reminded him that he had reached the five-shilling limit (or fifteen-shillings, for the three of us). Fechet nodded and went on. We ate well. Fechet then proceeded to re-fight the battle of El Guettar using salt and pepper shakers to mark positions on the table cloth. I remember he said that Tom Wells was a "tower of strength." I was puzzled; I couldn't imagine Col. Wells being a "tower of strength" to anybody.

He took us to see a musical, "Strike a New Note," at the Prince of Wales, with the comedian, Sid Fields. I loved this show so much that I went back to see it again when I was in London for my next leave. It had a singer, Zoe Gail, whom I was very much taken with. The hit of the show was a song she sang, "I'm going to get lit up when the lights go on in London –." The audience was almost one hundred percent American.

On the back of the playbill is written the notice:

If an Air Raid Warning be received during the performance the audience will be informed. The warning will not necessarily mean that a raid will take place. Those desiring to leave the Theatre may do so, but the performance will continue.

During this period the Germans were mounting what came to be known as the "Little Blitz" – "little" as compared to the big blitz during the winter of 1940-41. About fifty or sixty planes a night were raiding London, but London is so large that a raid of that size in one part of the city did not cause the other parts of the city to close down. I recall being in a theater when I heard the eerie sound of sirens in the distance, and a red light flashed a warning on the sidewall. Nobody made a move for the exits.

On another occasion that week, I was on Oxford Street when the sirens started, followed by a huge and noisy anti-aircraft barrage from the direction of Hyde Park. This time I was a little scared because the fragments from the bursting AA shells began raining down. I hastily looked for cover and made my way back to the club as quickly as possible.

My room in the club was on the top floor, and one night I was awakened by a very loud siren, apparently on the roof of a police station on our street. This time I could hear the planes. Their tactic was to have a "pathfinder" drop parachute flares over the intended target, and then the bombers dive-bombed the flares. I could distinctly hear them diving, but the anti-aircraft noise was so intense I couldn't distinguish bomb noise. I remember one morning hearing that a movie theater in South London had been hit with a large number of casualties. Many years later when I was living in South Croydon, I heard that a movie theater had been hit in the nearby suburb of Streatham – likely the same theater.

One night an air force officer took me to the American Melody Bar at 22 Brook Street (I still have their card; it says "Americans only"!) Here he introduced us to the girl behind the bar, Dolores. While we were drinking, we noticed two stern-looking men with hats and overcoats standing near the end of the bar. Finally they announced that they were from Scotland Yard and that the bar would have to close because they needed to take Dolores with them to provide some "assistance" to the police. We made a big fuss, and they finally relented and said that we could finish our drinks. Dolores was obviously very nervous and insisted that we accompany her to the police station, which was near my Red Cross club. The two gentlemen said they had no objection so we all set off down the street. At the police station they told us they had to question Dolores in private, but that we could wait in the "officers' mess." They took us upstairs and fed us Welsh Rarebit. We forgot all about Dolores.

I have another playbill for "Junior Miss" at the Saville Theater.

Needless to say, I loved London. It was the start of a love affair that has survived to this day.

Thursday night
January 20, 1944

Dear Mother, Dad, & Sis,

Well, here I am back again and London is nothing but a memory. But, what a memory! Why, in a week I just got to know the place. Hope you got my letter written from there. I had all kinds of wonderful intentions about writing letters while I was there, but somehow it was all over and I had written practically nothing. In six days I saw three stage shows, two movies, went to two dances, a night club, and any number of bars, not to mention shopping, sight-seeing, and calling on old friends. Saturday I went to U. S. Headquarters and called on Maj. Ralph Ingersoll and Col. Fechet under whom I served in the battle of El Guettar. You remember I told you about Ingersoll and his book, etc. He later took me out and bought me some of the best drinks I've had in an awful long time – namely some wonderful martinis. I think he'll prove to be a useful person to know. Col. Fechet took me and another officer to a stage show and dinner at a Chinese restaurant last Monday night. He's an amazing old coot. He's the darndest old woman you ever saw, but under fire he's afraid of nothing. He was wounded at El Guettar and has never completely recovered, so they won't let him go back into the field.

I set Sunday aside for sight-seeing, so London honored me with the kind of fog you read about. I'm telling the truth when I say that people would pass you on the sidewalk and you'd never see them. Busses and taxis stop running completely. I went to Trafalgar Square and didn't know where I was until I bumped into one of the huge lions at the base of the monument. However, I finally did get my sight-seeing in on Tuesday. In Westminster Abbey I saw a monument to Johnny's friend, Lord Robert Manners.

Due to the fact that it takes longer to get a letter thru to someone over here than it does to get one from home I missed connections with Bob. However, I have his phone number and I don't think he's too far from here. If I can get ahold of him I may be able to get a 48 hr. pass some weekend.

I did some stamping in London, as London is a wonderful place to stamp in, and will send them in due time. And, oh yes, I'll also send those belated Italian stamps I've been talking about for so long. I got my picture taken, but I wasn't too proud of the proofs. Due to the shortage of film they would only take two, and neither one was very good. I'll send one as soon as they arrive. Maybe they can fix it up so it doesn't look so terrible, or maybe I look that way, I dunno.

I've had several V-Mails lately (latest Jan 5) but no regular mail. For awhile the regular mail was ahead of the V-Mail.

Well, I've got a lot of the men's mail to censor so I'll close. I'm glad I wrote this before censoring mail because censoring mail makes you lose all interest in writing.

Love to all,
Bill

Soon after I returned from London we were told that plans had changed, we had been moved from 7th Corps to 5th Corps, and that we were going to be one of the assault divisions for the invasion of France. As I learned later, Eisenhower had been moved to London from the Mediterranean and given command of the pending invasion. When he examined the American attack plan he found that Omaha Beach was going to be assaulted by two National Guard Divisions, the 28th and 29th, neither of which had been in action yet. He decided, probably correctly in the end, that this was too risky. The 28th was removed from the plan and the 1st Infantry Division (ours) was substituted for it. In the end, the 1st Division was given total responsibility for Omaha and a regiment of the 29th was attached to the 1st Division until the beachhead had been secured.

This was obviously very distressing news, at least for me. This was the beginning of over four months of anticipation and specific training, and our minds were seldom on anything else. On about the 1st of February, "A" Company was sent, along with the 16th Infantry Regiment, to a newly established amphibious training center near the town of Woolacombe on the Irish Sea in North Devonshire. Now we were back in tents again and it was wet and cold. We must have spent about two weeks there making practice landings in freezing surf, and learning to do such things as blow up concrete obstacles with explosives. The infantry companies were completely reorganized into five assault teams in place of their traditional three platoons, the thirty-man assault teams being designed to fit the landing craft. They trained on the use of explosive charges and flame-throwers to attack concrete pill boxes, and were also taught how to use an explosive charge placed inside end of a long, extendible tube, called "bangalore torpedoes," to clear barbed wire. That, at least, was an improvement because previously it had been doctrine that the Engineers were supposed to be the people who used flame-throwers and placed explosive charges in the embrasures (windows) of concrete pill boxes. In fact, our original training of the "Hell Squads" at Tidworth the previous year had been based on that doctrine. Mercifully the training of the Hell Squads was never tested.

As the plan unfolded, it became clear that the 1st Division was going to attack in a column of three regiments instead of the conventional two regiments abreast and one behind. In other words, the attack was going to be made with a great amount of depth. It also became clear that the 16th would be the lead regiment, and this meant that our "A" Company would lead. I have always suspected that the 16th was chosen for this great honor simply because we were all billeted in the towns nearest to Woolacombe, where the amphibious training was taking place. The other regiments were at the other end of Dorset, thirty or forty miles farther east.

Woolacombe was something of a misery, although not quite as bad as I thought it was going to be. We had coal stoves in our pyramidal tents and we could get dry and warm in front of them. We had movies, in a tent, and I recall seeing "Casablanca" there. My health held up – it became clear that pneumonia wasn't going to get me out of the invasion.

The next letter was obviously written from Charmouth, so perhaps we left for Woolacombe during the last week of January. The letter gives no hint that we had been away, but there is a considerable gap between this and the preceding letter.

Sunday Feb. 6

Dear Mother, Dad, & Sis,

    This letter can't be very long as I am loading it down with scrap-book material from London.[2] I've finally gotten rid of a little inertia today and am going to pick up a lot of loose ends that I've left laying around. I'm burning up all kinds of junk that I've collected one way or another and in general streamlining my kit. (as the British say).

---

2   My mother created a scrapbook of all my war memorabilia. The original letters that are the basis of this book are still in that scrapbook.

Well, this house proposition looks pretty good. I've received several letters describing it in addition to a map so I feel pretty familiar with the place. I believe I could take a train out Claremont & find my way there with relative ease.

Of course it is quite a ways from a street-car or bus. There's one thing on the map that I can't figure out. There are a couple of purple lines winding from our house & also the campus up over the hills & back again. There seems to be no explanation.

I've been receiving my Readers' Digest lately which is very nice. My Feb. issue arrived just about the first of the month. I've received two letters dated Jan. 17. Right now the V-Mail & air-mail seem to be coming at about the same rate. However, I never get mail in any kind of straight order.

I got my pictures back from London. They're perfectly horrible, but I'll send them as soon as I can find something suitable for mailing.

When is Sis' graduation? It ought to be pretty soon, shouldn't it? I think the trip to Canada is a swell idea. There's no use getting tangled up in this war yet – there'll be plenty of war work to go around for a long time to come.

Went out to dinner last night at Col. Little's place.[3] Had a long discussion of the war with my good friend Capt. Brock-Burkett, late of His Majesty's navy. What a talker he is! Old Col. Little looks like "Esky" in Esquire. He apparently did his entire service in India and is full of all kinds of tales.

Well, so much for today.

Love to all,

Bill

My parents were in the process of buying a new house in Berkeley, and that is what all the conversation about a house is about. I seem to remember getting a letter while in Woolacombe with pictures of the new house. I tried to sound interested, but my mind was elsewhere, and my reference to "streamlining my kit" suggests that I was anticipating a move of some kind. The next letter is addressed to the new house.

Monday, Feb. 14, 1944

Dear Mother, Dad, & Sis, (and should I add Ed?)

Just received your letters of Jan. 25 and also one of Jan 10. What with a map of Berkeley, a floor plan, and the promised pictures, I ought to be able to find my way home & find my away around when I get home with relative ease.

I also received your box of cookies & whatnot that you packaged on Christmas day. Dad has concocted some amazing boxes for mailing, but that was the most extraordinary of all. It would have been OK if I had opened it the way you packed it, but as luck would have it, I opened it upside down & all the cookies went all over the table. Now I've also got to remember to write Pam, which reminds me that I am very much behind on my Xmas "thank you" notes.

I don't see how I can very well give you any addresses of British friends because it would be a violation of security regulations. (Not that I'm fooling anyone, but there are regulations.)

---

3   The Littles lived on High Street and had invited a couple of the officers to dinner more than once.

Sis, you asked what the Red Cross women do over here. Well, every hospital from the evacuation hospitals a few miles behind the front lines to the big general hospitals have Red Cross women who give out books, cigarettes, magazines, teach weaving, & in general try to keep the men amused. Then in every city where there are American Soldiers there are Red Cross Service Clubs & Red Cross Officers' Clubs which are staffed by regular Red Cross women. Then there are such things as mobile canteens which serve coffee & doughnuts & make the rounds of the camps. It's all apparently quite interesting except in the evacuation hospitals where (like the nurses) the Red Cross women wear regular GI coveralls and often sleep on the ground. These evacuation hospitals are pretty bloody places, anyway, but they comprise only a small percentage of the job openings.

I don't think I'm the one of the "five" who had engineer experience in civil life[4]. I think that was "Lt. Cobb", the CO. I think I was mentioned as the youngest of the "five." I don't have a copy handy at the moment, but I think that's the way it went. It doesn't seem possible that it was almost eleven months ago that all that was happening. In a little over two weeks I will have been overseas eighteen months. How about writing your congressman & telling him that eighteen months is plenty long enough! Maybe I'm unpatriotic, but I frankly don't think Hitler is worth all this and neither does a single other soldier who has been in active combat over here. People wonder what's the trouble in Italy – that's the whole blooming trouble in a nutshell, and it's something nobody behind the lines can understand. All the tanks & guns & planes in the world won't do you any good unless you have the will to use them. They try to get us to educate the man as to what he is fighting for – ridiculous – that should have started 15 years ago – it's too late now. There is only one thing the American soldier will "put out" for and that's the spirit of his organization, and they try their damndest to take that away from us. The Germans, Russians, & British learned that years ago, but you can't tell an American anything. You'll notice that the Russians let divisions that capture certain places take that name & wear it. They try to make us forget where we are & what we've done. Excuse me, but I feel very strongly about certain things and have to blow my top occasionally. Maybe they don't want people like me home because we'll talk too much. Well, I've about come to the end of my rope. I'll include a P.S. for socks at the end. I believe I have five pairs now.

Love to all,

Bill

P.S. Please send some wool socks & some cookies.

At this point, there seems to be a large gap in my letters. The realization that we were to lead the way into France had apparently sunk in. I was no longer terribly interested in what was going on at home.

---

4 This refers to Ralph Ingersoll's book *The Battle is the Payoff.*

13 March '44

Dear Mother, Dad, and Sis,
    (Whether or not Dad is there, I wouldn't know.)
    I hope you'll excuse the long gap in my correspondence. I think you understand, however, whenever I don't write.

    I got a whole mess of mail today dated from Feb. 7 to Feb. 28. And as usual, the most recent were straight airmail. I see you are finally in the house and I guess that by this time you are pretty well settled. I don't see exactly why Dad's orders were such a blow – you've been talking about it for a long time now. Honolulu sounds like a pretty good deal. You're near enough to be in on the know, and yet not near enough to be making the news.

    Congratulations on your graduation, Sis. So you're "footloose and fancy-free" eh. I'm quite anxious to hear what you're going to do.

    I'm now at least temporarily company executive officer. I say temporarily because the guy who has my old platoon spends about as much time in the hospital as out and I may have to take over at any time. Anyhow I have my fingers crossed. I've at least begun the long trail away from the front lines. That's one thing about the army – the higher up you go, the farther back you go (with exceptions of course). In the navy if the ship sinks, the admiral is no better off than anyone else. I was sort of sorry to leave the platoon, though, after almost 13 months in which time we only had two men killed and three wounded.

    As soon as I get time I'm once more going to make an attempt to locate Bob. D. Locating people over here is not the easiest thing in the world.

    I'm really going to try to do something about this correspondence situation in the next few days. I've got so many people I should write that the thought of it discourages me.

    Well, this is all I can think of for the present, so I'll write soon – I hope.
    Much love to all,
    Bill

An interesting footnote to the news that my parents had moved into a new house, at 160 Vicente Road in Berkeley, is that the house was completely destroyed in the great Oakland/Berkeley fire of 1991. However, my parents had sold the house many years before.

My father was at that time in command of the Naval ROTC at Berkeley. He had apparently been eager to get closer to the action in the Pacific and had applied for some kind of duty farther west. He got orders to go to Pearl Harbor where he was to be President of the General Court Martial, an absolutely ideal job for him. It would take advantage of his forty years of naval experience, but he would be very comfortable. And best of all, he would be very close to where the decisions were being made, because the fleet headquarters was at Pearl Harbor. In fact, he saw a good deal of Admiral Nimitz, commander in chief of the U.S. fleet, who was a classmate and close friend, during the next year and a half.

Near the end of February we had more changes in officers in the company. Bill Barnum left to join the battalion staff, and that is why I became company executive officer. Bob Conant took over my 3rd Platoon, although his health, mentioned in the letter, was a concern right up until D-Day. Phil Suna left, but I am not sure where he went.

Ed Sherburne left to take a job in the intelligence section of 1st Army. Ed had been trying to get out of the 1st Division from almost the day he arrived in Sicily. His father was an army colonel and a good friend of General Huebner's. I guess Huebner thought he was doing Ed a favor by getting him assigned to the Division in the first place. Ed finally pulled strings with some other friends of his father, and Huebner ultimately let him go. Ordinarily division commanders had absolute authority on these things and were very reluctant to let anybody go. I was distressed to see him go; we had become close friends. His background was very similar to mine and we had similar interests. But the fact that I don't even recall where Ed went to college is an indication of the extent to which we lived in the present, not the past. We simply never discussed our past lives. I think he had been in the 4th Infantry Division before coming overseas, but that is about all I knew of his past. He taught me some things about firing a rifle, so he was not without experience in the Army. Another example of this phenomenon is the case of Doug Forbes, who was CO of our "B" Company during most of the war. Since we were in different companies I didn't see that much of Doug, but over three years we did have a lot of contact. It was at a reunion twenty-five years later that I discovered that he and I had attended the same school, Punahou, in Honolulu. Another interesting footnote is that this was the same high school attended by President Barack Obama!

After Sherburne left, Valerie Kosorek was assigned to "A" Company and took over the 2nd Platoon (Kosorek went by the name of "Streaky"). He had been a master sergeant in the Regular Army, was a magnificent soldier, and was given a battlefield promotion to 2nd Lieutenant in Sicily. During the war the battalion promoted a number of NCOs to 2nd Lieutenant. Not all were great successes, but Streaky Kosorek certainly was. A major part of the problem was a social one. This system was set up so that officers were privileged and existed in a separate social class from enlisted men, and many of them, no matter how competent, found it very difficult to make the transition.

I kept referring to my good intentions about writing letters. Apparently all the boxes of cookies at Christmas time had produced a lot of obligations for me. I don't know whether I ever thanked everybody.

At about this time Murph's friend Joan Everett invited me to spend an evening at her house across the street, along with Murph and Pat Baker, the young mother whom I had met at the Battisil party at Christmas. Pat and I hit it off immediately, and I wondered why I had wasted the whole winter. I was amazed to find that I could be very aggressive with women; I certainly hadn't been so previously. After that, and especially in late April and May, I used to go frequently to Pat's house in the evenings, up near the cliffs on Upper Sea Lane, often following a supper at Joan's. Pat had a baby son, Alvin, but as I recall he was virtually always asleep when I arrived. Her husband was a British Army officer stationed somewhere in the north of England, but he didn't get to Charmouth often. Despite the depressing thought of the battle that lay ahead, my life at this point took a turn for the better. I discovered there was more to life than fighting or preparing for the next battle.

25 March 1944

Dear Mother, Dad, & Sis,

I'm at the present moment trying to find some envelopes in which to send pictures. I have all kinds of pictures now. A big one which I don't like – some little ones which are better, – and even some snaps which a guy took for me. Incidentally, before I go any further I should mention that I've spent the whole week in dear old London. I was a good boy and the Colonel gave me five days leave which I immediately put to good use. Went into London Sunday and got back last night (Friday). A wonderful place, London. I'm getting to be quite a connasuer (sp?) of the London theater. I can tell you what's good, who the best actresses are, where the best chorus girls are, and anything else you want to know. Went out one night with Ingersoll. What a layout he has! He has an apartment and his girl cooked us dinner after a show. And amongst other things I got my picture taken again - this time one of these high-speed joints. This picture will probably be the first and last time you'll ever see me decked out like a 1st Division soldier should be decked out. I borrowed all the insignias just for the picture.

London isn't so crowded as it used to be thanks to the Luftwaffe. It sure seems funny after those alerts we had at home to watch how they handle the situation here. The taxis & buses keep going and keep their dimmed out headlights on even after the siren blows, and they don't turn them out until the shooting starts. The people clear the streets pretty well, though.

I tried out some of the better eating places this time. You can't get very much to eat anywhere, but the quality & atmosphere make some of the places very nice.

This is just a note because I want to get it off. I'll write more later.

Much love,
Bill

I must have run into Tom Crowley in London again, because he and I looked up Ralph Ingersoll, who was by now on duty at ETOUSA (Eisenhower's headquarters). He invited us to dinner at his flat, to be followed by the theater. We took a taxi and I don't quite know where we went, but I think it was probably in Kensington. He had a nice apartment, complete with live-in girlfriend. He had another guest who I later discovered was the writer A.J. Liebling. I remember talking to Ingersoll about General Roosevelt. He said, "The only trouble is that he is dumb as hell."

26 Mar. '44

Dear Sis,

Here's another installment of the pictures I just got in London and which Mother should already have received. I've at last found envelopes that will hold the big pictures I got the first time I was in London, so they'll be along pretty soon, too.

I had a letter from your friend, Pam, the other day. Apparently I'm supposed to urge you to go to Canada. She didn't say that in so many words, but that's what I gathered.

I'm going to write an airmail letter in a day or so, so this isn't intended to be any more than a note. I'm looking forward with interest to see what you're going to do.

You'd better be sure you want to go to Honolulu before you go because they only give you a one way ticket on these overseas deals.

Much love,

Bill

During my second leave in London I also ran into Fred Finley and Harold Haas. One night around midnight we were on the south side of Piccadilly Circus when we started talking to a couple of girls. Where can we get a drink? They suggested that we get a taxi and have him take us to an "after hours" club where liquor was available. We did so and seemed to drive for a long time. We were let out in a residential neighborhood, and while Harold and the girls and I scampered into a basement, Fred stayed behind to pay the taxi. He joined us, furious, a few minutes later. The taxi driver held us up for some outrageous amount. Inside the club we had to pay some kind of fee to join, and then we bought a quart of gin at a terrible price. Haas then spent the next hour trying to proposition one of the girls, to no avail.

I also recall during this London visit having a late night snack at a large restaurant on the east side of Piccadilly Circus. I drank too much, got desperately sick, and ran out into Piccadilly. I puked into the gutter, but because of the blackout nobody saw me.

Sometime near the end of March we went on the first of two practice assault landings. We first moved to an assembly area near Dorchester where we stayed for several days, leaving all our trucks and heavy equipment behind. Then we loaded aboard transports at Weymouth. To my delight my transport was the Chase, which I had known so well in Africa. We sailed in the evening with a feint toward France, and then turned right and went along the coast of England, landing at dawn at a beach called Slapton Sands in Devonshire, southeast of Exeter. I don't remember much more about this maneuver except that we spent the next night in the field. This was the first time I had slept on the ground in England and I had been concerned about the wet and cold. Actually it turned out to be easy. The days were now rapidly getting longer and warmer. I had not experienced England in the spring before; all my previous experience had been in autumn and winter, and I had no idea that the weather could actually be quite pleasant.

April 7, 1944

Dear Mother, Dad, and Sis,

Well, I've finally sent all the pictures. It's only taken me three months to do it – I think that's pretty good.

Mail has been pretty slow lately. I get a letter or two about once a week and that's all. I believe the latest is dated the 13th of March. You were all busy fixing up the house. I guess now Dad is packing up.

Mother, there's one thing to remember about Dad's going away. We're a military family and have been so for a long time. We've reaped all the benefits of peacetime life in the service and during war we should expect to have to put out a little more than other people. The Navy is Dad's life and certainly a war is no time to be staying home. I've hated and detested every moment I've been overseas, but I know perfectly well that if I'd stayed home I'd be terribly restless to get overseas. It's because I've been brought up on uniforms and parades and I guess it gets into your blood. I think Dad probably feels the same way. I can remember only one incident where I've felt like I thought I'd feel before I came across. It was on about the 22nd or 23rd of April last year and it was the night we started the attack that ended with the capture of Hill 609. It was a bright moonlight night and I climbed a rather high hill from which we could look out over the country we had to cross. I was with an infantry battalion commander and some other officers and after they'd seen all they wanted to see they went down & I, having nothing to do for the time being, stayed there. It was one of those bare African hills with nothing but short grass on it and all I had to do was lay there with my chin in my hands and I could see the whole battlefield. I remember thinking, "I wouldn't miss this for all the world, despite all the complaining I've done and all the horrible experiences I've been through & the horrible sights I've seen. When H-hour arrived I listened as the whole air became alive with the characteristically low whistle of friendly artillery. Then I watched as the country ahead of me and for miles to the right and left lit up with flashes of artillery shells and I felt good because I knew what those people over there were going through. That was the only time (except when I first arrived in England) that I recall being excited in the way I thought I'd be. The rest has all been serious business in which you have too much to worry about to be excited.

I see by "Time" that Admiral Fechteler has made an invasion. I didn't even know he was an Admiral.

I'm sure getting awful about letter writing. I decide to write a letter after supper and then I lay down and take a nap & then somebody says, "let's go out and have a beer," and thus the days go by.

Noma tells me she is considering joining the Marines. I don't know why the Marines exactly, except that they have the "cutest" uniforms.

Well, that's about all I can think of at present, so I'll close.
Love to all,
Bill

The Admiral Fechteler referred to was my mother's brother. He was to eventually become, several years later, Chief of Naval Operations – in other words, the top man in the Navy.

During April we did a lot of specialized training; now that we knew what lay ahead the training schedule was not such a chore. In fact I rather enjoyed it. We built a Bailey bridge across the stream in Charmouth, a British structural steel bridge that you could assemble in hours and stretch across a river. It was one of the few pieces of British equipment that was truly superior to anything that we, or the Germans for that matter, had. We also set up a demolition training course on the beach where there were a number of concrete anti-tank obstacles that had been hastily constructed in the summer of 1940, and managed at the same time to blow up the wooden bath houses that were evidently used in the summer for people going swimming. This caused a row with the local authorities.

We set up a rifle-assault training course on the hillside on the other side of the valley from Charmouth. It was arranged so that the rifle bullets would go over the cliffs and out to sea. The coast is somewhat curved inwards there, and we found that our bullets were hitting the water and ricocheting to the right into the neighboring town of Lyme Regis.

Of course this caused more trouble with the locals. I remember the local constable, P.C. 205 Hapgood. He was forever coming around with problems of one type or another, and since I was now executive officer, I had to deal with him.

We originally had thought that the attack would take place around the 1st of May. But for some reason it was delayed a month and another practice landing was scheduled for early May.

Wednesday, April 19

Dear Mother, Dad & Sis,

    I'm lumping you all together although there's no telling how long it will be before you all get this letter. Pop, I'm anxious to hear from you & find out how you like the new job and the new atmosphere. And Mother, I think it would be a wonderful idea if you went to Canada with Sis. This family is doing enough for this war without you sitting home and stewing and fretting. Get out & enjoy yourself while you've got the chance

    Enclosed are a couple of pictures of the battalion officers. You'll probably notice that the turnover in officers in "A" Co is pretty large. Murphy & I seem to be the only ones that stay put. Finley, Haas, Barnum, & Dolega are the guys that I started at Leonard Wood with.

    I've been doing a little gadding about lately. The women are married, but that doesn't seem to make much difference in this country. However, my Number 1 girl who lives up the hill here a ways finally had a stroke of conscience & decided it was becoming too much of a good thing and won't let me come up any more. Guess I was breaking up a happy family. Murphy and I often go across the street where a girl fixes us fried eggs & fried potatoes (all home grown) and also she's quite a fiend on lobster which is plentiful. We go down there & eat, listen to the radio, sit in front of the fire, & in general relax. Sunday I think Murph & I are going out to the Pass' estate & have lunch & ride horseback. They are always complaining about their horses not getting enough exercise.

    I was interested when you said you heard Churchill's speech because I was having supper with the Littles that night & we listened to it in front of the fire. I believe it was about eight in the evening.

    Recently we blew three rather large craters on top of a hill near here while doing some experimenting & we had a big joke when we discovered that my friend Captain Brock-Burkett had found them while walking the dog one day & immediately decided they must have been some bombs dropped in a raid we had some time ago. He went & got the bomb experts and they were all baffled because they couldn't find any steel splinters.

    I'm sorry there's such a long gap in my correspondence but that's just the way things are. I've been receiving a good deal of mail from you and the latest which I got yesterday was dated April 8 which isn't so bad.

    Love to all,
    Bill

The "gap" in my correspondence was due more to my "gadding about" than anything else. As the next letter will indicate, Pat's "stroke of conscience" didn't last very long. I recall about this time taking her to a dance put on by the 2nd Battalion of the 16th Infantry in Bridport, the next town to the east. One thing I cannot remember is ever seeing a baby-sitter for Alvin, nor do I remember seeing much of Alvin at all. He must have been walking by that time, but this is all a blank. When we had our little parties at Joan's house I think that Pat probably brought Alvin in his pram, and he slept the whole time.

At about this time I was horrified to hear that Pat's husband, Nigel, was going to pay a quick visit. She brought him along for an evening at Joan's and introduced me to him. I can remember her smirking in the background while I was talking to him. He was a Captain in the British Army, and he complained to me about the promotion system. He had a typical little British mustache.

The reference in the letter to Captain Brock-Burkett and the "bomb" craters and a "raid" brings up a funny story. A couple of months previously we had been awakened in the middle of the night by a loud clatter of what must have been either gunfire or bombs. It turned out that a small British warship had come into the comparative shelter of the concave coast that evening and anchored for the night, about a half-mile from Charmouth. A German plane, evidently on a reconnaissance mission, had come over and had been picked up by the ship's radar. The ship opened fire on it, and in the extreme quiet of our little village, it sounded as if the sky was falling in. This was Brock-Burkett's raid that I spoke about in my letter. But the remainder of the story is that one of our men on guard duty, simply as a joke, took his rifle and dragged the rifle butt rapidly along the outside of the corrugated metal surface of the Nissen hut in which our company cooks were sleeping. Inside the hut it must have sounded like machine gun fire. The door burst open and all the cooks in their "long Johns" came running out into the cold wet night.

Monday, 8 May

Dear Mother & Sis,

Since this may reach you in Canada (or at least I hope it does) I'm not including Dad as I will write him separately.

I got a terrific stack of mail yesterday with letters dated as late as April 27 from you and April 28 from Noma. The mail service is really in good shape. I got one letter from Dad which was written the day before he got to Honolulu. I haven't yet heard from him there, although in one of your letters you mentioned hearing from him after he had landed.

We just got our new liquor ration – two bottles of Scotch, one gin, and two wines, so we'll be having some rip-roaring times for the next few days.

I'm getting to be quite a lobster eater. Murphy's girl knows a fisherman who gets them for her and every few nights I bring my girl (purely temporary) down and we have a lobster supper. If we have a liquor ration available then it's all the better. Of course we don't tell Noma about this sort of thing – I don't think it would go over very well. I think the quadruplet story has got her worried.

I'm going to be very disappointed if I find that you didn't go to Canada. The whole idea sounds wonderful.

I'm glad you liked the pictures. I guess when I see them again they'll always remind me of London.

We had another widow in town yesterday. That's the way it goes in this country. A guy will come home on leave from the RAF or what have you, and the next week you'll hear that he's missing over Germany or some such place. It's amazing how little it affects these British people, though. They go about their business as if nothing had happened at all. The only possible difference is that the wife snipes possibly a little more energetically at the available males. I think a good many of the younger couples over here were married when the war started and really never expected to carry on after the war.

It doesn't get dark around here until about 9:45 nowadays. Of course the double summer time we have is mostly responsible for that. It's now 8 o'clock & the sun is shining in my window like mid-day.

You'd really enjoy this country at this time of year. Everything is always green, but now all the flowers are out and the trees are in blossom and it's really beautiful.

Well, more later.

Much love,

Bill

On about the 12th of May we went to Devonshire for a second Slapton Sands practice landing, starting again with a move to the same assembly area near Dorchester. My principal recollection of this landing is an incident that occurred the day we were taken from the assembly area to Weymouth. Our battalion had prepared a large and elaborate set of field orders – a document about an inch thick. It was of course a very secret document and I carried it in my arms. In the hands of enemy intelligence it could provide a great deal of information about the coming invasion. I rode in the cab of a truck, and when we got out of the trucks in downtown Weymouth I accidentally left it on the seat of the truck. What to do? After agonizing for a moment or so I spotted an MP on a motorcycle. I told him my problem and he sped off in the direction that the trucks had taken. After about fifteen minutes, during which time I felt like dying, he returned with my field order.

This time we thought that we had left Charmouth for good, but to our complete surprise and delight we again returned to Charmouth.

Under the plan executed at Slapton, our battalion had been reinforced by another independent engineer battalion. A Provisional Company was formed with our 1st Platoon, under George Johnson, and a platoon from this new battalion was led by a guy named Polino. I was appointed commanding officer of the Provisional Company, and the plan was that we would be attached to the 1st Battalion of the 16th Infantry for the landing. In other words, we simply doubled the number of engineers attached to the infantry. The 1st Battalion was to be the second "wave" of the 16th Infantry's attack, with the 2nd and 3rd Battalions leading the way. My dream of bringing up the rear with the headquarters group of our company was now shattered!

Soon after our return from Slapton, since I was now a "company commander," I was asked to come for a briefing at our battalion headquarters near Blandford. There, with much attention to security, I was shown the whole plan. The landing was to be made on the coast of Normandy, and the 16th Infantry's initial objective was to be the little town of St. Laurent sur Mer, about a half mile inland. The beach was given the code name OMAHA.

We studied maps and examined hundreds of aerial photos. We had stereo viewers and could see everything in three dimensions. I would soon know every square inch of the beach and the road leading up to St. Laurent.

Between the time of my briefing and our final departure, I recall sitting on a couch on the back porch of Pat's house and looking out over the English Channel. I now knew what lay over the horizon. I was dying to tell her, but I managed to restrain myself, although I probably did give some hints.

21 May 1944

Dear Mother & Sis,

The mail service is now truly wonderful. I've received letters as quick as eight days (and not V-Mails, either). I'm afraid the mail going the other way hasn't been so regular, has it. Well, there really isn't much news that I can give you. I'm in good shape, but would feel much better if I knew you weren't fussing and fretting about me. Why don't you stop putting off this Canadian trip and get the hell up there. You're not going to do yourselves any good hanging around Berkeley feeling sorry for yourselves. And don't let anyone try to appeal to your patriotism as far as travelling is concerned.

Been having a good time lately. Had a supper last night of fried eggs and french fried potatoes. And I ate it on a soft chair in front of a nice hot fire. Boy oh boy, what a life! These people have sure been swell to us. I sort of feel guilty about eating things like eggs but Murph's girl has six chickens so I guess it's OK. We bring lard from our kitchen and my girl does the cooking. It's all very convenient.

I'm beginning to get a pretty fair idea of what the house looks like with the help of your pictures. In fact I think I could almost find my way around with a little help.

Well, this sheet is much too large for me to write a letter on, 'cause this is about all I can think of.

Love to all,
Bill

21 May 1944

Dear Dad,

Altho Mother & Sis are sending their letters on to you I thought I'd try one straight to you to see how fast it got there. I received about three letters from you to date, I believe. The service seems quite fast. About two weeks as I remember.

I'm glad you like your quarters. They sound very nice. Have you been out to Kahala yet? I'd like to hear how the old house looks.

Who are all these old friends you are running into? Or can't you mention names?

Mother and Sis are still fretting about going to Canada. I wish to heck they'd go ahead and stop putting it off. Only, please don't let Sister get away from Mother. That's one reason why I don't particularly approve of her going to Honolulu. I don't want Mother alone, for the time being anyway.

It's kind of difficult to write you and not repeat the stuff I write in the letters home. I've been having a pretty good time lately, but I've talked all about that in other letters. We've all got lots of friends very close by so we don't have to go off to a city to enjoy ourselves.

Well, that's about all there is for the present so I'll close.

Love,

Bill

The discerning reader of my letters may detect some changes in my attitudes. The griping and self-pity have disappeared. The depression that was evident in many earlier letters is gone. I sound almost light-hearted. Two things had happened. First, I had finally accepted the fact that I was a soldier, that the army and the war were now my life, my only life, and there was likely going to be no hereafter. I would probably die on that beach, but there was no alternative. I remember being over in Bridport one day with some of the infantry assault teams from the 2nd Battalion, including my friend, John Kersey. One Lieutenant said. "I hope the first shell that comes into that beach lands right on my head." That's how we all felt, but interestingly it didn't cause depression. Ironically, this guy probably got his wish, because virtually all of the Lieutenants in the two assault companies of the 2nd Battalion, "E" and "F," died on the beach – all except one, as we shall hear later.

The second "event" that obviously contributed to my light-heartedness was Pat Baker. After almost fifty years it is difficult for me to visualize Pat, and I have no pictures. She was a brunette, I think, certainly not a blond. She was perhaps slightly overweight, but pleasingly so. Her face was rather round with color in her cheeks, very red lips, a lovely smile. All I knew about her background was that she was from somewhere in Norfolk, in the Southeast of England. I think she had worked at least briefly in London near the start of the war. She spoke fondly of her "Mum," but I recall hearing nothing of her father. We exchanged a couple of letters when I got to Normandy, but after that she didn't answer.

By this time the weather had become truly delightful, and in England this makes everyone feel good. The sun didn't set until after nine o'clock pm, so the evenings were long. It seems to me that a certain sense of euphoria settled in over the entire army; everybody felt good and we were evidently ready to fight.

Within a day or two of the previous two letters, we were moved for the third and last time to the assembly areas (or marshalling areas, as they were called). First we went to the same place near Dorchester, and then a few days later we were moved to another place near Bournemouth. This final marshalling area was tightly fenced off by barbed wire, and we were locked in. Here we showed the whole plan to everybody and made all our final arrangements. As a matter of fact, all of southern England was now a restricted zone, with nobody allowed to leave or enter except on military business.

I got some final mail from home, including one letter from Noma. It ended with, "Good luck on the invasion!" It sounded to me like, "Good luck on the Big Game!" She "didn't grasp the concept!"

About this time I began to hear a song that became for all intents and purposes the theme song of the invasion. I think we picked it up from the British troops. At any rate, whenever you saw a group of soldiers together, in a truck, for example, you would be sure to hear, "Roll me over in the clover –". You would hear it on the highways, and in the streets of the towns, and they loaded up on the ships singing it.

During this period we were having a problem with men coming down with recurrences of malaria, which required that they be hospitalized. We also had a problem with Bob Conant, who was having trouble with either his stomach or with his back, which had been hurt in Sicily. He too was hospitalized. For a time it appeared that I might have to take his platoon (my old platoon), because my job as commander of the Provisional Company wasn't very important and could probably be dispensed with. Most of our missing men were in a hospital in the city of Axminster, west of Charmouth. Murphy told me to take a jeep and go to Axminster to check on our people and bring some back if I could. Since going to Axminster involved going through Charmouth, I grabbed a driver and a jeep and was gone before Murph could grasp that fact and change his mind.

We went to the hospital in Axminster and did manage to pick up a couple of men. (Conant also returned, but I believe that was a few days later.) In the evening we came back and of course stopped in Charmouth. I told the others that we would meet at about one o'clock a.m. For some reason that I have never completely understood, I went to Joan Everett's house first. I suspect I wanted to ask her how things were with Pat, and whether the coast was clear. She had been sort of my "confidant" with respect to Pat. I stayed there talking for a while, and suddenly had a severe case of chills. It got worse, and Joan wrapped me in blankets and turned an electric heater on me. Malaria! The chills lasted a couple of hours, followed by severe sweating as my temperature returned to normal. Joan eventually went out and returned with Pat. (Where was Alvin?) Around midnight I had recovered sufficiently to leave, and Pat and I went back to her house. But I couldn't stay long. Pat couldn't understand why I had gone to Joan's in the first place, instead of directly to her house, and I guess I was hard put to explain. I said good-by to Pat for the last time.

The next is a V-Mail letter. We were given one last time to write, but were told that the letters would not be sent until after D-Day.

May 31, 1944

Dear Mother, Dad, & Sis,

This isn't going to be much of a letter as you can see. I hate these things, anyway. I just wanted to let you all know that I'm thinking of you and although I'd like to be with you, I want you to know that I sincerely feel that I'm in my right place. I would never feel right if I was home now. I guess the Army eventually instills a sense of duty in one that overcomes the temptations to condemn those who we feel aren't carrying their full share of the load. This war isn't going to be won by machines but by men, and I mean real men. If I can be one of those men then I'll have something that I can carry with me for the rest of my life. I wish I could impart to you some of the confidence that I have in our ability to finish this thing. I feel so immeasurably better about it all than I did a year ago.

I hope to hear that you are in Canada by the time you get this. If you aren't, get the hell up there.

Love to all,
Bill

This letter reminds me of the Civil War song, "Just before the battle, Mother -."

On the 1st of June we were trucked to Weymouth and boarded the Chase for the final time. This time we were taken out into the harbor in small boats and had to climb aboard the ship by way of landing nets – rope nets hanging over the side. We were heavily loaded with weapons and junk and when I got two-thirds of the way up my strength gave out. For a brief moment I thought I was going to let go and fall back down into the boat. I would have been injured and would have had to be taken ashore – no invasion! The thought passed, and I struggled up.

My cabin-mate on the Chase was none other than T. J. Obrian. After hearing about him for almost two years and seeing him occasionally from afar, I finally became acquainted with him. We talked for hours. We talked about Jimmy Dowd, and about Boston and the Boston Irish. We talked about infantry and artillery tactics and colonels and generals, and how he hated the latter.

We stayed in the harbor for several days. And again we ate well.

The Chase had a gymnasium down below someplace and a huge relief map of the entire invasion area had been set up. I went down to take a look at it with some of the officers of the 1st Battalion. I noticed a well-known news photographer, Robert Capa of *Life Magazine*. He was trying to take a picture of the officers examining the terrain. I deliberately worked myself into the group. Years later I saw the picture in a book he wrote. I am right in the center.

At first it seemed that the landing was going to take place on June 5th, but the 4th came and went and nothing happened. Then finally late in the afternoon of the 5th we hauled up anchor and pulled out into the Channel. There we joined an armada of ships that extended over the horizon in all directions. I recall being up on the top deck that evening with Tom Crowley (our Battalion Headquarters group was also on the Chase). We both dumped our field orders into an incinerator near one of the smokestacks. I don't remember trying to get any sleep – I probably didn't. I do remember being on deck with Tom at about two o'clock in the morning, because at that time we saw, in the distance to the southeast, tracers from hundreds of anti-aircraft guns. The paratroops from the 82nd and 101st Airborne were landing behind Utah Beach, the code name for the beach tour right. The battle had started.

Soon after that the ship stopped and dropped anchor. I recall another small ship coming by and somebody called over a loudspeaker to our ship, asking where he was. I hoped this guy wasn't going to be the one to lead us in. By about three o'clock we were in the landing boats and were lowered over the side. All of the boats from the Chase formed a circle, and then we went around and around for what seemed an eternity. It was June 6, 1944: D-Day.

High Street, Charmouth (about 1988)

Blandford, England, March 1944;
First row: Sammy Gregg (Adjutant), Bill Barnum.
Second row: George Johnson, Charlie Murphy, "Streaky" Kosorek.
Back row: John Oxford.

Sicily, August 1943;
George Johnson

Blandford, March 1944; Tom Crowley, "Smokey" Stowell (Battalion Executive Officer), Bill Gara, Art Hoffman (Battalion Supply Officer).

London, March 1944; My "formal" por-triat, an improvement over an earlier one.

Blandford, March 1944; me.

Woolacomb, England, February 1944; Me, with Murphy.

CHAPTER EIGHT

OMAHA BEACH AND NORMANDY
JUNE 6 - JULY 25, 1944

Two dates stand out above all others in people's memory of World War II: December 7, 1941 and June 6, 1944. The first was unexpected, the second had been anticipated for at least two years, and this anticipation had worked itself into a frenzy in the press as June 1944 approached. Stalin had been demanding a "second front" in Europe since the summer of 1942 and was very upset when it hadn't happened in 1943. I recall when I was at Ft. Leonard Wood there was much talk in the papers about the "second front" and I assumed when I was shipped out that I was somehow going to be involved. But never in my wildest dreams did I imagine that I was going to be involved to the extent that I ultimately was.

This was the largest single American/British operation of the entire war. Success or failure would have enormous implications on everything that followed. It was what we had been working toward all winter, and what made it very special was that it all was to come down to one day -- "D-Day", "The Invasion", "The Second Front", June 6, 1944. It thus seems appropriate that I provide more extensive background and details than I have for the preceding chapters. Besides which, there is now a considerable gap in my letters.

The Tunisian campaign had taken months longer than anticipated. Sicily had been taken rapidly, but the resignation of Mussolini provided an opportunity to get Italy out of the war and it seemed foolish not to grab that opportunity, invade mainland Italy, and clean up the Mediterranean for good. But all of this activity in the Mediterranean made a simultaneous crossing of the English Channel impossible, primarily because of a shortage of landing craft. And the Pacific war was also making its demands on landing craft, and the American public in general was more sympathetic to attacks on the Japanese.

Once mainland Italy had been invaded and a beachhead established at Salerno in September 1943, there was no question but that a cross-channel operation would take place early in 1944. The American high command had insisted since 1942 that the decisive battle against Hitler would have to take place in northern France. The British had always favored a Mediterranean approach, but it was clear that ultimately the Americans would supply most of the troops, so the American view prevailed. The only question now was precisely where and when.

The build-up of troops and the other preparations in England had been staggeringly large. By June nobody could doubt that something big was about to happen. The whole world was waiting.

The Germans were also waiting. Field Marshall Rommel had been brought back from Africa when it became apparent that Africa was a lost cause, and he took command over the entire defense of Western Europe. He was dissatisfied with the defenses that he found and he immediately put people to work strengthening them. Every beach and harbor from Holland to Spain was prepared with all manner of obstacles and gun emplacements. Rommel felt that the best opportunity to defeat his enemy was at the water's edge, not after a beachhead had been established. But he didn't know where and when it was going to happen. Conventional wisdom suggested that a landing in the area of Calais was most probable, and here he concentrated his main forces. Normandy seemed less likely, particularly because there were no major harbors on the Normandy coast, and the Germans felt that a harbor would be needed early on to sustain an amphibious attack. But nevertheless Rommel did order major improvements in the defenses of every Normandy beach where a landing seemed possible. During the winter of 1943/44 aerial photographs began to reveal these new defenses.

In the English Channel the tide is extremely large -- perhaps 30 feet. On Omaha Beach at high tide the water extended to a low bank of gravel (or shingle, as it was called), but at low tide two or three hundred yards of flat sand beach were exposed. Between the high water and low water extremes the Germans, during the winter, installed a variety of obstacles designed to stop tanks and to rip the bottoms out of boats. As a counter to this threat it was decided that the first assault wave (the term "wave" will be used here to denote a group of landing craft sailing parallel to one another, perhaps 30 or 40 yards apart) would land at low tide just outside of the first obstacles. But of course they then were expected to cross two or three hundred yards of open flat beach before they reached the partial cover of the shingle bank, beyond which lay barbed wire, mines, anti-tank ditches, concrete pill boxes, and untold numbers of well-emplaced machine guns. Following about a minute behind the first infantry wave, a specially trained battalion of engineer troops was to land. Their objective was to blow lanes through the obstacles, using explosives, so that when the tide came in the boats could still land. This plan had been hastily put together when the obstacles were discovered during the winter. Before that, we, that is the 1st Engineers, had the responsibility for the obstacles. Fortunately I didn't learn of the plan until this special battalion had been designated to do the job, or I would have had a much less happy time in Charmouth. A more futile plan could never have been devised. It's only hope for success lay in the assumption that the Air Force and the Navy would lay such fire on the beach defenses that they would be at least temporarily neutralized. Nothing we had seen before suggested that this would indeed happen, and of course it didn't. And what if the first wave of infantry was wiped out, what then?

The plan also called for tanks to land on the beach, some of them just before the first infantry wave. These first tanks were fitted out with floats and propellers and literally "swam" in after being dumped from LCTs (landing craft tank) a mile or so out from the coast. Apparently most of these promptly sank in the rough sea as soon as they left the LCTs, but some did actually make it in. They can be seen in the pictures of the landing with their peculiar float shrouds and these few may have actually been landed directly on the beach when it was found that the first tanks sank when launched in deep water. A second wave of tanks were to land directly on the beach from LCTs, evidently before the tide came up too high.

In my sector the initial infantry assault was to be made by "E" and "F" companies of the 2nd Battalion, 16th Infantry Regiment. The 3rd Battalion was to land at the same time to the left of the 2nd. During the next hour all kinds of people were to come in, including "G" Company of the 2nd Battalion, and our own 2nd and 3rd Platoons, along with Charlie Murphy. At about H + 1 hour (one hour after the initial landing) two companies of the 1st Battalion, to which I was attached, were to land, followed a few minutes later by the remainder of the 1st Battalion. This latter wave would include the Battalion Commander, Ed Driscoll, me and my Provisional Company, and it also was to include Bill Gara, Tom Crowley, and our own engineer battalion headquarters group. Our wave would be followed by wave after wave of various kinds of specialized troops, artillery, anti-aircraft, trucks, bulldozers, regimental and division headquarters, and then a few hours later by the entire 18th Infantry Regiment. Behind the 18th, the 26th Infantry Regiment would land late in the afternoon. It was a very ambitious schedule and would lead to chaos if something went wrong. It was an attack in very great depth, which of course provided little comfort to those in the first waves. But such depth increased the chances for ultimate success, regardless of what happened to the first waves.

My company "headquarters" consisted of me, a radio-man, and a runner. My only mission was to stick close to Col. Driscoll so that he could have communication with some engineers if he needed them. Otherwise George Johnson and Polino and their two platoons were on their own. Our assumption was that the beach would be secure by the time we landed and our work would start a few hundred yards inland.

Something now should be said about the topography of Omaha Beach. The coast of France consists of a plateau about 100 feet above the ocean. Part of it starts with steep chalk cliffs near the water's edge, but here and there shallow valleys have been cut by streams, and these valleys provide access to the beaches and generally have a road coming down to intersect another road which parallels the water. We spoke of these as the beach "exits" and they were given names E1, E2, etc. The bank of gravel, or shingle at the high water point on Omaha Beach has already been described. The beach road, a dirt road, lay a few yards behind the shingle. Beyond that the terrain was relatively flat where the valleys were located, but between the valleys there was a flat area for perhaps a hundred yards, and then the ground sloped up at about a 45 degree angle to the plateau. There were no steep chalk cliffs except to the left of the next valley to our left. In our area the valleys were two or three hundred yards wide, and the valleys were spaced about a half-mile apart.

The 2nd Battalion of the 16th Infantry Regiment, and the 1st behind it, was to land in front of one of the valleys, opposite the E1 exit, and the 3rd Battalion to our left would land before the E3 exit. The E1 exit road led up the right side of the valley and emerged on the plateau near the village of St. Laurent-sur-Mer. The enemy defenses were generally sited with the assumption that the main attacks would come at these valleys, and large concrete pill boxes and gun emplacements were located on the shoulders of each of the valleys.

Our company plan ("A" Company and Murphy) was that we would meet at the point where the E1 exit road came out onto the plateau, assuming that by this time the beach was secure and it was no longer necessary to operate as small units attached to the infantry. I guess I thought this would happen sometime in mid-morning.

So now let's go back to about 3:00 or 4:00 am and we are in the landing craft in the water and going around in circles. It is overcast and very dark and the sea is rough. Men are getting sea-sick.

I was in a boat with the 1st Battalion Headquarters. The battalion commander, Colonel Ed Driscoll, along with the Operations Officer (the S3 he was called), Dave Milotta, were at the front right behind the landing ramp; I was at the very rear. I found myself standing next to the *Life* photographer, Robert Capa, who had taken my picture the night before. Interestingly, Capa was virtually the only photographer of any kind to land that morning. I have seen a few pictures that were evidently taken by naval personnel from the boats, but nothing from the beach except Capa's pictures which even today provide the cover picture and frontispiece of virtually every book written about the landing.

Finally we stopped going around in circles and headed for the beach. It was probably 15 miles away. Dawn broke and we could see other landing craft and a few naval vessels. Our column of boats deployed into a wave of parallel boats. It was very overcast. Nobody talked much and nobody cracked jokes. As H-hour approached we looked up, expecting to see the "armada" of bombers that were going to devastate the beach, but saw nothing but low gray clouds. It was hard to see straight ahead because of the landing ramp on our craft; at H-hour some of us leaned over the side to see what was going on ahead, but could see nothing but mist.

We passed a U.S. Navy cruiser firing toward the beach. I looked at the boat to our left and saw Bill Gara. He smiled, gave me a "high-sign", and pointed to the cruiser.

At this point I was of course a bit apprehensive, but not terribly so. I was confident that the Air Force and the Navy would by now have pulverized the beach defensives so completely that our main difficulties would be a secondary line of defenses and the inevitable counterattacks. The bombing alone would leave the beach area a maze of craters with all the barbed wire gone and all the mines detonated.

When we were 2 or 3 miles from shore Capa and I looked toward the beach and we both saw here and there puffs of black smoke and towers of water. Capa said to me, "That must the beach engineers blowing up the obstacles." He was talking about the plan for the specially trained battalion of engineers who were supposed to land a minute after the first wave. It looked like something more ominous to me, but I didn't say anything. Soon after I saw what appeared to be a Navy launch running across our front, perhaps a mile ahead. It was probably a launch used to control the landing craft traffic. As I watched I saw the puffs of smoke and the splashes hitting ahead of and behind the launch. I suddenly had a terrible feeling that things weren't as they should have been! Why would enemy guns be chasing a little launch when the beach was by that time alive with our tanks? Our wave of landing craft would soon be in range, so evidently we were going to have to go through some kind of artillery barrage while still at sea. I closed my eyes and what raced through my head was, "Yea, though I walk through the valley of the shadow of death, I shall fear no evil ---." Capa said nothing.

From then on we mostly stayed hunkered down and didn't see much. All seemed to be smoke and mist ahead anyway. Suddenly I heard machine-gun fire, very loud. Bullets were bouncing off our boat. I looked up and barely made out the outline of a hill, or bluff. What the hell! We were supposed to land opposite the E1 exit, not the bluffs. The coxswain of the boat, right behind me, yelled, "Where do you want to land, Colonel?" Our boat, carrying the battalion commander, was evidently free to land wherever Driscoll wanted. Driscoll waved frantically to the right -- he evidently felt that we were to the left of where we belonged and that his rifle companies would be to our right. I don't recall the exact time, but it was supposed to be H+1 hour and 20 minutes, about 7:30 am.

The boat swerved to the right, and in so doing it tipped far to the left so that the whole scene opened up for an instant before our eyes. There were the anti-tank and anti-boat obstacles, all intact, and now with a foot or so of water swirling around them. Some were hedgehogs, large steel structures that looked like the jacks from the children's game; others were wooden structures designed to overturn a boat, and still others were simply large wooden poles set at an angle towards the sea with anti-tank mines attached to their ends. There were several tanks in the water, but what really caught my eye in that brief instant were men (and the bodies of men) lying on the shingle bank just beyond the water's edge. In a flash I knew this was the front line. The initial assault had failed! We had been stopped at the water's edge just as Rommel had promised.

The boat righted itself and more machine gun bullets bounced off the hull. The coxswain maneuvered a few yards to the right and then did a good job of working the boat between some of the obstacles. In the meantime we saw men apparently drowning in the water next to us and my radio operator, Doyle, panicked. He was carrying a heavy radio on his back and he and Fitzwater, my runner, took off the radio and decided to carry it between them rather than on Doyle's back. The ramp dropped and we all rushed out into about two or three feet of water and headed for the beach.

I had read in awe of the Charge of the Light Brigade, Pickett's charge at Gettyburg, the Anzac charge at Gallipoli, and the first hour of the Battle of the Somme. (All disasters, I should add.) And I remembered both the French and Germans going "over the top" in *All Quiet on the Western Front*. But those ghosts of the past weren't real people with flesh and blood and feelings -- in my mind they were some kind of iron men who felt no pain! By what infernal stroke of fate was I, who had always been so careful, now involved in the same thing? How had I so carelessly thrown away what had been a good life?

Capa and I were at the rear of the boat on the right side. Our instructions were to run down the ramp of the boat on the right side and leave at the right corner of the ramp. This I did and I thought my two men and Capa were right behind me. (Capa's pictures seem to show that he must have stopped on the ramp and shot two or three pictures.)

I ran through the water towards a couple of the hedgehogs. I saw men and bodies behind them and for a brief instant I had the thought to join them. The thought passed and I ran to the right and then headed towards a tank about 50 yards ahead. I don't recall the noise, but at that moment I saw the splashes of machine gun bullets hitting the water immediately in front of me. The fire was coming from the right front. I remember the thought, "What is it going to feel like when they hit me?" It was hard going through the deep water, but I ran on and pulled up on the left side of the first of several tanks that were just our side of the shingle bank. The tide was coming in rapidly and the water was now lapping at the edge of the shingle bank. I looked around and found Doyle and Fitzwater right behind me. It was time to assess the situation.

There were no bomb craters or shell holes anywhere. I was to see later that the barbed wire was all intact. And the mines? Who knows? I didn't even think about them.

I looked up to the left front and on the banks of the bluff saw a huge concrete block-house, perhaps 150 yards away. But I immediately sensed that it was dead -- the machine gun fire was coming from my right front, and that was why I was on the left side of the tank. No more than 10 yards ahead of me was the shingle bank which afforded a little cover to the many men lying on it. The tanks could see and fire over it, but apparently couldn't negotiate it themselves. Forty years later I examined that blockhouse; it was apparent that it had been knocked out by fire from the tanks, probably the ones in the group I was now with. There are several places where tank shells had hit and it appeared that at least one shell had entered the embrasure and probably killed everybody inside.

I looked to my left and saw another tank about 20 or 30 yards away and there was Robert Capa behind it, his camera to his eyes, shooting in all directions. He pointed it straight at me. A few weeks later I saw Life Magazine and Capa's pictures. He apparently lost part of them in the darkroom, but there are about eight or ten that survived. Three were apparently taken from the landing craft just before he jumped into the water. The scene shows our boat group running through the obstacles toward several tanks in the background. I am somewhere in the pictures. In the first photo, I am at the upper right corner, with Doyle and Fitzwater, dragging the radio, right behind me. The others were all taken from behind the tank where I saw him, but I am not in them. None are from the beach. The Life article says he was on the beach, but I doubt that he ever got out of the water. I think he probably climbed aboard a boat in the very next wave. I wouldn't have blamed him. What good is a dead photographer?

I don't know how long I stayed behind that tank. It moved once and I discovered that my foot had sunk into the sand and I had a brief scare when I had trouble getting out of the way. The tide had risen about a foot. My overwhelming feeling at the time was that this whole enormous national effort was ending in an incredible disaster. I looked up and saw one of our P-51s circling overhead. I thought, "You lucky bastards!" Well, at least we had air cover, and that was a change.

At about that time I became aware of little splashes and puffs of black smoke near me every now and then. They were lobbing rifle grenades onto us, probably trying to hit the tank that I was crouching behind. There were apparently a lot of Germans up there somewhere on that bluff and they were shooting with everything they had. I have no recollection of any noise, but artillery and mortar shells were coming in here and there as they attempted to get at the men on the shingle bank.

There was another tank just ahead and to the right. I motioned to Doyle and Fitz-water and we ran to it, again staying on its left side. Now we were right at the base of the shingle bank. And then I was struck by a piece of irony. During the preparations for the invasion we had to paint all of our vehicles and equipment with some numbers and bar codes which evidently identified them in some way. If we didn't do it correctly and neatly we had to do it over again, and this all became a big issue to the people at the various echelons of command above us. Our equipment was forever being inspected to see if we had done it properly, with great threats of mayhem if we had not. While I was cowering behind this tank I saw at the water's edge, a few feet ahead, one of our mine-detector boxes standing perfectly upright, and there were the bar codes and numbers in all their pristine beauty. On either side of the box lay a dead soldier, both pitched forward with their faces in the gravel.

Soon after I spotted Ed Driscoll and Dave Milotta just ahead on the shingle bank. I motioned to Doyle and Fitzwater and we joined them. Still confused about where we had landed, I said, "Where are we, Colonel?" I guess it made me feel good to at least say something, or to discover that I was capable of saying something. He replied, "I don't know, but I know we've got to get the hell off this beach."

I peered over the shingle bank and could only see smoke and the bare outlines of the bluff ahead. Grass and brush were burning and of course the shells from both sides added to the smoke.

I looked to the left and saw George Johnson. He was about 20 yards away, peering over the top of the shingle bank.

We all were wearing inflatable life belts and the pictures show them scattered all around. I kept mine on. I had a feeling I was still going to need it.

Shortly thereafter Driscoll and Dave Milotta stood up and Dave turned to me and said, "Come on, Kays, let's go." We stepped back to the water's edge and then ran along the beach to the right for about 100 yards. There I saw the beach and all its horror, dead men, wounded men, some mangled by artillery shells, others running out in little teams into the water to rescue men, and also to pull in wheeled carts of ammunition. I heard no sounds of crying men -- in fact I recall no sounds at all -- everybody seemed stunned and traumatized and strangely quiet. And then Driscoll veered to his left and up over the shingle towards the bluffs. In another memory from All Quiet on the Western Front I thought, "It's 1917 and I'm going 'over the top'". But I followed. We ran across the dirt road that paralleled the beach, and then there was barbed wire and two dead American soldiers lying over the wire. There were also anti-personnel mines everywhere, but I didn't realize this until later. We picked our way over the bodies and in a few yards came to the ruined foundations of what had evidently been a house at the base of the bluff or hill. The Germans had apparently blown down the house to clear a lane of fire. We stopped on the left side of the brick foundations, and here with some temporary cover Driscoll set up a command post. It was now clear that there were others ahead of us. A trail led up a rather shallow ravine to the top of the bluff. (See the pictures at the end of the chapter.)

But who were these "others" and how did they get there? Here I must digress a bit.

Many years later I found on the Internet the personal recollections of some of them. Although Companies "E" and "F" of the 2nd Battalion, 16th Infantry, the two lead companies in that sector, had been almost wiped out, amazingly the right-most boat group from "E" under Lt. John Spalding had landed at the low water mark and had managed to walk (not run) the 200 or 300 yards through the obstacles to the shingle bank with only one or two casualties. This was almost exactly where I landed an hour or so later. It was about half way between the E1 and E3 exits while most of the German guns were concentrated in strong-points above the two exits in the two little valleys. Spalding described the machine gun fire as long range and inaccurate. In other words this was an unexpected "soft" spot in the defenses. Spalding's men then sat down on the shingle bank and cleaned their rifles. They had initially been in water up to their shoulders and had lost a good deal of equipment. After that they went right over the shingle bank for a dozen yards and reached the shelter of what they called the "Roman ruins", undoubtedly the same foundation wall that Col. Driscoll and I sheltered behind an hour later. Spalding apparently saw no Americans on either side of him but nevertheless he attacked up the shallow ravine, laying a base of rifle fire at the shrubs at the top. The shallow ravine shielded this small sector from other fire from up and down the ridge. They successfully attacked a machine-gun at the top and captured a couple of soldiers who turned out to be Polish. They apparently weren't much interested in dying for Hitler. But Spalding's platoon sergeant, Sgt. Phil Streczyk, who apparently led the attack, could speak Polish, and obtained information from them about the German defenses nearby. Since there were at least three tanks in the water behind them, there may have been machine fire from the tanks that helped out at this point, but Spalding doesn't mention the tanks. Perhaps they had come in later.

At about this time "G" Company, coming in about 30 minutes behind "E" and "F", landed at about the same spot. "G" was commanded by Joe Dawson, one of Murphy's carousing friends from those nights with the nurses in North Africa. Dawson apparently saw Spalding's group and started his men up the same path. They evidently conferred somewhere near the top of the ravine and agreed that Spalding would go over the ridge and work to the right along the ridge coming in behind the German trenches and dug-outs, with one platoon of Dawson's men providing covering fire. I don't know whether anyone at that time tried to attack along the ridge to the left. But Spalding reported that he and his couple dozen men (and most especially Sgt. Streczyk) cleaned out the gun positions along the ridge and then came in behind the fairly formidable set of trenches and concrete underground positions that overlooked the E1 exit. They discovered a concrete stairway leading down a hole. Sgt. Streczyk decided not to waste a hand grenade, and instead fired a couple of bursts of automatic rifle fire down the stairs. Out came a group of Germans (or Poles) with hands up. They knew they were hopelessly trapped and saw no purpose in dying.

In the meantime Dawson, finding virtually no opposition straight inland, led his entire "G" company inland up a road about a half-mile to the little village of Coleville. There appeared to be no immediate 2nd line of resistance behind the beach.

In his personal recollections, Captain Ed Wozenski, the CO of "E" Company, said that his company suffered 51 dead and 54 wounded that day (out of 150), but Spalding's boat section in the company had only two dead and 8 wounded out of about 30. The other four boat sections of "E" had been decimated by the murderous fire from the enemy E3 strongpoint to Spalding's left. "F" Company still further to the left suffered a similar fate. Captain John Finke, CO of "F," said that all his officers were killed, including my friend, John Kersey (an infantry lieutenant that I had met in Tunisia), and he thinks that at least three never even made it to the shingle-bank. Finke himself was wounded around noon and at the end of the day the remnants of "F" were commanded by a sergeant.

I believe this was the first significant penetration inland from Omaha Beach; I had been lucky enough to have landed close by.

The greatest heroes of Omaha Beach were these men in "E" and "G" companies led by Spalding and Dawson. Dawson received the DSC (Distinguished Service Cross), and Spalding and five of his men likewise got the DSC, personally awarded by General Eisenhower. But all accounts suggest that the greatest of all was Sgt. Phil Streczyk of "E" company. He got his second DSC for this action, having also received the DSC for action at the Battle of El Guettar in Tunisia, and a Silver Star for action in Sicily. Not to mention two Purple Hearts. He was somebody very special. Capt. Wozenski spoke of him as "the greatest unsung hero of WWII." He was later wounded in the Battle of the Hurtgen Forest in Germany, and sent home. Dawson and Spalding also survived the war, Spalding being evacuated in September suffering from "battle fatigue", as well he might.

Now let's go back to my own experiences.

Driscoll, while still on the shingle bank, had evidently seen Americans moving up the ravine, and that is why he led us to this spot beside the house foundations. Now I threw away my life belt.

Machine gun bullets chipped dust and brick fragments from a foot above our heads in our temporary haven on the left side of the foundation wall, but I don't recall worrying at all. Driscoll had lost his radio operator and asked to use my radio to contact his companies. We tuned it to his frequency, but then Doyle jerked the handset out of the radio container and broke a connecting wire, so my radio didn't work (at least we found later that this was the problem.) Staff officers and runners were sent back to the beach to attempt to round up the battalion and bring them forward. Men on the trail ahead began shouting, "Hold the fire", because machine gun fire from the tanks was now hitting our own people near the top of the bluff. So Spalding and Dawson may at this time have just reached the ridge at the top of the ravine. Spalding's recollection of the time he reached the top would seem to confirm this timing.

I must have stayed there behind the wall for at least half an hour. At one point three or four glum-looking German (or Polish) prisoners were brought down. The various elements of the 1st Battalion followed "G" Company up over the ridge and along the road to Coleville. But at Coleville it was clear that it would be dangerous to attempt to go farther with this small force, especially with no knowledge of what the enemy was going to be able to bring up. So everybody dug in to await the arrival of the 18th Infantry Regiment, due in a few hours.

Soon Driscoll and his staff moved up the bluff and onto the plateau and headed up the road toward Coleville. I followed.

At this point I felt that the battle for the beach was over and that I should think about making contact with Murphy and our "A" Company. It was now apparent that we had landed about 500 yards to the left of where we should have, and that the E1 exit and our rendezvous point was to the right. Part way along the road to Coleville I got the idiotic idea that I should take off to the right through the hedgerows, to the edge of the valley where the E1 exit was located, assuming that I would be able to see across to our rendezvous point on the road leading to St. Laurent-sur-Mer. At that time I didn't even know whether the landing had been successful in the sector opposite St. Laurent, but I wasn't thinking very clearly and evidently completely forgot that there was an enemy. I don't know what I was thinking, but I was so traumatized by the beach experience that I apparently thought I was immortal.

The fact is that for the first, and undoubtedly the last time during the war, I had reached a mental state where I was oblivious to bullets and shells. I suppose I would have been psychologically capable at that moment of some great heroic feat. Perhaps it is this particular state of excitement that makes it possible for men to engage in something like Pickett's Charge or the Charge of the Light Brigade or to do something that wins a posthumous Medal of Honor. But the problem was that I really didn't know what to do. I didn't know where Johnson and Polino were, and my radio didn't work. What good was it for me to be with Driscoll if I didn't have any communication? Our plan had been that I would leave Driscoll and the 1st Battalion and meet Murphy at the rendezvous point after the actual beach had been secured. But we were 500 yards to the left of where we were supposed to be and the plan had gone awry. Had anybody else actually crossed the beach and made it up the bluffs? I hadn't a clue!

I left Doyle and Fitzwater on the road and plunged off through the hedgerows and intervening fields all by myself. The fields were cattle meadows and apple orchards. I guess I thought I would take a look and then come back. However, luck had not deserted me for at about the third field I ran straight into an assault section from one of the 1st Battalion infantry companies. There was a 2nd Lieutenant whom I vaguely knew, and about a dozen men. They had come up against an enemy gun position in a hedgerow at the corner of one of the fields. Not knowing what else to do, I simply joined them. They were trying to get a good bazooka shot at the point where they thought the gun was located. A dead American soldier not far from where we were was obviously what had provoked this little battle. I spent quite a while with them while they attempted to get at the enemy position, but they couldn't tell whether they were doing any damage or not and were reluctant to go through the hedgerow and into the open field with such a small force. This was my first (and their first) encounter with the hedgerow fighting of Normandy and the peculiar problems it posed to infantry on the attack. Ultimately it was found that it was almost impossible to attack a defended position in the hedgerow country without tanks to provide covering fire, or better still to lead the way.

What I had not appreciated was that our little salient, or outward projection of the battle line to Coleville, was very narrow. I could just as well have blundered right into a German position.

After awhile they abandoned the attempt to attack the enemy position and moved farther to the right and then circled back to where we met a lot more soldiers. I sat down and smoked a couple of cigarettes and even cleaned my fingernails. A nearby soldier thought I was out of my mind. "Look at this guy; cleaning his fingernails!" It was now approaching noon and I decided to go back to the edge of the bluff where we had originally come up and see what was going on.

The scene below me on the beach was appalling. There was wreckage of boats and vehicles as far as you could see in both directions, and many fires and much smoke. Artillery shells were still coming in and hitting boats. I watched an LCT loaded with anti-aircraft guns turn sideways and come in broadside and hit a mine on one of the beach obstacles. Virtually all of the tanks in the little group where I had landed were still there but were now burning. They were being picked off one by one by anti-tank guns up the beach located in block houses behind thick concrete walls and sited so that they could fire along the beach, not straight out to sea. Until infantry working to our right opposite the E1 exit could overrun these emplacements they were able to exact a terrible toll. Some destroyers had come in close and were firing point blank at the cliffs to the east (left) of us. I still couldn't tell what was going on to the west of us opposite the E1 exit, although I understand that they eventually brought a Navy destroyer in close and blasted the concrete gun emplacement that was holding things up.

Today the Normandy American Cemetery and monument is located at the spot where I was now standing. In fact, the main path from the cemetery to the beach, which is now paved, follows the line of the trail we came up.

It appeared to me that it was much healthier to be up front with the infantry at that moment. I went back toward Coleville, picked up Doyle and Fitzwater, and followed the road until I found Driscoll and the 1st Battalion CP behind a hedgerow just short of Coleville, and a little way off the road to the right.

I must have spent most of the afternoon there. I munched a "D" ration, a bar of hard chocolate. I still didn't know where George Johnson and Polino were. It turned out that Polino had landed in pretty good shape, had been pressed into service as infantry, and was now digging in near Coleville, just ahead of where I now was. George had in the meantime reached our rendezvous point with Murphy, after having spent some time clearing lanes through the mines and barbed wire near where we originally came off the beach.

Around 6:00 pm I decided to once again try to contact Murphy and "A" Company. Once more I walked back to the top of the bluff and then followed the ridge towards the E1 exit, a little smarter route than on my previous attempt. I reached the edge of the E1 valley and could see the E1 exit road coming up from the beach to the plateau on the far side of the valley. It was crowded with tanks and all manner of vehicles moving up off the beach. It was now apparent that we were here to stay. The 18th Infantry Regiment was by now ashore, and I believe that the 26th was starting to come in.

I quickly got across to the road (and probably walked through a minefield) and went up towards St. Laurent-sur-Mer. Just after the road emerged onto the plateau, on the outskirts of St. Laurent, I found my company and also our battalion headquarters. The "A" Company casualties had not been bad -- about 10 killed. The only officer hit had been Murph. As he ran across the beach a machine gun bullet hit him on his side, grazed a rib, and came out again. He had a bloody shirt and two little holes in his side which he proudly exhibited. I guess it must have knocked him down and probably knocked the wind out of him, but the water quickly revived him and he was now in fine fettle. The same burst of machine-gun fire killed ex-1st Sergeant Wood who was right behind him. Our worst officer casualties had been with a part of the battalion staff who were on an LCI (a large landing craft carrying about 200 men). They had come in long after me but the ship was hit by artillery (or anti-tank guns) before it could land, and had to back away from the beach without landing anybody. Among others, Bill Barnum was badly wounded.

There was a lot of excitement when I arrived because they were having trouble with snipers. I talked with Murph, and with Gara and Tom Crowley, and they told me to return and spend the night with Driscoll and the 1st Battalion. So I hiked back and settled down behind the hedgerow outside of Coleville.

Late in the day, looking back towards the beach, we saw a barrage balloon go up untethered and disappear into the clouds. Then there was another, and then another. Apparently there was still a bit of panic on the beach!

It didn't become fully dark until almost 11:00 pm, partially because we were on double British summer time. Soon after dark, German planes came over very low and dropped bombs on the beach, but we were safe from that. I don't know what they hit, but it would have been hard to miss hitting something. I recall the white flashes and the deafening cracks of the bombs.

Everybody was very concerned about counterattacks, and from our previous experience in Sicily we expected to be hit hard at dawn. But dawn came and nothing happened. We didn't realize that the Germans were in a complete state of disarray and had nobody available for a quick attack. We had evidently caught a division on some kind of maneuvers at the beach, and this division was supposed to be the local reserve. At the same time our Air Corps had made movement on the roads very difficult for them and the nights at that time of the year were very short.

We just sat there for a good part of the day. The 18th and 26th Infantry Regiments had passed through us and were moving rapidly inland. As a Battalion Commander in the 16th, I remember Driscoll saying, "I'm not used to having somebody else do my fighting for me." The 16th Infantry Regiment had lost 1,000 men on D-Day, mostly in the first hour, and were not to really fight again until the St. Lô breakthrough near the end of July. I returned to our "A" Company.

So what had I contributed on D-Day? Actually not much. I provided one additional target for the Germans to shoot at, but that was about it.

I am not too clear about the activities of the two platoons of "A" Company that landed with Murphy in support of the 2nd Battalion of the 16th Infantry. These were the 2nd and 3rd Platoons under Kosorek and Conant. They were in larger boats called LCT's because they each had with them a bulldozer. Streaky Kosorek's boat got hit by anti-tank fire and they took casualties before they even landed. My impression is that they landed nearer to their original objectives than I did, i.e. more to the right and opposite the low lands at the E1 Exit rather than below the bluffs. By the time they landed (which was about a half hour before me) the 2nd Battalion of the 16th Infantry had virtually ceased to exist so I suspect they simply ignored their connection with the 2nd Battalion and went about their job which was to open the E1 Exit so that the tanks and other vehicles could get off the beach. This involved clearing mines and other obstacles and filling in an anti-tank ditch. I know that they, along with many others, were involved with opening E1, but I don't know exactly when that was finally accomplished, but certainly several hours after the initial landings. At any rate, they made a lot more useful contribution than did I.

I don't recall much about the next couple of weeks. My battalion, i.e., the First Engineers, came together and we stayed under battalion control. With the 16th Infantry out of action, "A" Company had little to do but follow along and try to make ourselves comfortable. I do recall a minor incident a few days after D-Day. Murphy and I went out to investigate a small bridge somewhere between Omaha Beach and Bayeaux. It was just at dusk. We parked and walked to the bridge and satisfied ourselves that it was intact and was not prepared for demolition by the Germans, that being the principal reason for our interest. Just then we heard what was obviously a German plane overhead flying rather low, although we couldn't see him in what was now semi-darkness. He seemed to circle us and I was reminded of the incident in *All Quiet on the Western Front* when Paul and Kat were walking along and a lone plane circled and then dropped a bomb which killed Kat. It had seemed to me to be a rather improbable event. Suddenly to my astonishment the plane went into a dive (at least the engine noise suggested a dive) and soon after a bomb went off about 100 yards away. I could only conclude that this was a plane that got scared away from the beaches and didn't dare return to base with his bomb still aboard.

The advance straight inland was fairly rapid. My first letter home was apparently written during this period. The letter gets a little dramatic, but I knew what my very religious mother wanted to hear, and I also relished the thought of the sensation it would cause when it arrived. It was written eight days after the landing; I presume we didn't have mail service earlier than that.

14 June 1944

Dear Mother, Dad, and Sis:

Well, you can rest at ease and go on up to Canada. You can't kill an old soldier, although I'll admit they sure tried hard on that beach. Boy oh boy, that was an experience I'll never forget. When I got out of my boat the water was kicking up all around me from machine gun bullets and mortar shells and I headed for a tank which was at the water's edge. Temporarily safe I couldn't see how we were going to get across the beach & inland. Then I thought of a passage from the 23rd Psalm --"Yea though I walk in the valley of the shadow of death I will fear no evil." I took my men and walked thru all that fire, stumbling and stepping over the dead all the way. Well, so much for the landing, I just wanted you to tell you about that incident.

Life is not at all bad now. The country is beautiful and we always have good bivouac areas. It is slightly rolling country with thousands of hedged in fields and orchards. Also lots of dairy cattle. Being executive officer I don't do much except hang around the company area and tend to administrative duties, so for gosh sakes don't worry about me.

We're expecting our kitchen in today which will be a blessing. I'm getting awful hungry. "C" ration gets a little monotonous after a while. I also would like to wash up, but we move so much I haven't had much time. I guess when you take out a map of France it looks like we aren't going very fast, but the doughboy can only move so fast and even if you make an armored break-thru, they've got to stop somewhere & wait for the doughboy to catch up. On the whole things are going OK. In fact considering the difficulty we had getting across that blooming beach, it has been remarkably easy.

We see a good deal of the "master race" marching to the rear. Most of them are very young, some only 15 or 16. These are all products of the Hitler youth business and are tough little fighters. Incidently, this letter paper is courtesy of the "master race".

By the way, could you get me another pair of glasses. Mine are OK but I'd feel better with another pair.

The mail hasn't come in yet, and I don't know when this will go out. However, I imagine that after a while the service should get pretty good.

Loads of love,
Bill

By the time the next letter was written I believe we had reached the town of Caumont, 20 or 25 miles inland. By this time the 1st Division was out ahead of the British on our left and the 2nd Infantry Division on our right, and we were ordered to stop. The important thing now was to secure the beachhead and build up for the next phase. As it turned out, we were to be in this position for almost a month.

We had been moving very rapidly and Gara began moving the battalion as far forward as possible in anticipation of the next move. At Caumont, which was on a little ridge, we bivouacked just behind the town, only a few hundred yards behind the front lines, assuming that we would move again the next day. But we didn't move and we soon found that we were unnecessarily close. Artillery shells and even mortar shells began falling on the battalion area as the enemy built up his defenses and became more active. One day I was sitting in an apple orchard eating a K-ration for lunch when a shell came screaming in and burst in the air not 30 feet above my head. Miraculously nobody was hit but that was enough. We spread out the battalion a bit and "A" Company moved back a couple hundred yards into an adjoining farm. We were still bugged by occasional shells, but I guess our "manhood" required that we move back no more.

France
June 25

Dear Mother, Dad, and Sis,

I'm addressing this letter to Berkeley because I still don't know whether you ever went to Canada. We've received some mail recently but I haven't got anything from you that was written since D-day. I got a letter from Sis written on June 5, however.

I meant to ask you in my last letter to get me another pair of glasses, but I don't remember whether I did or not. I only have one good pair and I should have an extra.

Things are rather quiet here now after several days of terrible weather. This sure isn't the "sunny" France I'd heard so much about. However, today is beautiful for a change and I stripped down and washed and put on clean under clothes.

Life photographer Robert Capa was next to me in the boat that I landed in and the last I saw of him he was behind a tank snapping pictures in all directions, so you may see me in Life huddled behind a tank. It will all look very silly because you won't be able to appreciate the hail of M.G. fire all around us. Nobody ever saw Capa ashore, but he may have hopped on one of the returning boats and gone back to the ship -- I wouldn't have blamed him.

I haven't got a worry in the world right now. This darn invasion has hung over my head for the last two years and now that it's over I feel that I'm really over the hump. Everything is going to seem simple after that mess. If they would just bring me a little more mail I'd be completely happy. Incidentally, I keep forgetting to request cookies -- consider this a request. I could really go for any kind of cookies.

We get lots of mail from our little English village. They sort of adopted us and speak of the company as "our boys". Now they're all in a big sweat about the casualties. We're not allowed to give names or numbers in letters.

You may have read that some of the beaches were easier than expected and others were a lot tougher than expected. As luck would have it ours was that tough one. At the end of D-day our progress could be measured in hundreds of yards.

Well, write soon and I'll try to write at least once a week. I think I'll send a letter to Dad in a day or so.

Love to all,
Bill

The "terrible weather" I refer to was evidently the very large storm which wrecked the artificial harbor at Omaha Beach and had a major effect on the supply situation. I was totally unaware of all of this.

26 June 1944

Dear Dad,

I guess this is the first letter I've written to you since I landed in France. I presume Mother & Sis have forwarded my letters to them, however. I got a letter from you yesterday dated 5 June, which isn't bad considering the distance. I've received two from Mother & Sis dated since D-day.

As I suspected, Mother & Sis apparently aren't going to Canada for the time being despite all my urging. Gosh knows when my first letters will get to them. They're going to drive themselves crazy sitting around listening to the radio & haunting the mail box.

Raining again today and the shelling on both sides is fairly heavy which is a bad combination. There's nothing more discouraging than flopping into a slit-trench with 6 inches of water in it. I'm beginning to regret that I didn't pitch my tent over my hole & sleep in the hole as many of the men are doing. This business of piling out of bed in the middle of the night and into a hole is sort of hard on your sleep.

Don't see much of the Luftwaffe during the daytime, although he's fairly active at night. Fortunately the nights are only about six hours long now. It doesn't get dark until about 2330 and it's light again before 0600.

You sound like you're having an interesting time. Apparently your friend who "should know" wasn't far off about the invasion. I guess you hear a lot more out there about what's going on than you would in Berkeley.

I guess on a map this still looks like just a beachhead, but things are now no different than if we were operating in the middle of a continent. I don't have very much to do as executive officer. I mostly stay around the company bivouac and keep things going. Every now and then I get the urge and I go out and see what's going on.

I hope we can finish off this show before winter. I don't relish a winter in this country. The French say that summer doesn't start until July, and that it's hot during July, August, and September, so we have three good months ahead of us. I hear that the Russians have started moving. I believe that once we get a broad front we can push these people back relatively easily by just weight of numbers if nothing more.

Well, that's about all the news for the present. I'll try to write as often as I can.

Love,
Bill

It was now evident that we were going to be at Caumont for an extended period. At about this time the Germans started bringing up some kind of very large rocket mortars during the night, and setting them off just before dawn. Some came uncomfortably close. Murphy and I decided that we were fed up with the anxiety of shelling during our sleep, so we dug a long and fairly deep trench, buttoned our pup-tents together, and pitched them over the trench. With my air mattress, I now had a comfortable haven and spent a lot of time there reading as well as sleeping. Even the rain didn't bother me much.

The battalion brought in a movie projector and set up a theater in the barn of our farm. Movie films were apparently now available. But I do recall watching a movie while shells fell so close that they knocked tiles off the roof. I liked my hole better.

A British division was on our left flank and for at least a week they were attempting to move forward to come up parallel to us -- we were in a salient. Night and day we could hear their artillery, but they were evidently having tough going. One day in broad daylight they brought on what seemed like the entire British night bomber force to lay a carpet of bombs on the German positions. These were big black night bombers, Lancasters and Halifaxes, and they flew singly rather than in formation, because that was the way they did night bombing on German cities. The sky was black with planes slowly flying in all directions and the German anti-aircraft fire was overwhelmed by them. But the Germans were scoring hits and I recall one incident where a large plane was coming down in a very slow and tight spin, virtually pivoting on one wing tip. We held our breaths waiting for parachutes to open, but suddenly the plane disappeared in a cloud of black smoke. The only recognizable thing that emerged was the tail section, which also slowly spun down. No parachutes.

On another occasion I took a detail of men back a mile or so to dig a dugout for General Huebner. I met him and he seemed a nice enough guy. He was sunning himself in a chair on the lawn of a house and seemed a bit old and tired.

France
July 2

Dear Mother, Dad, and Sis,

I got ahold of the company typewriter for a little while so I thought I'd try this out for a change and see if it doesn't improve my letter writing. It seems to have done wonders for Sister.

Today is Sister's birthday. Sorry I can't do anything else for you, but maybe a letter will be sufficient, considering the situation. Your mail is coming thru pretty well now, but I'm afraid that mine isn't doing so well. I got your letter of June 18 today which isn't bad at all. I guess they saved up so much mail prior to D-day that they had more than they could handle when the time came to send it. None of the people in Charmouth have heard from us either although the company has had many letters from them and it is just across the channel. Maybe the establishment of Cherbourg as a port will help out the situation.

The main news here is the rain. We've been here for twenty-six days now and for twenty-six days it has rained. It doesn't rain hard and it doesn't rain continually but it has never missed a day. The ground gets soaked and then the water seeps into your foxhole from the bottom and sides and it takes forever to get your blankets dried out. Outside of the rain we take a little shelling each day, but I'm getting used to that. You have to either get used to it or go crazy.

Sis, I'm glad to hear you have a job. It sounds like a good one from what you say. I hope you get the trip to Chicago. It will be a good experience for you. If you get some schooling in the type of work you are going to do it will make it a lot easier to start out. I suppose that means the trip to Canada is off for good. I wish Mother would take a vacation of some kind, but I guess there's no chance of that.

Well, my first adventure with the typewriter in quite some time has turned out fairly well, but I guess it isn't going to be as long as I had hoped. My typing hasn't suffered too much as I am rattling along at a pretty good pace. I have a tough time keeping from looking at the keys, though.

Love to all,
Bill

The next letter is typewritten, single spaced, and extremely long. Apparently I had time on my hands. It has to do with the landing and repeats some of the descriptions I have already given. But this is at least how it seemed a few weeks after the event. It is very pretentious; somehow I had become an "expert". It contains the kind of discussion I longed to have with my father after the war was over, but I could never interest him. My mother embarrassed me by sending it to my uncle who was an Admiral working with MacArthur in the South Pacific. The reader not interested in technical details may want to skip it.

4 July 1944

Dear Dad,

Today is the fourth of July. Two years ago today I reported for duty at Ft. Leonard Wood. One year ago today I was getting ready to embark the following day for the invasion of Sicily. Today is just like the fourth ought to be -- lots of noise. That's about all the news here. Just a lot of shelling by both sides and everybody sticking pretty close to their holes. I saw a great sight the other day. Hundreds of RAF heavy night bombers came over in a daylight attack. As far as the eye could see the sky was full of planes at all altitudes. They fly very slowly and unlike American bombers they fly in no formation. They weave and turn to avoid the AA fire and they are so big it all looks like slow motion. The German AA was completely overwhelmed and they acted as if they didn't know who to shoot at there were so many planes. I saw one get hit and go into a spin with two motors burning. It was a very tight spin and very slow. Then all of a sudden it burst into a thousand smoking pieces. The pieces seemed to just float away from it. Everybody held their breaths and watched for parachutes, but none appeared.

After the initial landing I didn't feel much like talking about it, but after reading all the newspaper and magazine accounts I feel like blowing off a little steam. I don't quite understand the American habit of trying to make everything look easy, especially after spending months talking about how difficult it was going to be. Then as soon as we get ashore they immediately proclaim the Atlantic Wall a myth. If the Atlantic Wall was a myth I'll eat my hat. Hell, you can take any position you want if you are willing to sacrifice the men. We had a lot of fancy plans but our success can be completely attributed to the very oldest of battle tactics. We simply landed more men than they could hit. It was a type of battle that we have never fought before and I hope we never have to do it again. Masses of men just had to get up and walk into the most terrible hail of fire that I have heard of. In ordinary battle the men just won't do it, but in a landing operation there is no place to stop or go back to. The defenses were roughly as follows: From the high water mark to about 400 yards out were underwater obstacles consisting of principally steel hedgehogs and log posts leaning seaward with a big fat Tellermine on the end of each one. At the high water line there was a bank of shingle (stones about 2 or 3 inches in diameter) and behind that a fairly level stretch for about a hundred yards leading to the base of a bluff about 200 ft high which overlooked the entire beach. In this particular sector there was a small valley opening through the bluff about every 1000 yards, and providing the only possible vehicle exits. In some places there was a certain amount of vegetation on the bluff and in other places it was pretty bare. In most places it could be easily climbed -- it was by no means a cliff. In the flat area behind the beach there was barbed wire enclosing both anti-tank and anti-personnel mine fields. In addition to the wire and mines there were anti-tank ditches across the entrance to each exit valley. The sides to these valleys were heavily defended by pill boxes housing MGs and AT guns of various calibers. Most of these positions we had picked up from aerial photos and they were still in the process of constructing many of them. What we had not picked up were an extraordinary number of well concealed dugouts and log emplacements along the entire ridge of the bluff. There must have been a machine gun emplacement every 10 yards, all looking down on the beach. Behind these defenses were mortar positions along with a good many well concealed MG positions that formed something of a secondary line, although they were more or less isolated with apparently little coordination between them. There were a certain number of rockets of very large caliber registered on the beach exits, and then well inland there were artillery positions. Fortunately there wasn't very much artillery and it appeared to be of very small caliber (probably 75mm). The surprising thing was the lack of tactical reserves of any size. At no time during D-day were we in any position to take a counterattack of any size. Rommel apparently held his reserves well inland and when the time came to use them they simply couldn't move because of the complete inability of the Luftwaffe to keep our planes from shooting them up on the roads. Anyhow, I believe the handling of his reserves was "The Fox's" great undoing.

Now, as to what happened. It is now a published fact that neither the British nor the other American forces had the difficulty forcing a landing as we had. I don't exactly know the reason why, because I feel sure the defenses were very similar, although I understand the forces holding the beaches were much smaller. There were things wrong with our plans that many of us could foresee, but it is a peculiarity among Americans that you have got to have a little combat experience before you can visualize what it is possible and not possible to do when someone is shooting at you. Our plans were handed down to us by staffs who had been working on them for a long time, but none of them had any combat experience to speak of. In an operation so vast as this was it was of course necessary for security reasons for the plans to be made almost to the last detail by the supreme command and then handed down to the lower echelons. In all battle plans, everything is supposedly figured out so that if everything goes according to plan nobody is going to get hurt. Contrary to the popular idea, soldiers are seldom asked to do something that is on the surface impossible. It is the unknown factor of the enemy plus the failure of certain people to do their job that causes casualties and failures. Inexperienced people fail to appreciate the importance of this unknown factor, and fail to appreciate the fact that no matter how good the plan looks, somebody is going to fall down, and therefore a battle plan should be very flexible and have a tremendous factor of safety. Especially a plan for a landing operation. Our only factor of safety was in the mass of men instead of in the mass of fire power where it should have been. We accomplished our mission, but it cost too much in my estimation. The other landings had no more than we had, but their plans must have worked a little better. I felt from the first that our naval support was inadequate. True, it was all figured out in advance how much was needed, but, as you people have apparently found out in the Pacific, you've got to multiply that by ten in order to do the job. Admiral Nimitz apparently learned at Tarawa what I sincerely hope we learned on the beaches of Normandy. You probably know better than I do just what our naval support was and I'll let you compare it with the terrible plastering that a tiny island in the Pacific is given before anyone goes ashore. It's all right to figure out how many rockets it will take to pound into submission a certain strong point, but one should also figure out what will happen when the sea is rough and the target is obscured by smoke and the rocket barrage lands a quarter mile from the strong point in a harmless pasture. That happened. The destroyers and cruisers should have come in closer so that they could see what they were shooting at. They did do that about noon of D-day when we found there were some positions on the bluffs that we couldn't handle. They can't expect to stand out of range of the enemy fire and do much good. There was not a position on that beach that couldn't have been completely destroyed by destroyer fire if they had had enough of them and they had gone in close.

It was apparently felt in many quarters that our tremendous air force made it unnecessary to call for any more naval forces than were immediately available in the Atlantic. It was true, we couldn't have asked for any more air force, but in my mind, a properly used destroyer is worth a hundred bombers in this type of job. The Aircorps almost completely neutralized the Luftwaffe and apparently did a marvelous job of disrupting the German communications. As we went inland we found mute evidence of that on every road. They shouldn't have been asked to do anything else, or they shouldn't claim they could do anything else. Mass pattern bombing of area targets is their meat, and they shouldn't be expected to do the job of artillery. Then too, there is the factor of uncertainty in air operations. There is the uncertainty of the weather and of inexperienced navigators and a thousand other things. In a plan that calls for split-second timing and the absolute certainty of a mission being accomplished the airplane cannot be relied upon. When you are invading something like an island it is OK because you can stand off and watch their bombing until you are satisfied with the results and then go in, but in this sort of operation once you have shown your hand you've got to go on in on schedule because it's a race between you and the enemy's reserves to get there first.

Well, the results of all this were simply that to my knowledge, in our sector, not a single enemy emplacement was knocked out by either naval fire or bombing. When we got in they were all blazing away for all they were worth. Tanks which came in with the leading infantry waves provided the heavy support and the doughboys finally forced their way up the bluff at one point, fanned out, and closed in on the enemy emplacements from behind. The entire D-day was spent expanding this one tiny sector where any substantial force had been able to get inland, and at the end of D-day we had a beachhead about a thousand yards deep and a couple of miles long. (And those are very generous figures.) There was heavy machine-gun fire on the entire beach until about noon, when sufficient emplacements were taken out to make a part of the beach reasonably safe to walk around on. The boats coming in were under artillery, mortar, and 88 fire till about evening. Didn't the President say something about naval losses being two destroyers and one landing craft? Well, one platoon in our company came in on an LCT at H plus 1 hour and took six hits from an 88 before they decided to give it up and come in later. All but one of the officer casualties in our battalion was caused by a shell hitting an LCI. It was just murder in anything larger than an LCVP. By D plus 1 there was so much wreckage on the beach that the boats had a difficult time finding a place to land. Many gave it up during the night and waited till daylight so they could find a place. Many people landing the second day with vehicles tell of having to get out of their boats and pull bodies out of the way to make a vehicle lane.

I landed at H plus 80 min and had the combined good fortune to be in a small boat and to land opposite the only place on the whole beach that any penetration had been made at that time. A few men had reached the top of the bluff to my front but there was terrific MG fire from both flanks. For the last 1000 yards in we were under mortar fire but they couldn't seem to hit much. We had no idea what was going on at the beach because we had been in the water since before H-hour and there was too much smoke to see anything. One thing we were pretty sure of was that we weren't landing at the right place, but as it turned out we were lucky that we did land at the wrong place. There had been a goof-off at the very beginning apparently, and everyone was about 500 yards to the left, and the unit on our right flank was so far to the left that they were on top of us. The MGs opened up on the boats as they dropped their ramps and caught a lot of people before they even got out of the boats. The worst agony was trying to wade thru the water with a tremendous load on our backs and people being picked off all around you. You couldn't run and there was nothing to hide behind so you just had to keep on, wondering which one was going to hit you. The tide was pretty well in by the time I landed and the coxswain of my boat did a marvelous job of wiggling thru the obstacles, so I didn't have far to go before I reached the shingle bank which afforded a little cover. As it was I stopped to catch my breath behind a tank. When the boats of our wave pulled out again the machine gun fire let up because they couldn't hit behind the bank, but any time one put his head over the top it started in again. The shingle bank was a mass of humanity, dead, wounded, and alive. At that time all I could see was disaster. On the other side of the bank in addition to the machine gun fire was a minefield before you could get to any kind of cover at all. If we all became paralyzed with fear, it wasn't for long because they began lobbing mortar shells and rifle grenades on the shingle and it was obvious that it was going to be safer to go forward than stay there. The infantry battalion commander that I was with then discovered that some of the men in the leading waves had got across about 50 yards to the right of where we were and were already at the top of the bluff, so we decided to make a break for it. They had blazed something of a trail thru the minefield by the simple expedient of stepping on enough mines to make a path. As far as I was concerned that was the end of the battle. 100 yards off the beach and in a defiladed place I sat down and smoked a cigarette. Our job was to open the vehicle exits at one of the valleys, but that was obviously impossible at the moment as the fire was terrific over there and there were no bulldozers in yet. I moved inland with the infantry battalion so as to maintain contact because we were to build a road to them and I knew they were not going where they had planned to go. The vehicle exit was finally opened at about 1400, and with the tanks and artillery rolling in the battle was won. A great deal of this equipment had been lost due to enemy fire as well as overturned boats, but there was enough to do the job. The heavy sea was something that I forgot to mention. Whole boatloads of men capsized and the DUKWs had a particularly rough time of it. I don't suppose it will ever be revealed how many tanks and artillery pieces are at the bottom of the channel.

This letter seems to have turned out a bit more lengthy than I had anticipated. Maybe I'd better use this typewriter more often. However, I thought you'd be interested in getting a first hand and reasonably accurate account of one small part of this greatest of all invasions in place of all the baloney the newspapers hand out. Now I hope I don't get hung for talking too much.

Have letters from Mother and Sis up to June 18. What do you think about Sister working for United Airlines? It sounds pretty good to me.

Much love,
Bill

We were still at the Caumont location when the next two letters were written. The Germans in front of us were now fairly active. I recall one day they mounted a small company-sized probing attack. It was very noisy and in a situation like that, if you are not at some kind of command post you don't know whether it's just a small affair or something very major for which you should be making some kind of contingency plans. Nobody ever tells you what is going on.

France
11 July, 1944

Dear Mother, Dad, and Sis,

I received Mother's letter yesterday, dated 27 June, and also Sister's dated 26 June from Ogden, Utah. At that time nobody had heard from me since D-day, but I hope you have by this time. I understand they censored all the first mail, so maybe some of my letters bounced. I'm really sweating out the long one I sent to Dad.

As usual the only news here is the weather. The Frenchman who said that July would be a dry month is a fraud. It's worse yet. We have now had 35 days of rain and it looks like we're in for 35 more. Everything is lush and green but I'd trade it right now for heat and dryness of an African summer.

Yesterday was the anniversary of our landing in Sicily. I fully expect that a year from now the old First Division will be sitting somewhere in Japan and looking back on this landing. We'll have some new Generals then and they'll need some medals.

I'll be anxious to hear how Sis is making out in Chicago. It ought to be an interesting trip.

I've taken up bridge again. All the officers in the company play so we don't have any trouble making up a foursome. I haven't been doing very well but I think I'm getting back my old touch. We have terrible arguments but we have a lot of fun.

We have a company radio that we keep going most of the day. They have an American Forces program which puts out satisfactory music and on the whole it's pretty nice. The news commentators with their usual baloney come on every hour, but outside of that it's OK.

After asking you for glasses I went back to a hospital and had two pairs made in about half an hour for nothing. Sorry I asked you now, but you've probably already had a pair made.

I think I goofed off badly by single spacing this letter because I can't for the life of me think of anything else to say. How about letting me know what you want me to say. I can't say much about what I'm actually doing and there really isn't much else to talk about except the weather and I think you're getting tired of hearing me gripe about that.

Love to all,
WMKays

France
12 July 1944

Dear Dad,

I just heard some Hawaiian music on the radio, so I thought of you and decided to write. I've received several airmail letters from you lately; the latest written on June 28, which isn't too bad. As a matter of fact I get them only two days later than from Berkeley.

I hope you got my last letter. It will probably be a long time before I cut loose with another like that. The papers and magazines are now coming out with pictures that will illustrate the story. (If you didn't get that last letter this won't make much sense to you.) The June 19 Time has a few fairly good ones. At the top of page 9 is a fairly good picture of the beach about 1000 yards to the right of where I landed. It gives some idea of the bluff I spoke of. From the looks of the way the men are walking I'd say it was taken near the end of D-day. The picture at the bottom of page 9 is especially interesting to me because in the corner it says "Life." That was the first indication I've had that Bob Capa, the Life photographer who came in with me, had made the grade. When he took that picture he was hiding behind a tank in knee deep water and looking out to sea. I was behind another tank about 20 yards from him. That is apparently my wave of boats pulling out. Notice the bodies and equipment in the water. If you look carefully you'll see men hiding behind the obstacles. It's hard to visualize the murderous machine gun fire that those men are trying to get away from. On the top of page 10 (left) is a picture of a pill box housing a 47 mm anti-tank gun that was about 500 yards to my right as I landed. The ocean is to the right and the gun fired enfilade fire down the beach. The walking soldier in the foreground is on the road that we built, the only beach exit that was opened that day. That particular emplacement was clearly visible on aerial photos and could have been easily destroyed by destroyer fire from close range. As it was, tanks finally got it from the flank. I hate to think of the number of small boats and tanks that that damn thing got before it was hit. On the top of page 7 is a picture that shows the shingle bank that I spoke of that provided a certain amount of cover at the water's edge. Incidentally, all these pages refer to the pony edition[1].

There is no other news to speak of. The weather let up a little and it didn't rain today. We're getting 'B' rations now and the kitchen is doing a pretty good job of baking. About every other day we get pie or cake or something like that.

Every once in a while some "SeaBees" come riding up here to take a look at the "Front". There's a good sized town up here that sits right on the front lines and they like to go up into it and poke around. Usually after they've been there a few minutes a couple of shells come wailing into town and the next thing you see is a truck roaring out of town with "SeaBees" hanging all over it.

Well, I hear Bob Hope on the radio so I'll have to close. Hope to hear from you soon.

Love,
Bill

On about the 14th of July we were finally relieved by the 5th Division (I think). I remember that the Germans were apparently very well aware of what was going on because they spent the day laying artillery fire on the road leading to the rear from Caumont. The poor guys from the 5th, never having heard a shot fired in anger, had to approach in virtually a skirmish line and did take casualties. We were sent back to near a town called Columbières, near St. Lô, where we cleaned up and got ready for the next operation.

This was to be a large attack just west of St. Lô with the objective of making some kind of breakthrough to the other coast of Normandy and cut off the Germans who were facing the Cherbourg area. But that was the start of the Battle of France and a new chapter. A strong beachhead had been established and The Battle of Normandy was coming to a close. The attack was scheduled to kick off on about the 25th or 26th, so the next letter was probably written just before we moved out of Columbières.

24 July 1944

Dear Mother, Dad, and Sis,

I'll have to admit that my letter writing hasn't been what it might have been lately. I'll try to do better.

Since I last wrote we had a few days of beautiful weather, but it has sure made up for it lately. This is undoubtedly the muddiest, wettest, nastiest country I've ever seen,

---

1   A physically smaller version of the magazine used for overseas mailing.

and that almost includes Tunisia in the winter. It doesn't do us much good to have the biggest airforce if they can't see, and it doesn't do much good to have the most tanks if they get stuck in the mud. The only thing we don't have is waterproof clothes. For days on end my feet have been wet and my clothes and blankets damp. You know it's funny; when I've been living in a warm house and get wet for any length of time I catch cold invariably, but I've never had a cold all the time I've been in the field. When I move into a new area I sometimes get hay fever, but I soon get immune to that. The only trouble I have is an occasional attack of malaria which is still the main casualty producer in all the outfits that were in Sicily. During warm weather we all keep pretty well dosed up with atabrine. In seems funny to be getting malaria in this country.

Things seem to be breaking in Germany at last, if you can believe the papers. Maybe this affair will be over before winter. I hope so, anyway. I'd hate to be in the field in this country in the winter.

After about a week of almost no mail I today received your letters of July 4, 5, and 9. Also Dad's of the 4th. Incidentally his had been opened by the censor but not disturbed. I had a letter from Sis from Chicago a couple of days ago. I guess she ought to be home by now and starting work.

You speak of having sent me some socks and cookies fairly recently. I don't recall receiving anything since February. However, once more consider this a request for cookies, cake, nut-bread, and socks. I'm getting awfully hungry. Or do you have to have a more formal request?

We still get letters from our friends in Charmouth. Now they all want to know when we are going to get leaves back to England. Fat chance.

This typewriter of ours is getting a little beat up. I may soon have to go back to writing my letters by hand. I had one of the carpenters convert one of our trailers into a rolling office and that's where I'm writing this. Two minutes after we pull into cover somewhere we can open up the back of the trailer and carry on the mess of paper-work that goes along with a modern army. For one little company we sure have an overhead. In the infantry apparently their battalion and regimental headquarters take care of all that, but we live a little more comfortably than they do, so they make us work as if we were in garrison. There is mail to take care of, poop-sheets to be complied with and filed, pay-rolls to be prepared, court charges to be prepared, activity reports to be turned in, supply requisitions to be made up, maps to be handled, and gosh knows what else. We used to think that those things weren't necessary and in Tunisia we had practically no paper work, but after coming out of action we found that our records were all balled up, men were just throwing away equipment because there were no records kept, and in general it was found best to operate as close to a garrison standard as possible, although I do think that our battalion does overdo it.

Well, that's all for now.

Love to all,
Bill

The attempt on Hitler's life took place at just about that time, and that may be what I was referring to in the letter. At any rate we began to feel that maybe the war was nearing its end, and the events of the next few weeks certainly reinforced that notion.

Probably the next day, we moved to a position just behind the 9th Division which was dug in along the St. Lô-Périers highway. Big things were again about to happen.

Robert Capa, Magnum Photos

On the USS Chase, English Channel, June 5, 1944; "C" Company (16th Infantry) officers examining a relief map of Omaha Beach. Captain Victor Briggs in center of picture. I am looking in from the left (in glasses).

This is an aerial photo of the E1 Exit, probably taken the year before. The exit road and the corner of the top of the hill where I agreed to meet Murphy show clearly in the center of the picture. St Laurant-sur-mer is at the upper right. The fortifications and the anti-tank ditch have not yet appeared. This is where we were supposed to have landed, but the 1st and 2nd battalions of the 16th Infantry (and I with them) all landed about 500 yards to the left, off the picture.

This is a low altitude picture of the E1 Exit taken a few months before D-Day, showing the flat beach at low tide. The various obstacles are just being installed (see the horses in the distance). This is the open beach over which the first waves of infantry had to run/walk before reaching the relative cover of the shingle bank seen here just this side of the house.

Robert Capa, Magnum Photos

Omaha Beach, June 6, 1944; I am somewhere in this group with Fitzwater and Doyle behind me dragging the radio.

Robert Capa, Magnum Photos

Same scene, a few seconds later; I am heading for the tank in the center of the picture. The shingle bank and the bluff beyond can be easily seen. A little later I saw Capa behind Tank No. 10 to the left.

This is what Lt. Spalding apparently referred to as the "Roman Ruins". It is the foundation of a house a few yards from the beach that the Germans evidently tore down to clean lanes of fire. Spalding stopped in the shelter of these walls before attacking up the ravine to the left. About an hour later I sheltered on the near side of this wall along with the 1st Battalion Commander.

This is the path up the ravine where Spalding and his men attacked, finally reaching the crest where they successfully cleared out a machine gun position. I followed about an hour later, and ultimately almost the entire 16th Infantry Regiment went up this path. The tape was probably by George Johnson's men. The present cemetery is just beyond the ridge.

Sgt. Phil Streczyk's platoon (Streczyk standing proudly at right.) Picture apparently taken in England at a pub in the Spring of 1944 before D-Day. This is the platoon commanded by Lt. Spalding on D-Day. These men, who earned 6 DSC's that day, were the first men to crack the German defenses of Omaha Beach.

CHAPTER NINE

THE BATTLE OF FRANCE

JULY 25 – SEPTEMBER 23, 1944

Until July of 1944 the war had been grim and foreboding, seldom exciting, and certainly not what one would describe as fun. The early days in Tunisia could be described as exciting, but also scary, and then horrifying. The Battle of France was to be something that we had not before experienced. We were to participate in the complete rout of a formidable army. It was awesome, it was truly exciting, and it was actually enjoyable.

I suppose the generals dreamed of battles in which they accomplished an armored breakthrough, moved at will behind enemy lines, and surrounded large numbers of troops. Obviously the Germans had done this in France in 1940, and also in Russia in the summer of 1941. But after two years of fighting, our thinking, or at least mine, was still mired in the fixed and impenetrable lines of trenches of World War I. You won by simply pushing the enemy back. We had seen the enemy in retreat, certainly in Sicily, but it was always a very organized retreat and the rear-guard fights were always deadly little battles with the retreating forces taking few casualties. I was not prepared for the success of the St. Lô Breakthrough and its consequences. The Battle of France was both exciting and fun and being a soldier didn't seem such a bad thing after all.

As will be apparent in the letters, we sensed that the war was nearing its end; in fact we began to think it would all be over by September. I would not have been so lighthearted had I known that another winter of warfare lay ahead, with some of the worst fighting of the entire war.

To pick up the story again, we had withdrawn from the Caumont salient and had moved over behind the 9th Division in an area slightly west of St. Lô. A very large attack had been planned, and at the time it was explained as an attempt to drive through to the other (southwest) coast of the Normandy peninsula and cut off the Germans facing Cherbourg. Nobody said anything about collapsing the entire German position in Normandy; in fact it seemed unlikely that an attack at the western end of our line would be the chosen way to break out to the east. But I don't suppose any general would ever admit that the whole thing wasn't planned from the very beginning to do just what it did!

However there is no question that the planned operation was to be a big one. Three infantry divisions, the 4th, 9th, and 30th, were to initially attack abreast along a relatively short line with great superiority of numbers. These divisions were expected to make a penetration of the enemy positions, and at that point the 3rd Armored Division was to dive into the hole that had been made by the penetration. The 1st Infantry Division was to be loaded into trucks and follow closely on the heels of the armor to exploit whatever the 3rd Armored was able to accomplish. As I understood the plan, the armor was to go straight south about ten miles to the town of Marigny, then turn right and proceed to the town of Coutances on the coast, about 20 miles farther on.

The unique feature of the whole operation was to be the use of 3,400 heavy bombers from the 8th Air Force, laying thousands of medium-sized bombs on a rectangular area some miles deep in front of the attacking infantry. One thing that made this experiment attractive was the fact that the front lines in this sector lay virtually along a straight section of paved highway, the St. Lô-Périers Highway. The idea was that the highway would provide a definite and unambiguous bomb line that the bombardiers could easily identify.

I was our company liaison at the 16th Infantry Headquarters. I remember being there on the day before the attack, when Ralph Ingersoll showed up. He was now a Lt. Colonel in the Intelligence Section of 1st Army. We were one of several divisions in the 1st Army. Our brass fawned all over him so I didn't even get a chance to say hello. But I recall hearing him say the Germans knew more about our plans than we did. So it wasn't encouraging.

The day of the attack, which I believe was July 25th, turned out to be overcast, which was nothing new. We were well behind the front lines, but everybody went outside of the tents to watch the planes. We heard them but saw nothing; they were all above the clouds. We could then hear the rumble of the bombs and saw smoke ahead. Then everybody waited to hear how the three infantry divisions were doing. Towards evening, we got word that the bomb drop had been carried out some hundreds of yards short of the St. Lô-Pèriers highway, and that the infantry attack had either been held up or at least had been slow getting started.

It was only later that we learned the true scale of the short drop. The infantry had been heavily concentrated just behind the front lines, ready to assault, and they were not dug in. This made them particularly vulnerable. Apparently the short drop extended for a considerable distance along the highway, because both the 4th and 9th Divisions (I don't know about the 30th) suffered terrible casualties amongst their assault troops. Among the dead was General Lesley McNair, Chief of the Army Ground Forces, the same General McNair who was badly wounded in Tunisia when he attempted to observe a battle from close up. He was once more "observing," and that was his last time. The journalist Ernie Pyle got caught in the bombing and described it with his usual skill.

The short drop of bombs completely disrupted the infantry attack, and I am not sure when it finally got started. My impression is that there was a several-hour delay, and it was late afternoon before things got moving. But when it did, it soon became apparent that the Germans had also been badly hurt. Not only had their front line men been roughed up, but what turned out to be more important was the damage that had been done extending two or three miles back from the front lines. Their telephone wires were apparently completely knocked out so that their artillery was almost helpless. Their vehicles were damaged so that they couldn't move. The three American infantry divisions were able to move rather easily, and then, the next morning, part of the 3rd Armored Division, along with our 18th Infantry Regiment, were committed with the remainder of the 3rd Armored and the 1st Infantry Division right behind them. The armor sliced through and they were in Marigny by the end of the day. In the meantime the Air Force had cleared the air of German planes so that they couldn't even see what was happening, much less interfere.

That first day of the armored attack, we moved our company and bivouacked at the highway right on the original front lines of the day before. The 47th Infantry of the 9th Division had been hit by the bombs there, and the area was a mess of dropped equipment and bomb craters, with a scattering of bodies still lying around, some American, some German.

The next day we moved through the hole in the lines and bivouacked just beyond Marigny. In the meantime, the 3rd Armored Division had moved on toward Coutance and I think they were at the coast by the end of the day. I don't remember much fighting that day; it seemed as if we had simply moved into a vacuum. There were no "front lines" anywhere and the enemy was obviously in a state of total confusion, intent primarily on trying to withdraw whatever they could so they could make a stand somewhere. We had an abundance of air cover and our P47s were dive-bombing every German vehicle that attempted to use the roads.

During the next few days our armor moved down to the town of Avranches at the southeast corner of the Normandy peninsula. After Avranches there was nothing but open space for hundreds of miles. At this point the 3rd Army under Patton was activated, and they took off south from Avranches toward the Brittany peninsula, with the 4th Armored Division leading the way.

We, the engineers, didn't have too much to do because the enemy didn't have time to blow bridges or sow mines while in retreat. We spent most of our time clearing roads of the wreckage of German vehicles and equipment, most of which had been destroyed by our fighter-bombers. The Germans made one determined effort to stem the tide. On about the 10th of August, they mounted a strong attack on the town of Mortain, just north of Avranches, in an attempt to reach the sea and cut off the troops that had already passed that point. The attack missed us, as we had already gone by the day before, but the 30th Division behind us beat them back. It was a peculiar sensation to be lying around in the sun in the pretty French countryside with no enemy around, hearing the booming of the guns a few miles behind us.

4 August 1944

Dear Mother, Dad, and Sis,

I guess you can figure out why I haven't been able to write lately. I've unrolled and rolled up my bedding roll so many times in the last week or so that I could do it in my sleep. This is really the way to fight a war. What happened was roughly this. The first two months here was characterized by slow cautious moves. Our armored divisions weren't committed and the infantry just carefully moved forward being careful never to have exposed flanks and never to be over extended. The beachhead was too precious to take any chances. Then after taking Cherbourg came the build-up period. Finally we had the beach-head firmly established and the time came to try some risky stuff. The break-thru was made by a couple of infantry divisions and was preceded by the greatest aerial bombardment in history. The air corps as usual made a couple of mistakes and dropped them on our troops but on the whole it accomplished its purpose. The attack didn't get off to a very good start because it was necessary to bring some other units in to take over the job of the one that was practically wiped out by the air corps, but when it did get going the enemy was found to be completely disorganized and unable to put up anything but harassing resistance. In about 12 hours the breakthru was complete and the armor and motorized infantry was able to pour thru into the virtually unprotected enemy rear areas. The sky was continually black with fighters that jump on anything they see moving and the result was that the enemy was unable to withdraw or bring up reinforcements. The 2nd SS Panzer Division Das Reich tried a withdrawal during the daylight and there is a stretch of back road about four or five miles long on which their convoy was caught. I've never seen such wreckage. For the entire distance there is nothing but burned up tanks, halftracks, artillery and other vehicles. In some places they were bumper to bumper. Lots of the vehicles weren't even touched, the drivers just went into a panic and left them. I've started a collection of German uniform insignias which I will send home eventually[1]. The 2nd SS has made the initial contribution to it.

We see a lot more of the Luftwaffe now, or rather we hear a lot more of it. They come over all night and drop flares and make a general nuisance of themselves. They still don't show themselves much in the daylight.

The weather has definitely taken a turn for the better with only occasional rain and a couple of cloudless days to our credit. The country is a little more hilly but is the same patch-work of small fields and hedges. The war has moved so rapidly over most of the people here that they never even had to leave their homes. One kid almost broke my glasses the other day when he threw a bouquet of flowers at my jeep. They seem a little more glad to see us than those near the coast. I guess the reason is that we didn't have to tear up their country so much.

Mail seems to be coming thru pretty well, but still no packages. I get Dad's letters almost as soon as the ones from Berkeley.

Well, I think the end is in sight over here. We haven't moved very far geographically but the enemy is hurting much more than most people realize and I'm pretty sure he can't replace his losses. I think you'll find that we can move almost at will now. The only thing that's going to hold us up is the 3000 miles of ocean that hold up our supplies and reinforcements. As the front broadens we've got to have more troops and it takes time to get them here.

That's all for now. There isn't any other news. I'm fine so don't worry about me.
Much love to all,
Bill

P.S. Please send cookies

P.S.S. If you'll look at the picture on the top of page 26 in the June 19 "Life" you may be able to find me. I know I'm in the scene somewhere.

5 August 1944

Dear Dad,

---

1 My mother put these insignias in my scrapbook, where they remain today.

I wrote home yesterday but I got such a pile of mail this morning that I just had to write again while I'm inspired. The mail sure is coming fast for a change. I got your letter of July 24 and two from Mother and Sis dated July 29. I wonder if mine are doing as well. They are apparently flying the mail all the way now.

In my letter to Mother yesterday I told her about our new offensive and I assume she will pass it on to you. I think these people are licked now unless they do something drastic like pulling out of Italy. I believe that resistance in the northern part of the front will continue to be tough because they can't afford to let us go that way, but we will be able to go south almost at will. It's just a matter of bringing in enough men to occupy the ground we take. I believe we will eventually form a line between the Seine and Loire rivers and then push towards Paris with the right flank pushing far ahead of the left.

This business of exploiting a breakthru is a new type of warfare for us. Everywhere there are small pockets of resistance and when you ride down a road Germans are likely to step out of the bushes and try to surrender to you. Or else they hide themselves and snipe which is a terrible nuisance. When we pick a new bivouac area we usually flush a few out. I can't say too much for the Air Corps Fighter Command. The enemy is absolutely unable to move in the daylight. It reminds me of our plight in the early days of Tunisia. On the other hand we find it a little difficult to move after dark, especially now since we have clear night and a full moon. They moan and drone around all night and drop whole clusters of bright amber flares. The AA cuts loose all over the place firing wildly and unfortunately obeys the law that everything that goes up has to come down somewhere. I'm more afraid of that stuff than of the bombs. Every now and then you see a string of tracers go across the sky and then a great burst of flame as a night fighter does its stuff. I have great faith in those people — they seldom seem to miss. I knew our bombers did a lot of damage the other day when they made their little error, but I had no idea that they had killed General McNair. He had an unfortunate habit of wanting to see the fighting first hand and generals are too valuable to do that. It's very difficult to see any fighting in this country without getting into the fight yourself. The Germans dig themselves into the hedge rows and are impossible to find until they have fired quite a bit. The artillery isn't playing such an important role as they did in the open country of Africa and Sicily because when you find the enemy strong points you are too close to him to use artillery. At that though, our artillery is plenty active and we are now getting into more hilly country where we have more distant observation.

I at last saw the June 19 Life and Capa's pictures. I'm somewhere in the blurred picture at the top of page 26. In the June 26 issue there are some more pictures of our beach. The two page spread of vehicles coming off the beach is the beach exit road that we built. When I feel that the censors will stand for it I will send you an aerial photo that I used before the operation and which shows the same place.

Well, I've got to do some more washing so I'll have to close. More later.
Much love,
Bill

Curiously I refer in this letter to "forming a line between the Seine and Loire rivers." I still didn't grasp the concept of open warfare with rapid movement and exposed flanks.

While we were basking in the sun I recall taking the company to a large municipal swimming pool near a small town. Life had definitely improved.

The next letter was written from our bivouac near the town of Mayenne.

9 August 1944

Dear Mother, Dad, and Sis,

This is one of these lazy afternoons that we get every once in a while. There is nothing to do and I am sprawled out on a blanket in the hot sun with my shirt off trying to get a little tan. Things are very quiet and I haven't heard a gun fire all day. We are way out by ourselves and it is very nice not to have millions of troops everywhere and the roads clogged with dust-razing vehicles. Our company has the best bivouac area we've ever had. We're on a little farm covered with nice shady apple trees. The ground is covered with grass that is almost as good as a lawn. The battalion has set up a big tent in a sunken road and we are now showing movies three times a day. We get pretty up to date movies now.

Yesterday I did a lot of laundry. You ought to have seen me scrubbing everything from OD pants to underdrawers. I have a little shoe brush that is just about perfect for scrubbing. With a bar of GI soap, a wooden box, and a bucket of boiling water I'm all set.

The only trouble with this place here is that we are pretty thinly spread and the front line is kind of vague. You have to be very careful at night because the enemy can come in and wander around at will. The other night they dropped some paratroopers behind us, captured a bulldozer and some rear area engineers, and made off with them scot free. However, the war is going on well, and as I predicted before the only thing that is going to hold us up is the time it takes to bring in enough new troops to man our expanding lines. The other day the enemy tried the only thing that he could do to stop us, to take Avranches, and he got his nose pretty well bloodied.

You asked about the French people. Well, these people in the inland are a lot more glad to see us than those out at the coast. However, here is a typical conversation between a GI and a Frenchman and gives the general feeling not only here but every other place we've been.

Frenchman: "Americain comerade, Bosch (Germans) no comerade, Anglais no comerade."

GI: "Aw nuts, Americain here, Americain comerade; Bosch here, Bosch comerade; Anglais here, Anglais comerade."

Frenchman: "Ah, vous ne connaissez pas, comerade (plus much other jabber)."

Incidentally, that word "comerade" seems to be a universal European word. In North Africa the Arabs yelled "comerade, cigareet", and the Germans surrender with "komerade, mercy". The Italian children yelled "comerade, beesqueet".

Well, it's getting near supper time and I have yet to shave, so I'd better bring this to a close. I got some more mail from you yesterday, but it was older than the mail I got several days ago.

Much love to all,

Bill

Again I speak of a "front line." I'm obviously not comfortable with the open spaces all around us. I'm still thinking of World War I and the distinct lines of combatants in trench warfare.

Around the 15th of August, we swung around to the north and were involved with the attempt to close the "Falaise Gap"[2] and trap the bulk of the German army facing the British south of Caen. This was only partly successful. In the meantime, Patton and the 3rd Army were racing south and east into the center of France and the Germans were only concerned with getting out of Normandy and re-grouping for their next stand. Whether that was to be along the Seine or at the German border wasn't clear to me, although I imagine that the high command by this time was pretty sure that we were going to sweep completely through France. There was going to be no repeat of World War I in northern France.

The next letter was written during the Falaise Gap affair, but we didn't have much to do and were enjoying the fruits of victory. We were bivouacked at a place called Bagnolles in a pine forest. One of the main things I remember about Bagnolles was that we had recovered a quantity of French wine and liquors and had an officer's party one night. I drank Quantro like it was beer and suffered for it.

19 August 1944

Dear Mother, Dad, and Sis,

I can't remember when I last wrote, but I have a suspicion that it was some time ago. I've been getting a peculiar assortment of mail lately. Some of it has been as far back as 17 July, and some has been as recent as 11 August. Nothing unusual has happened, however, now that Sis is back.

Since I last wrote things have progressed very well here. There has been another invasion, though why I'm not quite sure. If we hadn't made our breakthru it would have been very important, but as it is now there isn't much to be gained by it. The German field forces pulled out of Southern France some time ago and all there is a lot of static garrisons that may be tough to dig out. I suppose they had the invasion all mounted and decided to go through with it. The German army has already been decisively beaten in France and probably will not be able to make a stand this side of the Siegfried Line[3], although they may put up a fight to the north of the Seine in order to save their rocket installations. I don't expect any great news over here for awhile as it will take time to build up a supply system for our over-extended forces. The railroads look almost useless, but they may be able to fix them up in time. We need Brest[4] badly now as Cherbourg is way overworked. I imagine the Russians are now in a similar situation and will be able to move again when they get organized. I see little use in pushing the Italian campaign any further and hope to see most of those troops moved over into France. That may be the principle object of the new landing.

In the meantime we are having movies, listening to the radio, and cleaning up. I'm

---

2 The battle was named after a corridor the Germans tried to maintain to allow their escape.
3 A German defense system along their western border.
4 The French port.

hoping for more mail soon. I still haven't received any packages although they seem to be coming through.

I see that Time predicts that we will keep a 2,000,000 man army of occupation in Europe. Oh, me! And then General Lear says most of the troops in Europe will come home via the Suez Canal and Tokio. OH, ME!

I wonder if Dad saw the President when he was at Pearl Harbor. I hope they can get the Pacific War going on a large scale before I have to get mixed up in it. If we can get them out of the jungles and turn our armor loose on them it's going to be a different story. It's a funny thing about these armored divisions. The new ones are showing up much better than the ones that had experience in Africa and Sicily. The reason apparently is that the ones that fought there got badly beaten up by 88's and developed a terrible fear of mines. These new divisions weren't committed until they could be thrown into the open, and have moved very fast because they literally don't know what it is to be afraid, whereas the other people are cautious and stop and think about it when someone shoots at them.

We are now bivouacked in a place that used to be a German base of some sort. Nearby is a German QM salvage dump and all the men are loading themselves with souvenirs. We mail home on the average of a dozen helmets a day. My collection of insignias is coming along very well and I now have a shoulder patch from every branch of the German Army.

A Red Cross doughnut wagon is due here soon so we will have coffee and dough-nuts. See you later.

Love to all,
Bill

While we were at Bagnolles, the 7th Armored Division had started to move east-ward toward Paris. Between the preceding and the next letter we also started moving in the same direction, with the 3rd Armored Division out ahead of us. There was virtually no opposition and all we did was ride in our vehicles and camp. My principal duty, outside of ordinary company administration, was to ride out each day with our Battalion Adjutant as part of an advance party to pick out the next bivouac area. We went out in a string of jeeps, and when the spot was picked I then had to decide where each of our platoons would be located, where the company headquarters would be, etc.

We passed south of Paris. Ironically, the division that got to parade through Paris (their picture is on a commemorative stamp) was the 28th Infantry Division, which was the division we replaced back in January in the original invasion plan. I don't think they had even been in combat yet. Such were the little injustices of the Army. There would be others.

I recall going through Chartres (I didn't even notice the cathedral!) and then camp-ing near a town called Étampes, a few miles south of Paris. Somebody had recovered a large quantity of champagne from a German cache. I went over to our Battalion Head-quarters that night and drank quantities of champagne from my canteen cup. The result was too much. I staggered back to the company and collapsed into my pup-tent. I was awakened early the next morning to go out again with the advance party. I had the most terrible headache I've ever experienced, together with all the other symptoms of an awful hangover. There was no time to get aspirin from the medics, so I rolled up my tent and bedroll and crawled into my jeep. The road was rough and every bump went to my head. That morning we crossed the Seine at a place called Melun, east of Paris, and then headed north, ultimately locating the bivouac area at Château-Thierry. I remember seeing French Forces of the Interior (FFI) people near the outskirts of Paris, running around and apparently trying to round up scattered Germans, but scaring everybody by shooting at every bush and tree.

We continued north towards the Belgian border at Mons, following the 3rd Armored Division. I recall at this time trying to buy eggs for the company at a French farm. Despite my "excellent" French the farmer thought I wanted to steal his eggs. He invited me and the jeep driver into his house and his wife prepared fried eggs for us. After eating the fried eggs I think we finally did manage to buy a couple hundred eggs, but it had been easier to do so in North Africa.

The next letter was written a few days before we reached the Belgian border.

1 September 1944

Dear Mother, Dad, and Sis,

This is just going to be a short note as usual I haven't much time. You haven't heard from me for a long time for more than one reason. One is that all I've done for the last two weeks is roll up and unpack again, sometimes more than once a day. Another is that my mail has to travel a lot further than it used to have to.

The war is going very well. The big question in everybody's mind is where are the Germans going to make a stand, if any. I'm afraid it will be on the German border which was something I didn't think was going to happen. However, they are a very beat up army and unless they can pull reserves from someplace else they are going to have a tough time of it. They are no longer putting up anything but a weak rear guard fight here.

Haven't received much mail lately, but that ought to be coming thru pretty soon. As a matter of fact ammunition and gas are the only things with any kind of priority and the food hasn't been any too good. However, I'd just as soon not eat well for a month if we can move this fast.

Two years ago yesterday I sailed out of New York harbor. Boy, I sure didn't know what was ahead of me then. I remember then we were in a big sweat about getting in on the Second Front. Then when we went to Africa we thought all our worries were over. Outside of D-day this campaign has been a breeze compared to Tunisia and Sicily. Right now we in the infantry divisions are of secondary importance to the armored divisions and all we do is follow along and occupy the ground. When the going gets slow I imagine we'll get into the thick of it again.

Well, it's about chow time and I'll probably be running out right after chow so I'd better close.

Love to all,
Bill

P.S. I almost forgot. I received your cookie package dated July 17. Many thanks. It was a wonderful supplement to our rather meager rations.

P.S.S. Here is a picture of a party we had during a few day's rest a couple of weeks ago.

The drinks are from a German wine cellar. You may not be able to recognize me. It's a rather extraordinary picture. Also just had a haircut.

The day following the preceding letter we had an exciting experience that is described in the next letter. The 3rd Armored had reached Mons, in Belgium, and we were a few miles behind at the town of Maubeuge in Northern France. Our column had been moving straight north, and at the same time a German corps had been moving parallel to us but to our west. Something obviously had to happen if they were to make their way back to Germany. They turned east and attempted to cross between us and the 3rd Armored Division. The Air Force caught them on the road and by bombing and strafing stopped and jammed up their convoy. They abandoned their vehicles and attempted to cross our column in small groups during the night. It was a wild night, but I'll leave more of the description to the letter.

We then proceeded to Mons, but now everything stopped. We had outrun our supply lines, and in particular had run out of gasoline. I believe that at this time there was a big controversy between Patton and the 1st Army commander, Hodges. Patton had been moving straight east, south of Paris, was making good progress, and demanded all the gasoline. I guess he won the argument, as we sat there for several days. It is interesting to contemplate what might have happened had the fuel been given to Hodges instead, because the traditional military gateway to Germany had always been through Belgium, not straight east from France.

While at Mons we had a chance to do some reorganizing. "C" Company had had a lot of officer casualties and Fred Finley, commander of that Company, prevailed upon Gara to give him George Johnson. At the same time Gonzalo Martinez was transferred to us from "B" Company. The "A" Company officer complement then became Charlie Murphy, CO; me, Executive Officer; Martinez, 1st Platoon; Streaky Kosorek, 2nd Platoon; and Bob Conant, 3rd Platoon. It would stay this way until December. I was distressed to see George go, but Fred argued that if he was going to have few officers, he needed good ones.

About the 6th of September we started to the east, following along the north bank of the Meuse River, with Aachen, Germany, as the objective. My impression is that we no longer had the 3rd Armored ahead of us. We broke down into regimental combat teams and as I recall, I was company liaison with the headquarters of the 16th Infantry during this period. We passed through Namur, Huy, and Liège.

I remember talking with John Lauten, the S2 (Intelligence Officer) of the 16th Infantry while we were at Huy. We were all concerned about what we would encounter when we reached the German border and the vaunted "Siegfried Line," with its concrete pill-boxes and its rows of concrete "dragons teeth," which were anti-tank obstacles. John said that maybe the "momentum" of this drive was so great that we would drive right on to the Rhine. I couldn't see what "momentum" had to do with it. The Germans were either going to assemble enough troops to man the line, or they weren't.

The next letter must have been written at about this time.

13 September 1944

Dear Mother, Dad, and Sis,

I think the time has come for another letter. I can't tell at this point whether it will be a long one or not. Depends upon the situation, as they say in the army.

The mail at last began to come thru and today I got a letter dated 2 Sept. I was sorry to hear about Geary. Please express my sympathy to Mrs. Howard.

You always want to know where I am. Well, take a look at the map and somewhere on it you will see a salient of some kind. That's us. If there are two salients, then look at the longest one. You will always be correct, I assure you. It has never failed. There is only one exception. If the salient enters some important city then we aren't there; we're out in the sticks. We completely crossed France and yet I have no stamps to send home. I have no idea what a French city looks like, although I can tell you a hell of lot about their farms. In Belgium I've been through a couple of small cities principally because it's hard to avoid them. Southeastern Belgium is mining country and is almost one continual town. However, it's nothing as compared to what lays directly ahead of us.

We had an interesting time a week or so ago. As we were chasing the Germans up past Soissons and the British began to push up on the left side of Paris we knew that sooner or later we were going to catch up with them. It happened on about the 3rd of September. An armored division was ahead of us, and on the morning of the 3rd they were in Mons, Belgium, and we were well behind them. As we closed on them the remnants of five German divisions tried to cross in front of us going east for all they were worth. The wildest battle and the worst slaughter of human beings that I've ever seen followed. There were terrible traffic jams and the aircorps was called in to make the best of it. The Germans were completely disorganized and scattered. That night more Germans came thru our battalion bivouac than there were American in it. All night long our machine-guns were going and we were taking small bodies of prisoners. At dawn every ditch and every clump of trees was full of Germans that had to be cleaned out. The fool Frenchmen would shoot every time one of them stuck his head out so it was hard to make them surrender. Everybody including the Medics and the QM took prisoners. When we finally moved on the division had taken 15,000 prisoners and left about 3,000 German dead behind. All of which spelled just about fini to the German army in the west. They're going to have a rough time manning the Siegfried Line with the old men and boys they have left.

Sister's schedule sounds a bit extraordinary. Does it always add up to the same number of hours every week? They must have a large department that does nothing but figure out work schedules.

It's getting cold as the very dickens and for me it is a race against the weather to get the war over with. I think in another week we'll know a lot more about when this thing is going to end. That means that by the time you get this letter we ought to know one way or another.

Well, that's about all for the present. I won't send any requests with this because you say you don't need them for the next month.

Much love to all,

Bill

Somewhere between Liège and the German border near Aachen, the infantry dismounted from the trucks and started on foot. The Siegfried line was manned, but only lightly by local garrison troops, and was penetrated easily. But soon after, and before Aachen was reached, they were hit with a strong counter-attack by the German 12th

Infantry Division. The party was over!

23 September, 1944

Dear Mother, Dad, and Sis,

I can no longer give as an excuse for not writing that I'm moving so fast that I don't have time. The chase is over and the enemy is not far ahead in great strength. He definitely doesn't want us to come into Germany and has made that known in no uncertain terms. The Siegfried Line is not an impenetrable barrier as we have already gone through it partially with no great difficulty, but a lot of Germans fighting for every inch of the ground and supported by a great amount of artillery and mortars does form something of a barrier. If he has any secret weapon it's a rain machine. We spend most of our time pulling trucks and tanks out of the mud and keeping the roads open. Our company was fortunate in finding a house that had been left by a German colonel and we are living in pretty good style. Most other people didn't fare so well and the poor old infantry is sleeping in foxholes half full of water. One satisfying thing about fighting on German soil is that the people who live here will have no taste for war for a long time. What these people think they are going to gain by another winter of war beats me. With the airpower we've got this winter and the bases right on the German border we can systematically level every German city and maybe it'd be a good thing if we did. However, most of the troops ahead of us are old men and boys and even if we're not moving they are getting the worst of it so maybe they'll cave in before too long. If this affair up in Holland works out OK we may be able to move across to the Rhine in which case they will have lost the bulk of the most important industrial section of Germany. Maybe they'll see the light then. I'm afraid though that they landed the airborne forces too far ahead of the British. Airborne troops just don't have the weapons to hold out long against organized armored attacks.

I'm patiently awaiting the arrival of some more cookies. Since I've been on the continent I've received one package that was postmarked sometime in July. How many have you sent? The mail has been coming through pretty well and I've received letters as late as the 3rd of September. Although the company gets mail every couple of days I usually seem to get mine in bunches of several letters at a time, sometimes two or three weeks apart. Dad's letters seem to average about a week behind the others.

The enclosed citation I've hesitated to send because I know you will go crowing all over the place (this is for Mother's benefit) and it really doesn't amount to much. The Bronze Star is a very low medal and practically everyone has one. It was just instituted a few months ago and we've been trying to find an excuse to get one for everyone that's been through the whole business because the campaign ribbons and battle stars mean so little since the rear area troops get the same thing as the combat troops. I don't know how many battle stars I rate now. I got two out of the Mediterranean Theater and I don't know whether I'll get more than one out of this campaign or not. I now rate a unit citation ribbon (to be worn over the right pocket) with two clusters. They finally authorized overseas stripes after Ernie Pyle put up such a fuss and I should be wearing four of them. By the time I get home I ought to have them half way up my sleeve.

You asked if I'd ever seen Ernie Pyle. He spent the better part of the Tunisian Campaign with this division, but we haven't seen much of him since then.

That's all for now.

Much love to all,

Bill

Our company, "A," had moved onto a small estate near the town of Eynatten, Belgium, a mile or two short of the border. Because it was getting cooler and we found ourselves with a nice two-story country house, we moved indoors for the first time, or at least we moved the company headquarters indoors. Murphy and I shared the master bedroom upstairs. The house had been occupied by a German officer, a Colonel Schmidt (or maybe he was a Major), and he and his wife had evidently departed in a hurry and left most of their personal effects behind. We had an interesting time pawing through their stuff. After a few days a Belgian woman and her daughter showed up and said the house was theirs. We turned over an apartment in the basement to them.

I remember in particular looking through the Schmidt's phonograph records. They had an English record with a song entitled "I'm going to hang my washing on the Siegfried Line if the Siegfried Line's still there." (At least that was the first line of the song.) Obviously it was a record recovered from the British retreat to Dunkirk in 1940. One of the little ironies of the war!

There were also photographs of the Schmidts in the backyard naked. Oh, we got to know the Schmidts very well!

We had originally expected to be in the Schmidt house for one night. We were there at least two weeks. Very tough fighting was taking place just across the border ahead of us as the infantry slowly slipped around to the right of Aachen, but little progress was made directly into the city. Other divisions moved up on our flanks and encountered the same fierce opposition. The Germans were obviously going to defend Germany, and had brought new troops in from the east to do just that. The Battle of France was over. The war was not going to end soon, despite all my heady prognostications.

Bagnolles, France, August 1944; Drinking captured German liquor after Battle of Falaise Gap. Left to Right: Crowley, Kays, Murphy.

Somewhere in France, Summer 1944; Some members of my old 3rd Platoon with a Nazi flag. Left to Right: Cendroski, unknown, King, Orehowski, Beardsworth, Sgt. Lowe, Sgt. Graham (partially hidden), Libby.

CHAPTER TEN

THE WINTER WAR

SEPTEMBER 23, 1944 – MARCH 10, 1945

We were still living in the Schmidt house in Belgium, near the German border, when the next letter was written. Things had changed. Five months of some of the toughest and costliest fighting of the war lay ahead. However, I still seemed not to comprehend that fact, and was positively lighthearted. I was even starting to think about what I was going to do when the war was over, so I evidently thought that I was at least going to live. This was a big contrast to my attitude the previous spring.

2 Oct., 1944

Dear Mother, Dad, and Sis

I just received some mail so I'm going to write a letter while I'm still hot, so to speak. It was a letter from Mom dated 19 September which is pretty good, but of course still no packages. I guess I asked you in my last letter for an accounting of what you have sent and when. Speaking of accounts, how about a financial statement. I'm beginning to think vaguely of the post war world. Not that the war is over or any thing like that, but it's nice to think about.

Well, here's the latest war communique from your front line correspondent. Can't tell you where from but Dad seems to figure out where I am anyway. It is obvious to you by this time that our joy ride through France and Belgium came to a muddy, sloppy halt in and about the Siegfried Line. Since then we've been locked in the meanest battle since D-day. I know I don't sound like I'm fighting much of a war when I sit here and type a letter and as a matter of fact I'm not. We're still in a very nice house and the artillery has let us alone and everyone is quite happy. Now and then we have to go up front and lay mines or fix up a torn up road or bridge, but that isn't very often. Last week we had to blow up a lot of pill boxes because every time the Germans gained anything in their counterattacks they would come back and re-man their blooming Siegfried Line so we blew them up so they couldn't reuse them. It was kind of ticklish business wandering around the front lines carrying cases of TNT, but once again that's the beauty of being an executive officer — I only go out when the company commander isn't available. The worst thing about this battle is the artillery fire. It's an ordeal to drive on any of the roads within five miles of the front. It's something we haven't had to put up with so much in this campaign because artillery doesn't like to shoot with planes hovering overhead, but now this weather is so lousy that the advantage of our overwhelming air superiority is lost. It used to rain a lot in Normandy, but it was in the form of showers and visibility was pretty good, but here we've had just one real storm after another. The Germans move about in daylight with relative ease which is something they never used to be able to do.

3 October, 1944

I got interrupted yesterday and I couldn't finish this. I'll have to finish it quickly now because the clerk wants to use the typewriter to make out the morning report.

I have reason to believe that in the last two months the official German Army attitude in regard to the outcome of the war has completely changed. Before then they were certain of victory. Now they are certain of defeat. The question is why do they still fight? Apparently the idea is to try to salvage what they can, and possibly get a negotiated peace, and also there is no doubt that the army and Hitler do not share the same views. The Army would just as soon quit now in order to save some material for the next war which they openly speak of. Hitler of course has no interest in the next war.

I haven't got time to start another page so I'll quit. Everything is OK and I don't think there is much to talk about anyhow.

Much love to all,
Bill

Between the preceding letter and the next, we moved the company east into the town of Brand, an industrial suburb of Aachen around to the right (south) side. We were now fully in Germany. Our whole battalion was brought together and moved into some apartment houses. The local inhabitants, Germans, had mostly moved out and the buildings were empty. Here we were much closer to the front lines and there was considerable enemy shelling. As I recall, we moved the company headquarters into an apartment on the second floor, but on the rear side of the building to at least partially protect us. We kept the apartment very warm because there was a coal-fired stove and we found lots of briquettes (pressed powdered coal) at the back of the building. From somewhere we got cots and the officers, at least, slept on them.

15 October, 1944

Dear Mother, Dad, and Sis,

I'm trying out a German typewriter, so the results may be a little interesting. The keyboard is standard except that the y and z are interchanged. Of course all the symbols are changed around and you have to hunt to even find a period. Then there are such symbols as - [symbol missing].

I don't remember when I last wrote, but I have a suspicion that it wasn't recently. I can say I'm in Germany now - I don't remember if that was permissible in the last letter. The mail has been coming through fairly well, although no packages.

I'll have to admit that I'm getting just a wee bit war weary now. I had no idea at the beginning of this thing that they would keep us in it so continually. After about 30 days in the line the troops lose all the enthusiasm they might have had and from then on they just exist. A week or so in which they are allowed to relax, clean up, and enjoy a certain amount of entertainment will usually put them back in good shape, but we are now in the middle of our fifth month during which time we have been on several occasions out of contact with the enemy, but we've never had what could be strictly called a planned rest. We were pulled out of the line at Caumont, but it was only so we could participate in the St. Lô breakthrough. We were actually out of action for about ten days then because we had to wait for the weather in order to attack, but that is hardly a rest. During these long periods the men get more and more difficult to handle and you get so you would give anything in the world for just one day to call your own in which you wouldn't have to bawl someone out or get bawled out yourself for something your men did. I think the handling of men overseas would make good material for a book someday. It's really a problem. Not a single one of them wants to fight, or feels that he has anything to fight for. There is nothing overseas for them to spend their money on so most of them don't care if they are court martialed and fined. They won't jail a front line soldier because they feel that is too good for him. He'd like that because it gets him away from the front lines. Most of them don't want any rank because that involves responsibility and there aren't enough advantages to being an NCO to warrant the responsibility. So all in all fighting the war with the "citizen army" is an endless headache of nagging, begging, and leading by the hand. What a joy it must be to serve in a volunteer outfit where you can get rid of a man who doesn't want to play the game.

There's not much news so that's the reason I launched off into the foregoing discussion to fill space. The Luftwaffe is beginning to be a little more active at night again, which is hard on sleep, but I refuse to sleep under ground in this weather, so I just sweat them out. Otherwise everything is OK.

Much love to all,
Bill

During the next week or so the division was involved in surrounding and then finally capturing Aachen. Our company stayed in the apartment house in Brand. We had men out virtually every day, mostly clearing the roads and in general keeping the lines of communication open. But we didn't need to move the company because progress was slow, as the infantry and tanks methodically reduced the city block by block. It was the Division's first experience with street fighting. The German Army had removed the civilian population and contested every city block. The 26th Infantry Regiment was doing most of the fighting, and the 16th, with which our "A" Company was generally associated, was holding a flank position to the south of the city.

My duties were primarily administrative so I seldom left the company area.

23 October 1944

Dear Dad,

I haven't written a letter directly to you for some time so I thought I'd try it again. I've been getting your mail pretty regularly and only a few days behind the ones from home. I got three letters from home yesterday dated the 12th and 14th of September and they were all wet, so that accounts for the gap I had in the mail.

Murphy is away for a couple of days so I have the company. I have to keep a little more on my toes, but it's a nice change not to have him around for awhile. It's infinitely more quiet.

The war is a little quieter now. We've captured our city and the pressure is off. I get a kick out of all the fantastic reports the German radio puts out about the terrible losses we took in the street fighting. As a matter of fact in this winter warfare fighting in a city is a lot easier than fighting out in the country. The only difference is that it is slower, but you don't have the mud to contend with and the men can get under cover. The real tough battle here was getting around behind the place. Once we isolated the city it was just a matter of blasting them out. We have big self-propelled 155 mm rifles that we bring up to reduce the more obstinate emplacements. You can imagine what it's like being shot at from a few hundred yards by 6 inch guns. I don't understand why the Russians say that the tank is no good for street fighting. It's our principle weapon. There's no sense in the infantry running around throwing hand grenades in windows when you can knock the whole building down with tanks or these bigger weapons. The result of course is that the entire city is a shambles, but maybe the next time they think about making war they'll remember this place and the others to come. We had planned to systematically blow up every building in the city with TNT but we found it was unnecessary.

The Germans that we are fighting now are a peculiar mixture. The Regular Army units have deteriorated a lot in the last year and their desire to fight isn't what it might be. Some of the prisoners are amazingly young. However you run into more and more SS outfits which are about the best troops you can find. We first met them near the end of the Tunisian affair. We had the idea at that time that because they were mixed up with the Nazi party they wouldn't be much as soldiers. We found that each one of them had to be individually licked. Most of them are graduates of the Hitler Jungend movement and have been Nazi and militarily educated since they were very young. The reason we see more and more of them is that these boys just began to come of military age when the war started, and instead of putting them in the Regular Army they organized these special divisions. Their equipment is the same as the army's and the only difference in uniform is that they wear an SS on their right collar and a death's head on their caps. They fight right along side the other divisions but there seems to be a certain amount of friction between them as the Army feels that they get preferential treatment and they probably do. They definitely tried to get the SS divisions out of France in preference to the others. Most of the SS divisions are Panzers (i.e., armored divisions.).

A lot of people wonder why it is that we were able to actually crack the Siegfried Line and then not go much farther. What actually happened was that when we got to the line it was only held by what local troops they could dig up. Some of the pillboxes weren't even occupied and those that were fairly easy to reduce because of the caliber of the troops and the fact that the defense was too hastily organized. Also the anti-tank defense was very inadequate. Men inside of a pillbox tend to get panicky when a lot of fire is put on them because they can't see very well what's going on. Some of the hardest to reduce are those in which they built outside emplacements and merely used the pillbox as shelter from artillery fire. We've used them for the same purpose in which case it doesn't make a difference which way they face. After we got thru the line they hit us with a series of vicious counterattacks with a fairly fresh division. Although they weren't able to push us back they were able to stop us and hold, and therefore the line had served the purpose of slowing down our attack until they could organize their defense.

It is now obvious that they are going to fight for every foot of ground, but if they do so I think they will expend what's left of their army long before we have to fight our way into Berlin or anywhere near that far. It may be that by the time we get to the Rhine (and that will probably be quite awhile) they will be exhausted. They are now crowing about a homeguard called the Volksturm which Himmler is organizing, but a lot of old men and boys are going to get hurt if they throw something like that at us. The whole war is now rather maddening because the end is so obviously in sight for them and yet I think they will be able to prolong it into next spring and they're not going to hurt anybody but themselves. They've been convinced for so long that they were going to win that they just can't conceive that somehow they're not going to come out on top.

I've got some work to do now so I'll have to close. I still haven't figured out how to use this German typewriter properly. It keeps skipping spaces and yet it doesn't do it for anyone else. Maybe I can do better next time.

Much love,

Bill

When we passed through Liège, Belgium, the previous month, our Battalion had commandeered a nice fully-furnished apartment in the city in a building facing onto the Meuse River. It was then used as a place to send Battalion officers for a couple of days of R&R during quiet periods. Liège was a rather pleasant little city and had not been damaged by the war. As these things usually went, the apartment was used primarily for Headquarters Company and the Battalion staff, but sometimes officers from line companies got a chance to go. I think that is where Murphy probably was when I referred to his being away for a couple of days.

About this time I began to realize that staying back in the rear and administering the company all the time was developing in me something we called "CP-itis," an increasing reluctance to go out where the shooting was taking place. It was perhaps during the couple of days that Murph was away that I decided I had better try to shake it off. Although the bulk of the company was in Brand (and under a little shellfire), the 3rd Platoon under Bob Conant was on the front line with the 16th Infantry in the industrial suburb of Stolberg, a few miles away. I decided to go out and visit Conant and see what he was doing. It was a very quiet morning. Bob took me on a walk down a gently sloping street and soon we were passing sand-bagged machine-gun emplacements with a few soldiers here and there but all in holes or in well protected places. There were only a few houses interspersed with vacant lots. I asked Bob where the Germans were and he pointed to a row of shrubs and trees, a few hundred yards ahead. I was confident they wouldn't shoot machine-guns at just the pair of us, but I expected at any moment to hear the gentle rustle of a mortar shell. We continued walking down to a railroad line that paralleled the front. This was the outpost line; just a few men in foxholes with telephones. The riflemen looked at us obviously wondering who these two idiot officers were. Now I realized that

Conant was playing a game of "chicken" with me. We turned right and walked along the outpost line for a couple of hundred yards. No way would my pride let me say a word of protest. We then turned right and walked up another street towards the rear, my back now to the enemy. I didn't dare look back, and I tried to crack a feeble joke or two. I could have wrung Conant's neck!

At Brand we got another officer. The Battalion had once more decided to make some so-called "battlefield promotions," i.e., to make 2nd Lieutenants out of NCOs. We got a guy named Leuschner who had been a very fine squad sergeant in "B" Company. Leuschner was a fairly competent guy, but I don't think he ever completely made the transition from enlisted man to officer. He was just socially uncomfortable with the other officers. I believe he was wounded soon after, but interestingly he has never attended any of the Battalion officer reunions since the war.

The preceding letter provides a good excuse to digress and discuss something else. At the beginning of this book I mentioned that one of my biggest disappointments after the war was that my father was never interested in sitting down and discussing the details of my experiences. This letter, and many of the others that I sent, contained the sort of stuff I wanted to talk about. I think that at least part of his problem stemmed from an attitude about the European war of which I had little awareness at the time, and which I have only comprehended fully in recent years. My father was in the Navy, and the Navy regarded the Pacific war against Japan as "their war." Pearl Harbor had been an affront to the Navy, and they wanted revenge. The European war against Germany was the "Army's war," and the extent that it siphoned off men and equipment that could have been used against Japan, which it certainly did, was deeply resented. Germany was England's and Russia's problem, and all we were doing was pulling British chestnuts out of the fire. Admiral Ernest King, the Chief of Naval Operations, hated the British and made no bones about his desire to commit all resources against Japan. The fact that the Navy had to mount a very large effort against the German submarines in the Atlantic went against all of King's strategic beliefs. There were continual battles between King and the Army's General Marshall over allocation of supplies, especially landing craft.

When the European war did not end in September of 1944, and it became obvious that it was going to continue until at least the spring, the Navy resentment of the European war intensified. There was a feeling that it was Army incompetence that was prolonging it and thus preventing the United States from concentrating on the "real" enemy. These feelings intensified further when we took a big set-back in December during the Battle of the Bulge, when the Germans made a last intense stand to push back Allied progress into Germany.

My father was at this time on duty at Pearl Harbor, and had almost daily contact with the people commanding the Pacific Theater. Admiral Nimitz, for instance, was an old friend and classmate and my father saw him frequently. I am sure that my father became caught up in this inter-service rivalry and the attitudes that it generated. And of course there was the prevailing Navy myth that only the Marines did any real fighting on the ground. How could my father take what we were doing seriously?

But these attitudes were not confined to the Navy. In fact, the whole west coast of the U.S. regarded the Japanese as the enemy. In that sense, the European war was an east coast war. I began to pick up some of this from the letters from my mother. She was always heavily influenced by the people with whom she talked, and on more than one occasion (probably during the Battle of the Bulge) she made statements suggesting that her friends were getting increasingly critical of the Army and the apparent lack of progress in defeating Germany.

When I went home the next year, it took me a long time to realize that I had been fighting the wrong war. In fact, it took me years to fully grasp it. People, at least in California, were just not interested in our experiences in Europe and Africa. And unfortunately this seemed to include even my father. So I continued to write letters to him full of details about tactics and strategy and technical things, but they seldom provoked any comments from him, either then or later.

28 October, 1944

Dear Mother, Dad, and Sis,

I wrote to Dad the other day, but I believe it's been some time since I wrote home. I guess I didn't tell you that I received two packages of cookies which were certainly welcome. They didn't last very long, though. Anyhow, many thanks and while I think of it I'd better include a request for more cookies and also socks. I'll try to remember to include a request in every letter.

There's not much news of interest that I can think of. As a matter of fact life has been unusually uneventful of late. Winter is gradually setting in but it actually hasn't rained as much lately as it did in September. Today is a relatively clear day but it's quite cold. It is always muddy because it never gets warm enough to dry the ground up. I guess it won't dry up until spring. At home I never remember being very interested in the mud, but I guess it is about the same.

The enclosed picture is the A Company officers about a month ago. We are sitting on the porch of the mansion we lived in at that time. My hair has grown enough so that I can make a stab at combing it.

The Germans send flying bombs over in this direction nowadays. I don't know what they aim at; they don't bother us. We saw them once before when we were around Soissons. They were sending them to Paris. When you hear it coming it sounds like a fast moving bomber. When it gets overhead it sounds like the bomber is missing on about three-fourths of its cylinders. Or as one fellow put it — it sounds like it burns coal and the coal goes thru the carburetor in chunks.

I see that Paris is on limits now and they are going to make a lot of space for passes from combat outfits. However there are an awful lot of divisions over here now so the chance of getting there is probably rather slim.

About the only song I hear over the radio has to do with turning into a mule or some such thing. Fine stuff!! Then there's some other one about a milkman that sounds sort of silly.

This doesn't seem to be much of a letter but as I said there just isn't any news.
Much love to all,
Bill

I recall that at this time the principal action was up in Holland where the British were trying to clear out the Scheldt estuary so as to open up Antwerp as a port. Supply was still a major problem and stuff was still being brought by truck all the way from the Normandy beaches. I think that was the reason that we were for the moment not very active. I can remember listening to the Armed Forces Radio and hearing each day about some place called Bergen op Zoom. (I thought it was a very funny name.)

10 November 1944

Dear Mother, Dad, and Sis,

I have no news of particular interest, but I thought I'd better write because I can't remember when I last wrote. It seems like just a few days ago, but time goes so fast now that it's hard to tell. I just got a letter from Sis dated 30 October which ain't so bad.

The weather steals the headlines today, or rather I should say yesterday. It snowed!! In other words things are rough all over. It didn't stick for long but it's a sign of things to come. And you know what I think of cold weather. It isn't so bad when you can find a house to live in, but of course that can't always be done. The whole of Germany is one sea of mud now. There are few places where you can dig a foxhole more than a foot without having it fill up with water. All of which makes it especially tough on the infantry.

(Since starting this letter gun-fire shook this house just once too often and part of the ceiling fell down right on top of the typewriter.)

Outside of the weather things have been pretty quiet. The food is pretty good with fresh meat every day or so. They've finally got the cigarette situation straightened out so we get a pretty good ration. For one period of five weeks we got none at all. The solution was very simple when the brass began running out of cigarettes. They just cut down on the ration of the rear area people.

We have all sorts of involved rules about not fraternizing with the German people all of which is very fine but very hard to enforce. Being an officer is OK but this business of being a policeman 24 hours of the day becomes an awful pain in the neck after a while. And this fraternizing law is going to be the greatest cause of grief that we've ever had. The American soldier just isn't hard-boiled and he's going to give little kids candy even if he does get fined $50. If people are starving he's going to feed them even if he has to eat short rations. It's a very peculiar phenomenon.

One of the most striking features of the German people is their scrupulous cleanliness. The house we live in has a coal burning stove like in England and yet instead of being black and sooty every metal part of it is so shiny you can see yourself in it. The same goes for all the large utensils which hang on the wall. The people are extraordinarily friendly and helpful and yet we know that they direct artillery fire on us and shoot us at night when an AA barrage makes so much noise that you can't hear their shots. There are plenty of women and children around but very few men. Those that are here are quite old. I've seen very few boys over 10 years old. The husbands of virtually all the women are in the army and most of the houses have German uniforms in the closets.

11 November

Armistice Day! I wish it really was. This is enough for now.
Love to all,
Bill

At about this time, Bob Conant was transferred to "C" Company. They had taken more officer casualties. So now they had both George Johnson and Bob. I think Leuschner took over Conant's 3rd Platoon.

Soon after, the entire division moved ten or twenty miles south of Aachen to take part in a major offensive, the objective being to drive to the Rhine. The entire 1st and 9th Armies were to be involved. Our company was once again attached to the 16th Infantry Regiment and I again became the company liaison officer with the headquarters of the 16th.

The attack kicked off on the 16th of November – what became the infamous Battle of the Hurtgen Forest. The attack was preceded by a "carpet bombing" employing 2,500 American bombers, but this time it was totally ineffective. The country was cut by hills and valleys and covered by evergreen forest. The weather was atrocious - rain, mud, and cold. It was El Guettar all over again, but in the mud and wet and against a lot more German artillery. I now had some idea of what the battles of World War I were like. A continuous stream of ambulances struggled back from the front, along with trucks loaded with the dead. The advances each day were measured in yards. The booming of the artillery went on hour after hour, day after day. The heavy forest added another horror; the artillery shells frequently burst overhead in the trees and a foxhole was little protection. The infantrymen did not have proper clothing or boots and suffered terribly from the continuous wet and cold. The tanks were absolutely essential, but had an awful time with the mud. I heard that in our corps sector (two divisions) we were sending out 80,000 artillery shells a day, and the Germans were answering with 20,000 shells. It was miserable.

The infantry tactics were fairly simple. The objective was pounded with artillery, and then tanks were sent forward, guns blazing, each followed by a squad of infantry. A telephone at the rear of each tank allowed the infantry to communicate with the tankers and tell them what to do. The enemy's machine guns might by this time be closed down, but he responded with artillery and mortars and anti-tank guns. If the tanks didn't get stuck in the mud, or hit mines, or get hit by artillery, and if the following infantry didn't all get hit by the bursting artillery shells, then the enemy position would be overrun. A few arms of survivors would go up and some lucky prisoners would be taken. But then the position had to be held. At first there would be enemy artillery fire, and then frequently a counter-attack, using more or less the same tactics that we used, except they probably used more of their very superior machine guns. This went on day after day, and along a front now hundreds of miles long. Take away the tanks, and the battle scenes in *All Quiet on the Western Front* would still provide a pretty good description. The Flanders Fields of 1917 couldn't have been much different.

General Huebner, the Division Commander, came into the regimental headquarters one day and said, "This is the Battle of the Argonne[1] all over again; we have to keep driving no matter what the casualties."

The engineer work was the usual - keeping the roads open for the tanks and jeeps, and sometimes creating new roads. This was largely a battle against the mud, but now included cutting down trees as we were partially in a dense forest. Throwing gravel on the road was the best weapon against mud, and the best gravel was often that used to support railway rails. There was lots of bulldozer work as we cut through new roads.

I, at least, was very lucky. Colonel Gibbs, the CO of the 16th, lived in great luxury, in stark contrast to Colonel Fechet at El Guettar. I stayed in the headquarters, a large dugout on the side of a little valley, well back from the front, and pretty immune from shellfire. Gibbs fought the battle mostly by telephone, only occasionally venturing out to an observation post. I suppose this was actually the most effective way to lead a regiment under the circumstances. The battle went forward so slowly that we only once moved the regimental headquarters.

I remember listening to Major Smith (also known as Smitty), the S3 (Operations Officer) of the 16th, talking on the telephone. This was the most effective way for me to find out what was going on. Now and then he would get reports on casualties and I began to hear names of officers I had known all the way back in Africa. I saw him look up from the phone and say, "Victor Briggs is dead." Briggs was the CO of "C" company (of the 16th Infantry, not our "C" Company); I had gotten to know him well on the USS Chase. Smitty almost cried when he looked up and said, "T.J. Obrian has just died." The old regiment was disappearing.

I would shuttle back and forth in a jeep to our own company headquarters and get the news there. George Johnson was wounded and evacuated. Bob Conant was with an infantry battalion that got surrounded and cut off. They, or at least the survivors, ultimately surrendered and Bob became a POW. Of course, Bob and George were now in "C" Company. I think Leuschner became a casualty at this time because I don't remember ever seeing him after the battle was over.

We worried about Conant after he was captured. With his fussy stomach how was he going to survive on POW rations? He ended up spending the entire winter walking east through Germany, and then the spring walking west after the Russians entered Germany from the east. His stomach was apparently not a problem.

The next letter is the only one I wrote during this period, and in fact it is the only letter outside of a Christmas card that I wrote for an entire month. It was hand written – no typewriter now.

20 November 1944

Dear Mother, Dad, and Sis,

I'm in sort of a hurry and this ain't too good a time to be writing, but from your last letter you complained about not hearing from me for a long time which I can't quite understand unless they're stopping some of my letters somewhere along the line. Your letters seem to get here in two weeks.

You've asked for "requests" so here are some. First, can you get me some leather fur

---

1   Part of the final Allied offensive of World War I in 1918.

lined gloves? Don't bother if you can't get just that because I have a pretty good pair of wool leather-palmed ones. Also I can of course always use wool socks. And I might as well request some more cookies. Outside of the items mentioned above I'm pretty well off for clothes. They finally got us overshoes which makes all the difference in the world as far as comfort is concerned. The country is still a sea of mud and probably will remain like that until next summer. It hasn't been so cold lately and there's been no more snow, but it still rains every day. The Germans say that we should have an average of 1-1/2 hours of sunlight a day but I suppose as usual this will be an unusual winter.

Received some very nice cookies from Mrs. Lindley. I'm not sure I know her, but I will write and thank her in due course.

At the present time I am acting as a liaison officer with an infantry regiment which is a soft job and quite interesting. We are involved in a mean battle and if we have to fight like this all the way across Germany there won't be any Germany or Germans left.

So long for now and I'll try to write a little more regularly.

Love to all,
Bill

On this letter the Berkeley post office stamp says Dec 9, 1944, so apparently my letters were coming through fairly quickly.

I remember having a conversation about turkey for Thanksgiving. They had turkey all right, but how to get it to the front line troops was the problem. Ultimately they made turkey sandwiches and took them forward in a type of semi-insulated can that was used to get hot food to the front.

The next letter is actually a Christmas card and is not dated, but the mention of Thanksgiving Day dates it.

Dear Mother, Dad, and Sis,
I wrote you the other day so this is just to say hello & Merry Christmas. Begins to look like I'll have a very "White Christmas." Today is Thanksgiving Day and we actually got our turkey. Best meal I've had in many a day. I just hope they were able to carry it up to the boys on the line.

Love to all,
Bill

I mentioned before the luxury in which Colonel Gibbs lived. The dugout had a small dining room and he and his immediate staff ate like royalty. They had fresh meat and vegetables that somebody was apparently purchasing from the local farmers, all served in great style. Gibbs had previously been the G3 (Operations Officer) for the Division, and I guess he picked up his lifestyle there. The whole scene disgusted me. (I was definitely not invited to eat with them.)

After about ten days the regimental headquarters for the 16th moved forward and was relocated to a sort of castle. At least, it was a house with thick stone walls surrounded by substantial external walls. For about the only time when I was in the field, I caught a cold, and felt lousy for a couple of days. I slept in my sleeping bag under a table in the headquarters room, and didn't see any particular reason to crawl out of the sack in the morning. The Colonel spotted me and told somebody to "get that guy out of here."

A little later I moved back to my "A" Company; for some reason we didn't need a liaison officer any more; perhaps it was because the 16th stopped attacking. The Company had moved forward fairly close to the front lines and headquarters was located as usual in a little house. We were right on a main supply road and at night the Germans kept a slow but steady stream of shells coming in on and near the road. I remember one dark and wet night when a dozen or more of us sat in a room close to a stove, each of us holding our breath as every shell announced its pending arrival by its characteristic whine, followed by a crack and flash as it hit nearby (and these were big shells). There was a small basement, but there was no way we could all fit in, so nobody made a move for it. I remember thinking, "This must be what it feels like to be in a submerged and stationary submarine and listening as the depth charges dropped from enemy ships above went off."

The Battle of the Hurtgen Forest went on for twenty days. We finally emerged at the other side of the forest and reached the Roer River, but there was to be no breakthrough to the Rhine, at least not yet. With 4,500 casualties since the 16th of November, the 1st Division was simply used up. I don't think the Division was ever the same again. Too many of the old timers, the backbone of the Division, were gone.

During the first week of December we were pulled out of the line and moved to a very quiet sector some miles to the south. We were in and about a small town called Rotgen, just inside the German border. The company moved into nice houses on the outskirts. No sooner did we get there than it snowed heavily, and this time it stuck. I remember that we had our usual slit-trench latrine in the backyard. After squatting over it in ten inches of snow I decided that the toilet inside the house was a better idea. There was no running water, but a bucket of water could be used to flush it, and for the rest of the winter this became our preferred procedure.

Officer changes took place. A 1st Lieutenant named Wooldridge joined us, probably a replacement for Leuschner. The high casualties throughout the Army that fall had not been anticipated, and the rear area outfits were combed for replacements, both officers and enlisted men, and I think that's where Wooldridge came from. Then a few days later, the Battalion was given the opportunity to send one officer back to the States with one month's leave. This had happened once before, in Sicily, and the Battalion Adjutant (S1), Len Cohn, had been chosen. But Len didn't go on leave - he was permanently rotated home. This time I guess they didn't dare send another member of the staff, and Murphy became the obvious choice. Murph was married and had a baby daughter. A few of the others were married, but none had children. So off went Murph.

As Executive Officer I suddenly inherited a company. I think that Fred Rutledge, then in "B" Company, was the next in line to be a company commander, but it was expected that Murphy would only be away for a couple of months, so it wasn't possible to create another company commander. I was now the "acting" "A" company commander, with all the responsibility and none of the rank. As it turned out, I held the job for four months. I was not particularly thrilled. I much preferred being Executive Officer, and after the Battle of the Hurtgen Forest it was obvious that being Exec was much safer than being a company commander. I didn't think about it at the time, but I was commanding the company led by Robert E. Lee in the Mexican War, almost exactly 100 years before. The company had had a continuous history as a Regular Army unit and probably fifty to 100 different commanding officers in the interim. Obviously some were more distinguished than others!

I was soon introduced to the frequent "company commander's meetings" at which we three commanders of "A", "B", and "C" companies were harangued by the colonel and the staff - at least five of them to us three, Kays, Forbes, and Finley. Fred Finley took me aside and suggested that I keep a good notebook and write down everything they say. "Otherwise they will later deny that they said it," added Fred.

We only stayed in Rotgen for about a week. For some reason I didn't write any letters home. Maybe the shock of finding myself with the responsibility of the Company kept my mind on other things. The Division was soon after pulled completely out of the line and moved back (and north) to Aachen, where we were billeted in some rather posh modern homes in a residential suburb. This was about the 11th or 12th of December. I remember that we had most of the company, about 200 men, in a large house with probably two or three acres of lawns and gardens. The house had large plate glass windows that were mostly broken, but otherwise it was in good shape.

I have no idea what had been planned for us - probably some new offensive - but that soon became irrelevant. The next day I was told that "A" Company could nominate an officer, and some enlisted men, to go to Paris for forty-eight hours leave. I looked around. I had Kosorek, Martinez (who had transferred to us from "B" company in France), and Wooldridge. Kosorek was my only experienced officer, but Wooldridge outranked him. My sense of self-sacrifice instantly vanished. I volunteered myself. Wooldridge, as senior officer, took over the company.

I took our Command Car, a driver, some NCOs from the various companies, and a truck. We headed back that same day to the Division rear headquarters, about half way between Aachen and Liège. There we got our orders and took off for Paris. I remember having supper in a little town on the Meuse at the French-Belgian border (I think it was Dinant), and then we drove well into the night. We went through Rheims around midnight - I recall the yellow mud and the sandbagged cathedral, all in a sort of eery glow from the temporary street lights that the Army had strung up. At about two o'clock in the morning we decided that we were lost, so we stopped in a town that turned out to be Château-Thierry. We found a little hotel and got rooms. I shared a room with Sgt. Francis, the Supply Sergeant of "C" Company. I got to know him very well a few months later. Somehow the other NCOs managed to find women - I never figured out how people did that sort of thing.

The next morning we got to Paris and went to a Red Cross club that was very close to American Express on Rue Scribe. I recall that we parked our vehicles in a lot behind the place, and when we came back we found that they had been robbed! I lost my bedroll, including my beloved air mattress (which I had inherited from Alex Box in Africa).

I don't recall much about my two days in Paris except that I ran into Murphy at the Red Cross Club. He was waiting for transportation to the U.S. The next day we ran into Tom Crowley. The Battalion had evidently been given another officer pass to Paris. Murph and Tom and I found a couple of girls and took them to dinner. After eating they lost all interest in us.

I visited Notre Dame and found it to be dark and dank and altogether a very depressing place. It was heavily sandbagged and the famous stained glass windows had been removed. In fact Paris in general was depressing, certainly not the gay "Paree" of 1917/18 that one had heard about. The people were obviously just struggling to find enough to eat.

We started home on the 16th of December. That night we decided to stay in the town of Laon, which is situated on top of a hill. The next morning, during breakfast, we sent the truck down the hill to a nearby American air base to get some cans of gasoline. The truck driver returned and said that the people at the air base had told him that a big German attack was taking place and that they had broken through the American lines. We scoffed and passed it off as typical Air Force exaggeration.

We proceeded up into Belgium and then followed our old route along the Meuse toward Aachen. I began to notice what seemed like an unusual number of vehicles moving westward, that is, in the opposite direction from us. I said nothing, but I began to think about the Air Force story of that morning. We passed Liège and I began to see vehicles that appeared to be hastily piled high with things like mattresses. I grew a bit more nervous, but we continued on to Aachen and to the place where the company was billeted. It was deserted.

We found what had been our Battalion Headquarters, and Bob Krucklin, the Battalion Supply Officer, was there with a small contingent of Headquarters Company people. They told us the story. The Germans had initiated a big attack somewhere to the south and had apparently made a breakthrough, and the 1st Division, including our battalion, had left that morning to counterattack. It was late in the afternoon and I decided that it would be best to stay there for the night and then try to find the Battalion in the morning. It was by no means certain where they were, and there were rumors of Germans everywhere. As a footnote, it might be added that in returning from Paris we had come within a few miles of the advance elements of the German Panzer Divisions. We had taken a slightly different route than we had on the way to Paris, actually more to the west. Had we retraced our original route we probably would have run right into them.

The next morning we headed south, following signs that the Battalion had posted indicating the direction that they had taken. At one point it was rather disconcerting to drive along a road and see a skirmish line of infantrymen lying on the ground a few yards to our left. However, we found Battalion Headquarters without incident. It was in a little railway station in the village of Sourbrodt, a few miles south of where we had been in Rotgen.

Tom Crowley showed me the map. (He must have returned from Paris before us). The front line was drawn in with grease pencil, and showed two huge indentations just to the south of where we now were, and extending fifty or sixty miles into Belgium. We, i.e., the 1st Division, had been sent in to hold and contain the north shoulder of the "Bulge," as it came to be called. Heavy fighting was taking place nearby, primarily involving the 26th Infantry Regiment that actually occupied the corner where the "bulge" commenced.

I found "A" company in a large farm complex. They were sharing it with the headquarters of the 99th Division, which had been partially overrun and was in a state of considerable confusion. Since the front lines at this point formed a right-angle corner, the rear area troops were all mixed up with each other.

Wooldridge was obviously happy to see me. Streaky Kosorek didn't have much confidence in Wooldridge, who was acting company commander in my absence.

Soon afterwards, we moved the company a few miles to a spot behind the sector held by the 16th Infantry, which was to the right of the 26th Infantry. The Division now held a line facing directly south, extending from the corner of the "bulge" to the town of Malmedy, a distance of several miles. Our mission for the moment was to simply hold on while the Germans were streaming past us moving west. The 82nd Airborne Division was being brought in to block the tip of the northern branch of what was now a two-pronged attack. The northern branch was a direct threat to Liège, and had they reached the Meuse at Liège, we would have been facing a major disaster.

In the meantime, the 7th Armored Division was holding out at the town of St. Vith, farther to the south, at the point that separated the two prongs of the attack. Farther south still, the 101st Airborne was entering Bastogne in preparation for their epic stand. The 30th Infantry Division moved in on our right at Malmedy and a solid line was gradually formed to prevent the enemy from moving north and enveloping the whole 1st and 9th Armies.

Heavy fighting continued for a few days in the 26th Infantry sector as the Germans made a major attempt to widen the "bulge," but our 16th Infantry sector was relatively quiet with mostly night patrol activity. We had moved the company into farm houses and soon after we got there it started to snow. The ground froze and we soon had six inches or more of snow. Suddenly mud was no longer a problem and we were using our bulldozers to move snow.

Our farm house was actually warm and cozy. We moved the owners into about a quarter of the house and we used the remainder. The barn was connected to the house with the hay stored in the attic of the main house, so that helped insulate us. I remember that we entered through the barn, which was full of cows. It was warm and muggy and my glasses always fogged up when I came in.

My first letter since Thanksgiving was written from this farmhouse. With all the activity of the previous three weeks I had neglected to write and my mother became very frantic. The newspaper headlines daily spoke of disaster, and she didn't finally hear from me until long after New Year's Day. In fact, the "request" in this letter has a Berkeley postmark of 26th January. It was evidently a bleak Christmas in Berkeley. To make matters worse, she apparently ran into Doug Forbes' wife in Berkeley (he was the CO of our "B" Company) and heard that we were fine and had even had turkey for Christmas dinner. At that point she really let me have it! I guess the fact of the matter was that the responsibility of being commander had made me so anxious that I couldn't get my mind onto anything else.

20 December 1944

Dear Mother, Dad, and Sis,
    So much has happened so fast in the last three weeks that every time I sit down to write something else happens and I decide to put it off. First of all the battalion got a chance to send one officer home & Murphy got to go. Rutledge is due to get the next

company but the Colonel doesn't want to send him over here until we know whether or not Murph will be back. That may take two or three months, so in the meantime I've got the company and all the headaches that go with it.

The next thing that happened was that we at last got a break and were pulled out of the line — our first break in 180 days of almost continual combat.

Next I got a 48 hr. pass to Paris which amounted to 5 days away. Had a great time there but 48 hrs is hardly enough to learn where everything is. Prices are terrific, but the army is gradually taking over various things to make things reasonable. For instance, the subway is free to American soldiers and is really simpler to figure out than the N.Y. subway. I stayed at a Red Cross club which is in a big hotel and I got a single room with a big double bed. Boy, what luxury. One night two of us with a couple of girls planked out 3300 francs for a black market dinner. I learned my lesson & didn't get stuck again though. All in all it was a successful but much too short trip.

I got back in time to discover that there is no rest for the weary — some green-horns who thought the war was over and all they were over here for was the kill found out differently and got us all into a terrible mess and now we and all the other veteran outfits that thought they were going to get a rest have got to rescue them. So everybody's mad and I guess it'll be a Christmas of mud and guns.

I'm sitting in a nice parlor on a sofa and the house shakes from our guns and across from me sits the cutest German girl you ever saw. To hell with non-fraternization!!

Much love to all,

Bill

P.S. I keep forgetting to include a request. Surely the postman will let me request some cookies even if it's in the P.S.

I don't suppose the complaint about "green-horns" helped my parents' attitudes about the competence of the Army.

I have forgotten what the exchange rate was at the time, but it was probably about two cents to the franc. In 1940's dollars, 3,300 francs would have been very expensive indeed. A good meal in a San Francisco hotel could be had for $1.25.

During Christmas week we were heavily involved in laying mines out in front of the infantry positions. It was always at night. The weather turned clear but there was still snow on the ground.

At about Christmas the moon came out full so that it seemed like daylight. In the meantime, the Army had arranged to have capes made from bed sheets for camouflage, so we went out each night dressed in these things. The front lines were about 1,000 yards apart and it was a sweaty palms affair. I can't believe they couldn't see us, despite the capes. One night a lone German plane came over and dropped flares (as if it weren't bright enough already). He then droned back and forth while we all stood perfectly still. Finally he came down low and strafed his own positions!

I recall that we laid mines on both Christmas Eve and Christmas night as well as several other nights. On both occasions I was offered a shot of Scotch at infantry company headquarters. The infantry, like everyone else, lived in farmhouses and simply rotated the men out into defensive foxhole positions. I remember being with a platoon of "I" Company in a stone farmhouse right on a little ridge where you could look out a window in the moonlight and see the German positions, or at least see where they were. The platoon commander was a lieutenant named Kestlinger whom I had met before and who had been around a long time (for an infantry platoon commander). He was a survivor of Omaha Beach but I don't know whether he was in the regiment in Sicily and Africa. They were using some kind of miner's lamps that they had picked up somewhere to provide enough light to read and write and things like that.

On one occasion, Martinez and his men were fired upon by our own troops. Marty had to charge across a field waving his arms to stop the machine gunner. He was a bit upset. I was with the infantry company commander at the time and he was furious. On another night I was with the same company commander when the Germans tried to pinch off one of his outposts that was about 500 yards in front of his main positions. He fought it all by telephone, laying mortar fire all around the outpost, and then sending out a patrol to make contact after the telephone wires had been broken. (As somebody once told me, "If you can talk you can fight.")

New Year's Eve

Dear Mother, Dad, and Sis,

At last another chance to write. I'm expecting to get beaucoups "sweat" letters from you during the next couple of weeks. Everything's OK, though. The krauts seem to have lost their drive for the time being. I guess they didn't figure they'd have to contend with the old First Division on this affair. However, I don't think this is any eleventh hour desperation drive as many contend. These stupes actually think they're going to cut us up and drive us out of Europe.

We have a light snow on the ground continually now and it's bitter cold. Gets down around zero every night. The streams and lakes are frozen over and everything is very dry. There is no such thing as mud any more which makes this weather a little more desirable than the warmer but sloppy fall weather.

I get Christmas packages in practically every mail now. Gosh, I get them from all kinds of people I've never heard of. And right now I'll put in a request for cookies and wool socks.

I never realized what a soft job I had until I got this company thrown into my lap. I keep on the go about 18 hours a day.

Christmas was just like any other day. We spent all night of both the 24th & 25th laying mines in no-mans land so most of Christmas day was spent sleeping.

I'm going over to Bn. Hq. in a little while to have a drink with the Colonel.

I just read in the papers where one of the Congressmen who made the inspection over here says the troops don't favor the rotation plan and he wagers not over a hundred out of the million and a half would go home now if given a chance. You should have seen the looks on the faces of my men when they read that. It was as if the last ray of hope had gone. What's the use of having a democracy if our representatives don't represent us?

That's about all for now.

Much love to all,

Bill

8 January 1945

Dear Mother, Dad, and Sis,

Time flies by and I don't ever realize how long it's been since I've written. Everything is OK and fairly quiet. I've still got the company. Murphy must be home by this time but we haven't heard from him so I still hang on. Right now there's a second captaincy open in the battalion which Rutledge, who's supposed to take "A" Co after we find out if Murphy isn't coming back, is holding down, but it may be only temporary. The guy went to the hospital with bad eyes and may be back.

We have about a foot of snow on the ground and it's still snowing. It's not quite as cold as it has been, but it'll probably really freeze when this storm blows over. The snow is drifting to several feet on the roads and we're having a hell of a time keeping them open. However, the days of mud are apparently over till spring, so that's something. We could go for some fur lined clothes, but I guess the powers that figure such things out figured the war would be over before winter. As long as you can get in a house now and then and near a stove it's not a bad life.

I don't know exactly what the Germans are up to now. Their breakthru is well taken care of but they may try to pull out their armor and try some place else. We could use a lot more troops. What they did was to spend the fall rebuilding the divisions that were practically wiped out in France and they are now in as good shape as before D-day. The German youth organization turns out good soldiers as fast as we capture or kill them. I didn't think it was possible to build up first class divisions as fast as they did it, but they had a certain number of experienced personnel to build on and that makes a lot of difference. How they managed to assemble such a large army and commit them without our G2 knowing anything about it is something that may cause some heads to fall but we probably won't know the full story until after the war. Here's how they planned it though: They attacked in two prongs, the northernmost one of which had the mission of taking Liège and coming in behind the bulk of the First Army which was concentrating on Duren. To shield this mission they dropped paratroopers to hamper reinforcements from pulling out and moving south. This accomplished, the southern attack could carry out the plan to swing through Belgium and seize Antwerp. This done, they could chop up the First Army and the British at leisure. The plan fouled from the very beginning. The paratroopers were a total failure. They made their breakthrus very easily but they underestimated our ability to move quickly and counter the northern salient for which we can take a certain amount of credit. The sector that they hit was very thinly held and there were no reserves immediately available to plug gaps. Once they broke through the crust they were in the clear for the time being. Rather than risk getting chewed up in a counterattack we built up along the northern side of the salient to keep them away from Liège but let them continue to move to the west virtually unhampered. They discovered too late that it was impractical to try to outflank this buildup and then they tried to break thru to the north by frontal assaults. By this time their plan was obvious and we stopped them cold. The western tip of the salient had entered some very rugged country that put their tanks at a disadvantage and it was easily chopped up and driven partway back. Liège was safe and troops could be pulled out of the line in the north and moved through Liège to take care of the enemy's main effort, the southern salient. The northern breakthru actually got farther in than has ever been admitted. Once more no premature attempt was made to counterattack it, but we just built up along the flanks and let them overextend themselves being careful not to let them fan out and outflank us at any point. Ground was sacrificed for time but there was nothing of any great importance in the path of their advance so that was OK. We finally got enough around them to stop them and some beautiful clear days around Christmas gave the Air Corps a chance to work them over. The stand made at Bastogne prevented them from using one of the main routes of communication in the bulge and must have proved quite a thorn in their side. The whole allied cause has had a very close call, but whether the attack speeded up or slowed down the war is still difficult to tell.

There's not much other news. I think I've about hit the end of the Christmas packages and I owe so many thank you letters that I don't know when I'll ever get them done. Tell Mrs. Howard that the slippers are swell and really make your feet feel good when you pull off a pair of wet boots.

The last letter I got is still the one of Dec. 19.

Love to all,

Bill

My "analysis" of the Battle of the Bulge was probably pretty accurate as far as the northern salient was concerned, but I seem not to have been aware of the attack by Patton's Third Army from the south, which was actually rather important.

Curiously, I don't recall the "slippers" at all. Those are the kinds of details that I usually remember.

It was probably at about this time that we got the opportunity to send one officer on leave to England for one week. Kosorek was the obvious choice, and off he went. He headed for Charmouth, and how I envied him. Although he was to have a week in England, he was in fact away for at least a month, and it may have been two. Streaky had acquired a dog that he called Siegfried (Siggy, for short). I inherited Siggy, or at least I promised to take care of him. He was a nasty little sort of miniature police dog, and was quite capable of biting the hands of those who fed him. I ultimately grew to dislike him very much.

On about the 17th of January we went over onto the offensive, the objective being to totally wipe out the remainder of the salient. The next letter describes a bit of it. One incident remains in my memory. I was driving along a road in a jeep. The snow was deep and we were passing a column of infantry heading toward the front (actually I think it was a part of the 82nd Airborne). A soldier reached out and tried to pet Siggy, who was behind me in the open jeep. Siggy snapped at him and ended up with a glove in his mouth. The soldier came running after us yelling for his glove. It was not a time to be without gloves.

26 January 1945

Dear Mother, Dad, and Sis,

If I never see any more snow I'll be a very happy man. The engineers have inherited the job of holding the roads open, or I should say opening them up as we advance and then holding them open. We've had two blizzards in the last week and I just about went out of my head trying to get the work done. To make matters worse the krauts lay their mines in the snow and they are very difficult to locate. Usually somebody has to get blown up before we know where they are. All of which has kept me very busy.

So far we've managed to find sufficient houses to live in so we keep warm. But from here on out all I see on the map are mountains and forests. You can make yourself fairly comfortable if you have time to build dugouts but they keep us so darn busy that if we have to move out in the woods it will take two or three days until we get comfortable. The snow is now about 18 inches deep and there's still a couple of months of winter to go and then of course the slush season to sweat out.

Otherwise everything is OK. The Russians seem to be going great guns but it is difficult to tell how much damage they are doing to the German army. The Germans may be just withdrawing, but it is hard to see how they can afford to do very much withdrawing unless they figure they can make the Russian offensive expend itself before crossing the Oder River and thereby delay a decisive battle until next spring or summer. An army can just move so far in a drive like that whether they meet any opposition or not and then they have to sit down and build up for another push. When you move fast you get ahead of such seemingly minor things as maps which makes a lot of difference.

My latest letter from home is dated about the 4th and since then I've received several letters that date back around the middle of December. By the way, I sent Mother and Sis a package and you have never mentioned receiving it. Didn't it get through, or am I just missing a letter?

That's all for now. It's snowing again.

Love to all,

Bill

On about the 1st of February we were pulled out and moved fifteen or twenty miles north to a position on the Roer River, a few miles south of Duren. This was about half way between Aachen and Bonn. At the same time it very suddenly became warmer, the snow melted, and once more we had to deal with mud. We were to be part of a major multi-army offensive that was supposed to take us to the Rhine. The crossing of the Roer was originally scheduled to take place on February 12th, but the thaw caused the river to become a raging torrent and everything became delayed.

10 February 1945

Dear Mother, Dad, and Sis,

When I think back I don't believe I've written since the thaw. When I calculate time now everything is based on before and after the thaw. It's just a different world now. Old "general mud" has taken over and it's no colder than it was in November. I had no idea that the winter would end so soon, but maybe we've got some more winter ahead anyway. I'll take the snow and frozen ground to this mess anytime.

So you finally heard from me after the breakthru. Gosh, it took enough time for the mail to go through. You see, you didn't have anything to worry about after all.

I'm so glad Dad got home. How often can he get leaves like that? My hope for leave is practically nil for a very long time. If they keep up the present rate of 3/4 of one percent per month it will amount to one officer in the battalion every three or four months. The battalion should get another officer home next month. I don't know who it will be but I think Doug Forbes would hold about the number 1 spot. What gripes us is that these outfits that have been overseas just a third of the time we have are getting virtually the same quota as us.

Right here I'll put in a request for some cookies and socks.

The Philippine Campaign sure has gone amazingly fast. I thought it was going to be a long drawn out affair like New Guinea. I think the whole hope over here is the Russians. We have too many natural obstacles ahead of us to do much good. About all we can do is keep up pressure & tie up troops so the Russians can keep going. At the first of the year we were faced by 75 German divisions here and 20 in Italy which is a good chunk of the German army. I believe the German gamble of attempting to crush us this winter and hold the eastern front lightly is going to prove one of the most costly blunders in military history.

Had a letter from Murphy yesterday. He definitely has an iron in the fire to get transferred to Ft. Belvoir. It will be interesting to see how he makes out.

We're living in the woods right now. What few houses there are in this neck of the woods are all completely destroyed. However, we found some Kraut-built dugouts that are quite comfortable. We have a stove, table, and triple bunks in the one I'm living in and it isn't half bad.

Well, that's all for now. Oh, incidentally, I'm receiving Time and Reader's Digest quite regularly.

Much love to all,
Bill

I recall that while living in this dugout I first began to dream seriously about going back to college for graduate work when the war was over. I think that it was at about this time that Congress passed the GI Bill, and after reading about it I could see that graduate work was financially feasible. I also remember thinking about getting married, and trying to figure out a family budget of $160 per month - and yet somehow the idea of getting married didn't particularly excite me.

The return of the mud meant that we had men out every day working to keep the roads to the front lines passable.

While we sat waiting for the water to subside in the Roer River, one incident stands out. The crossing of the Roer was to be by boat, each vessel holding about a dozen infantrymen and two Engineer soldiers to guide and steer. The river was less than 100 yards across, and in our sector the far side was bordered by the houses of the little town of Kreuznach. It was decided that we had better find out whether sending boats across the river was even physically possible. Accordingly, they proposed to put two boatloads across in the middle of the night. Essentially these were infantry patrols doing the kind of thing that they did routinely, probing and testing enemy defensive positions.

In the best of circumstances, a patrol probing enemy positions was a nightmare proposition, but in this case it appeared to be more suicidal than usual. The reason that

I got involved was that supplying the boats was an Engineer responsibility, and we also had to provide an NCO to be in charge of each boat and to steer with a paddle from the rear, and another man for the front position in the boat. The infantrymen each had a paddle and kneeled in the boat, providing the motive power.

We had a company from the 16th Infantry located in a factory building on the water's edge. To get to it, you had to walk down a steep hill, so it couldn't be reached by daylight without full and fairly close exposure to the enemy. Individual men may have gone up and down during the day, but certainly no vehicles. It was from this position that the two boats were to be launched. I arrived around midnight on a very dark night with the boats, two officers, and some enlisted men, including the two unfortunate NCOs and two other men from my company. We carried the boats down the hill to the factory where the two infantry squads were assembled.

The river flowed northward, from right to left. One boat group went out onto a sand bar to the right of the factory, the upstream side, and the other to a similar place to the left. I sent two of my men with each boat, and then joined the infantry company commander in his CP in a room in the factory, where he had telephone communication with everybody concerned, including people in OPs higher up in the building.

The houses on the other side of the river, held by the enemy, were close together and right on the water's edge. A baseball player could easily have thrown hand grenades into them, but their gun positions were well concealed, and they had evidently been very quiet so it wasn't known how strongly the place was held. If they were short-handed, we could hope that they did not consider a crossing likely at that point and would only have a small force there.

At around one o'clock a.m. the two boats were launched simultaneously by a signal from walkie-talkies. Complete silence followed for what seemed like an interminable time. I remember Martinez coming back into the CP, saying that his boat had been successfully launched and had slowly paddled off, fighting the strong current, but it was so dark he couldn't see much.

Suddenly the silence was broken by an almost deafening barrage of machine gun fire. It echoed through the building and sounded as if it were only a few feet away. The company commander was immediately on the phone and the OP reported that flares were lighting up the whole area and tracers from more than one machine gun were coming from directly opposite us. The company commander called for 81 mm mortars to pound the other bank of the river, and within half a minute the cracks of the mortar shells added to the racket. Then silence.

All we could do now was sit and wait. After about half an hour some men came into the CP. They were from the boat that had been sent to the left. They had managed to land on the other side just downstream of the town and had found an open field and barbed wire, but had not encountered any enemy. The sergeant in charge said he got out and poked around a bit, and then they pushed off and headed back. Because of the current they landed a half mile to our left. Apparently we had no troops along the bank, so they just walked upstream along the water's edge. A few minutes later a wet and bedraggled soldier walked in. He was bleeding from a wound but didn't even know it. He was from the other boat. According to his story, a flare went up before they ever reached the other side and the machine gun fire followed immediately. The men that weren't hit instantly went overboard into the water, and he assumed that he was the only survivor. During the next three-quarters of an hour more came in, some wounded, some not. About half of that boatload finally showed up. Neither my NCO nor the other guy under my command in that boat ever came back.

18 February 1945

Dear Mother, Dad, and Sis,

Surprisingly enough the most recent letter that I have is one from Dad dated 6 Feb. Very amazing! Not much news of interest. We've had almost spring weather for the last couple of days terminating today in a drizzling rain with its inevitable mud. The freezing weather and snow of a few weeks ago seems to be very unreal right now. I am very disappointed in the German winter. As a matter of fact last year in England the spring actually started in late February just like this one seems to be doing. After saying this I suppose we'll have another snowstorm in March.

The leave situation seems to be gradually getting a little better. They've now instituted leaves to England (1 week) which are parceled out in small quotas. I have one officer in England now, or at least on the way to England. The transportation delays take so long that not many men get a chance. Murphy left here on the 8th of December and didn't get home until the 17th of January. I only have two other officers now so I'm kind of short handed. The turnover of platoon commanders is pretty high in this type of warfare.

I've got to put in an evening on efficiency reports so I'll have to make this short. I'm in another fit of war-weariness now and could go for a break. Surely this thing can't last forever. I watch the Russian news with great interest. We aren't doing much good here. If the Russians make as much hash of a German village before they take it as we do there won't be any Germany left. That would sure be tough, wouldn't it?

Will try to write soon.

Love to all,

Bill

P.S. Got a nice long chatty letter from Mrs V the other day.

The next offensive kept being delayed because of the swollen river. We spent most of our time trying to keep the roads passable. I remember in one impossible place we built a "corduroy" road by cutting small trees and laying the trunks side by side. The dugout continued to be comfortable, although Siegfried used to keep me awake by barking all night. The letter speaks of my having only two officers. I presume these were Martinez and Wooldridge, with Kosorek still away in England. We were still at the same place when the next letter was written, so we were actually in the dugout for the better part of a month.

22 February 1945

Dear Mother, Dad, and Sis,

This is just going to be a note to enclose a couple of items before I lose them. I remember getting a report of payment last year but I don't remember whether I sent it to you or not. Figuring out my income tax when I have to pay it is going to be quite a little problem. The division "history" is kind of sketchy and also a little inaccurate, but it's of some interest.

Well, the war goes on without much signs of ending. I do hope the Russians haven't bogged down, but it's beginning to look like the Germans have the situation under control. It will probably take another big summer offensive to do the job.

Guess what!! We got a ration of Coca-Cola yesterday. I can't remember when it was that I last had a "coke" but it seemed perfectly natural to be drinking one. Maybe my "reconversion" to life back home won't be so difficult.

Please send cookies and socks.

Got a new officer this afternoon so I'm only short one now. Trouble is it will take me some little time to break him in. It's difficult to fit in an officer with a group of experienced men. His first impression makes such a great difference in their confidence in him that you can't give him any responsibility until you know something about him and get him wised up about a few things. Tonight I've got him out on a little job with another officer. Hope he draws a little fire. It'll help.

Well, that's about all the news. I see my Jan 29 Time has just arrived so I'll have to dig into it for awhile.

Much love to all,
Bill

The new officer was a guy named Dratz, from Oklahoma. He turned out to be very good, but he was wounded and evacuated within a month or so.

At about this time I had a bit of good luck. George Johnson returned from the hospital and I argued that I needed him more than "C" Company did. They had taken away George and then Conant. This time I prevailed. I made him my Executive Officer. Suddenly my life was much easier. George was just plain good.

Shortly after that letter things began to happen again when the water had finally subsided in the Roer River. The plan was that the 9th Army, and the 7th Corps of the 1st Army (we were in the 1st Army - not to be confused with our 1st Division), both on our left, were to attack first, and then we were to cross the river forty-eight hours later. The 8th Division on our immediate left crossed the river and attempted to take the city of Düren on the 23rd of February. They were unable to get a bridge across the river, and it wasn't until two days later that the 104th Division finally got a bridge into Düren. The whole affair had been so costly that it was decided that the 1st Division would cross on the 104th's bridge by truck and attack our objectives from the flank. This maneuver was very successful and within a day we were in control of Kreuznach and moving east with only moderate opposition.

Things now moved rapidly. We worked day and night building bridges, clearing obstacles, clearing mines and debris, and filling in craters. The Germans were in retreat and blew up everything, and several canals, small rivers, and things like railroad overpasses were destroyed and blocked our tanks. The infantry moved fairly easily, but they relied heavily on their accompanying tanks and the rate of progress was dependent largely on how fast the engineers could provide a way to get the tanks through. We frequently worked, especially at night, with the infantry just a few yards ahead.

I will describe a typical evening. Marty Martinez and his platoon were with the 2nd Battalion of the 16th Infantry and soon after dark I got word that they had run into some kind of obstacle and needed help. I drove in my jeep across two or three miles of open country to a small village that was now occupied by the 2nd Battalion. On the far side of the village there was a very small river and apparently a concrete bridge had been blown out. Beyond the river, the bank led up to higher ground, and here evidently the Germans were dug in. The infantry staff officer suggested I go take a look, so he gave me a guide and we walked almost to the bridge where we encountered a soldier who was manning the outpost position. The trouble was that it was pitch dark and we couldn't see a thing. It was very quiet and as we listened we could distinctly hear the motor of a German tank as it was most likely being slowly moved to a new position, perhaps a hundred feet ahead. I wasn't going any farther, so I returned to the infantry battalion headquarters which was in a house a couple of hundred yards back. There I phoned to our own engineer battalion headquarters and ordered a "treadway" bridge to be brought up in the morning. This was a simple type of portable bridge that could be installed from special trucks in about an hour.

The staff officer then took me to see Marty who was with his platoon in a nearby farmhouse. As we walked, he said to me, "I think Lt. Martinez needs a rest." I said, "Oh?" He replied, "Shells worry him."

After telling Marty that the bridge would be available in the morning, I checked again into the infantry battalion headquarters. They were getting ready to make a night attack and the plan was to have one infantry company move several hundred yards to the right of the town and then to wade across the very shallow "river," go up the bank, turn left and take the enemy positions opposite the village from the flank. They apparently had already determined that the river was very lightly held except at the village. This was very characteristic of the fighting at that time; the mud and cold wet weather tended to confine most of the operations to near the paved roads and the towns.

What really surprised me that night was that the battalion commander, Col. Grant, was also getting ready for bed. He had an elaborate bed roll and they were preparing him a nice place to sleep on a real bed. So while one of his companies was carrying out an attack operation, he was going to get a good night's sleep! I guess by this time operations like this had become so routine that it was to everybody's advantage to have a well-rested commander for whatever had to be faced the next morning. I then drove back to where the remainder of our company was located and also got in a night's sleep. As far as I know, the operation went off smoothly, and by the next morning the infantry had secured the bridge site. Marty built his bridge, and the tanks were able to join the foot soldiers and continue to the next objective. And so it went, day after day. The Germans were once more fighting a rear-guard action as they fell back onto the Rhine.

This was extremely flat farming country, and in the winter when the crops were flat you could often see clearly for considerable distances. One day I drove up to see what was going on. I recall watching tanks attack a village from a little ridge about a mile away. I was standing amongst a battery of 4.2-inch chemical mortars that were laying a very nice smoke screen to at least partially isolate that particular action. I saw a couple of tanks make a mad dash across an open stretch towards the village. About halfway across, one of them apparently hit a mine. When the smoke and dirt cleared the tank could be seen partly on its side and turned around more than ninety degrees. German mines were effective.

Near the end of this drive to the Rhine I had a series of experiences that made me wonder whether I was really cut out for this sort of business. The 16th Infantry had momentarily stopped and the 26th Infantry attacked at night across the Erp canal, which was a fairly formidable obstacle. The highway bridge across the canal was large and had been blown, and a battalion of the 26th found themselves at daylight without their tanks, anti-tank weapons, or any other vehicles. They called for engineer help. Our "C" Company ordinarily provided the engineer support for the 26th, but were evidently committed to something else. John Oxford, our S3, called me since my company was at the moment unoccupied, and told me to join him on a reconnaissance. We drove out to near the bridge site, but since it was on an elevated highway in full view of the enemy, we had to get out and walk to the canal by another route. From the side of the blown bridge we determined that a Bailey Bridge would be necessary; the gap was much too large for the little steel "treadway" bridges that we had been more frequently using. We calculated what was needed, and John went back and ordered bridge materials to be brought up. The materials were handled by other engineer units in the rear. John told the infantry that it would take all day to get it, which meant building the bridge at night. My men groused but this was fine by me - I didn't relish the idea of building a Bailey Bridge in full view of German artillery.

By that evening the 16th Infantry Regiment was planning an attack sometime after midnight, and of course they wanted engineer support. I decided that we could build the bridge with two platoons and that I would send our new guy, Dratz, and his platoon with the 16th. They had been up all night doing something else, so I told Dratz to get some sleep and I would let him know when to join the 16th, which was several miles to the right of our current location with the 26th.

The bridge material arrived at the site sometime after dark. I brought George Johnson out to supervise the bridge construction because I knew I would have to deal with the 16th before the night was over. Besides, I knew that, with George, the bridge would get built. They built a rather large Bailey Bridge without incident and completed it in the early hours of the morning. In the meantime, I went back to our battalion headquarters and found out what the 16th was up to and when they needed Dratz. I contacted Dratz sometime after midnight and told him to load up and proceed to wherever it was that the 16th wanted him.

I told George to bring back the two platoons who had built the bridge and let them get some sleep. Then I proceeded to the headquarters of the 16th Infantry in a building in a small town, and got there sometime before dawn. As I entered the town I saw Dratz' trucks heading out of town in the direction of the attack. Since this was hours after he had left the company area, I wondered where he had been all this time.

When I arrived at the 16th headquarters, I was greeted by my old friend Lt. Kestlinger, the infantry platoon commander with whom I had recently spent Christmas Eve. He had recently been moved up to the staff; infantry lieutenants who survived a long time were sometimes rewarded that way. He told me that I was in "deep trouble" and that Colonel Gibbs was in a rage because one of his battalions had run into an obstacle that the tanks couldn't pass and he had no engineer support, and at that moment he was on the phone venting his wrath to the General. I could hear Gibbs on the phone in the next room and it didn't sound good. I decided the best thing was to get out there myself and find what the problem was and find out what had happened to Dratz. Kestlinger agreed that it was better if I didn't face the Colonel; in might be dangerous to my health!

I found Dratz at the problem site at about dawn. He had simply become lost during the night and had only just arrived at the site - exactly where he had been, I never knew. The infantry had attacked in darkness from a town and had immediately encountered a blown bridge over a small canal. A hundred yards beyond the canal the highway passed under a raised railway line with very steep banks. The concrete underpass had been blown out and was a mess. To make matters worse, there were evidently anti-personnel mines everywhere. Two guys lying in a field between the canal and the railway underpass, each with a foot blown off, warned me to be careful. I found a phone and reached John Oxford at our Battalion Headquarters and told him we needed a treadway bridge. I called the company and ordered the bulldozer to be brought out.

In a couple of hours we got the treadway bridge completed and the bulldozer over to the railway underpass. In the meantime, the infantry was holding up a half mile or so ahead and screaming that they needed their tanks. But after struggling with the bulldozer for awhile it became apparent that more drastic measures were going to be needed to clear the underpass. There were huge chunks of concrete that our bulldozer couldn't budge. It was going to require a major demolition job and I was becoming frantic. I started back to call John Oxford for advice and help.

About this time George Johnson, bless his soul, arrived on the scene. Within half an hour George walked about half a mile along the canal to the right and found another small bridge across the canal at a point where it would not be necessary to get through the railroad underpass. The bridge had been wired for demolition but had not been blown. There was some question about whether it was strong enough to take a tank because it was pretty small, but they tried it and it didn't break. The tanks streamed across and everybody was happy. Except me - I felt like an idiot.

The incident with Dratz and Colonel Gibbs taught me a lesson that I have frequently used since - if you are responsible for something, never leave it to somebody else without checking, double checking, and triple checking. Actually Gibbs was in a rage because he wanted to be the first to reach the Rhine; the danger to his isolated battalion was minimal. I was more concerned about the underpass and the near paralysis I suffered when I couldn't figure out how to handle it. The final indignity was finding the other bridge - it had never entered my stupid head that there would be an alternative route, much less an intact bridge, close by. Those were not my "finest hours."

By the 9th of March we were on the Rhine at Bonn. The next morning I was told to go into the ruined and largely deserted city and report back on the condition of the main bridge across the Rhine. I found that the infantry hadn't yet completely occupied the city and had not yet reached the bridge. They gave me a patrol of several men and we picked our way through the rubble and finally got up onto the bridge at the first tower. The towers were all standing but the roadway was entirely in the water. As we stood there looking out over the Rhine we could see a couple of German soldiers at the foot of the tower in the middle of the river. They appeared to be trying to make a raft. I guess they were stranded there. One of the riflemen asked me if he should take a shot at them. I said, "No, leave them alone."

It was a bit awesome standing there in the complete quiet looking across the Rhine into the heart of Germany. We stayed quite awhile.

Our whole battalion moved into some fairly nice houses on the main highway just north of Bonn. The next letter is typewritten, the first since early November.

Germany
10 March 1944

Dear Mother, Dad, and Sis,

I can put that heading on my letter this time without feeling a little foolish because there is no doubt that we are really in Germany. I have only to climb up on the roof of our house and there before me lies the Rhine. It's taken us exactly six months to get from Aachen to here, but when the ball began to roll it really moved. The result [was] that the engineers had more work than ever before while the infantry sailed along fairly easily, at least as easily as the infantry can sail. Every bridge was of course blown and every town had huge log barricades and large craters that made the roads impassible. I've spent two rather sleepless weeks but things are now temporarily at a halt so I have some time for writing and relaxation. Hope I can get a bath soon.

The letters I'm now getting from home are now complaining bitterly about a gap in my writing which I can't quite understand unless it was during that attack in late January. During an attack I don't have time to shave more than once every three days much less write letters.

I got a V-mail from you recently that you forgot to address on the inside so it came straight mail and sadly behind the airmails. Don't get talked into using the V-mails unless they start sending the airmails by boat. Once in a great while they put a bunch in a ship and it arrives about two months late but that isn't very often.

I got a package of cookies the other day. They were those round powdered sugar things you used to make when I was young and they didn't last ten minutes. How about some more? They were really wonderful. If this has to be a formal request please send one box of cookies.

I'm amazed at how well preserved the houses are where we are now. You'd hardly know a war was going on. Of course in the last stage of this push we moved against practically no opposition which partially accounts for it. These houses are much nicer than anything I ever saw in England. Some of the household fittings and appliances would put a lot of our stuff to shame. The kraut family prefers to live in the basement so we take over all the upstairs with all the feather beds and all that. Not bad. I take a dim view of living out in pup tents when we can live like this.

After spending all month telling us how the rotation system was being stepped up we got fewer men to go home this time than last month- a total of 3 EM's (enlisted men) out of a battalion strength of 550. I often wonder how much they tell you about the wonders of this great rotation system. At the present rate I'll be home sometime in 1950.

Well, my eyes are just about ready to close on me for good so I'll close for now.
Love to all,
Bill

The reader is by this time tired of hearing about "cookies". The fact of the matter is that the army field diet was very short on sugar and one developed an incredible sweet tooth. Even the thought of something sweet was overwhelming.

I was at this time looking forward to a nice, long, and pleasant rest. The Rhine is a very formidable obstacle, and even the Romans didn't try to go farther. At this particular point (Bonn) there were hills on the other side but practically no signs of the enemy. Clearly the Germans did not expect an attack here. We could drive up and down the autobahn and nobody shot at us, although at night they sometimes sent over a few large caliber shells. The city was a mess, but we were in a suburban community, and as the letter described, the houses and buildings were intact. It was now the Russian's turn to do something - or was it?

Eynatten, Belgium, September 1944; Murph and I at the Schmidt house.

Eynatten, Belgium, September 1944; "A" Company officers at the Schmidt house. Left to Right:
Conant, Kays, Murphy, Kosorek, Martinez.

CHAPTER ELEVEN

UNCONDITIONAL SURRENDER

MARCH 10 – MAY 16, 1945

Although I didn't know it at the time, on the same day that we captured Bonn, the 9th Armored Division (evidently the next division to our right) captured the town of Remagen on the Rhine. Unbelievably, they found that a major bridge over the river had not been blown. They quickly sent some people across and established a bridgehead, and within a day or so had a firm hold. This was an area where nobody would attempt an assault crossing, so there were practically no German troops available to defend it, at least for the first twenty-four hours. I believe the bridge was captured on March 8th. It was one of the greatest pieces of pure luck in the entire war. Somebody had simply goofed - the German army was beginning to come to pieces.

It was now clear that we would not be in Bonn long, and on about the 10th of March we loaded up and drove to Remagen. There we crossed the river on a pontoon bridge that had been erected the day before. The main bridge had by that time been badly damaged by artillery fire and bombs, and I think it eventually fell down, but it was too late and we were across in force.

The infantry regiments quickly fanned out and enlarged the bridgehead. The country was very hilly with steep slopes down to the river, but they were soon over the initial hills and several miles inland. Our engineer battalion moved into a little town on the river bank just north of Remagen.

In Bonn I had come down with a touch of bronchitis and the battalion surgeon ordered me to bed. So, for a couple of days, I lay on a cot in our company headquarters in a nice house in the town. It was beginning to dawn on me that I was getting hay fever and/or bronchitis every time I slept in a real bed on a real mattress. It had all started on the Queen Elizabeth in 1942. I had no such problems when I slept on the ground in the worst of weather, or on an army cot. We were now living indoors most of the time, but from then on I avoided German mattresses.

The town we were now in was the first we had seen that was virtually untouched by the war and in which most of the inhabitants were still at home. All of the towns in the Rhineland had been largely evacuated and were completely smashed. Here we encountered a German population that had seen little of the war, although they undoubtedly had contributed soldiers and casualties. They were either old people or women and children, and were well dressed and well fed. They seemed bewildered and a bit frightened.

We were under strict orders not to fraternize with them, but we did take from them what houses we needed. I remember in particular a well-dressed young lady filling jars of water from the gutter in front of our company headquarters. Apparently the town water system was not operating. Our street was on a hill and water was trickling along the gutter. She had a determined look on her face, but she was obviously uncomfortable and fearful.

I don't remember much about the next couple of weeks except that the bridgehead was continuously being enlarged and the opposition was not great. I believe Marty Martinez was hit by artillery fire about that time, so we continued to take casualties. The engineer work consisted of the usual clearing of obstacles, but nothing very formidable.

25 March 1945

Dear Mother, Dad, and Sis:

The war couldn't sit down and relax so all my promises of beaucoup letters has gone for nil, and I'm scribbling off this in the midst of much hustle and bustle. Your letters have been coming through at a great rate lately, some of them being just over a week old, which is pretty good considering they have to travel considerably farther now. I don't understand why my letters get to you so irregularly.

We've been having wonderful weather lately. It's plenty warm enough to lie out in the grass and things like that. We've been shedding such winter junk as stoves and it makes picking up and moving a lot easier. We're still living in houses but that is more a matter of habit than anything else. If we have to go out into pup tents because of lack of housing it isn't going to work any hardship on anybody, I'm sure. Probably do us good.

Here are some pictures I've gathered together. The one of me and Murphy was taken last Sept. at our chateau near Aachen. The other rather ridiculous pictures were taken during a recent presentation of awards when I finally got my Bronze Star ribbon. There seems to be some kind of joke between me and the general — forgotten what.

We heard from Murphy's wife that he was on the way back but still no word or sign of him. Boy, what a racket these leaves to the States are.

Please send me some cookies. I'm getting very hungry.

Well, so much for now. More later.

Love to all,

Bill

The day that letter was written, we kicked off on the last big offensive of the war. To the north of us, the British and our 9th Army made an assault crossing of the Rhine, apparently using all the airborne forces of both armies. To the south, Patton's 3rd Army went across the river, apparently to everybody's surprise. We again followed the 3rd Armored Division in an attempt to break out of our bridgehead, and did so with ease. The crossing in the north was evidently originally supposed to be the big effort to finish the war, but the luck at Remagen, and Patton's crossing, took a lot of the "glory" away from the British and the 9th Army.

We headed east at great speed, similar to our movement after the St. Lô breakthrough the previous summer. Then we turned directly north and soon linked up with the 9th Army, trapping a considerable part of the German army in what became known as the Ruhr Pocket. But before this occurred, my own fortunes took a big turn, as described in the next letter.

11 April
Germany

Dear Mother, Dad, and Sis,

Many changes since I last wrote. First of all, Murphy came back and I left "A" Co and came to battalion headquarters as assistant S-3. About two days later the S-2 got sick and went to the hospital so now I'm acting S-2. It's not much work but I'm a little too close to the brass to be very comfortable. I guess I'll get used to it.

In the meantime the war has definitely taken a turn for the better. If only we can maintain our momentum and continue to out maneuver then I think we'll finish this thing off soon. The fact that we were even allowed to break out of the Remagen Bridgehead is an indication of how pitifully weak they are even when organized, and now they have lost all semblance of organization. So I'm keeping my fingers crossed.

The mail has been a little slow in catching up to us lately as we are getting farther and farther away from our division base where it is sorted. This move is very reminiscent of last summer in France. We're still living in houses and don't suppose we'll ever get out of that habit now. You just stake out your claim & tell the Krauts to move out & live with the neighbors & there's much weeping and wailing & a dozen reasons why they can't move, but then you bellow and stamp your fist on the table and they don't cause any more trouble. Practically every house you find is very comfortable and very well furnished. I've been through an industrial and coal mining section of Germany as well as a great deal of farm country and I have yet to see anything that could be classed as a slum by American standards. I don't think there is any doubt that these people were living well when the war started.

I forgot to tell you that the reason I didn't get any stamps while I was in Paris was because the exchange is so disadvantageous that the prices are absurd. However, in Germany there are other methods and I have quite a collection. Kind of difficult to mail it, though.

Oh, incidentally, Doug Forbes is on his way home. He left several days ago, so you should be seeing him pretty soon.

Love to all,
Bill

The Colonel of our Battalion decided that after having run the company for over four tough months I shouldn't have to step down again and serve under Murph. I didn't much care for the staff duty, but it was a rest.

Soon after joining the staff I was sleeping in a rather nice house and discovered in a desk next to my cot a wooden box full of booklets of stamps. The owner of the house was apparently a stamp dealer, since these were "approval" books. "Approval" books are sent to mail-order customers. Under each stamp is written the dealer's price and you pick out any that you want, returning the remainder and the payment. I immediately saw a lot of great looking stamps that I didn't have, and was first tempted to go through the books and pick some of them out. There were several dozen books and I didn't have much time. In the end I said to myself, "why not take them all?" The box was a bit bulky, but I got it into my back pack. I have it still. Looking into it recently I found the name and address of the owner - Herr Wilhelm Gumm, Weyerbusch (near Altenkirchen). Two or three invoices were signed by Herr Gumm, and above his signature is written "Heil Hitler."

I was not alone in the looting. As we moved into the undamaged houses of well-off people who had not had time to hide their possessions, the temptations mounted. Cameras became the prizes that everyone looked for. Sometimes a brown Nazi SA[1] uniform hanging in the closet would help convince us that looting was OK. I recall a couple of weeks later, when Tom Crowley and I were scouting out a good place to put the battalion headquarters in the Harz mountains, we found a large locked wooden chest. Without hesitation, we found a tool and pried it open. Just then he got called into the adjacent room. I opened the chest and on top of the pile of junk was an Exakta camera. I grabbed it instantly. It was my only camera for the next twelve years.

A short time before this incident, I was sent over to check out a small industrial town that we had bypassed. A shabbily dressed man hailed me, and speaking reasonable English, said that I should investigate a large multi-storied brick building nearby. He said it was a hospital for little boys who were used for forced labor. He said that the Germans who ran the place had all left town and the boys were on their own. "Oh, how they worked those boys," he said.

I went into this rather filthy place and found it full of boys about ten to thirteen years old. I gathered that they were Poles and Czechs and other "inferior" types. Many were in beds, while others were running around, some on crutches. Soup was being heated in what looked like a fifty-gallon drum, and some of them were ladling it out into tin cans. I walked into a ward where the boys were in bed. They all stared at me and it was apparent that they were completely terrified. The whole thing made me sick and furious. What kind of animals were we dealing with here?

Across the street there was a small German army hospital. There seemed to be few patients but a considerable number of nurses in white uniforms. I stormed in and demanded that they immediately do something about the little boys across the street. All I got was silence. In the end I could only report what I had seen and hope our military government people were close behind.

The next few weeks are only a jumble of memories. With no real responsibility I was hardly aware of where we were, and today I can barely trace our route on a map. I obviously wasn't much of an Intelligence Officer! We went north to Paderborn, and I only remember that because my grandfather (my mother's father) was born there. It was also in Paderborn that I ran into Fred Finley (at that point, CO of "C" Company) on the street and he said, "Did you hear that Roosevelt has died?"

The next day we headed east again. A few days later the Division made a daylight assault crossing of the Weser River. Our "A" Company (but now without me) handled the boats and supplied the boat crews (two men each, I believe). It was obviously a considerably easier job than the one we attempted at night on the Roer River in February. The opposition was light and the enemy positions on the far side were quickly overrun. But

---

1 Sterm Abteilung, or Storm Section: Hitler's private army.

even then we continued to take casualties. I was particularly distressed to hear that Cpl. Dan Bacinski was killed. Bacinski was one of the men in the 3rd Platoon when I took it over in Tunisia, over two years before. He was also one of the men who accompanied me in the halftrack during my little adventure in Alimena, Sicily. Also about this time Sgt. Rocco Resenik was killed. He had been one of my squad sergeants in the 3rd Platoon in Tunisia and Sicily. I had become used to seeing new recruits come into the company and be killed soon after. But somehow it didn't seem right when the people who had been through so much for so long, had to go down when the war was obviously nearing an end. But of course there is no justice in war, anyway. It's a lousy business.

As we continued east we began to see men walking along the roads, dressed in suits with vertical black stripes. We were nearing Nordhausen where there was an underground factory in which the V2 missile was being manufactured. The Germans had deserted the place and the slave laborers were on their own. I never saw Nordhausen, but I heard that there was a great mass grave at the factory with hundreds of bodies in various states of decay. The men were simply worked until they died. These were mostly Eastern Europeans of various nationalities.

A considerable number of German troops withdrew into the heavily wooded Harz Mountains in central Germany. While the war swirled on past us, the 1st Division was given the job of clearing out the Harz area. There was some sharp fighting but I managed to avoid it all by sticking around our Battalion Headquarters attending to "intelligence" matters. In fact, I don't even recall hearing any guns firing. We spent several days there, and when we had finished, other troops were at the Elbe River and it was at about that time that they made contact with the Russians.

But we weren't finished yet. We got word that the 1st Division had been transferred to Patton's 3rd Army and were going to move south and attack into Czechoslovakia.

At about this time our battalion got a chance to send another officer home. Doug Forbes, CO of "B" Company, had gone the month before, and Fred Finley was the logical choice this time. I was suddenly very concerned because if Fred left I would be the one to take over "C" Company. I was beginning to enjoy the soft life as Battalion S2, and I was not particularly eager to take over a new company, especially if we were going to go immediately into an attack. Fred actually hesitated a bit, but finally said, "I think the war's over; I'm going home." So I was once again a company commander. This must have been about the end of April.

"C" Company all through the war had suffered terrible officer casualties, and of the four officers in the company at this time - Owens, Long, Stark, and Sidlowski - only Joe Owens had been in the battalion more than a few months. He had joined us near the end of the Tunisian campaign along with George Johnson. I immediately made Joe the Executive Officer. I did at least know the First Sergeant, Francis. He and I had gone to Paris together in December. But otherwise the company was completely new to me.

The next day we loaded up and drove to a little town, Liebenstein, just over the Czechoslovakian border, in the old Sudetenland. In a sense this is where the war really started in 1938 when Hitler demanded, and got, the Sudetanland at the Munich Conference. It was remarkable that I should be there at the very end, seven years later.

Joe and I installed the company in a real castle. A day or two later our three platoons were assigned to support the three battalions of the 26th Infantry Regiment, and the final push began. Everybody was very cautious - nobody wanted to die on the last day of the war. But there was some opposition, usually machine gun positions in rather hilly and forested country. On about the second day the infantry started out at dawn, seeking out the next enemy positions, but at around eight o'clock a.m. orders came down to cease fire and withdraw to the starting point. It was May 7th, VE Day - Victory in Europe. The war was over.

It was eleven months since D-Day. It was two years, three months, and nine days since I had heard the first shots fired in the Ousseltia Valley in Tunisia. The Division had started out in Africa with about 13,500 men; we had since then taken over 20,000 casualties, 4,400 of whom were dead. Their names are now inscribed in bronze at the 1st Division monument just adjacent to the old executive office building in Washington, D.C.

There were evidently great scenes of jubilation in the large cities of Europe; for us it was like most other days. Everybody just went about the business of trying to get comfortable. I don't recall any shouting or hand shaking.

In a few days our battalion all came together and moved into the town of Franzenbad, Czechoslovakia.

Franzenbad, Czechoslovakia
16 May 1945

Dear Mother, Dad, and Sis,

Well, as the Krauts say "alles kaput." As you can probably gather from the address we were in it till the last shot. Right now we're busy trying to amuse ourselves and also handle tens of thousands of German prisoners. What a job! They all come in with their own officers and hundreds of different kinds of vehicles — all trying to get under our wing before the Russians get them. They are absolutely terrified at the thought of being captured by the Russians.

This country we are in is actually the German Sudetenland and the people are definitely German and not Czechs. It is quite hilly and there are lots of small lakes. Up till a week or so ago it was cold, but it is now hot and I've been trying to get the men out swimming as much as possible. I imagine we will move back pretty soon because I think the Russians own this place but they seem in no hurry to get here. They must have found good lootin' up forward somewhere.

I suppose the number one question is when do I come home. Well, General Eisenhower says no soldier who fought in North Africa will have to go to the Pacific but then again I'm an officer and not a soldier and officers are considered a special case because they are a small group who can be slipped the pickle without causing political excitement. All this points system and redeployment plans smells of propaganda to soothe the people at home. For instance, the division sent quite a sizable group of men home today. They aren't sent on the point system or any other system; they were just told to get going. I'll be willing to bet that a great hullaballoo will be made over "thousands" of men coming home from Europe so soon and they'll probably pick out some of them and immediately discharge them along with much publicity about the speed of this system. Then everybody quiets down and forgets about Europe and there is no more political pressure to bring people home quickly. Oh, the old U.S.A. is learning about this propaganda game.

We still don't know what the status of the Division is. All of the older men, I'm sure, will get home within the next 8 or 10 months, and many will undoubtedly be discharged, because some of the men with the highest number of points in the army are in this division. With so many high point holders it would seem logical to send the Division itself home and then reorganize it for the Pacific, especially since many of the men would like to stay in the First Division if they could get home for awhile, even if that meant going to war again. But in higher circles there seems to be a certain amount of aversion to sending a regular army division home at any costs so there's no telling. I don't know how I stand because all this propaganda refers to enlisted men only and when speaking of officers they use the term "military necessity."

In the meantime this last quota stripped me of half my NCO's and another one like it will leave me high and dry. I've got to send NCO's when I get a quota because they comprise most of the older men. The privates are practically all men who joined us since Africa. They tell us not to send any man who is essential but I'll be damned if I'll hang onto any man just because he's hard to replace. Of course when I have to make a 1st Sgt. out of a Pfc. things are going to be rough. I don't expect to lose any officers because my executive officer is the only one who's been around any time at all, and even he is quite a ways down the list. We expect to drop from rolls those men home on leave and if that happens the colonel says he'll put me in for my captaincy but I have a sneaking hunch they are going to freeze all promotions over here. In fact I wouldn't be surprised if they shipped captains in on us from these outfits that are undoubtedly going to be deactivated. Well, I guess that's the way it goes. Anyway, don't stop sending cookies and don't forget the films. I suspect I'll be home before too long and I'll keep you posted.

I'm getting to know my company better now and I'll have to admit that it's a much freer life in a company than in battalion headquarters. You're sort of a little king in your own right with only the staff to worry you and then only when they come around. If I want to take a nap I do so and I don't have to worry about somebody wondering why I'm not working. I've learned to pass down all the work so that all I have is the responsibility to worry me and things seem to be shaping up now so that shouldn't worry me too much. I have an Indian boy for a dog-robber whose principle worry seems to be that I'll do something for myself, so you see life isn't so bad.

This is my most formidable writing effort in a long time. Hope I can keep it up.

Love to all,
Bill

A "dog-robber" was a man assigned to be the officer's valet. The British call him a "batman." In the field, an officer was expected to devote all his time to his command, and not to waste time attending to personal details like packing and moving his baggage.

Life was indeed pretty good. The weather was nice, there was wine for parties, and I could have been content in Franzenbad for a considerable time.

Bonn, Germany, March 1945; I get a very minor medal from General Taylor.

Liebenstein, Czechoslovakia, May 1945; "C" Company officers two days before the end of the war.
Left to Right: Long, Owens, Kays, Sidlowski, Stark.

CHAPTER TWELVE

THE LONG ROAD HOME

MAY 17 – NOVEMBER 6, 1945

We stayed in Franzenbad, Czechoslovakia for the next few weeks. The weather was beautiful and warm; we had little to do once we had taken care of the German prisoners; and life was pleasant. The Battalion created a little officer's club and I spent lots of time just talking with friends.

The main thing on everybody's mind was "going home," and the letters I sent at this time are largely concerned with that subject. However, I decided to write a long account of the chronology of my adventures of the past three years and to fill in the names of the places where I had been. All through the war we had generally not been able to identify where we were and I assumed that my parents would want to get out a map and trace my route. Whether that was true or not, the next three letters are very long and repeat much of what has already been written. In fact, I used these three letters as a reference in writing this account. For this reason I will repeat here only the beginnings and endings of these letters, and omit the other details.

23 May 1945

Dear Mother, Dad, and Sis,

I just got very recent letters (1 week) from you and Noma, both of which make me very hot. It seems to be a foregone conclusion that I'm on my way home, the only question being whether it will be this week or next week. If I don't get you straightened out quickly you're going to be in for some awful disappointments. You've apparently been completely taken in by propaganda. Remember this, officers aren't soldiers, and as such don't constitute a political problem — in other words the army can do anything they want to an officer without fear of congressional interference. Read in the papers about the point system and you will see the word essential. There's the key. A twenty-five year old 1st Lt. who is in good health is not going to be discharged. This whole point system concerns discharging only and has nothing to do whatsoever with sending people home on leave. Therein they've missed the whole point it seems to me. Most of these men aren't interested in getting out of the army — they just want to get home for a month or so. Some units will go to the Pacific via the States and they'll get just that. Only the most recent arrivals over here are going direct to the Pacific so that doesn't worry me. However, other units are going to stay here and strip themselves of their high-point men, retrain with replacements, and then go to the Pacific. We apparently are either in that group or the Army of Occupation. We've already started a lot of men home and a few officers, very few. The difficulty is that the high-point men are the NCO's and the other old-timers that form the backbone of the 1st Division. All the division commander or any unit commander has to do is brand a man or officer essential and he doesn't go home. As soon as we get any hint that we are going to the Pacific there is going to be wholesale branding of people "essential," because no commander is going to let anyone take any shingles off his roof. The higher an officer gets the higher he wants to go, and altho you'd think two stars would be plenty for any man, that third star is always beckoning for those who are energetic and a little more ruthless than the others. We all do it. My 1st Sgt. is very unhappy because I won't let him go home, but I can't run the company without him. I'm new to the company and all but one of my officers are new and it will be some little time before I can let him go.

Oh, come now, it isn't as bad as all that. I know the army well enough to know that when we start getting replacement officers we'll get some rank and to keep peace in the family the Col. will have to get rid of his senior Lts. So I hope to get home sometime next fall, maybe sooner. Will that do?

I've got years to recount to you all of my experiences but you might be interested in hearing at this time just where I've been and how I got there because I'm sure there are some gaps that you haven't been able to fill so here goes.

[ommitted]

Well, this letter is getting too long for one envelope so I'll continue it next time. This is definitely my best effort in a long time.

Keep the cookies rolling because the food is rather mediocre at present. Don't forget the films.

Much love to all,
Bill

This letter was twelve pages long, so I obviously had lots of time on my hands.

I should make a comment or two about our earlier expectations about going home. About this time we (or somebody) got a letter from Doug Forbes, former CO of "B" Company, who had gone home a month or two earlier. He was excited about the ending of the European war and in his letter he said, "Hope I can join you for the big pee-rade in New York." Somehow we had always assumed that we would go home together and that it would of course involve a big parade down Broadway. That's what the movies had always told us about the ending of WWI. It was the one thing that would make it all worthwhile. By the time this last letter was written, it was apparent that we would go home in bits and pieces and there would be no parade. It was one of the big disappointments of my life. On the Fourth of July there was in fact a huge parade in New York with General Eisenhower and all the "brass," but the troops that participated were the 86th Infantry Division, a division that had been the last overseas and never in battle. Obviously this was because of the continuing war in the Pacific, but the mentality of the top command of the Army appalled me then, and has never ceased to amaze me since. Pride and morale are the names of the game in this business and one would think that the professionals would know this best.

Franzenbad, Czechoslovakia
28 May 1945

Dear Mother, Dad, and Sis,

Well, this is sort of an all-time record for consecutive letters, isn't it? However, I thought I'd continue my history while I'm still hot and have plenty of time. As I remember when I left off I was arriving in Liverpool in early November of 1943.

[ommitted]

Well, that's enough for this edition. More next time. In the meantime there's no other news so I'll close.

Love to all,
Bill

P.S. Here are some pictures in which I tried out my new camera. The results were a little disappointing, but I think the main trouble was a poor developing job.

Franzenbad, Czechoslovakia
31 May 1945

Dear Mother, Dad, and Sis,

I hadn't expected to write so soon again, but I forgot to ask for some film in the last one so here it is. Will you please send me two rolls of No. 127 film?

For want of better writing material I'll continue my travelogue — if you don't mind. As I remember, we had left off at Aachen where things had settled down to a sort of stalemate near the end of September.

[ommitted]

We don't know much about what lies ahead. All the emphasis is on getting the newest divisions over here home and to the Pacific so we have the peculiar situation of the units that arrived here last going home first. In the meantime we are sending a lot of men home individually to be discharged. I expect we'll at least temporarily be in the army of occupation. A few leaves to the Riviera and Paris and England are coming thru and my main hope now is a leave. I think I'd like to go to England. Right now I'm horribly bored with everything. I'd almost rather be in combat.

Well, this is long enough so I'll get it mailed.

Love to all,
Bill

Soon after this (sometime in June), the whole division loaded up on trucks and moved out of Czechoslovakia and back into Germany. We moved into some German army barracks near the town of Ansbach, west of Nürnberg. For the first time since Tidworth in England in 1942, we were in a strictly garrison situation, with all the spit and polish that goes with an army that is no longer in the field. It was a part of the Army that I had never really known.

More people went home. Murphy moved up to Battalion Headquarters as S3 and George Johnson took over "A" Company. So now our line company commanders were George in "A," Fred Rutledge in "B" and me in "C." All three of us had served together in "A" Company in Africa and Sicily.

Nürnberg, Germany
14 June 1945

Dear Mother, Dad, and Sis,

I've moved since I last wrote you, as you can see from the heading. We're not actually at Nürnberg, but it's the nearest identifiable place. We're out in the sticks about 25 miles west of the city. Looks like occupation for awhile, but they won't tell us anything definite. In the meantime we're busying ourselves fixing up a pretty good camp. The place is actually a German ammo dump and we're living in the barracks that the station complement lived in.

About the only thing around here that is plentiful is labor. Every day we send trucks out to the PW camps to bring back all the Krauts we need. We've got them doing all the horse work. Also I have four Polish boys that live right with us and do KP and things like that. They've been prisoners for five years so they are very glad to get a little freedom and good food and they work much harder than any soldier ever would. This wouldn't be too bad a life if there was something to do on off-duty hours. I still feel as if I'm sitting on a powder-keg in that respect. General Patton has put out orders about carrying out training and what not. Sounds good coming from him in California.

I got a lot of mail yesterday and a package of cookies the other day. Please send more cookies. I haven't received any films, but please send some more anyway. Remember No. 127. I don't know exactly how I'm going to get them processed. Our battalion photographer ruins them and the PX takes about five months to get them back. Maybe the service will improve, however.

Oh, incidentally, please address me as Captain Kays from now on. Date of rank, June 7. Now, all I've got to do is get home and everything will be rosy.

If I should ever go home as an individual, and not with an outfit as a unit, I've got a problem that does not lend itself to easy solution. When you leave you have to give an address you want to go to and they ship you direct to the nearest army post to that address, and you have to return there after your leave is over. If I give my correct home address, they'll ship me direct to California with no stop-over and Noma will never get over it. So Sis, how about giving me the dope on air priorities and the cost of flying across the country. I'd just as soon give New York as my address and travel on my own anyway, because I'd hate to be in charge of a train load of men going across the country. Now, will I run into difficulties trying to run around the country on leave orders that don't take me to the place I want to go? Of course all this is pleasant to think about, but I figure I've got to come home someday.

There's not much other news. I'm enclosing our June 6 special edition of the Division news rag. It probably will go well in the scrap book.

Love to all,

Bill

Evidently I did know that my mother was keeping a scrapbook. Was I consciously writing letters for the scrapbook? The other news of note in this letter was that I had finally been promoted. I had been a 1st Lieutenant for almost two years; something of a record I suspect.

Nürnberg, Germany
5 July 1945

Dear Mother, Dad, and Sis,

A good deal of time has elapsed and a lot has happened since I last wrote. I'll go thru it all in chronological order.

Capt. Rutledge and I took one look at the training schedule for last week and decided it was high time we left, so we cornered the Colonel and asked him for some leave. Ordinarily there is no such thing as regular leave over here as all recreation is done on a quota basis. However, last fall when things were fluid the battalion acquired an apartment in Liège, Belgium and when we were around Aachen officers used to go back there for an overnight stand. The Colonel gave us 7 days leave and his German "staff car" and we took off for Liège and had a wonderful week. Although Liège isn't a leave city there are plenty of army-run facilities for the local troops. You have to stay out of trouble because leave of that sort is illegal but Liège isn't very tightly controlled and our status was never questioned. We took one day and night off and went to Brussels. Brussels is a "little Paris" and that was the high point of the trip. In all these cities you can cook up a good story and get a meal ticket to army transient officer's messes and there are always night clubs turned into officer's clubs. All told I spent $100.00 so I couldn't stand a trip like that very often. Our little German car is fast and by using the Frankfurt-Cologne super-highway we made the trip in 10 hours. Brussels is only 1-1/2 hr ride from Liège. Seems funny how close everything over here is.

I got a good look at Cologne for the first time. For a one mile radius from the cathedral at the center of the city there isn't an inhabitable building. From one mile to three miles out every second or third building has one or more inhabitable rooms. After three miles you begin to see a house here and there in pretty good shape. Even in the suburbs which were once very beautiful residential sections and where the houses were well dispersed every second or third house is demolished. It doesn't seem possible that a city could ever be rebuilt on the same site. The downtown section is more burned out than bombed out and the buildings are just shells. The most pulverized cities I've seen are Duren and Julich which were in the path of last winter's battles. Those places were just ground to dust by artillery fire and the shells of the buildings aren't even standing.

The biggest news is that tomorrow I'm being transferred to the 16th Armored Division, a unit that is scheduled to be demobilized. I understand the 16th is scheduled to go home around January, but if things continue to go faster than anticipated it might leave sooner. They are in Czechoslovakia now but I don't imagine the Russians are going to let us stay there very long so I anticipate getting back to France in the next month or so. It's sort of tough to take the old Red One off, but if I can get a chance to get discharged I'm going to jump at it. As it stands now you can't be declared essential until you go before a board in the states, and that's a wonderful break. Incidentally, I have enough points if you were wondering about that. I would like to get home for Christmas but we'll see.

The films you sent have never arrived. I don't know why. However, in Liège I bought four rolls of Belgian film (for 50 francs a roll), and that ought to work OK. I'll enclose another request anyway. I'm going to get films developed by giving them to somebody going on leave because all over Belgium they have 24 hr service. Incidentally, the shops in Belgium are pretty well stocked and have in large quantities some things which seem to be scarce in the states. The prices are sky-high however and our rate of exchange is very disadvantageous. Is there anything you can think of that I could get you over here? I don't know thing one about linen, china, and stuff like that.

My principle pastime right now is stamp collecting. I've got so many stamps that I never know whether I've got a certain stamp or not. Sis, will you buy for me the latest edition of Scott's catalog and mail it to me pronto.

I saw a camera like mine advertised in a Liège second hand store for 15,000 francs. Not bad, eh?

I'll have to send my new address in a day or so as I don't know the APO.

Love to all

Bill

What I neglected to tell my parents about in that letter is a little adventure that Rutledge and I had in Brussels during the one night we were there. As we drove into Brussels we spotted an Army MP and asked him for a recommendation for a hotel. He gave us a card for a hotel on Rue de Lambermont, convenient to the downtown area. When we checked in we realized that this was a rather high-class brothel. So what the hell! The madam promised us two attractive girls for the night. Mine was named Niska, a Romanian girl. She didn't speak English but knew French. My long-neglected school-boy French served me very adequately!

The next day I left the 1st Division for good. I guess about two-thirds of our officers were exchanged for officers who had few "points" and thus were not scheduled to go home anytime soon. Most of our people were sent to the 99th Infantry Division; only the Colonel (Gara), George Johnson, and I were sent to the 16th Armored Division. The guys going to the 99th were furious because the 99th was one of the divisions that had been badly mauled at the beginning of the Battle of the Bulge, and the 1st Division had been sent to rescue them at the very beginning of the battle. We felt very superior!

Once we got to the 16th Armored I was given command of Company "C" of the 216th Engineers, George was given Company "A," and Gara was supposed to take over the battalion. However, he convinced the commanding general that he had so many "points" that he would soon be going home independently and it would be pointless for him to take over command of the battalion. Gara was therefore given a temporary position at division headquarters and the battalion was left in the hands of the guy who had been battalion executive officer.

My company was located in a little town called Weseritz in Czechoslovakia, miles from anybody else. We were billeted in a school building and my room had been the principal's office. I had one other officer, a guy named Alter from New York, and I may have had others but I don't recall them. We had a pretty good First Sergeant and the men were reasonably cooperative. At this particular time I'm not sure whether the men were mostly from the original company or had been exchanged for men due to go home. Ultimately we were almost entirely made up of men transferred from either the 77th Division or some such number.

I remember in my room/office there was a picture of Konrad Henlein on the wall, and various references to him in other papers and documents in the room. Konrad Henlein had had his day in the sun in 1938 when he was the leader of the Sudeten Germans, and Hitler was daily ranting about the necessity of transferring the area to Germany. His name was in the news every day at about the time I started college.

Weserwitz, Czechoslovakia
23 July 1945

Dear Mother, Dad, and Sis,

My writing has fallen off to a very dismal state, I'll have to admit. I can't remember whether or not I've written since I joined this outfit or not, but I don't think I have. Anyway, to be sure I'm now in the 16th Armored Division and the days in the "Fighting First" are finished forever. I'm convinced I got a raw deal because this outfit seems to have about the last going home priority in the ETO. They are supposed to go home in January to be de-activated, but we are all keeping our fingers crossed and hoping they will get ahead of schedule so we can make it by December.

In the meantime we sit here and twiddle our thumbs. A company of men awaiting discharge is a very unhappy affair, especially when the officers don't want to do a damn bit of work and yours truly isn't very ambitious either. There's still an outside chance of getting on a "going home" quota, but I'm too far down the list to hold much hope. They work strictly from the point list, and not by time overseas, so guys that came over here years after me are going home before me because they stayed home and begot children (at 12 point per) while I was sweating it out in North Africa and Sicily. Well, I don't suppose they could have instituted a system that would make everybody happy.

Mail has been pretty slow since I moved over here. In three weeks I've had two letters. I have received two packages, though. No films yet, though.

Many happy returns, Ma. I just remembered. I wonder what you are all doing now.

I think I'll take a run down to Pilsen one of these days and see what cooks. That's fraternizing country, but I haven't much use for the Czechs. As a matter of fact the only people in Europe that I've seen that are of any account are the Germans, surprisingly enough. I'd better be careful what I say, but I'm afraid there's something all wrong over here. There's no doubt in my mind that [sentence is lined out] No, I won't say it.

Sister's dope on the travel situation at home is very discouraging. If I get 30 days leave it looks like I'll spend half of it travelling no matter what happens. From the way you talk about the food situation and the gas situation all is apparently not a bed of roses. We're having a gas shortage here now. I need 75 gallons a day to run my company properly and all I'm getting is 20. It takes 10 gallons to run the stoves and the rest will hardly keep the ration & water trucks running. I wonder how many years it will be before you can get what you want & not a ration. Our rations are on the whole plenty ample but they are still rations.

Well, that's enough for the present.

Love to all,

Bill

I should comment on my statement "there's something all wrong over here." What I was seeing, but not understanding, were the first signs of the new order in Europe: Communism was beginning to be forcibly imposed. The Czechs that I encountered were mostly young Communists from farther east who were seizing everything in sight, throwing people out of their homes, arresting and kidnapping, and in general getting ready to establish a Communist state, although that didn't really happen for another year or two. We were in what had been the German Sudetenland, that part of Czechoslovakia inhabited primarily by Germans, and of course taken by Germany at the time of the Munich crisis in 1938. Of course there was also a legitimate revenge motive in the behavior of the Czechs, but what we were hearing was primarily from the local Germans who were quite justifiably terrified.

During this period I remember seeing Colonel Gara at least once. He came by to visit, along with the acting battalion commander. He also talked to me in private and told me that he was trying to convince the acting battalion commander that his first priority should be to protect his men and not to please and impress the general. At that time we were daily sending out details to improve the roads and do all kinds of other bits of construction and maintenance, most of it just "make work" and not really necessary. I began to realize that the 1st Division and the 1st Engineers, and especially Bill Gara, were all something a little different from most of the Army, and rather special. "Take care of your men" was something that Gara continually preached; it was something I didn't see much of in the other units I was in. The 216th seemed to have some of the characteristics of the 361st QM Battalion with whom I had been in Scotland and in the early days of Africa - in both, the officers tended to prioritize their own comfort over that of the enlisted men under their charge.

On the other hand, I liked the enlisted men in the 216th. They were largely draftees from the Midwest and very different from the predominantly Brooklyn gang of roughnecks that I had become used to in the 1st. I don't have anything against Brooklyn, but let us say that my own background was a little different.

I should mention here that the war in the Pacific was still going on, the atomic bomb had not yet been dropped, and redeployment of the army to the Pacific was obviously the top priority. All this was to change dramatically in a few weeks. The next letter was written just two days before the Hiroshima bomb was dropped.

Weseritz, Czechoslovakia
6 August 1945

Dear Mother, Dad, and Sis,

I keep putting off writing in the hope that each day will bring more news of what's to become of me. I'm living a life of rumors and sweating. Recently they said that everyone with over 85 points will be out of the division by the 15th. All the enlisted men have gone, but still no word on the officers. We're finally getting down to business turning in equipment, but it's quite difficult when they keep shifting personnel. I'm now on my 3rd motor sergeant, mess sergeant, and supply sergeant, and my 2nd 1st Sergeant. I'm initiating reports of survey for several hundred dollars worth of equipment that's missing, and if they ever bounce I'm going to be out a pretty penny. All of which makes me plenty mad, because with this terrific turnover of personnel and no really qualified men taking care of the various sections it has been impossible to account for everything. Every time you ship out a bunch of men they steal you blind.

I'm beginning to soak up a little culture. The Army is subsidizing a local symphony orchestra and I've been attending (and enjoying) the concerts. They have lots of guest artists which they pick up from the hordes of displaced persons who are wandering all over Europe. Some of them were apparently quite well known. For instance the guest conductor the other night was the former conductor of the Warsaw Opera who they found hiding around here somewhere.

I have lots of Germans working for me now. They are scared to death of the Czechs who are really on the rampage. If they work for the Americans the Czechs can't touch them so they all come flocking around willing to do anything for nothing and I'm taking full advantage of it.

The weather has been pretty good lately. At least there's more sunshine than rain. There is no such thing as a dry season in this part of the world.

I've been getting a little mail but in the latest letters you still knew nothing of my coming over here. I've had two boxes of cookies since I've been here. Once I leave this outfit I don't ever expect to get any more mail till I get home. This shift of personnel is more than the Army Postal Service can stand. They suddenly shift out mail clerks and when you try to break in a new one he finds the records all confused and the forwarding of mail stops right there.

That's all for now.

Love to all,

Bill

P.S. - Don't send any Christmas packages. I'll be home before then.

George Johnson's company had been running a recreation camp for our troops in Marienbad and it was there that I went to the concerts. I think I visited George at least once on a Sunday. Soon after he was sent home, as was Bill Gara.

My friend Alter, one of my officers, was a musician and this was probably the reason I went to a couple of concerts. However, even Alter was transferred out a little later.

It must have been the day after the last letter that my company was moved back from Weseritz to the town of Tachou where the entire battalion was billeted. The atomic bomb was dropped on Hiroshima on the 8th, and I definitely recall being in Tachou when I heard the news. I had evidently been in Weseritz for over a month. I can't imagine how I spent all my time that month. The town was a very small village with nothing whatsoever to offer. Outside of a couple of Sundays in Marienbad I don't recall doing much of anything. However, I do recall working on my stamp collection. I found in the office a blank hardbound book, and I began to mount all the stamps that I had bought in Belgium. I have the book still.

In Tachou I lived with other officers and made some new friends. We had a separate officer's mess and our standard of living was pretty good. All thought of training and stuff like that was forgotten. I don't even recall having much to do with the enlisted men in my company. Our battalion commanding officer was an idiot named Major Varnum who had never commanded anything before. I pretty much ignored him. My roommate was Captain Nelson Stark and we became great friends. He had come from the same outfit as had Varnum and most of the others. Another close friend was Lt. John Warga. Warga was very clever mechanically, and when my camera developed a mechanical problem he used the battalion dentist's tools to repair it. (We didn't have a dentist at the time.) Warga was what we would call a "facilitator." He was one of those guys who could always find food when none was available, or get a vehicle when the rules forbade it. Stark, Warga and I were then into photography and we made the acquaintance of a girl in town who ran a photo processing shop. She developed our films.

VJ Day — Victory in Japan — was on August 15th, and my next letter is dated August 27th. As was the case after VE Day, I apparently didn't feel any great urge to write.

Tachou, Czechoslovakia
27 August 1945

Dear Mother, Dad, and Sis,

Well, I'm still sitting here. That little sentence alone just about describes my present state of mind. They just announced today that all officers are frozen in place in the division, the enlisted men will once more have a mass reshuffle, and we go home in October. All of which wouldn't be so bad if it wasn't for the fact that every man I came overseas with is either home or on the way, and most of those who came over a year later are home.

The last two weekends a couple of other officers and I decided to see a little of Europe, regardless of regulations. On VJ holiday we drove down to the Danube at Passau on the German-Austrian border, and then took a cruise on the Danube quite a ways down into Austria. Had a nice day and I even got my face sunburned. At that point the Danube is very beautiful. The water is milky from the glaciers in Switzerland, and the river is bordered by quite high mountains which are forested right down to the water's edge.

This last weekend we really took a trip. Taking two days we drove to Berchtesgaden. In all the stories I've read about Berchtesgaden they seem to have omitted to mention that it is in some of the most beautiful mountain country in the world. It's like a dozen Yosemite Valleys all crisscrossing. We went up to Hitler's "eagle's nest" where you look almost straight down on the town of Berchtesgaden, 6000 feet below. I could easily have spent a week there. We stayed at a nice resort hotel taken over by the army. The people and their houses are very picturesque. The men all wear leather shorts and these Alpine hats with a whisk broom sticking out of them. The farm houses are all the same pattern — the first story is white plaster, the second is natural finished wood with large overhanging eaves and usually a narrow porch around the second story. Everything is spotlessly clean. The absolute lack of commercialization would make you think that there were never any tourists. I took two rolls of film which I'm getting developed now.

We went down by way of Regensburg and Wasserburg which is a pretty rough trip. We came back through Munich and Nurnburg, using the "Autobahn" which was much faster. We had originally planned to go from Berchtesgaden to Innsbruck and then back through Munich, but we decided there was too much to see around Berchtesgaden in the short time we had. I'd love some day to follow the Inn River from Wasserburg up to Innsbruck, altho the latter is now in French Occupation & it takes some fast talking to get thru.

Hope to have the pictures to send you soon. Meanwhile I hope to be home. I'm sure we'll have Christmas together, anyway.

Love to all,
Bill

Curiously I did not even mention the atomic bomb or the fact that the war was by then completely over.

The Berchtesgaden trip was slightly illegal. One was supposed to have valid Army orders to go anywhere. Nelson Stark wrote a set of orders for me, John Warga, and a Sgt. Millwood, who would be our driver. At six in the morning he woke up Major Varnum and thrust the orders and a pen under his nose. In some confusion Varnum signed them and we were instantly off in a jeep.

I was with the 216th for over four months and yet I have no recollection of ever discussing the war with any of the other officers. I think they all came overseas in 1944, but I have no idea where they fought or what kind of experiences they had. Outside of Stark and Warga I had no friends; the others considered me a conceited smart-ass from the 1st Division and usually wouldn't give me the time of day.

Tachou, Czechoslovakia
8 Sept., 1945

Dear Mother, Dad, and Sis,

Well, I guess I'm finally going home. Sometime between the 11th and the 21st we load up in box cars and head for Le Harve. Sometime after the 21st we embark and set sail. I won't believe it until it happens. You have no idea what it's like to live for three years with only one thought and ambition. You think and talk about it so much that you sometimes question your sanity. I hope it will be as exciting a moment as I have built it up to be.

In the last letter you were still sweating out Pop, but I expect he'll be home by the time I get there - hope so anyway. Hope you don't succumb to the shock of us both arriving so near together. Boy, what a Christmas this is going to be.

I figure I have 107 days of leave coming. Today they finally made up their minds about officers and the point system. I've got plenty to get discharged with, so I figure I should be out soon after I get to the States. With 107 days and mustering out pay I should pocket about $1000. I intend to be among the unemployed for awhile so let's load up the Olds and take off for the hills.

I was a bit worried about Sis when I read about the VJ riots in SF. Glad to hear that you didn't have any trouble. Somehow it never occurs to me to celebrate after a victory. I don't remember that VE Day was much different from any other over here. I feel like I want to relax rather than celebrate.

Enclosed are a few snaps of my recent ramblings. I have quite a few others that I'll show you when I get home.

I'm trying to write and listen to a mystery story on the radio at the same time. It's a bit difficult.

See you soon,
Love to all,
Bill

Despite all my complaints, I think the Army did a remarkable job of shifting gears and starting people home in large numbers very soon after VJ Day.

St. Valery, France
27 September 1945

Dear Mother, Dad, and Sis,

I had hoped by this time to be at least on the high seas, if not already home, but fate has me still in France so I'd better write a letter and get you up to date.

About 10 days ago we left Czechoslovakia on a "40 & 8"[1] and after a rather rugged 4 day trip arrived here at a staging area. If you'll look on the map you'll find St. Valery about 35 miles north of Le Havre on the coast. This is a miserable 55,000 man tent camp where you sit and wait for space on a ship. Soon after we arrived a big storm cut loose a lot of hitherto unknown mines so the port was closed and the whole redeployment schedule shoved back. Things seem to be rolling again but nobody seems to be able to find out when we sail. I hope by the time you get this I'll be well on the way.

I believe we go to Camp Kilmer, N.J., where we immediately break up into separation center groups. I'll then go to Ft. Dix. If I don't get a discharge right away I'll at least get some substantial leave. However, I can't see much excuse for my not being a civilian within a month unless Congress messes up the point system. I've got 111 points under the VE computation. Of course if they start discharging the coal miners and steel workers and WPA I may be out of luck. These occupational discharges are a lot of hooey because these guys haven't any intention of going back to work till they've run out of money and that may be a long way off the way Uncle Santa Claus is operating.

Don't ask me what my plans are when I get home because I haven't the vaguest idea. What I need most is some good advice. You might try to round up a little of

---

1   A "40 & 8" was the typical tiny four-wheeled European railroad freight car. This particular expression was left over from the First World War when in France the freight cars had been labeled "40 hommes ou 8 chevaux."

that for me. The educational part of the GI bill of rights looks too good to pass up, but that's the only idea I do have. Just don't rush me, 'cause first of all I want a good vacation.

Our APO closed down some time ago so I haven't had any news from home since the first of the month. I think the day Dad got home was the last. Sis should be on vacation about now. What are you going to do when I get there, go AWOL?

Dad, keep your eyes open for some good football games because that's one of my major ambitions — to see a football game.

Well, that's all for now. I sincerely hope this will be the last letter. The next should be a telephone call.

Love to all,
Bill

And that was the last letter, number 123. The next was in fact a telephone call.

I particularly remember one incident on the train trip. The train was forever stopping and starting, and when it started in the middle of about the second night the brakes on one of the pairs of wheels on our car apparently froze. The two wheels simply slipped along the tracks for many miles making a terrible screeching noise. Finally they broke loose, but by that time a large flat area had been worn on each wheel. For the remainder of the trip we had to endure a continuous pounding and clattering beneath us, all of which made sleep difficult. Nobody complained because we were heading in the right direction.

While waiting for our ship in St. Valery, Stark, Warga, and I managed to get a jeep one day and take a little trip up the coast to see Dieppe. I had been curious about the place ever since the infamous "Dieppe Raid" in August 1942.

On October 4th, I was able to send a telegram:

EXPECT SAIL NEXT TWO OR THREE DAYS ARRIVE US AROUND 15TH
BILL

We finally loaded up on a small transport, the SS Exchange, and sailed about the 8th or 9th. The trip across the Atlantic was uneventful and easy. I always liked sailing on transports, and this time we had none of the usual disciplinary problems. I don't recall I had to think about anything but myself and my comfort. I loved it.

On Saturday October 13th, the ship's loud speaker system tuned into the broadcast of a college football game. It was a lovely sound I hadn't heard for four years.

That night we saw a lighthouse off to the right. We were getting close. I believe it was on Sunday morning, October 14th, that we awoke to see the low outline of Long Island on our right. The excitement built up. That day turned out to be perhaps the most exciting of my life.

About mid-morning we turned into the Narrows and started into New York Harbor. We saw large American cars moving along a road on the land to the right, probably near Coney Island. The cheering started.

Then suddenly, through the mist, the skyline of Manhattan appeared dead ahead. I had dreamed about that sight for over three years. For hours we slowly cruised up the bay and then up the Hudson River past the whole length of Manhattan. Fire boats saluted us with jets of water sent into the air, and every ship we passed blew its whistles. I stood on deck all day with tears streaming down my cheeks. This was the parade that I had hoped for, although in a slightly different form. Manhattan seemed to embody everything that America stood for and for which the war had been fought. As I stood there my mind went back to Africa and Sicily and England and France and Germany and all the death and destruction. There was nothing like home, and New York was home even though I was a Californian. At one point Nelson Stark gave me a pat on the back; he knew, as the others probably didn't, that this was a somewhat more special day for me than for most of the others. Being overseas for over three years was very different than one year.

We continued to cruise up the Hudson all afternoon, and about nightfall we arrived at Camp Shanks, New York, where we disembarked. Telephones were plentiful and that night I phoned my family and Noma. Noma was at Sweet Briar College in Virginia. She immediately proposed coming to New York the following weekend. She had relatives in New York, and also an uncle who was manager of the McAlpin Hotel, so presumably there would be no problems finding a place to stay.

I spent a couple of days being "processed" at Camp Shanks, and then was put aboard a train for Ft. Dix, New Jersey. At Ft. Dix I then went through all the further "processing" for discharge from the Army, including physical exams and things like that. It was something that took a bit of time.

In the meantime, Noma came to New York on Thursday, although I was not going to be completely out until late on Friday. She went to her relative's apartment because even her hotel-manager uncle was unable to find a hotel room. She was a little put out that I didn't take the train into New York on Thursday night, which I suppose I could have done, but I would have had to return to Ft. Dix the next day.

On Friday night I arrived at Penn Station and called Noma's uncle. He told me that she was staying with her cousin and his wife and gave me a phone number. He said that he and his wife were about to leave for a party. I phoned the number and got no answer. For the next hour I continued phoning, becoming more desperate as time went on. Finally a man answered and said he didn't think this was the number I wanted. I didn't even know her cousin's name, but I did have an address, so I got a taxi and finally got to their apartment about eleven o'clock p.m.

We had a reasonably joyful reunion, but hardly a private one. Since I had no place to stay they decided to put us up as best they could in the tiny apartment using makeshift beds.

The next day, Saturday, Noma and I wandered around New York a bit and then called on some of my own relatives, the Dieckerhoffs, who had a large apartment on Madison Avenue. They offered me a room and that's where I stayed for the next two days, Noma returning to her cousin's apartment that night. Later in the afternoon we called on her aunt and uncle who had invited us over for drinks. He was a Wall Street stockbroker and they had a rather elegant apartment. He showed me to his bar and suggested that I mix the cocktails. I didn't have a clue how to mix a cocktail, and I was beginning to feel very awkward — perhaps this was not my world. He undoubtedly wondered what kind of farm boy his niece had brought in. I became miserable.

The fact was, I wanted to talk about my experiences but nobody was interested. Noma wanted to talk about Frank Sinatra or whatever band was playing at the various Manhattan night clubs! Her uncle talked about the stock market. I felt lonely and longed for my buddies in the 1st Division; they were my world now, not the world I had left behind three years before. I longed for Murph and Tom and Rut, and Bill Barnum and George and Conant and Fred Finley, and even Gara. Had I thought about it, I might have remembered another scene from *All Quiet on the Western Front*: Paul goes home on leave following discharge from a hospital, and after a few days he can't stand it, cuts short his leave, and returns to the trenches, the only world he still knew. My mind was still at Kassarine, El Guettar, Alimena, Sicily, Omaha Beach, the Hurtgen Forest and the Battle of the Bulge.

Noma wanted to go to a night club so we did go to one of the famous ones, but I don't recall it being much fun. I guess I then took her back to her cousin's apartment. I don't know what we did the next morning, but I put her on the train in the afternoon. It was agreed that I would visit some of my relatives during the coming week and then go to her home in Norfolk for the next weekend.

Back at the Dieckerhoff's apartment Sunday night, I shared a bedroom with my second cousin, Ned. He had just been discharged from the Navy and had been at Omaha Beach. We talked for hours about our experiences. Here was somebody I could talk to. For the first time I began to feel comfortable. In the meantime I called my Aunt Amy who lived in Cazenovia, a suburb of Syracuse. She said that another of my aunts, Liz, was visiting from California and suggested that I take the train up to Syracuse and spend a few days with them. These were my mother's sisters.

On Monday I sent a telegram home:

AM AT THE DIECKERHOFFS LEAVING FOR CAZENOVIA TODAY THEN
TO WASHINGTON NORFOLK AND HOME WILL COMMUNICATE
AGAIN LOVE
BILL

I took a train from Grand Central, and a few hours later my two aunts met me in Syracuse and drove me to Cazenovia. They made a big fuss over me; I was the center of attention. I remember going with them to a cocktail party where the people all seemed genuinely interested in me. They served martinis, and I remember my aunt saying that I had had "tee many martoonies." I had seldom tasted a martini before. I have tasted many since!

I believe it was on the next Friday that I took the train back down to New York City and spent the night again with the Dieckerhoffs. On Saturday I took the train to Washington, and then a six-hour bus trip to Norfolk. I remember calling Mrs. Greene, Noma's mother, from Washington, and she suggested that I fly to Norfolk to save time. I had never flown before (except on a stretcher, in Africa) and trying to arrange a flight by telephone sounded too complicated to me.

That evening when we were finally alone Noma suddenly announced to me, "I don't love you any more." Well, I guess she was more honest than I was. I was a bit shocked at the abruptness of it all, but also a little relieved. It had been clear that things were not as they had been, and after over three years it was foolish to think that they could possibly be the same. If I had been honest with myself I would have admitted at least two years earlier that it wasn't going to work with Noma. We had both grown but in different directions. What had I really expected? The warrior coming home to the faithful girl next door after years away was the romantic stuff of the movies and novels on which I had been brought up. What happened after he came home was never clear. During the past year I had certainly thought of marriage, but it was mostly in the abstract. When I thought about it seriously it was a little scary. My ego was damaged a bit, but that was about all.

The next morning, Sunday, I slept late and Noma apparently had a long talk with her mother. I think her mother must have persuaded her to give it another chance because she was all bouncy and suggested a day visiting some of the places we had known in the years before. I think we had a picnic on the beach. That evening we both boarded a train for an overnight trip to her college in the western part of the state. We sat up all night, arriving about six o'clock in the morning. At the station we said a rather sad good-by and she took some kind of transportation to the college. I waited and caught a train coming from Atlanta, going to Washington.

I wanted to stay in Washington for a few days so that I could look up a lot of old friends - I had attended three years of high school there. In those days the United States was a very large country, five days from coast to coast. Air travel was still in its infancy and the standard mode of transport was the train. One didn't get to the other coast often, so it seemed important to see people while I had the chance.

By this time my sister was working as a reservations agent for United Airlines (UAL) in San Francisco. She had suggested by phone when I called from Camp Shanks that she could probably get me a flight, although it was at that time very difficult to do. I was excited about the prospect and the first thing I did in Washington was go to the UAL office and try to make a reservation. She had told me to refer to her boss in San Francisco. They were skeptical, but told me to come back Friday.

I then went to the Pentagon to look up an old friend, Charlie Thomas, who was on duty there. He took me to an office that arranged hotel reservations and they soon told me that I had a room at the Statler. Later in the day I called the Statler to confirm. They had never heard of me and said a room reservation was impossible. Charlie was living at the Bachelor Officer Quarters at Ft. Myer, Virginia, so he took me there and ultimately fixed me up in the room of some other officer who was away. I don't know whether the guy ever knew I used his room, but I stayed there for a week.

That night I called Noma and we were both thinking the same thing. Since I expected to be in Washington through the next weekend, she suggested that she come to Washington where she could stay with some family friends. A faint flicker of the old spark was still there.

I then got down to seriously visiting old school friends and friends of my family. I sent the following telegram on Wednesday:

IN WASHINGTON STAYING AT FT MYER BUT YOU CANT CONTACT ME THERE. FIGURE TENTATIVELY ON GETTING PLANE RESERVATIONS

MONDAY. SORRY I AM TAKING SO LONG BUT I MIGHT AS WELL SEE
EVERYONE AND SETTLE MY MIND ON MY DOMESTIC PROBLEMS
BEFORE I LEAVE. HAVE SEEN LEES, FECHTELERS, GLENNONS, AND
SCHOOL FRIENDS. LOVE
BILL

It seems curious today that I sent telegrams rather that phoning, but in those days
a transcontinental phone call was expensive and not something you used except in great
emergencies.

I had dinner at the Army-Navy Country Club with my uncle, Admiral Fechteler,
my aunt, and two cousins that I hadn't seen since they were quite young. I learned from
my uncle, who had just returned from the South Pacific, that only the Marines did any
serious land fighting during the war. Well, bully for them!

On Friday I checked in with UAL and they still didn't have anything for me, but
told me to check again on Monday morning. In the meantime, unbeknownst to me, my
sister had been pulling strings on the UAL internal communication system.

Noma took a morning train on Saturday and arrived around noon. I don't recall
where I met her, but she was staying with friends in Chevy Chase. We wandered around
and called on some mutual friends and ended up spending the evening at a friend's
house. But the spark never ignited anything. I took her, probably by bus, to her friend's
house late that night (Saturday) and we said good-bye again. This time we both knew
it was for good and I never saw her again. Her friends must have taken her to the train
Sunday morning.

By now I was very relieved and had no regrets. I was ready to go home.

On Monday morning I returned to the UAL office on 14th Street and they were
very surprised to find that I was on a flight. My sister's "pull" had worked. I sent the
following telegram home:

AM IN. ARRIVE SF AIRPORT TUESDAY UAL FLIGHT 21. SEE YOU SOON.
LOVE,
BILL

I boarded Flight 21 at National Airport at seven o'clock p.m. that Monday. The
plane was an old propeller-driven Douglas DC3 carrying twenty-one passengers. I was
very excited. The flight stopped at Toledo, Chicago, Omaha, Cheyenne, Salt Lake City,
Reno, Sacramento, and finally San Francisco. Dawn broke as we left Cheyenne. The
flight gradually lost time and we didn't get to San Francisco until four o'clock p.m. on
Tuesday, November 6th.

I should mention that the 6th of the month seemed to be my magic date. I had
landed in Scotland on the 6th of September, and in Oran on the 6th of December. We
had returned to England on the 6th of November, and of course we had landed in France
on the 6th of June.

Landing in Reno I got a terrible pain in my sinuses above my right eye. It went
away when we gained altitude again, but hit me once more when we landed in Sacra-

mento. The pain was excruciating. From Sacramento to San Francisco I was terrified that I would arrive on a stretcher, but fortunately we didn't climb very high and I was in reasonable shape when we landed.

The plane pulled up to a low chain-link fence and through the window I could see Mother, Dad, and Sis behind the fence. I had a hard time choking back the tears.

It had been forty months and five days. It was a long war.

Nürnberg, Germany, August 1945; With John Warga during our trip to Berchtesgaden.

Cheb (Eger), Czechoslovakia, May 1945; With my command car.

Tachau, Czechoslovakia, September 1945; Showing off my overseas stripes.

*Tachau, Czechoslovakia, August 1945;
Nelson Stark*

On the North Atlantic, October 1945; Nearing home.

The "A" Company officers at the Battle of El Guettar reunite 47 years later. Left to Right: Barnum, Crowley, Murphy, Rutledge, Kays.

ORGANIZATION OF THE AMERICAN ARMY

The organization of the American Army is central to my story, yet it can be an enigma to those who have not participated in the armed services. Below I include a very general description of the organization of the army, at least those parts that are pertinent to my story.

Enlisted personnel are personnel below the commissioned ranks and make up the vast majority of military personnel. This includes three ranks of **Private (Pvt.)**, **Corporal (Cpl.)**, and multiple ranks of **Sergeant (Sgt.)**.

Commissioned Officers are drawn typically from soldiers who have graduated from a military academy, i.e. West Point, or **Officer Candidates Schools (OCS)**, or who have attended the **Reserve Officers' Training Corps (ROTC)** in a civilian college. The ranks of **Commissioned Officers** flow from **2nd Lieutenant (Lt.)**, **1st Lieutenant (Lt.)**, **Captain**, **Major** (generally a staff position), **Lieutenant (Lt.) Colonel**, **Colonel**, to the various ranks of **General**.

Non-commissioned Officers, **Non-Coms**, or **NCO's**, are enlisted personnel, who have risen up through the ranks of the enlisted personnel to be **Corporals** or **Sergeants**. Occasionally, especially towards the end of the 2nd World War, an NCO could be promoted into the rank of **Lieutenant**.

Executive Officers are officers who are second in command of a given organization. **Commanding Officers** or **CO's** have ultimate authority over the unit under command. A **Squad** is the smallest unit of the military, and usually consists of about 12 soldiers. They are led by a **Sergeant** from the ranks of the NCO's. A **Platoon** consists of three or four **Squads** and is led by a **1st** or **2nd Lieutenant**. A **Company** consists of two or more **Platoons** and is led by a **Captain**. A **Battalion** is comprised of two or more **Companies** and is led by a **Lieutenant Colonel**. An **Infantry Regiment** contains two or more **Battalions** and is led by a **Colonel**. A **Division** consists of multiple **Regiments**. A **Division** is led by a **Major General**.

During the 2nd World War, the U.S. had about 70 Infantry Divisions, over 50 of which served in the European theater of Operations. **Armored Divisions** were army divisions consisting primarily of tanks. During 2nd World War, there were 16 **Armored Divisions**.

Multiple Divisions make up a **Corp**, and multiple **Corps** makes up an **Army**. During the war, the **1st Infantry Division** was variously in the 2nd Corps, 5th Corps, and the 7th Corps, which in turn were variously in the 7th Army, the 1st Army, and the 3rd Army.

My division, the **1st Infantry Division**, consisted of three **Infantry Regiments**, four **Artillery Battalions**, and **Special Troops**, including the **1st Engineer Battalion** of which I was a part. In its entirety, it consisted of about 13,000 soldiers. During most of my story, I was in **"A" Company** of the **1st Engineer Battalion**. In addition, often **"A" Company** would be attached to the **16th Infantry Regiment**, providing engineering support for their missions.

LIST OF ACRONYMS

AA	Anti-Aircraft Guns
AEF	American Expeditionary Forces
APO	Army Postal Service
AT	Anti-tank Guns
CO	Commanding Officer
CP	Command Post
DSC	Distinguished Service Cross
DUKW	Amphibious Vehicle
EM	Enlisted Men
ERTC	Engineer Replacement Training Center
ETO	European Theater of Operations
ETOUSA	European Theater of Operations, United States Army
FA	Field Artillery
FFI	French Forces of the Interior
Halftrack	An open-topped armored car, with quarter-inch armor plating on the sides and half-inch armor over the windshield, truck wheels and tires in front, and tank tracks in the rear
H&S	Headquarters & Service
JG	Lieutenant, Junior Grade
KIA	Killed in Action
KP	Kitchen duty
LCI	Landing Craft Infantry
LCT	Landing Craft Tank
LCVP	Landing Craft Vehicle, Personnel
LST	Landing Ship Tank
MG	Machine Gun
MP	Military Police
NAAFI	Navy, Army, Air Force Institute
NCO	Non-Commissioned Officer
OCS	Officer's Candidate School
OD	Officer of the Day
OD	Olive Drab
OP	Observation Point
Panzers	German tanks
POW, PW	Prisoner of War
PX	Post Exchange
QM	Quartermaster, the supply branch of the army
QMC	Quartermaster Corps
RAF	Royal Air Force
Rangers	A special purpose force of highly trained "elite" infantry
SeeBee	Navy Construction Battalion
S2	Intelligence Officer
S3	Operations Officer
SA	Storm Section (German)
SOP	Standard Operating Procedure
SOS	Services of Supply
SS	Protective Squadron (German)
UAL	United Airlines
USO	American Entertainment Group
VE	Victory in Europe
VJ	Victory in Japan
WAAF	Women's Auxiliary Air Force
WPA	Works Progress Administration

INDEX OF PEOPLE

ABOUT THE AUTHOR

William Morrow Kays was born in 1920 in Norfolk, Virginia. His father, Herbert E. Kays, was a U.S. Navy captain, and the family lived in Virginia, Washington, D.C., San Diego, Palo Alto, San Francisco, Berkeley and Honolulu. After college at Stanford University, Kays began his active duty in the U.S. Army, starting in July 1942. After serving in the First Engineer Battalion of the Army's First Infantry Division ("The Big Red One") in Tunisia, Sicily, England, France, Belgium, Germany, and Czechoslovakia, he was discharged in November 1945. June 6, 1944 found him landing on Omaha Beach as part of the great Allied Invasion of France. Kays is among those pictured in the famous D-Day landing photos of Robert Capa, the Life Magazine photographer who had been with him on the U.S.S. Chase and the landing craft.

After the war, Kays returned to Stanford on the GI Bill, earning a PhD in Mechanical Engineering. He settled in Palo Alto with his wife Alma and four daughters, joining the Stanford Mechanical Engineering faculty in 1951. Kays' career led to chairmanship of his department as well as Dean of the School of Engineering from 1972-1984. After Alma's death in 1982, he retired from Stanford in 1990 and lived on campus with his second wife, Judith until his death in 2018. He had four children, two stepchildren, fifteen grandchildren, and many great-grandchildren. He was an avid fan of the Stanford football team for more than eighty years.

After the war, Kays attended numerous First Division reunions with his fellow officers. During a sabbatical leave to England in 1959-60, Kays and his family visited Omaha Beach as well as many of the other places he had been during the war.

Further inquiries may be directed to wimkepress@gmail.com

EXTRAS

©United Feature Syndicate, Inc. Used with permission.

©United Feature Syndicate, Inc. Used with permission.

```
WARTIME BROWNIES

1 15-ounce can sweetened condensed milk
2 squares melted chocolate
1¼ graham crackers, rolled fine (1 cup)
¼ tsp vanilla
salt
½ cup walnut meats
        Mix, spread thin in greased baking pan
and bake in 350 oven about 20 minutes.
```

Printed in Great Britain
by Amazon